'Demonstrating an extraordinary command of the literature, Greg Martin offers a fresh perspective on the cultural criminology project that is destined to become a classic in the field. *Crime, Media and Culture* is nuanced in historical specificity, broad in scope, and as timely as the morning news. Superb.'

—Mark S. Hamm, *Professor of Criminology, Department of Criminology and Criminal Justice, Indiana State University, USA*

'*Crime, Media and Culture* offers a fresh and invigorating push at the boundaries of cultural criminology. Greg Martin's book expands understandings of crime-media relations by drawing upon the sheer diversity of contemporary media forms to engage with crime and criminal justice in contemporary society.'

—Ruth Penfold-Mounce, *Senior Lecturer in Criminology, University of York, UK*

'*Crime, Media and Culture* is a landmark achievement. It provides a thorough, creative and boundary-pushing look at a rapidly changing field of study. For anyone seeking a comprehensive and authoritative guide to it, this is an essential book. Bold, critical and ambitious it will serve as a foundational text. By incorporating classic scholarship with the latest cutting-edge interventions, it does more than simply cover or define a field, it takes criminology into areas it urgently needs to go.'

—Eamonn Carrabine, *Professor, Department of Sociology, University of Essex, UK*

'Greg Martin's *Crime, Media and Culture* sparkles with theoretical insights and provocative case studies. Comprehensively outlining the foundations of crime/media analysis, it also traces the latest trajectories in cultural criminology and associated fields like visual and narrative criminology; chronicling long-standing substantive concerns in crime/media research, it also explores contemporary issues surrounding digital surveillance, gendered images of crime, representations of terrorism, and more. For anyone interested in the interplay of crime and media, it's required reading.'

—Jeff Ferrell, *author of* Drift: Illicit Mobility and Uncertain Knowledge

CRIME, MEDIA AND CULTURE

Working broadly from the perspective of cultural criminology, *Crime, Media and Culture* engages with theories and debates about the nature of media-audience relations, examines representations of crime and justice in news media and fiction, and considers the growing significance of digital technologies and social media.

The book discusses the multiple effects media representations of crime have on audiences but also the ways media portrayals of crime and disorder influence government policy and lawmaking. It also considers the processes by which certain stories are selected for their newsworthiness. Also examined are the theoretical, conceptual and methodological underpinnings of cultural criminology and its subfields of visual criminology and narrative criminology.

Drawing on case studies and empirical examples from the increasingly blurred worlds of reality and entertainment, the dynamics of crime, media and culture are illuminated across a range of chapters covering topics that include: moral panics/folk devils and trial by media; fear of crime; cop shows and courtroom dramas; female criminality and child-on-child killing; serial killers; surveillance, new media and policing; organized crime and state crime.

Crime, Media and Culture will be an invaluable resource for undergraduate and postgraduate students interested in criminology and media studies. The book will also prove useful for lecturers and academic researchers wishing to explore the intersections of crime, media and cultural inquiry.

Greg Martin is Associate Professor of Socio-Legal Studies in the Department of Sociology and Social Policy at the University of Sydney, Australia. He has published widely in criminology, law and sociology, and is author of *Understanding Social Movements* (Routledge, 2015) and co-editor of *Secrecy, Law and Society* (Routledge, 2015). He is an Editor of *The Sociological Review*, Associate Editor of *Crime Media Culture* and a member of the Editorial Advisory Board of *Social Movement Studies.*

CRIME, MEDIA AND CULTURE

Greg Martin

LONDON AND NEW YORK

First published 2019
by Routledge
2 Park Square, Milton Park, Abingdon, Oxon OX14 4RN

and by Routledge
52 Vanderbilt Avenue, New York, NY 10017

Routledge is an imprint of the Taylor & Francis Group, an informa business

British Library Cataloguing-in-Publication Data
A catalogue record for this book is available from the British Library

Library of Congress Cataloging-in-Publication Data
Names: Martin, Greg, 1951- author.
Title: Crime, media and culture / Greg Martin.
Description: Abingdon, Oxon ; New York, NY : Routledge, 2019.
Identifiers: LCCN 2018035726| ISBN 9781138945999 (hardback) |
ISBN 9781138946002 (pbk.) | ISBN 9781315671055 (ebook)
Subjects: LCSH: Mass media and crime. | Crime—Press coverage. |
Crime in mass media.
Classification: LCC P96.C74 M374 2019 | DDC 302.23—dc23
LC record available at https://lccn.loc.gov/2018035726

ISBN: 978-1-138-94599-9 (hbk)
ISBN: 978-1-138-94600-2 (pbk)
ISBN: 978-1-315-67105-5 (ebk)

Typeset in Bembo
by Apex CoVantage, LLC

In memory of my grans: Ellie & Alma

CONTENTS

DETAILED CONTENTS

FIGURES

BOXES

ACKNOWLEDGMENTS

To my partner in life, and in crime, Rebecca Scott Bray, for her love and support, and for providing me with up-to-the-moment newsfeeds, images and research. At Routledge, I'd like to thank commissioning editor, Tom Sutton, for editorial assistance, including much help with image permissions, Hannah Catterall, and with help in the final phases of production, Mihaela Diana Ciobotea. For always reminding me there is life beyond work, and book writing, thank you to my gorgeous daughters, Roxana and Maya. The cover illustration was created for the book by Terri Hawkins, an artist living and working in Glasgow, Scotland.

CHAPTER 1

Introduction

With the advent of 'post-truth' and 'fake news' it now seems hard to be certain about the veracity of anything we read, hear about or see in the news media, though, as we will see in this book, news media institutions have always been selective, rather than objective and impartial, when it comes to deciding what stories are 'newsworthy'. In fictional accounts as well the line traditionally drawn between entertainment and reality is now more fluid than ever, as an increasing number of television shows, for instance, blur those boundaries, providing varieties of 'infotainment', whether that assumes the form of reality TV, re-creations of true crime or fly-on-the-wall documentaries. Moreover, fictional representations of crime and justice are sometimes believed to be as real as real life itself, providing authentic accounts of street-level crime, or acting as vehicles to trace actual changes in police occupational culture and law enforcement strategies. These and many more themes pertinent to working at the intersections of crime, media and culture are considered throughout this book, which adopts an approach broadly aligned to a field of critical criminology known as 'cultural criminology', albeit one that is not uncritical of that perspective.

Cultural criminology is the focus of Chapter 2, which examines theoretical underpinnings, key concepts and methods used by cultural criminologists, as well as looking at what have become two more or less distinct sub-areas of cultural criminology: *visual criminology* and *narrative criminology*. While Chapter 2 is focused specifically on cultural inquiry relating to the crime-media nexus, the purpose of this introductory chapter is a little broader: it aims to provide some foundations for understanding media in society where the study of crime and media is the focus. To that end, the chapter considers some of the ways scholars have theorized the role and function of media institutions in society. It also looks at research that has attempted to comprehend the nature and extent of media reporting and fictional representations of crime, which focus largely on newsworthy or dramatic crime stories and events occurring relatively infrequently in the real world. What that might tell us not only about the nature and role of media in society but also about the possible effects crime news and fiction might have on audiences is, as we shall see over the course of this book, a source of much debate and contention.

THEORIZING THE NATURE, EXTENT AND ROLE OF MEDIA IN SOCIETY

From the outset it is important to recognize that what is frequently referred to as 'the media' is not monolithic, but diverse and multifarious. Hence, rather than referring to 'the media' or 'mass media', it is sometimes helpful to think in the plural about 'media', which denotes the existence of a multiplicity of institutions, organizations, processes and practices that are varied in composition, scope and purpose. Distinctions can now also be made between 'old' and 'new' media, as evident, for example, by the presence of different forms and formats, including the Internet, television, newspapers and mobile devices like phones and tablets. Media also include both factual and dramatized representations, although, as we have already seen, the boundaries between reality and fiction can be blurred and hazy.

We might also think of distinguishing between tabloid media and more 'serious' media, or even between mainstream media and 'alternative' media. These distinctions suggest some media institutions are conservative, tending to produce stories that reinforce prevailing power structures or perpetuate stereotypes about certain groups, while others are critical of the status quo or offer radical perspectives and accounts (see Box 1.1). In certain respects, this goes to what Aaron Doyle (2011: 290) suggests about treating the media as a *contested space*, albeit the mass media tend to frame stories around the immediacy of distinct dramatic events rather than examining long-term situations and focusing on broader social issues. That is because media accounts are underlain by 'an implicit, unquestioned belief system supporting the status quo', and as journalists produce stories in the context of that belief system, '[f]rames of meaning that resonate with dominant cultural beliefs may be more likely to make it into the media than those that involve dramatic paradigm shifts' (Doyle 2011: 291). However, while surveillance studies scholars have paid attention to resistance (Chapter 8), as Doyle notes, a similar approach should be adopted in thinking about the mass media. In particular, and given the premise that the media represents a contested space, media studies scholars should examine the potential openings that exist in getting oppositional messages into the media. For example, in Chapter 8, we will see how Copwatch groups, along with other video activists and 'citizen journalists' use video surveillance of police as a tool to both expose and resist police brutality and other misconduct, which they make available on social media and Internet platforms like YouTube.

As we will see later in this chapter, framing stories according to dominant cultural attitudes and beliefs also means that far from being objective and value-free, decisions made by professional journalists and editors entail normative judgments as to what constitutes 'news', and what items and stories will be included in media

BOX 1.1 EXPLORING THE CRIME-MEDIA NEXUS: KEY QUESTIONS

In a very useful summary, Chris Greer (2005: 158) suggests we ought to consider the following key questions, when examining the nexus between crime and the media:

- Can we discern a coherent picture of the 'crime problem' from the media? If we can, to what extent does this picture resemble what we might claim to know about the 'reality' of crime and disorder in society?
- Do media representations of crime merely reflect, objectively and impartially, what happens in the world, or are the media active agents in socially constructing 'media realities' wherein certain values, interests and beliefs are promoted, and others are downplayed, or maybe even suppressed?
- Do the media reproduce and reinforce prejudicial or stereotypical views about marginalized groups, or do they attempt to challenge those views?
- To what extent do the media undermine or bolster existing structures of power and authority?
- Does violence in the media influence us to such a degree that it makes us more aggressive, more fearful, or both?

reports. In both news reporting, and in fictional accounts, a primary driver is whether the material will appeal to a public audience, which is a decision-making process that also involves factoring in commercial considerations. These ideas are consistent with a Marxist perspective, which posits, as a capitalist institution, the mass media is required not only to make profit, but, as part of capitalism's ideological superstructure, it is also in the business of producing and reproducing dominant ideas, beliefs and perspectives, which functions to support (not challenge) the status quo (Box 1.1). Ultimately, so Marxists argue, media institutions act in the interests of the dominant class, and since those who own media companies form part of the ruling elite the situation becomes somewhat self-perpetuating.

In contrast to the Marxist perspective, the pluralist paradigm conceives of media in rather more 'neutral' terms, and is premised on the notion that media institutions operate freely and in open competition with one another – unhindered by state censorship and government regulation – providing the consuming public with an array choices in a 24–7 global mediasphere. This view is underpinned by liberal theory and attendant principles of freedom, choice and democracy, which lie at the heart of the idea of a 'free press'. According to the 'liberal pluralist' perspective, therefore,

> news selection and production is shaped by public interests and consumer demand, the sovereignty of professional journalistic values, equal competition for media access by a diversity of news sources, and the collective values of a society built around more or less organic consensus.
>
> (Greer 2010: 491)

The pluralist view is contested by Marxists and other proponents of 'radical' theories, such as critical theory, on the basis

> it does not take account of the many vested interests in media ownership and control, or of the fact that, for all the proliferation of new channels, media industries are still predominantly owned and controlled by a small handful of white, wealthy, middle class men (or corporations started by such men).
>
> (Jewkes 2015: 28)

Against liberal pluralism, Marxist-influenced 'control approaches' stress the uneven distribution of social, economic and cultural power in society, and it is for this reason that it has tended to appeal to academics interested in news media, crime and justice, whereas the liberal pluralist paradigm has been more popular with media practitioners (Greer 2010: 491).

Marxist-influenced theories, then, emphasize *conflict*, arguing the ideology of the mass media is the ideology of the ruling class, and that the media functions not to support the population as a whole, but instead serves the interests of a small section of that population: the ruling elite. Pluralism highlights the diversity of media in society, as well as crediting audiences with a degree of agency, autonomy and capacity to exercise free choice about what media they consume according to their preferences (Jewkes 2015: 27). And, along with other conservative perspectives, it stresses *consensus* and the positive role the media plays in espousing an ideology that is broadly supportive of society as a whole.

Conservative principles also unpin what is known as 'media effects' theory, although this perspective differs from pluralism because it tends to treat the media as an undifferentiated monolithic mass, as well as denying audience agency. In its most simplistic form, media effects theory is referred to as the 'hypodermic syringe model', since it conceives of the relationship between media and audience 'as a mechanistic and unsophisticated process, by which the media "inject" values, ideas and information directly into the passive receiver, producing direct and unmediated "effects" which, in turn, have a negative influence on thoughts and actions' (Jewkes 2015: 16). Another way of thinking about this is in terms of a 'pure media effect', which, Allen et al. (1998: 55) say, conceives somewhat implausibly of the media 'as an ideological hypodermic syringe injecting noxious emotions and values into a passive audience of cultural dopes'. The presupposition (and fear) of conservatives here is of the 'criminogenic consequences of media representations', whereby 'these "dopes" imitate in reality the thrilling crimes and deviant acts committed by their screen idols' (Allen et al. 1998: 55).

Although it is hard to provide empirical support for a pure or simple version of the media effects model, not least because, as we shall see at various points in the book, audiences are *actively engaged* in processes of *interpreting* mediated content, as Allen et al. (1998: 55) state, it is equally implausible to deny the existence of *any* media effects at all, simply because it is difficult to prove straightforward causal links between people's mediated experiences and their behavior. As we will see in Chapter 2, and again in Chapter 10, those working within the field of cultural criminology have been prone to do just that. Accordingly, in striving to break

BOX 1.2 THE *WAR OF THE WORLDS* EFFECT

The clearest example of a simple or 'pure media effect' is Orson Welles's radiobroadcast of H. G. Wells's *War of the Worlds*, on the night of Halloween 1938 (Figure 1.1). Although a fictitious story of Martian invasion, many believed it, and panicking, fled their homes or stayed put and prayed. Welles was also able to exacerbate the fear of invasion by drawing on expert opinion that advised people to evacuate and attack (Jewkes 2015: 16). Even with the advent of 'fake news', it is hard to imagine anyone being able to pull off such an audacious stunt nowadays, when so many people have access to so much information via the Internet and a panoply of media and news sources.

Indeed, as we will see at various points in the book, newer media spaces opened up by the increasing availability of digital technologies, social media platforms and the like have created opportunities for ordinary citizens to move from being consumers to producer-consumers or 'prosumers' (Ritzer and Jurgenson 2010); a process that involves a 'blurring of the lines between producers and consumers, writers and readers, actors and audiences' (Yardley et al. 2017: 469). Moreover, when these opportunities are harnessed in digital activism and online campaigning they can act as informal means of influencing formal criminal justice process, which, echoing Doyle's (2011) comment about getting oppositional viewpoints into the mainstream media, can happen either with or without the aid of older, more established media institutions.

© World History Archive/Alamy Stock Photo

Figure 1.1 *War of the Worlds* radiobroadcast and *New York Daily News* front-page headline, 31 October 1938

Average net paid circulation for September exceeded
Daily---1,800,000
Sunday-3,150,000

Vol. 20. No. 109 — New York, Monday, October 31, 1938* — 48 Pages — 2 Cents IN CITY LIMITS | 3 CENTS Elsewhere

FAKE RADIO 'WAR' STIRS TERROR THROUGH U.S.

Story on Page 2

(NEWS foto)

"War" Victim

Caroline Cantlon, WPA actress, listening to this radio in West 49th St., heard announcement of "smoke in Times Square." Running to street, she fell, broke her arm.

(By Associated Press)

"I Didn't Know". Orson Welles, after broadcast expresses amazement at public reaction. He adapted H. G. Wells' "War of the Worlds" for radio and played principal role. Left: a machine conceived for another H. G. Wells story. Dramatic description of landing of weird "machine from Mars" started last night's panic.

—Story on page 2.

Figure 1.1 (continued)

free from the limitations and constraints of orthodox criminology and existing scholarship on 'crime and the media', which they see as 'formulaic' and 'static' (Hayward 2010: 5), they tend to dismiss entirely the idea of media effects.

However, as we shall see, multiple media effects do exist, and they can be both positive and negative. In Chapter 4, for example, we see how people's fear of crime might be influenced by media exposure; however, the way those mediated experiences impact on people's behavior and everyday conduct is also affected by demographic factors like race, gender and age, as well as contextual factors, such as situated experiences in local communities or crime victim status. Similar arguments might also be applied to a variant of the media effect model known as 'cultivation analysis', which rather than seeing audiences as active interpreters of media messages, posits that televised depictions of violence *cultivates* – especially among heavy watchers – a 'mean world view', and that this contributes not only to widespread crime fear in a population, but is also instrumental in fostering a generalized 'culture of fear' in contemporary society.

In terms of positive effects, which also demonstrate audience agency/active interpretation, in Chapter 5 we will see how televised crime and legal dramas – from reality TV judge shows such as *Judge Judy* to *Crime Scene Investigation* (or *CSI*) – might educate members of the public, enabling them to comprehend specialized legal language and concepts, as well as help them understand crime investigations and criminal procedure. That in turn might have positive or negative effects. Hence, some believe the effect of watching forensic-themed television like *CSI* on real-life jurors is likely to result in them 'wrongly' acquitting defendants when scientific evidence presented in court is not of the quantity and quality of evidence shown on television. Others believe watching shows like *CSI* has the opposite effect, arguing, for example, that because those shows valorize forensic scientists, they act to bolster prosecution cases in real courtroom settings. Conversely, educative effects might be less positive, as *CSI* and similar shows are believed to inform criminals about ways to avoid detection, such as wearing gloves or cleaning crime scenes with bleach. As we shall see in Chapter 5, regardless of whether the effect is positive or negative, pro-defendant or pro-prosecution, *CSI* research indicates watching forensic crime shows has *some kind of effect* on audiences.

RESEARCHING CRIME-MEDIA CONTENT

As well as critiquing 'formulaic' and 'static' research on crime-media relations, such as media effects theory and cultivation analysis, cultural criminologists are generally critical of conventional criminological approaches that have tended to use quantitative methods and statistical data as 'reliable' techniques and 'objective' measures to understand crime causation and patterns of crime, as well as develop crime prevention initiatives. For cultural criminologists, however, such approaches are not reliable in the sense they tell us little, if anything, about the *phenomenology of transgression*; that is, the situated and visceral experience of committing criminal acts, including the emotions and feelings that occur 'inside the criminal event' (Ferrell 1997: 11). As we will see in Chapter 2, to overcome the methodological shortcomings of orthodox approaches cultural criminologists propose alternative methods and techniques be adopted that are capable of comprehending the *situated experience* of transgressive behavior, including qualitative approaches like 'criminological *verstehen*' (Ferrell 1997), which enables criminologists using 'participant observation' to understand the criminal moment by experiencing firsthand the adrenaline rushes, excitement and exhilaration of rule-breaking and thrill-seeking activities.

However, as most people have little or no direct experience of crime, but 'read about it in newspapers, hear about it on the radio, and see it on television' (Chadee and Ditton 2005: 324), criminologists have often been inclined to conduct content analysis studies to help discern the incidence or coverage of news reporting on crime and disorder, what types of crime/s might be reported on the most and what, if any, impact that might have on audiences. For news media reporting and fictional portrayals alike, studies have tended to reach the same conclusion: 'Crime drama is typically violent, but even when apparently factually reporting events, crime "news" tends to be selective and distorted with a general overemphasis on crimes involving sex and violence' (Chadee and Ditton 2005: 324).

Combining media effects perspectives with content analysis can prove useful too. For instance, if the news media is reporting on more crimes of a sexual and violent nature, that may cultivate a view, especially among certain sections of the population, as to the ubiquity of those kinds of crimes, and that might, in turn, fuel crime fear, which, depending on demographic and/or contextual factors, may (or may not) affect the way people behave and conduct themselves in their daily lives. Content analysis studies proffering information about the extent of media reporting on crime and disorder, and the types of crimes receiving the most coverage, can also help answer the first of Greer's (2005: 158) key questions for those interested in exploring the crime-media nexus (Box 1.1), namely to what extent do media portrayals provide a true or accurate account about the nature and incidence of crime in society?

Indeed, many studies using content analysis are premised on a suspicion that media representations of crime, both in fact and in fiction, do not reflect the reality of crime, nor does media reporting reflect the true nature and extent of crime in society. Generally speaking, these studies consist of *quantitative* analyses aimed at uncovering the *amount* of crime, violence or control that is depicted in the media, such as looking at the number of crime stories newspapers or television shows being reported in any given day, week or month (Greer 2005: 158). By contrast, *qualitative* studies seek to understand the *nature* of media portrayals of crime, violence or control, like 'exploring the use of language, the forces and constraints that shape media production, or the wider influence of the economic, political and cultural environment' (Greer 2005: 159).

Both approaches have pros and cons. While quantitative studies have the advantage of providing a more 'complete' picture of media reporting around crime, violence and control, as contended by cultural criminologists and others working from critical perspectives, statistical data gathered from quantitative studies also have limitations. For instance, official statistics around crime only tell us about the incidence of *reported* crime. They do not tell us about crimes that go unreported, such as domestic violence and sex crimes, which, unlike the majority of crimes making up the official data, are crimes that occur in private, rather than in public settings. That is why criminologists often supplement data from official crime statistics with *victimization surveys* that, among other things, ask respondents whether they have experienced crimes they have not reported to the police. Often those surveys will use qualitative methods, such as conducting research interviews with crime victims, to provide more nuanced accounts and information about unreported crimes, and why they might go unreported. In the case of sex crimes and domestic violence, victims often tell of how they feel a sense of shame at having suffered such crimes, and also how they have been reluctant to report those crimes to the police for fear of not being believed or taken seriously. In specific relation to sex crimes, Greer (2003) has shown how increased media coverage can have a positive effect here, bringing the problem of sexual violence to public attention, so it is no longer privatized or 'hidden' behind social awkwardness and cultural taboos.

Notwithstanding the limits of quantitative methods, content analysis studies with a quantitative focus have disclosed some interesting patterns and trends particularly in relation to the news media's reporting of crime. In his summary of content analysis studies, Robert Reiner (2007: 306) compares American and British results. In American studies, crime-related content in news stories is often found to be quite high. For instance, Graber (1980) discovered crime and justice topics made up 22 to 28 percent of total stories in newspapers, 20 percent of news in local television and 12 to 13 percent of network television news. Another study reviewed 36 American content analysis studies of crime news that were conducted between 1960 and 1989, revealing marked variation in the proportion of news coverage dedicated to crime: from 1.61 to 33.5 percent (Marsh 1991: 73).

In Britain, Roshier (1973) found an average proportion of crime news of 4 percent from 1938 to 1967. Like the US studies, more recent research has revealed higher proportions of news given over to crime than in earlier studies. For example, in their study of six Scottish newspapers conducted in 1981, Ditton and Duffy (1983) found an average of 6.5 percent of space devoted to crime. The rise in space given over to crime news was also confirmed in a study comparing coverage of crime in ten national daily newspapers for four weeks from 19 June 1989, which found that, on average, 12.7 percent of event-oriented news reports pertained to crime (Williams and Dickinson 1993). This research also showed that more space was given to crime in 'downmarket' newspapers, such as the *Sun* (30.4 percent), while crime news was less prominent in more 'upmarket' newspapers, with, for instance, the smallest proportion of 5.1 percent being present in the *Guardian* (Williams and Dickinson 1993: 41).

More recently, Allen et al. (1998) conducted a content analysis study of representations of crime in post-war cinema (1945–1991), using both qualitative and quantitative methods. They found there was a three-stage periodization of crime films, with the nature of crime changing, the violence and threat of crime also increasing, as well as there being increases in portrayals of suffering victims. Their study revealed that to combat these developments, police officers were depicted increasingly as heroes, who use vigilante and sometimes corrupt tactics to achieve their goals, though with diminishing chances of success at bringing criminals to justice. Among other things, that study serves to reinforce a key theme of this book in respect of the blurring or slippage of fact and fiction, and the suggestion that in referencing reality, dramatizations of crime can act as important cultural barometers, indexing broader social transformations in real life.

While cultural criminologists are critical of content analysis studies, as with media effects models, it is important not to dismiss them out of hand, but instead recognize their value for criminologists working at the intersections of crime, media and cultural inquiry. In Chapter 3, for example, we will see how Machado and Santos (2009) use a content analysis approach to compare reporting on the disappearance of Madeleine McCann in two Portuguese newspapers. Their study highlights the distinction made earlier in this chapter between tabloid and 'serious' journalism, which they see reflected in different reporting on scientific evidence in the case. On the one hand, the 'quality' status of *Público* was evident in it not presenting DNA evidence as categorical proof of murder, and in discussing the probabilistic nature of such evidence. On the other hand, the populist and sensationalist stance of *Correio da Manhã* meant it constructed a discourse built on images of the efficiency of forensic science and certainty of DNA evidence reminiscent of television shows like *CSI*.

Although not a content analysis study in the conventional sense, in Chapter 6 we will see how David Green (2008a: 201) uses a 'text-only approach' to explore the different responses to cases of child-on-child killing in England (the James Bulger case) and Norway (the Silje Marie Redergård case). Analyzing the content of tabloid and broadsheet newspapers in both countries, he explains the very different media reactions to what were two quite similar cases in terms of the relative importance of legitimate claims makers in each country, including the reception of expert evidence and scientific knowledge. According to Green, the higher prevalence of expert claims makers in the Norwegian press as compared to the English press can partly be accounted for by the fact that expert views were not valued by reporters and editors in England as they were in Norway.

In addition, the English newspaper market is overcrowded, while in Norway local newspapers dominate, and there are only two daily national papers. Newspapers in England tend also to be sold at newsstands, whereas in Norway they are sold via subscription. All of this means English editors and journalists operating in an intensely competitive environment tend, more than their Norwegian counterparts, to be enticed to capitalize on scandalous, sensationalist and provocative stories to sell newspapers. The highly competitive nature of the media market in Britain is also mirrored in the country's political system, which is highly adversarial in comparison to the Norwegian model that stresses consensus, inclusivity, bargaining and compromise. Hence, Green's argument is that the differing responses to the killings in each country – punitive in Britain and welfare-driven in Norway – were not only a function of different *press cultures* but also contrasting *political-economic cultures*. By emphasizing the cultural aspects of the societal response, Green's analysis contributes to an understanding of the dynamics of crime, media and culture, saying less about the distinct reactions of tabloid and broadsheet newspapers than Machado and Santos (2009) do, and more about the broadly different cultures of Britain and Norway.

NEWSWORTHINESS AND NEWS VALUES

Among other things, Green's study of the case of the killing of 2-year-old James Bulger highlights its inherent 'newsworthiness' – a term referring to decisions journalists make regarding 'which events to select for inclusion as news, and how to present those events once selected' (Greer 2010: 502). Much of the value-laden content of stories in news media as well as in fictional accounts reflects its 'newsworthiness' or public appeal. Accordingly, what we see or read about is often more a function of editorial slants or the ideological stance of a particular media organization than it is objective reporting of facts or relaying of information. However, while media content can serve ideological or political purposes, the newsworthiness of stories is also driven by commercial imperatives to produce 'good copy' that sells and thus turns a profit. As we have seen, content analysis studies show how commercial imperatives associated with newsworthiness often cause media institutions to paint a distorted picture of crime in society – exaggerating the incidence of sexual and violent crime, for instance. Not only is this 'criminogenic' in the sense it provides a false or inaccurate account of the nature and occurrence of crime, it can also be criminogenic in its consequences because media reporting on crime can affect significantly people's behavior, such as not wanting to go out alone at night in certain areas for fear of victimization. In addition, as we shall see in Chapter 4, commentators argue that imagery and messaging about crime, disorder and violence emanating from the commercial media has contributed to the generation of a pervasive 'culture of fear' in contemporary society, which provides the context for politicians to criminalize more and more behavior.

Given this, one might be forgiven for thinking ethical considerations should be factored into decisions made by professional journalists and news editors when determining what news items are included in stories and reports. However, as Reiner (2007: 324) notes, journalists' sense of what is newsworthy has more to do with their sense of having a nose for what makes a *good story*, rather than, for example, any ethical or ideological considerations. In contrast, Jewkes (2015: 45) argues the process of determining the newsworthiness of story is an inherently ideological (though not necessarily ethical) process: deciding whether or not a story is newsworthy is by no means a random process or dependent on decisions made by individual journalists or editors, but is instead dependent upon 'a range on professional criteria that are used as benchmarks to determine a story's newsworthiness'. These criteria take the form of commercial, legislative and technical imperatives, as well as occupational conventions, which stem from journalists sharing ideological values with the majority of their audience, or, as Doyle (2011: 291) puts it, framing stories that resonate with dominant cultural beliefs. The result is 'a normalization of particular interests and values', which are distilled in 'news values', or 'the value judgments that journalists and editors make about the public appeal of a story and also whether it is in the public interest' (Jewkes 2015: 46). If we apply this idea to the aforementioned case of the disappearance of Madeleine McCann, we might observe a different set of news values reflected in the reporting styles of tabloid and 'serious' newspapers, whereas in the James Bulger case we see different news values residing in the respective press cultures of Britain and Norway, with the latter appearing to value more the potential contribution of expert claims makers than the former.

BOX 1.3 NEWSWORTHINESS AND CRIME NEWS VALUES

Although there are variations in emphasis and articulation across studies, as well as some substantive differences, Greer (2010: 503) claims 'the different accounts of newsworthiness are most notable for their similarities'. He cites the first study by Galtung and Ruge (1965) as continuing to influence researchers. In that study of four Norwegian newspapers reporting on foreign affairs, Galtung and Ruge (1965: 66–68) identified 12 news values, which have been neatly summarized by Harcup and O'Neill (2001: 262–264) as follows:

1. *Frequency* – events that unfold over a short time period in tune with the frequency of the news medium (e.g. murder) are more likely to be selected as news than events taking place over a long period of time.
2. *Threshold* – only after passing a threshold will events be recorded, with the greatest chance for news selection going to events of great intensity, gruesome events and those with more casualties.
3. *Unambiguity* – less ambiguous events, capable of being interpreted without multiple meanings, are more likely to become news.
4. *Meaningfulness* – events that are culturally similar to the news selector's own frame of reference are more likely to be selected. For instance, stories about British citizens involved in events in remote countries are more meaningful to British media, as is news about the US regarded more relevant to Britain than news from countries that are less culturally familiar.
5. *Consonance* – predicting or wanting something to happen, based on a mental 'pre-image' of an event, increases the chances a news selector will select it to become news.
6. *Unexpectedness* – so long as they are culturally familiar and/or consonant, the most unexpected or rare events will have the greatest chance of being selected as news.

7 *Continuity* – even if their amplitude has greatly reduced, events that have become headline news are likely to remain in the media spotlight for a while because they are familiar and interpreted easily. Continued coverage also justifies selection in the first place.
8 *Composition* – events are not always selected for their intrinsic news value, but might be chosen to fit the overall composition or balance of a newspaper or television broadcast. For example, news reports about institutional racism in the police force might include information about positive initiatives to tackle racism that would not ordinarily be reported.
9 *Reference to elite nations* – actions of elite nations are deemed more significant than those of other nations. Where definitions of elite nations are culturally, politically and economically determined, and vary from country to country, there may be general agreement about including nations like the US among the elite.
10 *Reference to elite people* – actions of elite people (often synonymous with the famous) are seen by news selectors as more significant than those of others. Audiences might also identify with them more.
11 *Reference to persons* – news tends to present events as being the result of the actions of named people rather than of social forces. Such personification goes beyond 'human interest' stories, and may relate to '*cultural idealism* according to which man is the master of his own destiny and events can be seen as the outcome of an act of free will' (Galtung and Ruge 1965: 68, original emphasis).
12 *Reference to something negative* – negative news can be presented as unambiguous and consensual, as well as generally more likely to be unexpected and to occur over a shorter time period than positive news.

Although the insights of Galtung and Ruge (1965) were based on content analysis, and did not include, for instance, interviews with journalists or sources, Greer (2010: 503) remarks it is striking that 'after much empirical testing . . . how well their framework still stands up to scrutiny'. Having said that, he also refers to Katz's (1987: 63) research on crime news, which challenges the news value of novelty, or in Galtung and Ruge's (1965: 67) terms, events that are 'unexpected or rare', on the basis 'especially newsworthy crimes do not appear to be especially unexpected, either to victims or to readers'. Indeed, political scandals, stories about high-level corruption and bank robberies all 'remain distinctively newsworthy sites of crime' (Katz 1987: 63).

Hence, Katz (1987: 63) argues rather than focusing on unexpected or rare criminal events, we ought instead to 'consider whether crime is newsworthy for its symbolic value in articulating the normatively expected'. From this perspective, audience interest in crime news is 'less morbid than inspirational' (Katz 1987: 67). Recognizing audience agency, then, Katz (1987: 67) proposes, '[t]he predominance of stories on violent crime in contemporary newspapers can be understood as serving readers' interests in re-creating daily their moral sensibilities through shock and impulses of outrage' (Katz 1987: 67). Concomitantly, for researchers, interest in crime news should reside in 'a process through which adults in contemporary society work out individual perspectives on moral questions of a quite general yet eminently personal relevance' (Katz 1987: 67).

Along with Galtung and Ruge's (1965) influential account of news values and newsworthiness (Box 1.3) there is also Chibnall's (1977) classic study of journalistic priorities in post-war Britain (1945–1975), which found some of the core elements of newsworthiness were: novelty; simplification; dramatization; immediacy; personalization; graphic presentation; and titillation. While that study continues to inspire researchers, Jewkes (2015: 47) argues Britain is now a very different place to the one Chibnall researched more than half a century ago, with news reports containing stories about crimes that could never have been imagined only a few years ago, including road rage, identity theft and image-based sexual abuse. Accordingly, Jewkes (2015: 49–70) proposes 12 news structures and news values pertinent to the twenty-first century; some overlapping with the earlier accounts of Galtung and Ruge (1965) and Chibnall (1977). These are now considered in some detail, as they provide crucial background information for our analyses in subsequent chapters of the book.

Threshold

This is the level at which stories are deemed newsworthy. What Jewkes (2015: 50) calls 'supplementary thresholds' might also be required to keep stories fresh by providing a new angle. For example, stories of attacks on elderly people in their homes may be supplemented with new angles of *escalating drama* and *risk* ('Attacker of elderly "could kill" next time'), a *sexual component* ('A 93 year old woman has spoken of her bewilderment after a man conned his way into her home and raped her elderly daughter') or a *counter-story* ('Man, 76, stabs 21 year old neighbor to death for singing too loudly').

Predictability

Just as rare and extraordinary events make things newsworthy, as Katz (1987: 63) argues, stories, including those about crime, might be regarded newsworthy for articulating what is 'normatively expected' (see Box 1.3). To Jewkes, this relates to the predictability of a story that 'may be deemed newsworthy because news organizations can plan their coverage in advance and deploy their resources (e.g. reporters and photographers) accordingly' (Jewkes 2015: 50). For instance, criminal trials and government crime policy announcements provide a degree of predictability. Mainstream media might also set an agenda for reporting certain events that provide predictable content. For example, reports about carnivals and public protests (e.g. Mardi Gras parades or anti-capitalists demonstrations) tend to stress the criminal and violent aspects, even though these events tend to be peaceful and relatively crime free. In Chapter 8, we will see how news coverage of protest events might de-contextualize video footage, focusing on police brutality – violence or conflict being another news value discussed below – rather than the issues about which the protest and activism is organized (Wilson and Serisier 2010).

Simplification

To cater for the limited attention span of audiences, brevity is a key feature of news coverage. Simplification also means stories can be interpreted only in particular ways: communicating unambiguous news reports encourages a unanimous audience interpretation, which most often amounts to moral indignation at transgressive or criminal behavior. Tabloid media are most prone to present an (over) simplified world view, which might, for instance, equate asylum seekers with terrorists (see Martin 2015b), see the mentally ill as potential murderers or assume a form of unquestioning patriotism, which, for instance, regards as treacherous anyone who is unsympathetic to the 'war on terror'. Oversimplification usually involves the setting up of binary oppositions, presenting a polarized view of the world, e.g. good/evil, black/white, normal/deviant. In sum, says Jewkes (2015: 53), 'processes of oversimplification add up to a mediated vision of crime in which shades of grey are absent and a complex reality is substituted for a simple, incontestable and preferably bite-sized message'.

Individualism

Individual explanations about the causes of crime as well as responses to crime tend to be privileged above social, cultural and political-economic explanations. That is largely because 'human interest' stories have a mass appeal, and, accordingly, the media engages in a process of personalizing crime to provide the audience with simplified accounts. Individualizing criminality also absolves governments and politicians of responsibility for anti-social behavior and crime prevention. Such was the case during the 2011 English riots, with politicians and the press characterizing looters as 'mindless thugs' whose behavior constituted 'sheer criminality'. Criminologists contest such characterization of criminals and criminal activity, stressing the social not individual origins of crime and anti-social behavior, as well as the need to analyze crime trends and patterns, and engage in policy debates about crime prevention and so forth (Martin 2011a, 2011b, 2017a). Many of the points just raised are summarized in the following statement:

> Interpersonal crime of sex and violence can be more easily presented as dramatic and titillating than non-violent crimes – for example, most property and white-collar offences. By focusing on people (as victims and offenders) and events rather than abstract issues and debates, crime reporting is individualized and simplified, which also contributes to the common association of crime with individual pathology rather than wider social, structural and political influences.
> (Greer 2005: 165)

As Greer intimates, focusing on individuals and personalities also has the effect of exculpating corporations and other powerful institutions, which might be implicated in crimes, social harms or other injustices. For example, in the case of the collapse of Barings Bank in 1995, bank employee Nick Leeson was the 'rogue trader' who it was believed was solely to blame, while systemic failings, which subsequently became evident, were downplayed (Jewkes 2015: 54).

Risk

Most serious crimes, like rape, murder or sexual assault are committed by people known to the victim. Crime statistics also reveal victims are more likely to reside in particular geographic locations, as well as come from certain socio-economic groups. However, the view presented in the mainstream media is of the ubiquity of crime, and potential there is for everyone to become victims of crime. Jewkes (2015: 55) argues that where once news stories showed compassion for offenders and endorsed a rehabilitative ideal, we now live in 'retributive times', which are victim-centered and risk-obsessed. Moreover, and as Greer (2010: 503) notes, crime news is more likely to be reported if it features what Nils Christie (1986) calls 'ideal victims', such as young children or older people. The upshot is that people are increasingly fearful of becoming victims of crime, even though victimization is most unlikely. We will explore these ideas in more detail in Chapter 4.

Sex

Studies in numerous countries show how this is a persistent news value, not only in tabloid news media as one might expect, but also in more serious/upmarket broadsheet newspapers, as well as in 'alternative' media. Accordingly, it is proposed that the over-reporting of sex crime has the effect of distorting the true incidence of those crimes, and increasing fear of victimhood, especially among women (although, as the #MeToo movement has demonstrated, sexual harassment and assault are pervasive crimes in society). Moreover, the media often conflate crimes involving sex and violence, which according to a Scottish study accounted for only 2.4 percent of recorded crimes, but constituted 45.8 percent of total news coverage (Ditton and Duffy 1983).

The conflation of sex and violence also illustrates the news value of *risk* whereby stories present narratives of 'ordinary' women as victims of randomized stranger violence. Similar to other narratives around risk, the media's preoccupation with 'stranger-danger' does, in fact, present a statistically incorrect view of crime in society, giving the false impression that the public sphere is unsafe, while the private sphere is safe. As already mentioned, Greer's (2003) research provides an important corrective to what is often seen as the negative effect of sex crime reporting, showing how increased coverage of sex crime in the 1980s and 1990s impacted positively by exposing the problem of sexual violence as a public issue rather than a solely privatized concern.

Celebrity or high-status persons

People with a high profile attract media attention with lower levels of transgression than other members of the population. Accordingly, celebrities are often the focus of media attention for committing what ordinarily would be considered quite routine crimes. Moreover, what are normally under-represented crimes, such as embezzlement, libel, perjury, tend to be the focus of attention simply because of the celebrity status of the people committing them. However, as with other news, sexual deviance relating to celebrities is of enduring interest, where the focus is on 'a celebrity or high-status person who unexpectedly takes personal and professional risks by engaging in a sexually deviant act' (Jewkes 2015: 57).

Proximity

This has two dimensions: *spatial* and *cultural*. Spatial proximity refers to the geographic closeness of the reported events, while cultural proximity refers to the relevance an event has to a target audience. However, Jewkes (2015: 60) suggests these factors will often entwine, 'so that it is those news stories which are perceived to reflect the recipient's existing framework of values, beliefs and interests and occur within geographical proximity to them that are most likely to be reported'. Whether events are reported or not will also vary according to their local or national relevance. American media, in particular, is renowned for focusing only on stories and events that relate to the US, although that has changed in recent times with what Jewkes (2015: 61) calls, 'the domestication of foreign news whereby events in other areas of the world will receive media attention if they are perceived to impinge on the home culture of the reporter and his or her audience'. An example, here, is the increase in reports about events in Middle East since the terrorist attacks in the US on 11 September 2001. Interestingly, and similar to arguments about forensic crime shows having a *CSI* effect (mentioned earlier), some argue news coverage about foreign affairs of this sort has given rise to the 'CNN effect', which refers to the impact global television networks like Cable Network News (CNN) – with global reach and operating on a 24-hour news cycle – have on international relations and the foreign policymaking of Western governments (see Gilboa 2005a, 2005b; Livingston 1997; Robinson 1999, 2005).

Violence or conflict

Violence is arguably the most common news value because it enables the media to present stories about events in the most graphic ways possible. In fact, Jewkes argues the presentation of violence has become so commonplace in the media that it is now frequently reported in a mundane and routine fashion. This also means that unless a story containing violence corresponds to several other news values or provides a threshold sufficient to sustain audience interest, it will be relegated to 'filler'. Nevertheless, violence remains a persistent feature of news coverage, which also produces a distorted picture of crime in society. Hence, research conducted in Britain during the 1990s found 65 percent of press reports pertained to interpersonal violence, whereas police statistics indicated only 6 percent of crime involved interpersonal violence (Williams and Dickson 1993). More recent statistical data indicate violent crime is on the wane, yet media reports continue to suggest violence is widespread and increasing (Jewkes 2015: 64).

Visual spectacle or graphic imagery

The prominence of visual imagery is arguably the most significant recent transformation in media reporting. In a world cultural criminologists describe as being 'saturated with images of crime' (Carrabine 2012: 463), it is assumed audiences take for granted that news stories about crime will be accompanied by visual and often graphic imagery. Indeed, many of the most memorable events, criminal or otherwise, that have occurred in the past few years have involved spectacular imagery. Jewkes (2015: 66) gives the examples of the beating of Rodney King by LAPD officers, the police chase of O. J. Simpson, the CCTV footage of James Bulger being led out of a shopping mall in Bootle, England by the boys who killed him, and the shots of the final hours of Princess Diana's life at the Ritz Hotel, Paris. Above all, the images of passenger planes crashing into the Twin Towers on 11 September 2001 are probably the most shockingly graphic of all the images yet witnessed.

Significantly, Jewkes (2015: 65) suggests while contemporary visual culture means spectacular crimes get a lot of coverage, it also means crimes occurring behind closed doors, and in the private sphere (e.g. domestic violence, white-collar and corporate crime, state violence and the abuse of human rights), are less likely to attract attention. This is worrying because the commission of these crimes may no longer be subject to public scrutiny, and they may therefore become even more peripheral, eventually disappearing from public view altogether.

Children

As we shall see in Chapter 6, any stories involving children as either victims or perpetrators of crime are eminently newsworthy. More often than not these stories will contain a strong moral element, which stems from the social construction of childhood as separate from adulthood, as well as historic ideas of children being innocent and in need of nurture and protection. Crimes where children are offenders are especially newsworthy. Indeed, the notion of childhood innocence was discarded in the case of James Bulger, who was killed in 1993 by two 10-year-old boys subsequently characterized as 'evil little monsters'. The case was doubly newsworthy in the sense it was not only a story about the murder of a young child, but also about the two young boys who had killed him. As discussed in Chapter 6, the case was seen as symptomatic of moral decay in British society, and also proved a watershed moment with lasting effects for the administration of criminal justice in Britain, which became increasingly affected by 'law and order' politics.

Indeed, Green (2008a: 198) shows how the Bulger case helped pave the way for the landslide election victory in 1997 of New Labour, with Tony Blair proclaiming, when in opposition, that, if elected, his party would be 'tough on crime, tough on the causes of crime'. (Note the order, and stress first on being *tough on crime*, only then being tough on its *causes*.) Hence, the Bulger murder was seminal for fostering a cultural and political appetite for punishing children in England and Wales, such that in the immediate aftermath of the case:

> public concern about crime immediately doubled and sentences reflected this concern in their decisions. The adult prison population in England and Wales has since 1993 risen almost inexorably, increasing by 80 per cent over the last 14 years after the reversal of a brief downward trend that had begun one year before James Bulger was killed. The number of youths aged 15 to 17 held in prisons rose from 769 to 2089 between 1993 and 2002.
>
> (Green 2008a: 197–198)

Conservative ideology and political diversion

Many of the news values discussed above resonate with a right-wing/conservative world view, which is present in most parts of the mass media, but especially the tabloid press. Over the past few decades, a symbiotic relationship appears to have developed between the rhetoric of politicians and opinions published in the press around issues of law and order. Broadly speaking, these views are supportive of law enforcement agencies and approaches that are tough on offenders and sympathetic to crime victims. They also tend to support the view that 'prison works', and advocate accordingly for the construction of more prisons to mete out retributive justice. Any form of transgression or deviation from what the media defines as the norms of a conventional way of life is deemed ripe for punitive treatment (Pratt 2007), and is increasingly accompanied by new police powers or the introduction of very specific offenses (Loughnan 2010): from curfews designed to curb the 'anti-social' behavior of young people (Martin 2011a) to legislation that criminalizes public protest (Martin 2017d).

One significant effect of this 'punitive turn' has been generalized hostility towards minority and marginalized groups (Bhatia et al. 2018), which is an aspect of a broader culture of fear in contemporary society (discussed in Chapter 4). Fear of migrants as terrorists is a particular manifestation of these developments (Martin 2015b), so is fear of migrants generally, as demonstrated in the 2016 Brexit vote where, in an example of 'fake news', the UK Independence Party, or UKIP, launched a highly controversial poster (Figure 1.2) showing a line of Syrian refugees at the Croatia-Slovenia border (not trying to enter Britain) to highlight concerns over immigration in the European Union (Grice 2017). Media hysteria and political rhetoric around this and other issues where there is a degree of moral indignation about behavior labeled 'deviant' may give rise to 'moral panics', where 'folk devil' groups are blamed for the ills of society. As we will see in Chapter 3, by scapegoating particular groups in this way the response of politicians and the media functions to divert attention from real and serious issues. For example, the construction of immigrants-as-terrorists diverts attention from some of the ways interventionist foreign policies in the Middle East impacts domestically on Muslim communities (Kundnani 2014).

© Mark Thomas/Alamy Stock Photo

Figure 1.2 On 16 June 2016, Nigel Farage unveils and discusses UKIP's 'Breaking Point' poster highlighting concerns about immigration ahead of the Brexit vote on 23 June 2018

BOX 1.4 A SUMMARY OF MEDIA REPRESENTATIONS OF CRIME

Although it is not as comprehensive as Jewkes's (2015) list of news values and news structures, Reiner (2007: 315) nevertheless provides a useful précis of some of the ways the mainstream media represents crime, including the following:

- Stories about crime figure prominently in all media, whether in news or fictional accounts. Although evidence suggests there is increasing attention on crime in some parts of the media,. overall the fascination with crime has been constant in media history.
- The proportion of different crimes represented in the media is the inverse of official statistics. Moreover, news stories and fiction concentrate overwhelmingly on serious violent crimes against individuals, albeit with some variation according to medium. For instance, '[b]roadcast news generally devotes more attention to crime reports than newspapers' (Reiner 2007: 307). The proportion of crime news items also varies according to different markets: '[c]ommercial radio and television broadcast a higher proportion of crime news stories overall than the BBC [British Broadcasting Corporation], although the latter carried more reports about crime in general and criminal justice' (Reiner 2007: 307).

- The demographic profile of offenders and victims in the media differs from those actually processed by the criminal justice system, tending to be older and of higher status; child victims and perpetrators are also represented disproportionately.
- Media portrayals of crime risks are both quantitatively and qualitatively more serious than the picture reported in official statistics, while the media tend to downplay the risk of falling victim to other crimes, such as property offenses.
- Although the media conveys a positive image of the success and integrity of the police and criminal justice in general, in both news and fiction there is also a tendency to criticize law enforcement in respect of its effectiveness as well as its adherence to principles of justice and its honesty/integrity.
- Media coverage of crime is motivated increasingly by 'human interest' stories, focusing on the suffering of individual victims. Although Reiner does not extend his observation here, as Jewkes (2015: 68–70) notes, this style of media reporting, which focuses on the suffering of individual crime victims, has the effect of fueling populist politics and punitive policies around crime and justice, while obscuring issues and debate engaging with the causes of crime and the formulation of better government policies that might prevent crime from occurring in the first place.

CRIME, MEDIA AND CULTURE

The notion that there is some kind of symbiotic relationship between the mainstream mass media and politicians is something we consider in Chapter 9, when we look at some of the ties that can exist between media, corporate business, politics and organized crime. At the heart of this type of argument is the idea just canvassed that far from acting as neutral conveyers of information, media institutions are driven by a set of norms and values when determining the newsworthiness of stories. However, while this frequently serves to reinforce the status quo and bolster dominant cultural beliefs, alternative voices have a growing presence in the 24–7 global mediasphere. Using social media and online platforms those expressing views and perspectives different from the media mainstream can have a positive impact on crime and justice issues. And given many using new media and digital technologies in this way are ordinary citizens, not professional journalists, their actions can also affect the ways older media actors and institutions engage with those issues.

A key aim of this book is to explore some of the ways criminal justice processes might be affected by this changing media and cultural landscape using perspective fitting loosely within the framework of cultural criminology. As mentioned at the beginning of this chapter, Chapter 2 offers a review of some of the key insights afforded by cultural criminology, including material on what might be regarded two of its subfields: *visual criminology* and *narrative criminology*. However, it is also argued that we must be circumspect about cultural criminologists' somewhat dismissive characterization of existing scholarship on 'crime and the media', such as media effects and content analysis studies, which, they say, constitute a relatively 'formulaic' and 'static' body of work (Hayward 2010: 5). We must be critical of that characterization because throughout the book we will encounter examples of multiple media effects, which require we adopt a broad and inclusive conception of media effects beyond what cultural criminologists and other critics quite rightly see as a simplistic (and implausible) model of a 'pure media effect' (Allen et al. 1998: 55), with the media being seen as analogous to a hypodermic syringe injecting passive audiences with noxious ideas and messages.

In Chapter 3, we look at moral panics and folk devils, which have become a staple of cultural criminological analysis. Among other things, our discussion looks at some of the more recent developments and extensions of moral panic theory, including the idea that, although classically conceived as episodic, moral panics might nevertheless have long-lasting effects or legacies in areas such as law and crime policy. We also consider some of the ways moral panics might be resisted, and how 'good moral panics' might emerge to confront issues of legitimate public concern. In that chapter, we also look at the concept of trial by media, which is linked to the moral panic-folk devil couplet in the sense it also involves a process of demonization, though one that is directed at individuals rather than groups.

The role the media plays in generating crime fear and a more generalized 'culture of fear' in contemporary societies is the focus in Chapter 4. It considers the idea that media portrayals of a mean and violent world *cultivate* fear in audiences, and especially heavy television watchers, which, in turn, affect people's behavior in everyday life. However, research shows how audience responses derive not only from mediated exposure to crime and violence but also, and significantly, how they are affected by demographic factors, like gender and age, as well as contextual factors, such as degree of community attachment and real-life experiences of criminal justice. The chapter also examines the paradox of why some groups, such as women and the elderly, are more likely to fear crime even though they are statistically less likely to be crime victims. Finally, as with our analysis of moral panics, the chapter considers some of the real and lasting effects of crime fear and research relating to it in respect of crime policy formation and lawmaking.

Chapter 5 considers portrayals of criminal justice and law enforcement in popular culture, with a focus on television and film. Addressing a key theme of the book, it shows how fictional and real-life representations of crime, justice and law are often blurred, and how, in the process, law films, crime movies and televised police dramas can provide valuable insights into the current state of society, as well as chart some of the ways society has changed. The chapter looks in some depth at the so-called '*CSI* effect', which, as discussed earlier refers to the perceived tendency of jurors who have watched forensic science television dramas to acquit defendants on the basis that the evidence presented in real courtrooms is not of sufficient quantity or quality as compared to evidence portrayed on television shows. The chapter discusses a number of other effects of watching shows like *CSI*, which might be positive or negative, including that heroic portrayals of state-employed forensic scientists might cause jurors to adopt pro-prosecution attitudes. Watching forensic-themed television might also educate audiences about criminal procedures and forensic investigations, but it can equally inform criminals about some of the methods that can be used to avoid detection. Regardless of whether there are positive or negative effects, the research indicates watching forensic crime dramas, and other formats, like reality TV judge shows, does have some kind of effect.

In Chapter 6, we look at media representations of female criminality, showing how violent women, and particularly those who harm or kill children, are regarded 'doubly deviant', since they violate laws of nature *and* criminal law. Moreover, those who deviate from stereotypical feminine behavior, such as not showing the requisite signs of grief or remorse, or dressing inappropriately, are subject to especially harsh media treatment, which sometimes amounts to a media trial. Focusing on Green's (2008a) comparative analysis of child-on-child killing in England and Norway, the chapter also shows how the treatment of children in those jurisdictions can provide cross-cultural insights into their distinct press cultures and, more broadly, the different political and economic structures of the two countries. Comparing media reporting on two female killers in England and Finland, Berrington and Honkatukia (2002) similarly show how the different press responses to female criminal violence can be explained via a political-economic analysis of crime and the media, which, like Green, contrasts the highly competitive media market in Britain with the less competitive, subscription-based market in Finland.

Rather than focusing on the psychological roots of serial killing, which stresses individual pathology, biography or dysfunctional family background, Chapter 7 situates serial killing and serial killers in socio-historical context. It shows how serial killing can be conceived as a product of modernizing processes, which have provided a number of preconditions for serial killing, such as: the anonymity afforded by urban environments that are the hunting ground for serial killers; the prevalence of a mean/ends rationality, which tends to instrumentalize social relationships; and notions, dating back to Enlightenment thinking, of social progress and visions of utopia that are enacted by serial killers who, in an effort to rid society of its detritus, prey disproportionately on modernity's devalued, denigrated and dispossessed populations. The presence of a mass media and attendant celebrity culture is another precondition for serial killing. Here a symbiotic relationship exists between serial killers who revel in their notoriety and celebrity status (sometimes mimicking fictional killers or being inspired by accounts of real killers preceding them) and the media, which capitalizes on public fascination with crime of this kind. Also part of the 'serial killer industry' (Soothill 1993) are law enforcement agencies and professional profilers who stand to benefit from the public's continued interest in serial killing, and who, it has been observed, actually invented the serial killer category having been influenced by popular culture and detective fiction. In contrast to the reading of serial killing as modern, another perspective regards serial killing as a reaction against modernity. On this view, serial killers are the antithesis of the unified, centered and rational modern self; a postmodern self destabilized by consumer capitalism, free to consume unshackled from the constraints and controls of modern institutions, yet flattened and thinned through immediate and repeated acts of consumption.

While modern notions of privacy and increased social anonymity help shield the activities of serial killers, in Chapter 8 we consider a countervailing tendency in modern societies, whereby the ubiquity of surveillance technologies now makes it almost impossible to remain anonymous and disappear from view. These developments have partly been enabled by the emergence of a 'surveillant assemblage', which, in contrast to hierarchical forms of top-down surveillance (e.g. panopticism), consists of a fractured rhizomatic criss-crossing of the surveillant gaze across state, police and corporate monitoring systems. Having the capacity to affect the powerful and powerless alike, it would seem that under these conditions resistance is futile. However, the chapter shows how the surveillant gaze of the state and its agents, for instance, can be reversed via bottom-up modes of observation or 'counterveillance'. Though these moves do not constitute a total democratic leveling of the surveillance hierarchy, they are made increasingly possible through citizen use of new digital technologies (e.g. mobile phone cameras), online activism and social media, which, when harnessed, are capable of exposing police misconduct and state abuses of power.

Continuing the theme of symbiosis, discussed in Chapter 7 with regard to serial killers, Chapter 9 considers the 'symbiotic model' of organized crime, which identifies a blurring between legitimate business activity and organized crime. In so doing, it inverts stereotypical images of organized criminals as underworld mobsters, although, as we see in the chapter, fictional portrayals adhering to those stereotypes can serve as a useful means of indexing social change. The symbiotic perspective, then, asks us to broaden our definition of what constitutes 'crime' to include those activities resulting in social harm or other kinds of injustice, rather than equating crime strictly with the violation of criminal law. It also seeks to reconceive of the actors involved in organized and systemic acts causing harm and injustice to include corporations, states and state officials, politicians and the media. Linking back to Chapter 8, the chapter shows how 'state-organized crime' and other abuses of state power might be exposed by citizen journalists and activists using digital technologies to post images and video footage online and in social media feeds in the hope they will contribute to greater transparency and accountability of future state operations.

The book concludes in Chapter 10 by drawing out some of the more prominent themes that have emerged in our explorations at the intersections of crime, media and culture. It begins by proposing that rather than treat media effects in its most simplistic form as denoting a direct causal relationship between media messaging and passive audiences, the media effects concept should be applied broadly and inclusively to an array of phenomena, recognizing the multiple ways both news reporting and crime drama affect not only audiences but also legal institutions and government crime policy. The chapter also considers the numerous ways the boundaries between real crime and fictional depictions are increasingly blurred, and what that might tell us, for example, about the possible ways dramatized representations can help audiences understand the operation of the criminal justice system within the context of broader social and cultural transformations. Blurring is also evident in the various symbiotic relationships identified in the book, including in the slippage between factual and fiction representations of serial killing, which serves to reinforce mutually beneficial relations between media institutions, law enforcement agencies and serial killers themselves. A symbiotic model can also be used to analyze organized crime, highlighting the gray zone that exists between legitimate and illicit business activities, which requires we widen the scope of organized crime beyond stereotypical depictions of mobsters to include corporate crime, state crime and harms perpetrated by the mainstream mass media.

Towards the end of Chapter 10 we look at some of the ways the mass media can be read as 'criminogenic' in nature, function and consequence. For instance, to compete with rivals, and maximize profit, mainstream media institutions produce sensationalist and provocative stories that sell. Given we know those stories also focus disproportionately on sex and violent crimes this only provides a false and misleading account of crime in society, but it can also have the *effect* of fueling fear of crime, which is exploited by politicians using it as a pretext to introduce punitive 'law and order' measures. That, in turn, leads to increasing criminalization, or 'overcriminalization', giving the impression there is a serious 'crime problem' in need of resolving via harsh treatment, which fuels crime fear again, and that is then used to justify the further implementation of punitive measures. The book concludes on a more sanguine note, showing how citizen-led digital activism and online/social media campaigning around crime and justice issues might provide important correctives to the criminogenic tendencies of the media mainstream.

SUGGESTED FURTHER READING

The following chapters provide useful overviews of key ideas and concepts, and offer summaries of some of the classic studies in crime and media research:

Greer, C. (2005) 'Crime and media: Understanding the connections' in C. Hale, K. Hayward, A. Wahadin and E. Wincup (eds) *Criminology*. Oxford: Oxford University Press, pp. 157–182.

Greer, C. (2010) 'News media criminology' in E. McLaughlin and T. Newburn (eds) *The Sage Handbook of Criminological Theory*. London: Sage, pp. 490–513.

Reiner, R. (2007) 'Media-made criminality: The representation of crime in the mass media' in M. Maguire, R. Morgan and R. Reiner (eds) *The Oxford Handbook of Criminology* (4th edition). Oxford: Oxford University Press, pp. 302–337.

On newsworthiness and news values it is always worth revisiting the following pioneering studies:

Chibnall, S. (1977) *Law and Order News: Crime Reporting in the British Press*. London: Tavistock.

Galtung, J. and Ruge, M. H. (1965) 'The structure of foreign news: The presentation of the Congo, Cuba and Cyprus crises in four Norwegian newspapers' *Journal of Peace Research* 2(1): 64–91.

CHAPTER 2

Studying crime and culture

INTRODUCTION

As we saw in Chapter 1, the killing of James Bulger was a doubly newsworthy event because it was a story not only about the murder of a young child but also about the two 10-year-old boys who killed him. In his study of the case, and its comparison with the similar case of the killing of Silje Marie Redergård in Norway, David Green (2008a) shows how the media and political responses reflected the very different cultures of Britain and Norway. It will be recalled that in Britain the media marketplace is densely populated and highly competitive, which leads to the production of sensationalist news stories. Likewise, the adversarial nature of the British political system means politicians frequently fight with one another so as to be seen to be the toughest on crime, which, in the Bulger case, was reflected in the punitive treatment of the child killers. By contrast, the Norwegian newspaper market is less crowded and less competitive, and instead of being sold at newsstands, newspapers are sold via subscription, which decreases the need for highly sensationalist and provocative stories. The political system is also modeled on a form of democracy that privileges compromise and consensus, which tends toward a more welfare-driven approach to crime.

Green's study, which we will consider in greater depth in Chapter 6, is poignant not only for highlighting the newsworthiness of stories about child-on-child killing, but also, for our purposes in this book, because it illuminates some intersections between crime, media and culture. Similarly, John Pratt (2006) explores connections between culture and crime, analyzing the cultural (and historical-colonial) roots of punitiveness and high imprisonment rates in New Zealand, which, he says, are paradoxical when considered alongside New

Zealand's reputation as a friendly and hospitable place. To Pratt (2006: 545), New Zealand's lesser known history of intolerance and excessive punitiveness ought to be placed in the context of the cultural values of social cohesion, homogeneity, security and conformity that have led to the country being described regularly as a 'paradise'. Pratt's (2006: 545) contention is that over time those cultural values have been 'reasserted and affirmed by sanctioning the transgressors' through punishment and imprisonment:

> In effect, the very qualities that had brought about stability and social cohesion had also brought about a crushing conformity, enforced by intense levels of formal and informal social control and fear of appearing different, fear of not belonging to and fear of being rejected by this tightly drawn homogeneous community.
>
> (Pratt 2006: 553)

Pratt (2006: 553) adds that, '[t]hroughout the history of New Zealand, the famed qualities of friendliness and openness have been denied to those who were outside its narrow parameters of acceptability'. Moreover, in recent times, intolerance to those who threaten social cohesion and excessively punitive responses to criminal acts have assumed 'a new ethnic toxicity', such that '50 per cent of the prison population are indigenous Maori, even though they make up only 15 per cent of the population' (Pratt 2006: 542).

Exploring links between crime and culture, the works by Green and Pratt clearly fall within the ambit of what has become known as 'cultural criminology', which is now a key framework used by critical criminologists working at the intersections of crime and cultural inquiry, including those with a specific interest in crime-media relations. Nonetheless, the two quite distinct studies also exemplify what Jeff Ferrell (2010) says about cultural criminology being a 'loose canon', which in part derives from its highly interdisciplinary nature, having 'developed from a synthesis of theoretical traditions, including symbolic interactionism/labelling theory, critical and cultural theory, and cultural geography' (Ferrell 2015: 293). Accordingly, not only does cultural criminology contain ideas from within criminology (e.g. symbolic interactionism, labeling theory), but it also 'incorporates perspectives from urban studies, media studies, existential philosophy, cultural and human geography, postmodern critical theory, anthropology and social movements theory' (Ferrell et al. 2015: 8).

Related to these points about the interdisciplinary origins of cultural criminology, as well as its antecedents in mainstream criminology and the sociology of deviance, is the criticism cultural criminology repeats what others have done before, or that it (re)presents 'new wine in old bottles' (Hayward 2016: 301, 304). However, despite its interdisciplinary influences, and notwithstanding questions pertaining to its novelty, over the past two decades or so cultural criminology has developed a relatively distinct character in terms of both theory and method. In respect of methodology, for instance, we shall see how cultural criminology has taken 'shape as a distinctive methodological sensibility – a sensibility attuned to qualitative inquiry in general, and ethnographic inquiry in particular' (Ferrell 2015: 293). The theoretical and methodological origins of cultural criminology are also evident in what have become two relatively discrete though, as we shall see, sometimes interconnected, offshoots of the field: *visual criminology* and *narrative criminology*.

Given the crime-media nexus is a core concern of cultural criminology (Hayward 2016: 301, 2017: 136), and that, as we saw in Chapter 1, visual spectacle and graphic imagery are key news values in contemporary societies, it is unsurprising that studying images and the visual has always interested cultural criminologists. In fact, some would even contest there is any distinction between cultural and visual criminology on the basis 'the story of crime' is one that is 'imaged, constructed, and "framed" within modern society' (Hayward 2010: 9). In keeping with a theme of this book – that is, the slippage between fact and fiction – that view of crime as constituted through images applies to the line between 'real' crime and 'unreal' images of crime, which, accordingly to Ferrell and Van de Voorde (2010: 36) is increasingly blurred, such that it is now impossible to divorce crime and crime control from their visual representations (see also Carrabine 2012: 463).

Moreover, in light of Hayward's (2010: 9) assertion that images are a key element in the *story* of crime, we might conclude not only that there is little, if any, distinction between cultural and visual criminology, but also that there is some blurring of the lines between visual criminology and narrative criminology. That there are links between storytelling and crime should not be surprising given, as we saw in Chapter 1, stories about crime constitute staples of news media, works of fiction and popular culture (see also Katz 2016: 235; Presser 2016: 139). Indeed, according to Katz (2016: 235), studies of culture *about* crime, which includes visual *and* textual representations in popular culture as well as news media reporting, 'make up a great bulk of cultural criminology'.

Cultural criminology, then, is one of the principal ways of approaching the study of crime and culture, particularly where the focus is on exploring relationships between crime, media and culture, as in the case of this book. That being said, the purpose of this chapter is not to provide an exhaustive account of cultural criminology, which since 2005 has had its own dedicated journal, *Crime Media Culture*, and has also been the subject of entire books; most notably Ferrell et al.'s (2015) *Cultural Criminology: An Invitation* (now in its second edition). Rather, we will consider key theoretical, conceptual and methodological issues in cultural criminology in order to establish some foundations for our analyses in subsequent chapters. We begin by considering briefly the political orientation of cultural criminology, and its relationship to orthodox criminological perspectives.

CULTURAL CRIMINOLOGY

Noting the interdisciplinarity of cultural criminology, Ferrell (2015: 304) says it 'is among the most porous of criminological perspectives, readily moving beyond the theoretical boundaries of contemporary criminology to welcome insights from cultural geography, cultural studies, political theory, and other perspectives'. In other words, it is a form of criminological investigation that has 'torn itself away from the moorings of conventional criminological practice' (Ferrell 2010: 305–306), which has traditionally been of an 'administrative' nature, using, for example, surveys and official statistics to advise government departments on matters such as the causes of crime, patterns of crime and crime prevention (see Presdee 2004a). Challenging this 'scientific' approach, 'cultural criminology rests on an understanding that the reality of crime and control – their meanings and consequences – emerges from an interplay of representation, interpretation, and emotion' (Ferrell 2010: 308). Similarly, Carrabine (2016a: 852) describes the 'revival of interest in cultural criminology over the last two decades' as constituting 'an approach that has attempted to place the study of crime and its control firmly in the context of culture, viewing them as creative constructs full of energy and meaning'.

In an instance of breaking free from orthodox approaches, cultural criminologists have been critical of 'broken windows theory', which posits broken windows and other physical signs of neighborhood neglect, like graffiti, act as invitations for further neglect, disorder and criminality (Kelling and Wilson 1982); and, moreover, they are perceived by residents themselves as indicators of increasing levels of crime and decay. That, in turn, has provided 'a simplistic justification for policies of urban exclusion and low-level "order maintenance policing"' (Ferrell 2010: 307). However, as Freiberg (2001: 269) observes, 'deviant or criminal effects do not occur in a vacuum but are embedded in the larger social environment and where this environment is itself also threatening, unstable and insecure a multiplier effect will occur'.

Thus, according to Ferrell (2010: 307), broken windows theory is incapable of conceiving of 'complex cultural dynamics of display, symbolism and perception' so much as assuming them, 'constructing a series of one-dimensional meanings and then arbitrarily assigning them to physical phenomenon and imagined public audiences'. In other words, and as Kubrin (2008: 207, added emphasis) says, the broken windows approach relies on objective indicators of disorder, instead of interrogating 'the *social meaning* ascribed to disorder by community residents that may trigger the broken windows process'. Hence, broken windows theory strays into the territory of cultural criminology, though by imposing objective measures of neighborhood decline and so forth, it ignores, somewhat ironically, the importance of residents' own perceptions and interpretations of their communities, as well as would-be offenders' 'reading culture in public space (graffiti, trash, loitering, open contraband marketing) for signs of official indifference' (Katz 2016: 237).

At the heart of cultural criminology, then, is a 'political' project to debunk conventional criminological approaches, which are themselves political in the sense they entail 'a closing down of theory and critique in the interest of quantification and criminal justice' (Ferrell 2010: 304). But Martin O'Brien (2005) has critiqued cultural criminology's political rather than analytical orientation to studying connections between culture and crime. In the case of graffiti, for example, he argues Ferrell (1996) produces an imbalanced account, giving 'detailed and celebratory empirical attention' to the graffiti-writing culture, yet does not give the same attention to 'those who resist the writers and motivate themselves to produce alternative aesthetic motifs in the same urban environment' (O'Brien 2005: 603–604). As there is no analytical or methodological rationale for that imbalance, O'Brien (2005: 604) concludes, '[t]he only justification there can be is political'.

However, the political 'bias' of cultural criminology constitutes an important and quite legitimate antidote to the conservative and overly rationalistic tendencies of conventional criminology. After all, Ferrell (1997: 16) states, '[a]s all criminologists know, criminality is decided as much by legal and political authorities, and by their strategies of criminalization, enforcement, and control, as by criminals themselves'. So, just as the high standard of proof in criminal trials of 'beyond reasonable doubt' is designed to safeguard the rights of relatively powerless and far less well-resourced defendants vis-à-vis the power of the state and its agents, so cultural criminologists are inclined to represent or 'defend' the perspectives of transgressive lawbreakers and members of deviant subcultures. In so doing, though, they have been accused of glorifying resistance (Webber 2007: 143), celebrating the activities of 'criminal edgeworkers' (Hayward 2016: 303) or idealizing and romanticizing the offender (Carrabine 2016a: 854), which has meant they have supposedly failed to consider the messy and tragic outcomes of transgression (Webber 2007: 140), and have not developed a critique of state formations and state agents (Hayward 2016: 311), nor corporate crime (Carrabine 2016a: 854). In a more devastating appraisal, Hall and Winlow (2015: 52) claim cultural criminology is not really criminology at all, since it does little work on serious and 'harmful crimes such as domestic violence, homicide, and violent organized crime, yet it also fails to investigate state and corporate crime, which it leaves to more traditional critical criminologists'.

As we shall see in Chapter 9, however, recent lines of inquiry in cultural criminology have emerged that do focus on harms caused by states, including those relating to terrorism and 'state-organized crime' (Hamm 2007; Hayward 2011). Moreover, as Hayward (2016: 304–305) argues, rather than focusing on risk or excitement and the drama of criminality, some cultural criminologists, like Mike Presdee (2004b), for example, have explored *emotions* associated with the everyday lived realities of crime, such as loss, humiliation and resentment. And although there may be a tendency to romanticize low-level transgression and resistance (Hayward 2016: 304), or even seek revolutionary potential in delinquency (Martin 2002: 75), cultural criminology is equally concerned with the mundane (Ferrell 2013: 260), looking for instance to decode those activities that are 'so predictably routine, as to be all but unnoticeable', such as strategies of crime control and prevention aimed at 'designing out crime'.

We have already seen what a cultural criminological analysis might import into conventional approaches like broken windows theory. Similarly, cultural criminology can provide an interpretative framework for understanding how quotidian environments may be fashioned according to principles of 'situational crime prevention', whereby the prevention of crime is achieved through environmental design, incorporating seemingly innocuous features (e.g. hedge rows, park benches) intended to manipulate and control human behavior to prevent criminal activity:

> In these circumstances, cultural criminologists seek to penetrate the façades of 'civility' or 'urban development' behind which such control strategies are hidden; to decode the hidden meanings of hedge rows and park benches; and so expose the ways in which power and ideology operate at the level of everyday life.
>
> (Ferrell 2013: 260)

Thus, cultural criminology is not only a *loose cannon* set upon smashing the canonical core of orthodox criminology and the various mythologies sustaining it, but, according to Ferrell (2010: 311–312), it is also a *loose canon* aimed at reimagining the criminological enterprise by 'embracing an array of alternative theoretical and methodological approaches [and] investigating topics conventionally omitted from criminological analysis'. As such, it tends to defy definition (Ferrell 2010: 305, 2013: 257–258), although, as we will see in the remainder of this chapter, there are in fact some key elements constituting what has been called 'new cultural criminology' (Hayward and Young 2004: 263; Ferrell et al. 2015: 7–10; Martin 2009: 125). In the next section, we trace some of the theoretical and conceptual roots of contemporary cultural criminology, after which we examine its methodological approaches. In the final parts of the chapter, both theory and method figure prominently in our discussion of two relatively new strands of cultural criminology: visual and narrative criminology.

THEORETICAL FOUNDATIONS OF CULTURAL CRIMINOLOGY

The immediate origins of cultural criminology can be traced to the 'new criminology' and cultural studies perspectives that emerged in Britain from the 1970s. Many of the concerns of researchers back then have continued in contemporary (new) cultural criminology. For instance, cultural criminologists remain interested in deviant and criminal subcultures, though unlike those working under the auspices of Birmingham's Centre for Contemporary Cultural Studies (CCCS) in the 1970s, they are less concerned with notions of class and class-based identity (Martin 2009). In many respects, that has to do with the impact of postmodernism and post-structuralism – themselves part of a general 'cultural turn' in the social sciences and humanities – on the new cultural criminology, such that notions of class and social structure give way to more fluid ways of thinking about *style* and *identity*.

That is evident in the way contemporary cultural criminologists conceive of subcultures 'as "fluid, porous, amorphous and transitory"' (Ferrell et al. 2008: 53, quoting Martin 2004: 31). Likewise, whereas the CCCS saw style as a means of resolving, albeit symbolically, structural (i.e. class) contradictions (Martin 2002:

75), contemporary cultural criminologists define style as 'the fluid in which meaning floats, the essential medium for collective communication, the connecting tissue between individual and society' (Ferrell et al. 2008: 198). Accordingly, cultural criminology has been criticized on the basis that 'while "style" and "subculture" were formerly connected to broader structures, and social class in particular, they now appear autonomous, free-floating, decoupled from wider structural forces' (Martin 2009: 125).

Despite this objection, cultural criminologists remain interested in the wider social and structural contexts within which crime takes place, which has been the traditional preoccupation of a good deal of criminology. Hence, they are concerned with what they call the 'background' to crime and transgressive behavior, such as issues of relative deprivation, unemployment, poor neighborhoods and educational disadvantage. However, they are also critical of criminological analyses that ignore 'the foreground of experience and the existential psychodynamics of the actor' (Hayward and Young 2004: 266). In that regard, they have been influenced by Jack Katz (1988), whose work privileges the expressive and subjective *lived experience* of individuals, considering deviance in terms of the 'thrill of transgression' and 'self-transcendence', which are perceived as ways of 'overcoming the conventionality and mundanity typically associated with the banal routines and practicalities of everyday "regular life"' (Hayward 2004: 149). That central concern with excitement 'as the antidote to modern boredom' (Ferrell 2004: 294) is perhaps best captured by Steven Lyng's (1990) concept of 'edgework', which pertains to losing and regaining control in risky situations (and is the subject of examples in Boxes 2.1 and 2.2).

BOX 2.1 FIGHTING OFF BOREDOM: CULTURAL CRIMINOLOGY AND *FIGHT CLUB*

> The spreading disintegration of the work process, the growing confinement of youths and adults in fractured and relatively meaningless work situations (when they can find work at all), surely will continue to heighten the seduction of edgework and adrenaline rush experiences as moments of cleansing terror and desperate rehumanization.
>
> (Ferrell 1997: 19)

Throughout this chapter we will consider some of the contexts in which 'edgework' might occur in both fictional and real-world settings. The 1999 movie *Fight Club* provides a fictional example of what might be thought of as a type of edgework associated with some of the developments Ferrell is talking about in the above quotation. However, according to critics, like Henry Giroux (2000: 33), while the movie appears to offer 'a critique of late capitalist society and the misfortunes it generates out of its obsessive concern with profits, consumption, and the commercial values that underline its market-driven ethos', ultimately, it 'confirms capitalism's worst excesses and legitimates its ruling narratives'. In other terms, *Fight Club* is

> less interested in critiquing the broader material relations of power and strategies of domination and exploitation associated with neoliberal capitalism than it is in rebelling against a consumerist culture that dissolves the bonds of male sociality and puts into place an enervating notion of male identity and agency.
>
> (Giroux 2000: 33)

Among other things, then, Giroux (2000: 36) proposes *Fight Club* can be read as a response to the assault on masculinity, and domesticated masculinity, in particular, as exemplified by Jack (Edward Norton), who is 'a packaged representation of masculine crisis'. Although a character with a very different temperament, Tyler Durden (Brad Pitt) also 'rails against the boredom, shallowness, and emptiness of a stifling consumer culture and the ongoing feminization of men, both of which contribute to men's feelings of disenfranchisement' (Giroux 2000: 33). More than Jack, though, Durden 'represents the redemption of masculinity repackaged as the promise of violence in the interests of social and political anarchy' (Giroux 2000: 34).

The depiction of violence is also problematic to Giroux (2000: 36), in that the movie treats violence 'as a sport, a crucial component that lets men connect with each other

Figure 2.1 Scene from the 1999 movie *Fight Club*

through the overcoming of fear, pain, and fatigue, while reveling in the illusions of a paramilitary culture'. Moreover, Giroux (2000: 36) argues, '[b]y maximizing the pleasures of bodies, pain, and violence, *Fight Club* comes dangerously close to giving violence a glamorous and fascist edge'. However, not only does it romanticize violence, it also demonstrates a 'lack of discrimination for diverse forms of violence' (Giroux 2000: 37). For instance, misogynistic representations of women depict them as 'both the other and a form of pathology' (Giroux 2000: 38). Indeed, the only primary female character in the film, Marla, seems to exist to 'simultaneously make men unhappy and to service their sexual needs', having 'no identity outside of the needs of the warrior mentality, the chest-beating impulses of men who revel in patriarchy and enact all of the violence associated with such traditional, hyper-masculine stereotypes' (Giroux 2000: 38).

Given the absence of any critical analysis of gender or sexuality, Giroux (2000: 34) argues it is also not surprising that 'class as a critical category is non-existent in this film' (Giroux 2000: 34). Accordingly, the movie 'is marked by an absence of working men and women who embody a sense of agency and empowerment focusing, instead, on largely middle class heterosexual, white men who are suffering from a blocked hyper-masculinity' (Giroux 2000: 35). Race is also missing in *Fight Club*'s account of 'a society in which public space collapses and is filled by middle-class white men', who are 'disoriented in the pandemonium of conflicting social forces', and 'end up with a lot of opportunities for violence and little, perhaps none at all, for argument and social engagement' (Giroux 2000: 37).

Many of Giroux's criticisms of *Fight Club* have also been leveled at cultural criminology, including accusations it glamorizes transgression, and privileges the *foreground* of crime and exhilaration of thrill-seeking to the detriment of *background* factors, 'disregarding the wider social context in which all action takes place' (Carrabine 2016a: 853), including that linked to structural inequalities, such as class, gender, race and ethnicity. In response, Hayward (2002: 83) has argued those objections are flawed because they ignore 'the failure of "background" structural theories of crime to address the fundamental question of why (under shared social conditions) one person rather than another commits crime'. Specifically in relation to Katz's (1988) account of the sensuality of crime across a range of acts that means 'there remains a troubling split between structure and agency and a need to reconcile the rich, existential focus of his work with an understanding of structural forces and historical processes giving shape and meaning to lives that transgress' (Carrabine 2016a: 854). The remedy to that malady might be found, Carrabine (2016a: 854) believes, in the concept of edgework, which, as illustrated by our analysis *Fight Club*, seeks 'to place voluntary forms of risk taking in a broader social context'.

Cultural criminologists have also been accused of focusing on prototypically male subjects and their high-risk endeavors, and ignoring the concerns of feminist criminologists. In an early critique of Lyng's work, for instance, Eleanor Miller (1991: 1531) observes that nearly all examples of edgework involve 'activities that are engaged in primarily by white men with attachment to the labour force, those who by definition are not members of the underclass'. Drawing on her fieldwork exploring the underclass world of predominantly African American female street hustlers, she suggests they are a group that 'may engage in edgework to an extent that far exceeds that of working- and middle-class white men'

(Miller 1991: 1532). However, their edgework is *forced*, born not only of class oppression but also of oppression structured by race/ethnicity and gender. Indeed, she says, '[o]ne might argue that, because of their poverty, they are not totally free to engage in risk taking voluntarily, that they are forced by circumstance to hustle the streets, and that that activity per se is dangerous' (Miller 1991: 1532–1533).

Cultural criminology's focus on the situational and experiential aspects of criminality, such as the excitement associated with transgressive acts and rule-breaking, is intended to negate dominant ways of thinking about crime and deviance as acquisitive, utilitarian and instrumental (Martin 2017a: 115). That view has its origins in the work of Robert K. Merton (1938), who posited certain forms of anomie (or normlessness) arise from structural *strain* generated by differential access to opportunity structures, that is the discontinuity between American cultural values regarding the attainment of material goals and the legitimate-institutional means to achieve them. However, while the anomic condition of deviance is 'culturally induced' (Merton 1938: 676), strain leads to responses, or 'adaptations' as Merton called them, that are *individual* in nature.

Although this theory is probably regarded as a little antiquated, a version of the core disjunction between cultural-commercial inclusion and economic exclusion, as highlighted by Merton, has been applied by those working in cultural criminology to analyze anti-social behavior and the 'chav' phenomenon (Hayward and Yar 2006: 21; Martin 2009: 138; Martin 2011a), as well as being used to explain the collective looting that accompanied the English consumer riots of 2011 (Martin 2011b: cp.; Newburn et al. 2018; Winlow et al. 2015). Each of these examples highlight the contradictory practices and processes of consumer culture in late modernity, which have accentuated the polarization between the 'haves' and 'have-nots', training 'attention on the enhanced consumer expectations and new forms of desire that together constitute a profound, and arguably unprecedented, recipe for dissatisfaction, anxiety and, importantly, acute social strain' (Hayward 2004: 7).

While Merton emphasized the acquisitive and utilitarian nature of deviance and delinquency as *individual* solutions to systemic strain, later theorists, like Albert K. Cohen (1955: 25), claimed the 'status frustration' experienced by individuals suffering strain might lead to the formation of delinquent subcultures as a 'collaborative *social* activity' (Cohen 1965: 8, original emphasis). Moreover, Cohen (1955: 26) stated, delinquency could be 'non-utilitarian, malicious and negativistic', such that gang members may steal ' "for the hell of it" and apart from considerations of gain and profit'. Similarly, Walter B. Miller (1958: 9) considered 'the search for excitement or "thrill" ' among the 'focal concerns' of delinquent gangs in what he called 'lower class culture'.

In contrast to Miller (1958), Matza and Sykes (1961: 715) suggested that rather than there being a conflict between lower-class culture and middle-class culture, as evident in prevailing accounts stressing 'the delinquent's deviation from the dominant society', deviant and conventional values are not, in fact, that dissimilar. They contended the values of gang members (e.g. the search for adventure and excitement; a disdain for work, yet a desire for money; and aggression as an expression of masculinity) are not intrinsically 'deviant'. Rather it is the *mode of expression*, that is, delinquency, which tends to obscure the similarities between the values of delinquent gang members and those of conventional society.

The reason accounts of juvenile delinquency have tended to equate delinquency with deviance, and, in turn, opposition to the wider society is because they have 'reduced the value system of the whole society to that of the middle class' (Matza and Sykes 1961: 715). According to Matza and Sykes (1961: 716), however, the value system of society is not merely synonymous with middle-class values but is more complex, consisting of *subterranean values*, 'which are in conflict or in competition with other deeply held values but which are still recognized and accepted by many'. For instance, the search for adventure and excitement is by no means only a deviant value, as there are occasions when to be daring is acceptable, such as in sports and recreation; where there is 'a sort of periodic anomie, in which thrill-seeking is allowed to emerge' (Matza and Sykes 1961: 716). Here, then, there are clear parallels between the work of Matza and Sykes (1961) and the notion of 'edgework', which, as we have seen, was developed by Lyng (1990) to refer to the exhilaration associated with both transgressive behavior and non-transgressive leisure pursuits, including:

> Various types of dangerous sports (rock climbing, skydiving, downhill skiing, motor racing and so on), risky occupations (firefighting, test piloting, combat soldiering and police work) and illicit sensations (binge drinking, drug use, body modification, sadomasochistic sexualities, eating disorders and outlaw bikers).
>
> (Carrabine 2016a: 854)

As a case in point, when reflecting on what motivated him and his accomplices involved in the Great Train Robbery (Box 2.3), Bruce Reynolds has made a direct comparison between what they did and the practices of rock climbers:

> We wanted to do something as spectacular as that. . . . It's insanity, of course, and we knew we would be in the frame as soon as the robbery happened but it's the same madness, I suppose, that drives people to bivouac on the north face of the Eiger.
>
> (Reynolds, quoted in Campbell 2013: 36)

Likewise, to Matza and Sykes, certain middle-class leisure activities share values with delinquency, although it is the *context* in which the value is exercised, along with the 'appropriateness' of the activity, that defines it as deviant or not. Hence, the search for adventure and excitement can be thought of as a subterranean value, though '[i]t is not a deviant value, in any full sense, but it must be held in abeyance until the proper moment and circumstances for its expression to arrive'; therefore, insofar as the value is redefined or used inappropriately, it is simply the case that the delinquent suffers from 'bad timing' (Matza and Sykes 1961: 716).

BOX 2.2 THE THRILL OF THE CHASE: JOYRIDING AS 'EDGEWORK'

Mark Halsey (2008) has looked at young men involved in high-speed car pursuits with police as an example of edgework, or 'the exhilarating, momentary integration of danger, risk, and skill' that drives transgressive as well as non-deviant experiences (Ferrell 1997: 12). To Halsey, high-speed car chases are an example of edgework because: (i) they are to do with a particular kind of *risk*; and (ii) they are a particular mode of losing and gaining *control*. Conceived as edgework, high-speed chases also involve 'skills' and 'sensations'. *Skills* concern a 'desire to "discover the performance limits of a piece of technology or other form" ' (Halsey 2008: 109, quoting Lyng 1990: 859). *Sensations* entail dealing with fear, which, according to Lyng (1990: 860) 'gives way to a sense of exhilaration and omnipotence' as one moves to the final phases of the experience. Indeed, at the height of the experience – as the edge is approached – the perceptual field becomes highly focused, as one of Halsey's (2008: 110) interviewees recounts:

Interviewer: And how fast would you be going sometimes in these chases?
Participant: Oh, I'd be hittin' 200 to 220 kilometres, yeah . . .
Interviewer: Did you worry about what the police would do to you when they eventually caught you? . . . Did that cross your mind?
Participant: Nah, nothing's ever crossed my mind when I'm driving 'cause it's just the road. You just got to watch the road and handle – try to handle the car as good as you can 'cause nothing comes to your mind when you're [driving] . . .

As this excerpt suggests, another sensation associated with edgework is a feeling of 'one-ness' with the object or the environment. Another is the feeling of 'hyper-reality' whereby the attraction of the edge involves elevating oneself above the mundane dimensions of daily life. As one joyrider states:

> I was going flat out, you know. Like this is brilliant, you know, and looking behind me. . . . One copper's turned into two, two's turned into four, you know, there was so many. In the end I had . . . 18 police cars and a helicopter chasing me. . . . Yeah, it was unreal. . . . I was loving it.
>
> (Halsey 2008: 110)

Some research participants also reported being highly focused, having a 'streamlining of vision' and attention to the smallest detail, which, in turn, brought about as sense of the loss of time: 'the inability to say just how long one was at or near the edge' (Halsey

2008: 110). Hence, the young men Halsey (2008: 110) interviewed 'can recall the specifics of the chase (down to which wheel was on its rim) but not the length of time they were pursued for (beyond saying a few minutes or a long time)'.

Crucially, Halsey argues that in giving chase the police play a role in amplifying and intensifying the visceral elements of high-speed pursuits. And by participating in the pursuits, they too become edgeworkers, risking humiliation and 'damage to their reputations depending on how the chase unfolds' (Halsey 2008: 115). In another study comparing outlaw motorcycle gangs and police motorcycle clubs, Librett (2008: 259) similarly found both outlaw gangs and police clubs

> express a transgressive yearning for freedom from the stultifying doldrums of late modernity – and the influence of the 'seductions of the edge' [which] is evidenced by a common obsession with volitional risk-taking and the rush of raw, transcendent emotional power that is the reward of survival.

As well as being of theoretical significance, Halsey's research raises important concerns of public policy, namely under what conditions might the parties involved in high-speed pursuits be prepared to pull back? To be sure, contrary to police policy, the accounts of the young men in the study suggest safety is sometimes being subverted by police desire to capture suspects. And, while Lyng's initial interest in edgework was sparked by the activities of rock climbers and skydivers, all of whom are involved in risky activities, which mean they approach the edge but have a fair degree of control over their equipment, as well as the conditions they choose to perform in, as Halsey (2008: 112) states, '[s]uspects in high-speed pursuits [. . .] do not have these same "luxuries" '.

Hence, beyond the spectacle, Halsey argues (2008: 107) we must recognize the devastating consequences of car chases, and specifically that between 1990 and 2005, 136 people died in such scenarios. This goes to Craig Webber's (2007: 140, original emphasis) critique of cultural criminology, namely that in favoring 'foreground', and the spectacular, it glamorizes crime, and therefore fails to examine 'those whose lives are filled with mess and tragedy as an *outcome* of transgression'. In order to plug the 'reality gap', Webber proposes using ethnographic data – as Halsey (2008) has done – and that to 'foreground' and 'background' we should add 'foresight' as a third analytical category to account for the tragic outcomes of crime and transgression.

Regardless of their differing emphases, early subcultural theorists recognized the *social* and *cultural* nature of both the origins and character of delinquent gangs, which they regarded as groups of individuals who experience similar problems, and, in an attempt to solve them, 'initiate a process of *mutual* exploration and *joint* elaboration of a new solution' (Cohen 1955: 60, original emphasis). Members of the CCCS were clearly influenced by this view, and newer cultural criminologists, too, follow in this tradition, adapting earlier ideas to 'read' conditions of crime and deviance in late modernity. In particular, they are interested in examining how contradictions inherent in capitalist consumer culture may give rise to transgressive acts as attempts to solve subcultural problems (Hayward and Young 2004: 226). At the same time, contemporary cultural criminologists recognize subcultural activity may not necessarily be instrumental and acquisitive, or a means of attaining any material reward, but is entered into instead as a means of thrill-seeking to transcend and escape the mundane routines of everyday life:

> Teenage criminal practices such as vandalism, theft and destruction of cars, fire-starting, mugging, hoax emergency service call-outs, car 'cruising', peer group violence and other forms of street delinquency all have much to do with youth expression and exerting control in neighbourhoods where, more often than not, traditional avenues for youthful stimulation and endeavour have long since evaporated.
>
> (Hayward 2004: 149–150)

METHODOLOGIES OF CULTURAL CRIMINOLOGY: ETHNOGRAPHY, FIELDWORK AND CRIMINOLOGICAL *VERSTEHEN*

To understand the phenomenology of crime and deviance – that is, the *situated experience* of transgressive acts – cultural criminologists have devised specific methodological approaches. While Halsey's (2008) research on edgework and joyriding draws on the relatively conventional method of conducting qualitative in-depth interviews (see Box 2.2), others have proposed more unconventional, even radical approaches. Largely to counter what Kane (2004: 306) sees as criminology's obsession with quantitative methods, cultural criminology has tended to draw on the ethnographic tradition of anthropology, using the technique of *participant observation*, which 'remains the touchstone of the culture-worker'. While criminology's focus on 'quantitative measures of significance', and the concomitant emphasis on 'reliability', arguably derives from insecurity about its disciplinary authority, Kane (2004: 304) argues the focus on the *quality* of insights afforded by ethnographic techniques has had a moderating effect on the 'blind obsession with quantitative (in) significance', which has constituted a 'dominant cultural force in mainstream criminology'. Moreover, although interviews might provide a 'snap shot . . . along with some of the richness and surprise of experience' (Kane 2004: 312), ethnography can provide powerful insights from serendipitous and accidental experiences, such as walking down a street by mistake, that 'can realign data to reveal key patterns linking empirical patterns in novel ways' (Kane 2004: 317; see also Ferrell 2015: 301).

Messy and 'improvisatory modes of ethnographic knowledge production' (Kane 2004: 311) such as these do not tally with the aims and scope of highly risk-averse human research ethics committees in contemporary university contexts. However, information gleaned from this type of research, says Kane (2004: 317), might still be 'directly or indirectly useful to practitioners'; especially when '[a] ssessing the particular needs of practitioners as points of departure, cultural criminologists can offer guiding insights about culture and crime from a wide and rich

ground'. Similarly, Ferrell (1997: 16) contends that, since criminality is as much an invention of legal and political authorities as it is the commission of certain acts by criminals, cultural criminologists should seek to participate in (potentially) illegal fields of action 'to engage a larger set of moral issues and political dynamics, and to confront one's own theoretical and political responses to those dynamics'.

Ferrell proposes the way to provide such insights is via the method of 'criminological *verstehen*', which, following in the sociological footsteps of Max Weber (1949), requires criminological researchers to develop an emphatic understanding and appreciation of criminality by participating in, or being as close as possible to crime and transgression. This research technique therefore complements cultural criminologists' focus on the 'foreground' of criminality and the immediacy of crime, which, after Katz (1988), hinges 'on a particular etiology of crime – an etiology that locates the origins and meanings of crime largely inside the criminal event' (Ferrell 1997: 11).

In contrast to the 'place of safety distanced survey research or statistical analysis' affords, like Weber's interpretative approach, cultural criminologists, such as Ferrell (1997: 9), question 'the façade of objectivity' contained in accounts that claim to be 'value-free'. Accordingly, criminological *verstehen* implores criminologists 'develop a certain intimacy with illegality' in order to 'begin in part to feel and understand the situated logic and emotion of crime' (Ferrell 1997: 11). In this enterprise, researchers seek to 'achieve a deep, reflexive, and theoretically informed subjectivity whereby their own meanings, emotions, and understandings emerge in concert with those of their subjects' (Ferrell 2015: 301). Accordingly, research becomes a collaborative process, which sets out to achieve *intersubjectivity* between researchers and those under study (Ferrell 2015: 305). That, in turn, inverts prior notions of methodological rigor, which instead of being defined in terms of 'objectively and quantitative precision', now defines accuracy according to 'phenomenological precision and emotional exactitude' (Ferrell 2015: 300–301).

However, such a methodological orientation – involving deep immersion in the social setting under investigation – also means criminologists will almost inevitably encounter 'a troubling tangle of ethical contradictions and legal ambiguities' (Ferrell 1997: 4). Hence, risks to personal responsibility and professional integrity/identity will accompany criminological field research, which, because it often involves criminologists working on the edge of legality, means they too can be thought of as edgeworkers. That is apparent in a brief extract Ferrell himself provides from his field notes while hanging out with graffiti writers in Denver, Colorado (see also Ferrell 1996). He recounts how being almost out of malt liquor, paint and energy, they pack up for the night only to be surprised by the sudden appearance of two cars accelerating towards them at high speed. Not knowing whether these are gangsters or police, and overcome by 'a remarkably powerful rush of adrenaline and fear', Ferrell (1997: 5) and the other writers run for it:

> I run out of the alley and down the street, intending to turn towards the dark salvation of the railyards, which lie only a couple of blocks to my left. A high fence blocks my way, though, and as I continue down the street, I hear a high-performance engine closing on me and decide that it must be the police behind me.

> In the next instant, I am pinned against the fence by a policeman, whose partner has caught up with Toon nearby. There follow barrages of questions about my accomplices (which I decline to answer), a seemingly endless string of derogations about the sort of university professor who would vandalize private property, threats of jailing, photographs of me and Toon, and finally a summons and complaint ordering me to court on charges of 'destruction of private property'.
>
> (Ferrell 1997: 6)

This incident highlights some of the ethical dilemmas and risks posed to (un) professional identity criminological *verstehen* can entail. However, while to Ferrell (1999: 400), and others, the 'deep participatory immersion in criminal worlds' of criminological *verstehen* is the best, if not most extreme way to experience and understand the criminal moment, it is not the only methodological approach available. That is because the loose can[n]on of cultural criminology possesses a mélange of methodologies, though two broad frameworks predominate: 'methodologies oriented towards ethnography and field work practice, and those oriented towards media and textual analysis' (Ferrell 1999: 399).

BOX 2.3 ECSTASY AT THE EDGE OF WHITE-COLLAR CRIME

In Chapter 3, we will consider whether or not the banking crisis of 2008 can be considered a moral panic in the proper sense, given the backlash against bankers as white-collar criminals raised *real* issues of global import and public concern that were not in the least disproportionate to the deviance they condemned (as occurs in classic cases of moral panic). While it might be somewhat counter-intuitive to think of white-collar crime in terms of exhilaration and excitement as compared to more 'spectacular' and audacious acts of criminality, like the infamous Great Train Robbery (Campbell 2013), even seemingly mundane acts of transgression can be conceived as 'edgework' (Lyng 1990).

A poignant example involves the banker, Fabrice Tourre, who was at the center of the collapse of Goldman Sachs, which dealt in subprime mortgages that sparked the 2008 global financial crisis (GFC). In an email sent to a colleague on 23 January 2007, Tourre wrote, 'I am at this aca Paulson meeting, this is surreal' (Treanor 2010). And, on the same day, as the financial markets were on the verge of panic, he sent another email to his girlfriend, using the moniker, Fabulous Fab, clearly expressing the ecstasy he was experiencing as an edgeworker:

> The whole building is about to collapse anytime now. . . . Only potential survivor, the fabulous Fab . . . standing in the middle of all these complex, highly leveraged, exotic trades he created without necessarily understanding all of the implications of those monstruosities [*sic*]!!!
>
> (Rushe 2013)

CONSTRUCTIONS UPWARDS-DOWNWARDS, LOOPS AND SPIRALS

Whereas exploring the phenomenology of crime and transgression via ethnographic fieldwork or criminological *verstehen* involves an examination of the *action* or agency associated with criminal behavior, criminologists, including cultural criminologists, have been interested equally in the social *reaction* to deviance and transgression. And, insofar as the focus here is on the relationship between action and reaction, the aforementioned influence of symbolic interactionism and labeling theory is evident once more (Ferrell 2015). Hence, criminologists have been concerned with the ways people defined as deviant might assume that definition as the basis for adopting a deviant identity or lifestyle; perhaps going on to develop 'criminal careers' as a result (Lemert 1951). Accordingly, it is argued that social control may itself cause deviance via a process of 'secondary deviation', whereby people develop a deviant identity as a consequence of the social reaction to the initial 'primary deviation', or original deviant act (Lemert 1964).

Similarly, what Leslie T. Wilkins (1964) termed 'deviancy amplification' considers the ways action and reaction produce a spiraling chain of events, whereby '[s]ome slight initial difference in dress, expression, or conduct can lead to a sequence of events which magnifies, exaggerates and creates deviance' (Downes and Rock 2007: 171). In his seminal study of the clashes that occurred between mods and rockers in English seaside towns during the 1960s (discussed further in Chapter 3), Stanley Cohen (1972/2002) showed how the press exaggerated and distorted the clashes, creating a 'moral panic' (which led to targeting of mods and rockers by the police and courts), and how this societal reaction to the two subcultures 'amplified their deviance, such that they assumed elements of their socially defined deviant or "folk devil" identity' (Martin 2017a: 112).

Howard S. Becker (1963) was also interested in action-reaction relationships. On the action side, he looked at the processes of social learning involved in becoming deviant. In his study of marijuana subcultures, for instance, he showed how becoming a marijuana user is less a consequence of the pharmacological effects of the drug than an outcome of the social processes involved in learning about the techniques of smoking marijuana and how to experience the drug's effects via symbolic (i.e. face-to-face) interaction (see also Martin 2017a: 112). In respect of social reaction, Becker (1963: 9) was interested in the processes by which deviance is socially constructed by 'moral entrepreneurs' (e.g. politicians and journalists) and agencies of social control (e.g. the courts and police), as summed up in his observation that, '[t]he deviant is one to whom that label has successfully been applied'.

Given cultural criminology rests on the supposition that criminality is largely determined by political and legal authorities (Ferrell 1997: 16), Becker's conclusion here is to be taken as read. However, like those earlier theorists, cultural criminologists are not only concerned with what they call 'constructions downwards', or 'the various mediated texts that circulate images of crime and crime control' (Ferrell 1999: 400). Rather, they seek to interrogate the *interrelationship* between two elements, that is 'the relationship and the interaction between constructions upwards and constructions downwards' (Hayward and Young 2007: 102).

This perspective has arisen largely out of disillusionment with orthodox approaches to studying 'crime and the media' (Hayward 2010: 5, 2017: 136), some of which were discussed in Chapter 1, including content analysis, media effects and cultivation theory. For cultural criminologists, this 'relatively formulaic [and] static received body of knowledge' (Hayward 2010: 5) is incapable of making sense of a world now 'saturated with images of crime' (Carrabine 2012: 463), resembling what Hayward (2010: 3) calls, 'a highly mediated "crime fest"'. In other words, these older theories present a rather rigid, one-dimensional view of the crime-media nexus, where, as if a hypodermic syringe, the mass media injects passive audiences with information about crime and crime control. Instead, what we need, argue cultural criminologists, is a far more dynamic approach that is capable of understanding 'a televised world of "media loops" whereby one image becomes the content of another' (Ferrell et al. 2015: 155). The study of crime then comes to resemble 'a walk down an infinite hall of mirrors where images created and consumed by criminals, criminal subcultures, control agents, media institutions, and audiences bounce endlessly one off the other' (Ferrell 1999: 397).

However, loops only offer 'a few frames from a longer film', which involves a series of loops spiraling 'on and away to new experiences and new perceptions, all the while echoing, or at other times undermining, meanings and experiences already constructed' (Ferrell et al. 2015: 158). Hence, loops and spirals between mass media formats and individual experience will become ever more significant in contemporary societies where mediated understandings of crime increasingly penetrate everyday life (Ferrell 2015: 298).

Accordingly, the task for cultural criminology is to 'go beyond simple analyses of the static image/picture and develop the theoretical and methodological tools necessary to understand the dynamic force and power of visual culture' (Hayward 2010: 3). However, simple importation of images will not suffice, because in a discipline dominated by 'words and numbers' that is 'likely to *retard* the development of visual criminology, since it will leave in place the ugly notion that written and numeric analysis can somehow penetrate the obfuscation, conquer the opaqueness, of the image' (Ferrell et al. 2015: 228, original emphasis). Given the centrality of powerful and emotional imagery in mediated worlds, a new branch of cultural criminology – 'visual criminology' – has emerged to make sense of the dynamics involved in the production and reception of images in contemporary *visual culture*, that is a culture which regards vision as culturally constructed (Carrabine 2017: 23–24).

VISUAL CRIMINOLOGY

The roots of visual criminology can be traced to the 1800s and Cesare Lombroso's 'criminal anthropology', which set out to use photography 'to classify bodies into distinguishable types' (Carrabine 2012: 470). Filling entire books with pictures of 'born' criminals, Rafter (2014: 130) notes that, '[n]o criminologist has ever drawn more heavily on the visual or reveled more in the imagery of crime'. Lombroso's influence, however, extends beyond phrenology. Hence, although photography has long been a part of police work, starting in 1851 with French police taking daguerreotypes of prisoners, and British police employing photographers from the 1840s (Carrabine 2014: 140), 'the photographs taken for police and prison records should be understood in relation to the boom in portraiture, whereby people were encouraged to measure the respectable citizen against the criminal body and visualize social difference' (Carrabine 2012: 470).

Another influence on visual criminology has been the way photography and film has been used in anthropology, which although a highly visualized practice – incorporating words like 'seeing', 'observing' and 'reading' to draw analogies between 'the anthropologist and camera as external observer and recorder' – remains a discipline wherein the use of visual material is contested (Carrabine 2017: 25; see also Pauwels 2017: 62). Having said that, Brown and Carrabine (2017a: 4) suggest most photographs in anthropology remain largely illustrative; a 'descriptive resource' intended to vivify the more serious ethnographic analysis contained in written anthropological texts.

Visual criminology has also been influenced by developments in sociology, such as in the work of Becker (1974) and Goffman (1979). According to Carrabine (2017: 29), Erving Goffman's book, *Gender Advertisements*, is 'one of the best examples of visual sociology'. In it, he uses an array of commercial advertisements as *visual data* to show how advertisements reflect gendered social relations in the wider society. In a now classic essay, Becker (1974) argues many photographers have sought to capture the ambience of cities in ways echoing Simmel's (1903/1950) analysis of life in the metropolis. Subsequently, he has argued that '[j]ust as paintings get their meaning in a world of painters, collectors, critics, and curators, so photographs get their meaning from the way the people involved with them understand them, use them, and thereby attribute meaning to them' (Becker 1995: 5). Accordingly, 'there is much to be gained from reading photographs against their generic grain to explore how "context gives images meaning"' (Carrabine 2017: 29, quoting Becker 1995: 9).

As with other fields that have experienced a 'cultural turn', and like cultural criminology in general, visual criminology stresses the emotion and moral sentiment images can provoke (Brown 2014: 182). Put another way, it 'privileges the emotive and affective life of the crimino-visual, including the assemblage of imagistic sensory elements that give meanings to crime and control and their relations to spectacle, power, transgression and resistance' (Brown and Carrabine 2017a: 2). Accordingly, Nicole Rafter (2014: 131) argues that notwithstanding other influences, cultural criminology has been the main influence on renewed interest in visual criminology, although, as Hayward (2010: 9) says, the ascendancy of images and the visual in contemporary culture, which increasingly informs the 'story of crime' as imaged, now tends to render any distinction between visual and cultural criminology irrelevant.

Similarly, in an earlier piece, Rafter (2007: 147) argues we should recognize 'popular criminology as a criminological discourse in its own right', and that 'popular criminology is integral to criminology'. As sources of 'cultural information' (Rafter 2007: 416), she proposes crime films should be conceived as an aspect of popular criminology, and that popular criminology ought to be considered an aspect of 'academic criminology' (Rafter 2007: 417). In summary, she states, '[i]f we define *criminology* as the study of crime and criminals, then it becomes clear that film is one of the primary sources (albeit an unscientific one) through which people get their ideas about the nature of crime' (Rafter 2007: 417, original emphasis).

Articulating a similar argument subsequently, she says if criminology is understood as the study of crime, 'then visual criminology is the study of the ways in which all things visual interact with crime and criminal justice, inventing and shaping one another' (Rafter 2014: 129). As we have seen, to Hayward (2010: 3) this requires developing new methodologies, as well as new theoretical and conceptual approaches, which, like cultural criminology generally (Ferrell 2015: 304), requires cross-disciplinary conversations:

> Like visual sociology and visual studies more generally, visual criminology draws on a wide range of fields including aesthetics, art and art history, comics, epistemology, ethics, ethnography, forensics, geography, history, movies, philosophy, photography and photographic theories, sociology, and textual and numerical documents, videos.
>
> (Rafter 2014: 130)

Importantly, then, according to Michelle Brown (2014: 181), the 'visual turn' in criminology allows not only for a broad reconfiguration of conventional ways of conducting criminological research, but it also requires criminologists take seriously ethical questions posed by visual representations of harm, punishment and violence (see also Carrabine 2012: 463). Accordingly, she says, '[a] visual criminology is a "visually attuned criminology" and this includes attention to the problems of theory, methods, ethical engagement, political reform, and social responsibilities that come with the production, representation, and analysis of images' (Brown 2014: 181).

At this juncture, we should distinguish the proliferation of forensic imaging and use of crime scene photography (and other 'CSI' techniques and practices) to help solve particular crimes from the focus of visual criminology (Pauwels 2017: 62). As a branch of cultural criminology, visual criminology veers away from 'scientific' forms of criminology, such as forensics, that are reliant on 'the exact and life sciences', although, as Pauwels (2017: 72) speculates, 'it is very likely that productive intersections between cultural and forensic aspects will further occur in the broader visual domain'.

Conceptually, visual criminology has also grappled with limitations associated with the term 'image', which, as Pauwels (2017: 63) points out, 'does not, in fact, include many types of visual representations'. For that reason, Hayward (2010: 1–2) proposes we 'expand and enhance the term', to accommodate, for instance, 'the increasing interchangeability of the terms "image" and "visual"', where 'the former relates to representation', and 'the latter (traditionally at least) relates to "seeing"'. Accordingly, we can appreciate that 'much of what we "see"', whether on the Internet, TV, film or in newspapers, 'is actually mediated by the image' (Hayward 2010: 2). Whether still (e.g. photographs, drawings) or moving images (e.g. film, video) (Hayward 2010: 2; Pauwels 2017: 65), visual criminology relies primarily on pre-existing or 'found' images. That, in turn, throws up the all-important issue of *context*, which, as we saw in the early work of Becker (1995) is key to understanding the meaning(s) of any image. However, the main problem with using existing visual data is that they 'lack contextual information to some degree, as researchers typically have no control over, nor complete knowledge about, the exact production circumstances (historical, technical, cultural), or the intended goals and uses' (Pauwels 2017: 64).

Context becomes important also when considering the ethics of delving into archival material, such as police photographs of gruesome crime scenes, and re-presenting them publicly. Invoking strong emotions, images of trauma and suffering, and even death, are more than 'just images' (Carrabine 2012; Scott Bray 2017: 149). Thus, it is incumbent upon criminologists using such images to be ethically responsive and sensitive to their various meanings, and the ways audiences might perceive them. For example, there are dangers inherent in aestheticizing crime or presenting trauma as art, including issues associated with voyeurism and turning pain and suffering into spectacle (Carrabine 2012: 467, 2014: 143–149; Scott Bray 2017: 144, 2018: 420). Although there are clearly 'markets' and 'consumer demand' for such material (Carrabine 2012: 469; Scott Bray 2017: 137, 146, 2018: 415), visual criminologists are mindful to be particularly attentive when working with sensitive material in law's archive, including 'police photographs, surveillance films, objects, statement and trial transcripts' (Scott Bray 2018: 417). Accordingly, Katherine Biber (2013: 1042–1043) proposes the development of a 'jurisprudence of sensitivity' or 'sensory jurisprudence; that is, a jurisprudence connected with the senses, perceptible by the senses, endowed with the faculty of sensation; a jurisprudence that feels quickly and acutely'.

Cultural criminologists working with disturbing and distressing images must therefore be attuned to the strong emotions those images can provoke and potential harm, or 'collateral damage', that may accrue to victims, eyewitnesses, bystanders and viewers (Scott Bray 2017: 138). Here, as with other work in visual criminology, context is vital, especially when one 'bears witness' to dreadful and traumatic events, where *bearing witness* means not only seeing an event firsthand, with one's own eyes, but testifying to what we cannot see or what lies beyond seeing (Carrabine 2012: 467–468).

Such issues related to the ethics of representation and working with sensitive images, argues Scott Bray (2014: 79, 82), resonate with the practice of 'dark tourism', which refers to 'the act of travel to sites associated with death, suffering and the seemingly macabre' (Stone 2006: 146), including sites of genocide and serial killing. As we shall see briefly in Chapter 9, that, in turn, has implications for education, awareness raising and even resistance. Hence, in the case of the role images, social activists may bear witness using 'visual strategies' (Brown 2014: 187): from producing 'counter-images' as part of the prison abolition movement (Brown 2014), including photo essays used to illustrate the problem of overcrowding (Pogue 1999; Figure 2.2), to reading certain acts of graffiti as political protest against dominant (legal) readings of graffiti as vandalism (Young 2014).

Interventions such as these are increasingly commonplace in a digital age marked by proliferating use of social media and ubiquity of miniature recording devices like mobile phone cameras. As we will see in Chapter 8, this means ordinary people can engage in what has been called 'street journalism' or 'citizen journalism', which in certain respects has the effect of undermining professional journalism, giving rise to what Altheide and Snow (1991) call an era of 'post-journalism'. Here, Carrabine (2012: 485) makes the point that in some ways these amateur photographers carry on the tradition of bearing witness to terrible events.

An example that touches on many of the issues just raised, including dark tourism, working with sensitive images, 'crime as art' and social media use, is Yolocaust. Created by Berlin-based Israeli artist and writer, Shahak Shapira, Yolocaust combined the popular social media hashtag, Yolo ('You only live once'), and Holocaust. Shapira launched the site (Yolocaust.de) after he noticed people posting selfies on Facebook, Instagram, Tinder and Grindr, depicting themselves smiling, juggling and doing yoga at Berlin's Holocaust memorial: *Memorial to the Murdered Jews of Europe*. Selecting only the most extreme selfies he found on social

Figure 2.2 Photograph of the 'gay wing' of a Texas state prison, 1984

media sites, Shapira deleted the background of the Memorial, and in its place superimposed shocking death scenes from Nazi concentration camps. He then posted the re-worked images on his site without the permission of social media account holders, but gave them an opportunity to 'undouche' (remove) themselves at the bottom of the site, if they sent him an email. Shapira said the project arose out of his concern that far-right politicians in Europe posed a threat to the lessons of the Holocaust (Gunter 2017), but said he also wanted to provoke thinking about appropriate ways to commemorate its legacy (Oltermann 2017). Less than a week after creating his website, all 12 of the people featured in the images had contacted Shapira to request they be removed from the webpage, which led him to take down the original site, replacing it with a letter describing only what the project was about (Ziv 2017).

NARRATIVE CRIMINOLOGY

As Pauwels (2017: 68–69) notes, 'visual essays' are one option for criminologists to express insights about crime and justice. But photographs can also tell stories. An example is Copes and Ragland's (2016) analysis of the story told by a photograph of a woman holding a small plastic bottle against the backdrop of a dirty kitchen area. The woman is a 38-year-old methamphetamine user who thinks the bottle is frozen urine, which she uses to pass drug tests. The bottle's contents are in fact leftover fluid from her niece's science project. To Copes and Ragland (2016: 271), signs and symbols of gender and poverty within the image 'both reproduce and undermine cultural narratives of what it means to be a woman who uses methamphetamine', which can be interpreted by viewers in a number of ways, including interpretations that can be stigmatizing, as well as those that 'can humanize people who use meth, thereby facilitating more complex, implicit narratives'.

A similar example of the 'interplay between words and photos' is Gumpert and Goodman's (2012: 96) photographic portraits of inmates in San Francisco County Jail. Robert Gumpert provides prisoners (and staff) with four portraits if they tell him a story about or from their lives. In conjunction with the images showing inmates 'freed from the bars of the prison and . . . humanized' (Gumpert and Goodman 2012: 96), the stories give voice to some of the most excluded, allowing 'those of us fortunate to have avoided such blighted opportunities to have an insight into this other world' (Gumpert and Goodman 2012: 95):

> From the testimonies we learn awful stories of deprivation, pain, cruelty and lack of opportunity. What comes across is that many did not have a chance of living a life that could in any way be construed as normal. They describe being born into families that were violent, drug-ridden and poor. The testimonies are given without self-pity or excuse. It is how it is. They are a living proof of the collateral damage suffered by some in society so that others can enjoy an excess of the resources on offer.
>
> (Gumpert and Goodman 2012: 96)

Given what was said in the introduction to this chapter regarding the various ways '"the story of crime" is imaged, constructed, and "framed" within modern society' (Hayward 2010: 9), it should come as little surprise that there is a degree of crossover between visual and narrative criminology. Indeed, this is something of a false distinction, recognized by Carrabine (2016b: 253) when he says integrating narrative and visual criminology 'can help inform how images should be read and interpreted', presupposing that 'many different kinds of texts can be understood narratively, including spoken, written and visual material' (see also Sandberg and Ugelvik 2016: 132). By this logic, '"images both tell stories and mobilize story making", revealing "taken-for-granted and dominant narratives" and thereby open up fresh possibilities for narrative criminologists to explore further' (Carrabine 2016b: 255, quoting Presser and Sandberg 2015b: 296).

As with visual criminology, interest in stories and narrative in criminology is part of a wider 'cultural turn' that has occurred in the humanities and social sciences, of which cultural criminology (and visual criminology) itself is also a part. However, unlike other areas, such as social movement studies (Martin 2015a), and despite the emergence of cultural criminology, criminology has only recently taken the 'narrative turn' (Presser 2016: 137, 140–141). That is not to say narrative and storytelling have not figured in criminology's past. Indeed, whereas visual criminology is arguably a more established strand of cultural criminology, which has influences *beyond* the realms of criminology (e.g. in sociology and anthropology), narrative criminology has clear antecedents *within* criminology.

Originally coined by Lois Presser (2009), narrative criminology 'refers to the study of the role the telling and sharing of stories play in committing, upholding and effecting desistance from crime and other harmful acts' (Sandberg and Ugelvik 2016: 129). Like cultural criminology more broadly (Ferrell 2015), and visual criminology too, Sandberg (2016) states narrative criminology is both a theoretical (Presser and Sandberg 2015a) and methodological approach (Presser and Sandberg 2015c). As we shall see, in terms of theory, there are various ways of conceptualizing narrative, including: (i) as a record of events; (ii) as a means of interpreting actions; and (iii) as a shaper of experience. In terms of method, many of the techniques of narrative criminology have changed little from those pioneered by the Chicago School of Sociology, which from the 1920s used ethnography and life-history methods to understand patterns of social disorganization, delinquency and subcultural formation in a rapidly changing urban environment. To date, most studies in narrative criminology have focused on offenders, often combining ethnography and life-story techniques:

> Ethnographic studies of offenders clarify how offenders view themselves, their actions and their communities. They reveal humans making choices from partial vantage points on complex and dynamic social forces. They also showcase intersections of personal and historical circumstance.
>
> (Presser 2009: 183)

Clifford R. Shaw (1930/1966: 21) famously used an oral history approach to understand the world from the perspective of a young delinquent boy, though he recognized the subjectivity of the individual delinquent's own story as a key limitation of his study. Another important antecedent of narrative criminology, which is still influential, is found in the work of Sykes and Matza (1957), who examined the 'techniques of neutralization' offenders use to justify their actions, including the following:

- *The denial of responsibility*: 'I didn't mean it' (delinquent acts are rationalized as the result of forces beyond the control of the individual, such as unloving parents or bad company);
- *The denial of injury*: 'I didn't really hurt anybody' (vandalism may be defined simply as 'mischief', theft may be viewed as 'borrowing');
- *The denial of the victim*: 'They had it coming to them' (the delinquent is the rightful avenger of the victim who deserves punishment);
- *The condemnation of the condemners*: 'Everybody's picking on me' (delinquents deflect attention away from their own deviant acts: police are corrupt, stupid and brutal; teachers always show favoritism; parents 'take it out' on their children);
- *The appeal to higher loyalties*: 'I didn't do it for myself' (faced with resolving a conflict between claims of friendship and claims of law, delinquents insist they must 'always help a buddy' or 'never squeal on a friend').

A contemporary application of this taxonomy can be found in Thomas Ugelvik's (2016) research on Trandum, Norway's only immigration detention center. As a highly controversial facility, and one with a legitimacy deficit, Ugelvik (2016: 216) shows how engaging in the telling and sharing of stories provides an important conduit for creating and shaping a 'staff culture of self-validation'. Put another way, he says, the narrative self-legitimation work of detention center officers 'in part is produced through the telling and sharing of stories' (Ugelvik 2016: 221). To demonstrate this, he shows how officers at Trandum use four techniques of legitimation:

> These are: (1) stories that attribute responsibility to individual detainees ('it's his own fault, he brought this on himself'); (2) cautionary tales about disturbed, risky, or dangerous detainees ('these are dangerous people, we must protect ourselves and the other detainees'); (3) stories about the proficiency/professionalism of staff ('we are trained to do this, we know what we're doing'); and finally (4) stories about Trandum as a humane and decent institution ('this is a decent place, we treat people properly, there's nothing really to complain about').
>
> (Ugelvik 2016: 221–222)

Moreover, while some of these stories resemble the neutralization techniques described by Sykes and Matza (1957), others do not:

> Officers tell stories about dangerous and violent detainees in a way that ascribes responsibility and denies victim status. But the self-legitimation work

> Trandum officers do also includes stories that seem far removed from Sykes and Matza's neutralizations, including stories about Trandum as a decent and (relatively) humane institution where people do a difficult job to the best of their abilities, acknowledging the common humanity they share with detainees in the process.
>
> (Ugelvik 2016: 217–218)

One legacy of the influence of Sykes and Matza (1957) has been the suspicion among laypeople and scholars that stories of offenders are inauthentic (see Presser 2010: 444), which, incidentally, has been a preoccupation of crime historians reliant on narrative accounts and textual interpretation (Gilman Srebnick 2005: 4–5). Nonetheless, criminologists have tended to use narrative as a report on individual lives (Presser and Sandberg 2015c: 85), and thereby have not been especially concerned with the veracity of such narratives, which are treated as *consequential*. Accepting offender stories at face value is also a criticism made of cultural criminology (Carrabine 2016a: 853), yet criminologists accept these stories may be 'strategically pitched and thus potentially inauthentic', acknowledging selectively and partiality are integral to *any* narrative, whether they be offenders' stories, victims' stories or the stories of police and other state officials (Presser 2009: 181). That is largely due to the practical necessity to be selective when recounting one's own life experiences to tell a story (Presser 2009: 180), which applies to both individual and group narratives:

> Witness the fact that groups such as nation-states and youth gangs tell stories of who the group is, judiciously presenting some life-world that group members share in common. Nor could individuals possibly include every life event for the sake of telling their story. It must start and end somewhere; it must emphasize some event(s) and not others to make its point.
>
> (Presser 2009: 179)

Among other things, group narratives are important when considering 'stories of change' (Davis 2002), which can ignite political action by, for instance, arousing strong *emotions*. Indeed, to narrative and cultural criminologists alike (including those working within visual criminology), grappling with emotion is seen to be something conventional criminology has not tended to do (Presser 2009: 179). While some have considered the role played by emotions in law and policy formation (Freiberg and Carson 2010), as well as the 'emotionalization' of public discourse about crime and justice (Karstedt 2002; Karstedt et al. 2014) – some of which causes *fear* (as examined in Chapter 4) leading to an increase in punitive attitudes and support for harsh criminal justice policies (Johnson 2009: 53) – in other fields the study of emotion and affect is a little more advanced. In social movement studies, for instance, it has been recognized for some time that, 'people are often motivated by anger, indignation, fear, compassion, or a sense of obligation, not optimism about the possibilities of securing political concessions through extra-institutional protest' (Polletta and Amenta 2001: 305).

As a wider field of inquiry than research into collective action, 'narrative criminology opens the inquiry to what individuals do, motivated by politics or anything else' (Presser 2016: 140). However, it can also realize the emancipatory potential of storytelling for marginalized narrators, or see narrative as 'a vehicle for resistance' (Presser 2016: 143). Attached to this can be the act of 'bearing witness', which we have seen is an important element of visual criminologists' work with distressing and traumatic images. An example in the field of narrative criminology could be the widespread recognition eventually gained by 'comfort women' after they recounted their stories as an act of bearing witness to the systematic exploitation and sexual abuse they suffered at the hands of Japanese soldiers during the Second World War (Martin 2015a: 245–247). Similarly, 'speak-outs' are a method of storytelling traditionally associated with feminist movements (Martin 2015a: 78).

As well as conceptualizing narrative as *record* – that is, to 'document what actually happened or is happening in someone's social world' – criminologists have also conceived of narrative as *interpretation*, or as 'a certain *rendering* of what is happening or has happened, including a rendering of one's own actions' (Presser 2009: 182, original emphasis). While some have been preoccupied with the authenticity of offenders' stories as record, by recognizing the subjectivity of accounts the latter conception of narrative as interpretation is unconcerned with notions of 'fact' or absolute truth, acknowledging 'it is the interpreted circumstances rather than "real" circumstances that are consequential' (Presser 2009: 183). Either way, both conceptualizations – narrative as record and narrative as interpretation – are 'representational', but 'with the gap between the representation and the event(s) estimated differently' (Presser 2009: 184). In contrast to both of these is a third view, which:

> values narrative for its ability to tell us about the past, present, *and* future according to the narrator. The emphasis in this view is on the reciprocal influence of discourse and action. Therefore, those who take the third view also tend to consider how broader (e.g. national) discourses shape the narrative. The veracity of the events recounted in the story is not central.
>
> (Presser 2010: 434, original emphasis)

This conception of narrative is premised on a post-structuralist philosophical position that regards narrative as a *shaper of experience*. It focuses on the telling of local stories to avoid global narratives, recognizes there are different levels of truth, so as to privilege agency in meaning-making, and aims 'to understand meaning-making as inevitably social, dynamic, and open-ended, and thus to doubt the possibilities of predicting human action' (Presser 2010: 434). In respect of offenders' stories, Presser (2010: 444) argues, this view highlights the *constitutive* nature of narratives, as opposed to the prevailing representational view, whereby narrative is regarded 'as a shaper of reality, which is concerned with how stories are put together and how they affect action, and not primarily or at all with the truth of those stories' (see also Presser 2016: 139).

While cultural criminology is more generally concerned with the various ways meaning is made, and how people make sense of their experiences, and is less concerned with discourse than constitutive criminology (and narrative criminology), both cultural and constitutive criminology nevertheless 'insist on culture as processual, performative, and dynamic' (Presser 2016: 145). As suggested above, a concern with emotion is also something connecting narrative and cultural criminology. However, while cultural criminology stresses 'the here-and-now of crime, including dynamic factors at the point of behaviour', narrative criminology recognizes a story 'references the past but is always tailored to the present, and specifically to the moment of narration' (Presser 2009: 179). In common with cultural criminology, then, narrative criminology acknowledges that 'both emotional state and story change too quickly to be captured and measured by the researcher', which, in the case of offender stories, highlights the fact that the 'life story, including its affective dimensions, has no fixed or necessary essence' (Presser 2009: 179). In these ways, both narrative and cultural criminology are critical of conventional criminological approaches that try to quantify lived experience, and thereby reduce it to 'manageable' statistical data.

CONCLUSION

Throughout this book we will encounter some of the many ways criminologists have used images or text, or both, to examine crime and justice issues. We have already mentioned the work of Green (2008a: 201), whose comparative study of news media reporting on child killings in Britain and Norway consists of a 'text-only approach'. In Chapter 6, we will see how Green's approach differs from Jones and Wardle's (2008, 2010) analysis of text *and* visual imagery in the case of news reporting about Maxine Carr. On the other hand, in Chapter 3, we will show how Machado and Santos (2009) use a content analysis approach (discussed in Chapter 1) to compare the very different approaches of two Portuguese newspapers when reporting on the disappearance of Madeleine McCann.

As one would expected in a book about crime and media, the role of the visual and the place of images in crime, crime control and criminal justice is evident throughout (Brown and Carrabine 2017a: 2; Carrabine 2017: 23). Often images (both still and moving) will be used to illustrate broader points. For instance, in Chapter 9, we consider Mark Hamm's (2007) argument that images of abuse and torture at Abu Ghraib provided photographic evidence of state crimes committed by American soldiers. In a similar vein, Wikileaks's video, *Collateral Murder*, taken from gunsight footage on board an Apache helicopter, shows the killing of a dozen civilians in a suburban street of New Baghdad in 2007 in clear breach of the military's rules of engagement (Martin 2015a: 204). The video's release led to the capture, detention and subsequent release of whistle-blower, Chelsea Manning, whose case is discussed briefly in Chapter 8.

These examples provide clear illustrations of what we discussed above in respect of the increased capacity in contemporary societies of citizen journalists using new digital technologies, such as mobile phone cameras, social media platforms and the Internet to expose abuses of power by governments and state agents. In some cases, these interventions have real impact, such as in the case of Ian Tomlinson. As we will see in Chapter 8, Tomlinson died after being struck and pushed to the ground by a police officer while walking home from work during protests at the G20 summit in London in 2009 (see Martin 2015a: 211–213; Scott Bray 2013). The incident was videoed on a mobile phone by an American tourist who, after realizing the significance of the footage, sent it to the *Guardian* newspaper, which posted it on its website. Publication of the video changed the course of legal proceedings, resulting in a new coronial verdict of 'unlawful killing', and prosecution for manslaughter of PC Simon Harwood, the police officer shown assaulting Tomlinson (a charge for which he was ultimately acquitted).

A more recent example, also illustrating the research potential of new technologies (Pauwels 2017: 71), and discussed briefly in Chapter 8, is the Black Lives Matter movement, which emerged in the US following the release of footage, sometimes from police's own 'dash-cams', showing police officers shooting black people (see Figure 2.3). In this way, the use of mobile, personal and wearable technologies and devices, often operating in tandem with social media, can enable 'informal' justice practices and community responses, as well as provide important 'digital evidence' to police and courts (Stratton et al. 2017: 25).

© Reuters/Jonathan Bachman

Figure 2.3 Black Lives Matter protestor Ieshia Evans is detained by law enforcement near the headquarters of the Baton Rouge Police Department in Louisiana, 9 July 2016

While these examples highlight citizen-instigated initiatives in what Altheide and Snow (1991) call the age of post-journalism, journalists themselves are also embracing new technologies, sometimes by reconfiguring existing formats. For instance, as a variant of 'visual cultural criminology' (Hayward 2017: 142), documentary film can involve *audiovisual verstehen*, which 'intensifies traditional ethnographic attempts to experience *verstehen* by employing digit technologies to simultaneously record sound, setting and sensory experience in a bid to fill in some of the gaps that . . . have traditionally been absent from criminological knowledge' (Hayward 2017: 144, original emphasis). Thought of in this way, documentaries can utilize new technologies to produce cultural products capable of influencing criminal justice processes.

A recent case in point is the true crime documentary, *Making a Murderer* (2015). Described as an example of 'trial-by-Netflix' (Timberg 2016), the show resulted in the overturning of Brendan Dassey's conviction for his part in the 2005 murder of Teresa Halbach, though the series failed to affect the conviction of Dassey's uncle, Steven Avery, for his role in the murder. In spite of viewers' near universal opinion Avery was framed, Schulz (2016) has pointed to certain failings of *Making a Murderer*, including the omission of inconvenient evidence, such as DNA from Avery's perspiration that would be virtually impossible to plant, and information about some less savory aspects of his past, such as multiple allegations of physical and sexual assault. Moreover, the show provides no coherent account of Halbach's murder, which remains a mystery, and far from being a one-off, Avery's case highlights systemic problems:

> Seventy-two per cent of wrongful convictions involve a mistaken eyewitness. Twenty-seven per cent involve false confessions. Nearly half involve scientific fraud or junk science. More than a third involve suppression of evidence by police.
>
> (Schulz 2016)

In contrast to *Making a Murderer*, and uncharacteristically for the genre of 'independent private investigate projects' (Schulz 2016), HBO's *The Jinx* (2015), sought to implicate rather than exonerate its subject, real estate heir, Robert Durst, who was arrested by the FBI on the eve of the documentary's final episode, after being caught muttering to himself in a bathroom: 'There it is. You're caught! What the hell did I do? Killed them all, of course' (Patterson 2016). Other documentaries have brought injustices to the fore without, as yet, having any impact or affecting any real change. For instance, *The Queen and Zak Grieve* highlights the controversy of mandatory sentencing in Australia's Northern Territory, telling the story of how Zak Grieve was sentenced to a mandatory 20 years imprisonment, despite withdrawing from a murder plot.

Stressing 'sound' over 'image', podcasts have also become a key tool in achieving justice in cases where the criminal justice system has seemingly failed. Here, podcasts might be considered part of what Hayward (2017: 146) calls 'sonic criminology', which 'is now being developed in innovative ways within documentary criminology'. An example of a podcast that has had an impact is, *Serial* (2014), which has led to the retrial of Adnan Syed, who was sentenced to life for the 1999 murder of his former girlfriend, 18-year-old Hae Min Lee. Beyond the formal post-conviction process, Yardley et al. (2017: 489) have shown how, as a newer media space, the online discussion forum, *Serial* Subreddit, has provided secondary victims – in this case, the younger brother of Lee and elder brother of Syed – with 'opportunities to express alternative narratives to those in existing mediated representations of homicide'. Among other things, Yardley et al. (2017: 486) say, producer-consumers, or 'prosumers' (Ritzer and Jurgenson 2010) in newer media spaces are able to exercise 'a greater degree of control in deciding how and when to tell their story than is true for encounters with older media', which tend to focus on emotive content rather than stories like the innocence of a perpetrator believed to be a victim of a miscarriage of justice.

Another podcast bringing matters of injustice to public attention is *Phoebe's Fall* (2016), which tells of the circumstances surrounding the death of 24-year-old Phoebe Handsjuk in 2010. Having been found dead at the bottom of a garbage chute at a luxury apartment tower in Melbourne, Australia, the coroner recorded a finding of death by misadventure. Phoebe's family seriously doubted this decision, given numerous anomalies, like the fact there were no fingerprints at the top of the chute (but Phoebe had gone down feet first), and that no CCTV footage had been recovered on the night of her death, and that the CCTV hard drive later went missing. Under existing legislation in the state of Victoria, coroners cannot be challenged for misinterpreting a fact or ignoring evidence; a coroner's finding can only be challenged if a perverse error of law has been made. However, following public concern at the coroner's finding in Phoebe's case, the Victorian Government directed the Coronial Council of Victoria to review relevant provisions of the Coroners Act 2008, and in its 2018 report, the Council made 11 recommendations to enhance the options for families seeking a review or appeal of coronial findings (Baker and Bachelard 2018).

The significance of these examples lies in their efficacy, or the power they have to 'make a case' (Pauwels 2017: 69). Moreover, insofar as they show how both mainstream and alternative media can play a positive role in rectifying injustices, they also highlight aforementioned synergies between the politics of cultural criminology and social movement theory. However, as we will see in the next chapter, and in Chapter 6, tabloid-driven 'media trials' can have equally negative and undesirable effects.

SUGGESTED FURTHER READING

The contents of the books listed below are indicative of the diverse range of research topics falling within the ambit of cultural criminology. The text by Ferrell et al. (2015) is particularly helpful as it situates cultural criminology within a broader tradition of cultural analysis in criminology, and provides key theoretical, conceptual and methodological insights.

Ferrell, J., Hayward, K., Morrison, W. and Presdee, M. (eds) (2004) *Cultural Criminology Unleashed*. London: Glasshouse Press.

Ferrell, J., Hayward, K. and Young, J. (2015) *Cultural Criminology: An Invitation* (2nd edition). Los Angeles, CA: Sage.

Ferrell, J. and Sanders, C. R. (eds) (1995) *Cultural Criminology*. Boston, MA: Northeastern University Press.

Useful overviews of the field of cultural criminology can be found in the following pieces:

Ferrell, J. (1999) 'Cultural criminology' *Annual Review of Sociology* 25: 395–418.

Hayward, K. (2016) 'Cultural criminology: Script rewrites' *Theoretical Criminology* 20(3): 297–321.

Hayward, K. and Young, J. (2007) 'Cultural criminology' in M. Maguire, R. Morgan and R. Reiner (eds) *The Oxford Handbook of Criminology* (4th edition). Oxford: Oxford University Press, pp. 102–121.

In his 2016 article, Keith Hayward takes stock of the field and responds to some criticisms of cultural criminology since he and Jock Young edited a special edition of *Theoretical Criminology* (8(3)) on cultural criminology in 2004. As well as looking at that special issue, it is worth perusing the pages of *Crime Media Culture* and related journals in the field, e.g. *Journal for Crime, Conflict and Media Culture*; *Continuum: Journal of Media & Cultural Studies*.

For readings on visual criminology see:

Brown, M. and Carrabine, E. (eds) (2017b) *Routledge International Handbook of Visual Criminology*. Abingdon: Routledge.

Hayward, K. and Presdee, M. (eds) (2010) *Framing Crime: Cultural Criminology and the Image*. New York, NY: Glasshouse Press.

See also the 2014 special issue of *Theoretical Criminology* (18(2)) on 'Visual Culture and the Iconography of Crime and Punishment'.

For readings on narrative criminology see:

Presser, L. and Sandberg, S. (eds) (2015a) *Narrative Criminology: Understanding Stories of Crime*. New York, NY: New York University Press.

See also the 2016 special issue of *Crime Media Culture* (12(2)) dedicated to narrative criminology.

CHAPTER 3

Moral panics, folk devils and trial by media

INTRODUCTION

Some two years after being exonerated for the sexual assault and attempted murder of Penny Beerntsen, for which he served 18 years in jail, Steven Avery was arrested in 2005 over the disappearance of Teresa Halbach, a local photographer based in the US state of Wisconsin. In 2007, Avery was convicted for his part in Halbach's murder, though, as we saw towards the end of the last chapter, following the 2015 airing of the Netflix documentary series, *Making a Murderer*, which dramatized his story, many now believe he was framed. Avery's case is significant for our purposes because it highlights the important role various media can play in framing crime stories and influencing formal justice processes. In Avery's case, it became clear he would struggle to get a fair trial given the media's presentation of what was determined to be critical DNA evidence that made the case against him and left little doubt as to the fate of Teresa Halbach. Speaking at the beginning of episode 3 ('Plight of the Accused') of *Making a Murderer*, this is how one of Avery's civil rights lawyers, Walter Kelly, saw it:

> The transformation from Steven Avery as wronged victim of a miscarriage of justice to Steven Avery the horrendous murderer of an innocent young women was breathtaking. It left me stunned. The absence of any serious commentary that the presumption of innocence that he enjoys might in fact be valid – that there should not be a rush to judgment. I thought it was just awesome how endangered he is as an accused.

Although as we shall see in this chapter, and at other points in the book, social media increasingly provide ordinary citizens with a means of challenging dominant narratives about crime and justice, and even intervening in formal justice processes, news media have long had a potentially powerful impact in exercising parallel functions of justice, often where the interests or capacities of formal institutional authority are seen in the eyes of the public as wanting because of incompetence, unwillingness or corruption and the like. In these cases, a 'trial by media' may ensue, in which individuals are charged, prosecuted and sentenced not in a court of law but in the 'court of public opinion'. This process may or may not focus on people who are publicly known, such as celebrity personalities. In Avery's case, the media trial focused not so much on a well-known celebrity, but someone who had a degree of notoriety and media presence as a consequence of his previous conviction and subsequent exoneration for a crime.

In many ways, what the media does in these circumstances is demonize particular individuals not only because it is believed they have offended societal values but also because the story of their 'offending' is regarded as newsworthy and possesses certain 'news values' journalists think will appeal to the public or will be in the public interest if reported (see Chapter 1). A similar process of demonization occurs when the mass media create 'folk devils' of groups regarded as deviants and a threat to established values and interests, and the moral order of society. In such cases, 'moral panics' may emerge, and it is to this topic that we now turn.

MORAL PANICS AND FOLK DEVILS

The term 'moral panic' was coined by Stanley Cohen in his now famous study of the clashes that occurred between mods and rockers in English seaside towns during the mid-1960s. At the very beginning of his book, first published in 1972, Cohen describes the moral panic concept as follows:

> Societies appear to be subject, every now and then, to periods of moral panic. A condition, episode, person or group of persons emerges to become defined as a threat to societal values and interests; its nature is presented in a stylized and stereotypical fashion by the mass media; the moral barricades are manned by editors, bishops, politicians and other right-thinking people; socially accredited experts pronounce their diagnoses and solutions; ways of coping are evolved or (more often) resorted to; the condition then disappears, submerges or deteriorates and becomes more visible.
>
> (Cohen 1972/2002: 1)

Crucial to this definition is the notion that moral panics are *episodic*, in that societies undergo *periods* of panic. Secondly, the role of the mass media and 'society's guardians', or 'moral entrepreneurs', is critical for moral panics to occur. And, thirdly, that a person or group is defined as a threat to dominant values is also key. By identifying this third element of moral panics, Cohen developed the accompanying concept of 'folk devils', which are the persons or groups that are demonized, and regarded as a threat to societal values and interests. In developing this idea, Cohen was indebted to labeling theory. It will be recalled from Chapter 2 that rather than seeing deviance as attributable to individual pathology or intrinsic to certain acts, labeling theorists argue deviance is *socially constructed*, as captured in Becker's (1963: 9) observation that, '[t]he deviant is one to whom that label has successfully been applied'. As we also in Chapter 2, moral entrepreneurs, including the media, play a pivotal role in labeling deviants, who, in moral panic terminology, assume the role of 'folk devils', and are subject to the attendant process of 'deviancy amplification' (see Box 3.1).

BOX 3.1 DEVIANCY AMPLIFICATION

Deviancy amplification refers to a 'hardening' of some original deviance, and was described initially by Leslie T. Wilkins (1964) as a process where action and reaction produce a spiraling chain of events. The typical sequence of events here would be: initial deviance, societal reaction, increase in deviance, increase in reaction, etc. (Cohen 1972/2002: 118). Since deviancy amplification is regarded a *social* process, it is founded upon the assumptions of labeling theory. And, in keeping with that approach, Cohen showed how the social reaction to mods and rockers tended to amplify their deviance, such that they came to assume elements of their socially defined deviant or 'folk devil' identity.

Figure 3.1 Policemen try to calm down confrontations between mods and rockers in the English seaside town of Hastings, 3 August 1964

The part played by the mass media in this process of *increasing* deviance rather than decreasing it, or holding it in check, was seen by Cohen as crucial. That is because the nature of information about deviance is the key variable in understanding a society's response to it. The media is pivotal here because it has a tendency to process and filter information about deviance in a highly selective and stereotypical manner. In Cohen's words:

> An initial act of deviance, or normative diversity (for example, in dress) is defined as being worthy of attention and is responded to punitively. The deviant or group of deviants is segregated or isolated and this operates to alienate them from conventional society. They perceive themselves as more deviant, group themselves with others in a similar position, and this leads to more deviance. This, in turn, exposes the group to further punitive sanctions and other forceful action by the conformists – and the system starts going round again.
>
> (Cohen 1972/2002: 8–9)

The process of deviancy amplification was demonstrated quite clearly in the BBC TV documentary, *Mods, Rockers and Bank Holiday Mayhem*, which was shown in 2014 to mark the 50th anniversary of the bank holiday 'battles of the beaches', when hundreds of mods and rockers flocked to seaside resorts on scooters and motorbikes in search of excitement. At one point in the documentary, a rocker tells of how she witnessed members of the press attempting to incite violence between mods and rockers, which soon became a regular part of their conduct, as another rocker explains:

> But we knew darn well that if we didn't go and support the rockers that lived down there, then they'd get knocked to hell. . . . It was a case of why should they take over the places that we always liked to go? Why should we let 'em? So, if we don't go down there, you know, they'd think they'd won.

Since Cohen's initial study, there has been a veritable avalanche of writing and research into moral panics/folk devils. For instance, Goode and Ben-Yehuda (1994) have provided a very useful outline of five key elements of the moral panic concept, which has been summarized as follows:

> (i) *concern* (some reported conduct or event sparks anxiety); (ii) *hostility* (the perpetrators are portrayed as folk devils); (iii) *consensus* (the negative reaction is broad and unified); (iv) *disproportionality* (the extent of the conduct, or the threat it poses, are exaggerated); (v) *volatility* (the media's reporting and the associated panic emerge suddenly, but can dissipate quickly too).
>
> (Garland 2008: 10–11, original emphasis)

In an influential article on the concept of moral panic, Garland (2008) sets out the qualities of a panic as being *disproportion*, *exaggeration* and *alarm*. Moreover, while he finds Goode and Ben-Yehuda's summary useful, he says Cohen's original conception also contained two further elements: '(i) the *moral dimension* of the social reaction, particularly the introspective soul-searching that accompanies these episodes; and (ii) the idea that the deviant conduct in question is somehow *symptomatic*' (Garland 2008: 11, original emphasis). For Garland, these two elements are significant because, taken together:

> they point to the true nature of the underlying disturbance; namely, the anxious concern on the part of certain social actors that an established value system is being threatened. This fear that a cherished way of life is in jeopardy is central to Cohen's account of moral panics, their nature and their genesis.
>
> (Garland 2008: 11)

Indeed, Cohen (1972/2002: xxx) has argued that, 'successful moral panics owe their appeal to their ability to find points of resonance with wider anxieties'. Garland (2008: 11–12) illustrates this point with the example of the moral panic that occurred over gang-related violence perpetrated by young people in Britain in 2007. Here, the alarm went beyond the immediate facts, with politicians and sections of the press stating that, among other things, Britain needed to be 'recivilized', and that the events were symptomatic of 'family breakdown' and 'absent fathers'.

This process of singling out specific groups as 'folk devils' is a deliberate means of creating 'cultural scapegoats', who are deemed 'a suitable screen upon which society can project sentiments of guilt and ambivalence', and 'whose deviant conduct appalls onlookers so powerfully precisely because it relates to personal fears and unconscious wishes' (Garland 2008: 15). The unconscious denial and projection that is involved in the generation of moral panics and folk devils is evident, for example, in recurring responses to pedophiles or child sex offenders, which, according to Garland (2008:15), 'seems to be connected to unconscious guilt about negligent parenting and widespread ambivalence about the sexualization of modern culture'.

It is here where Garland (2008: 15, 18, 26) argues Cohen's theory of moral panics is indebted to Durkheim's ideas about 'deviance reaction' insofar as that involves a 'collective effervescence' surrounding moments of 'passionate outrage'. It also owes a great deal to Freudian psychoanalytical approaches, for stressing 'the symptomatic character of panics, the projective nature of folk devil construction, the social and psychic conflicts that underlie these processes' (Garland 2008: 18). Hence, as with individual dreams, in collective nightmares there emerges a particular *bête noire* that is over-determined by prior conflicts. For Garland (2008: 15), then, the more cogent moral panic analyses 'render these involvements and anxieties conscious and intelligible', as well as connect them clearly to the outcry in question. Weaker analyses, by contrast, fail to proffer evidence as to the existence of these background anxieties, and are unable to show how they have contributed to the creation of a specific moral panic.

One contemporary example that has all of the hallmarks of a moral panic as described so far, are the numerous responses to refugees and asylum seekers across the globe. Indeed, Cohen (2011: 242) himself has said that, 'anything connected with immigration, migrants, multicultural absorption, refugees, border controls and asylum seekers' will be the most important site for moral panics, not least because these topics are 'more political, more edgy and more amenable to violence'. In the next section, this is discussed in relation to Martin's (2015b) study of moral panic over asylum seekers in Australia, which aims to remain as faithful as possible to Cohen's original conception of the moral panic concept.

MORAL PANIC OVER ASYLUM SEEKERS IN AUSTRALIA

> [T]the general public consume the emotive and inflammatory news headlines about 'boat people' and more easily form a view of asylum seekers arriving by boat as undeserving because they are believed to be exploiting an orderly migration system and conspiring with criminal elements, such as human smugglers.
>
> (Martin and Tazreiter 2017: 102–103)

While Cohen (1972/2002: xxxv) acknowledges that studying moral panics is 'easy and a lot of fun', equally it has been observed the moral panic concept is 'frequently misinterpreted' (Jewkes 2015: 105). Sometimes this is because people have looked at panics that have no moral dimension; at other times, accounts of moral panics have been provided where the allied concept of folk devils is missing. In light of these criticisms, Martin's (2015b) analysis of the moral panic over asylum seekers in Australia strives to remain true to the moral panic concept as originally conceived by Cohen, but also, where relevant and appropriate, seeks to apply some of the revisions that have been made to Cohen's earlier ideas by the likes of Goode and Ben-Yehuda (1994) and Garland (2008).

First, there are clear grounds for claiming this reaction to asylum seekers is *disproportionate* to the deviance it condemns, which is, for Garland (2008: 21), the point of departure for any analysis of moral panics. Indeed, according to David et al. (2011: 222), disproportionality 'might be considered to be a defining characteristic of any social phenomenon described as a "panic" of one sort or another', and is certainly a concept that 'has formed the central tenet in almost all conceptions of moral panics and in distinguishing them from "legitimate" public concerns'.

Interrogation of the statistical data reveals the Australian response to asylum seekers, and especially those arriving by boat, is disproportionate, given, for instance, 'boat people' represent as few as 0.01% of all arrivals, and that most 'illegals' are people who have overstayed their visit visas after having arrived by plane from places like Britain (Martin 2015b: 309). Interestingly, though, Garland (2008: 28) says the social reaction is often proportionate to the underlying anxieties expressed. In the Australian case, *concern* over boat people also reveals the *symptomatic quality* of the 'deviant' conduct in question, which 'reflects and resonates with broader historical processes and deep-rooted anxieties relating, among other things, to a longstanding fear of Asian "invasion", concern over multiculturalism and the perceived impact of these upon Australia's national character, identity and way of life' (Martin 2015b: 307–308).

Significantly, moral panics obfuscate 'real' issues (e.g. Britons overstaying visit visas), and thus serve a *diversionary function*, deflecting attention away from actual problems. In certain respects, the Australian case is analogous to the situation in 1970s Britain, as described in *Policing the Crisis* (Hall et al. 1978), where the 'black mugger' was created as a folk devil, and 'a pre-emptive escalation of social control against a minority [black] population served to divert public attention away from a looming socio-economic crisis that threatened the legitimacy of the state' (Martin 2015b: 310).

The *moral dimension* of the Australia panic over refugees is also evident in the fact that the negative social reaction is directed at non-white, mostly Muslim, people arriving by boat from countries like Afghanistan and Iraq, and how moral entrepreneurs, including politicians, members of the press and immigration officials appear to turn a blind eye to the bigger 'problem' of British nationals overstaying their visas. As Guild (2009: 15) says, '[i]f the category of illegal immigrant were one of neutral normative content then the efforts of the Australian authorities to reduce overstaying of visit visas would be directed against British citizens'. Accordingly, representations of border control create anxiety and ambivalence, since they disrupt the myth and the fantasy that Australia is a nation with a coherent white identity (Martin 2015b: 310).

The *hostility* and *volatility* elements of moral panics are particularly apparent when political opportunities exist for elites to exclude and demonize certain groups, such as during elections, which, for Garland (2008: 14), constitute a key 'precipitating cause' of moral panics, because they 'have to do with transitions in the social, economic or moral order of the society'. However, in Australia, as elsewhere, moral panics directed at refugees and asylum seekers are different from others, as they appear to be more permanent than they do episodic, which is an idea Cohen (1972/2002: xxx) has rejected as an oxymoron, although, in respect of social reactions to asylum seekers, he has also observed that while 'there have been intermittent panics about specific newsworthy episodes, the overall narrative is a single, virtually uninterrupted message of hostility and rejection' (Cohen 1972/2002: xix).

Thus, although moral panics are subject to volatility – exploding into the headlines at key strategic moments, like during election campaigns – Martin (2015b: 307) has argued refugee moral panics are fed by dormant moral sentiments and cultural sensibilities that *lay in abeyance* until resurrected by moral entrepreneurs when deemed ripe for invoking. Problems caused by what Cohen (1972/2002: xix) calls 'global political changes' have also contributed to the relative persistence of moral panics over asylum seekers and refugees. Most prominent among these are transformations occurring since the terror attacks of 11 September 2001, which have resulted in Islamophobia and increased hostility directed at the composite folk devil identity of the Muslim-terrorist-refugee (Martin 2015b: 308).

While negative social reactions to refugees and asylum seekers have a long history, which often involves politicians speaking 'with a voice indistinguishable from the tabloid press' (Cohen 1972/2002: xix), it is not necessarily the case that moral panics involve the formation of a *consensus* whereby the negative reaction is broad and unified. As McRobbie and Thornton (1995: 556) make clear, folk devils themselves may 'fight back', and, as Martin (2015b: 317) shows, moral panic might also be met with what Jasper (1997: 106) calls, 'moral shock', which is 'when an unexpected event or piece of information raises such a sense of outrage in a person that she becomes inclined toward political action'. This was true in the Australian case, when a group of protestors, responding to the federal government's asylum policy, produced three-meter tall posters, which appeared on Sydney's main thoroughfare, George Street, over one weekend in 2013. The message the posters intended to convey was that we should not forget the original unauthorized or 'illegal' invasion – euphemistically called 'settlement' or 'arrival' – of the British fleet on 26 January 1788 (Figure 3.2).

EXTENDING MORAL PANIC THEORY

To Garland (2008: 14–15), one of the key 'facilitating conditions' of moral panics is the presence of a sensationalist mass media, which are both the prime generators and prime beneficiaries of moral panics, as the sensation they create sells papers, entertains the public and makes more news and commentary as stories evolve. In short, folk devils and moral panics are newsworthy because they provide 'good copy', which goes to what was discussed in Chapter 1 regarding the criminogenic nature of the commercial mass media in capitalist societies. On this view, mass media institutions provide readers with highly dramatic and sensationalist stories, which sell and turn a profit. Accordingly, rather than seeking to tell the truth or provide factually based accounts or stories engaging with broader policy issues and debates, commercial media organizations have a tendency to produce stories about the ubiquity of crime and disorder in society, with a particular emphasis on sex and violent crime. Jock Young (1971: 37) has shown how this translates to moral panic generation, observing that, 'there is institutionalized into the media the need to create moral panics and issues which will seize the imagination of the public'. In this way, Garland (2008: 15) contends, 'the media "fan public indignation" and "engineer" moral panics in order to generate news and appeal to the imagination and concerns of their readers', which they do to fulfill a commercial imperative to make profit.

Another significant way Garland extends moral panic theory is by considering the *productivity of moral panics*, seeking to ask: what is it that moral panics produce, and what might be some of their lasting outcomes? Indeed, looking at the potentially long-term consequences of moral panics is an interesting point of analysis, given moral panics, as initially conceived by Cohen at least, are treated as episodic and therefore of relatively short duration. Nevertheless, that

© Dean Sewell/Andrew Quilty/Nic Walker/Jake Lloyd Jones/Jess Miller

Figure 3.2 Poster parodying the Australian government's 'no visa' campaign

moral panics have *effects* and leave a *legacy*, was in fact intimated originally by Cohen when he said:

> Sometimes the object of the panic is quite novel and at other times it is something which has been in existence long enough, but suddenly appears in the limelight. Sometimes the panic passes over and is forgotten, except in folklore and collective memory; at other times it has more serious and long-lasting repercussions and might produce such changes as those in legal and social policy or even in the way the society conceives itself.
>
> (Cohen 1972/2002: 1)

Examples of the productivity of moral panics include: (i) the drift to a 'law and order' society; (ii) mass incarceration; and (iii) an erosion of civil liberties, all of which, in one way or other, tend to involve the increased use of coercive measures employed by the state (see Hall et al. 1978: 221). Indeed, in the context of the 'war on terror' that has been waged since September 2001, it has been argued moral panics have been used to expand police powers, abrogate civil liberties and undermine the rule of law (Martin 2010, 2014, 2015b). In their study of the moral panic over 'bikie' gang wars in the Australian state of New South Wales, Morgan et al. (2010) highlight not only the part played by the tabloid press but also the orchestrating role of senior police officers in racializing the panic by equating 'bikies' with (Middle Eastern) terrorists to justify an escalation of police powers. This is how New South Wales Police Gang Squad chief, Scott Whyte, saw things in 2008:

> Like any well-run business, outlaw motorcycle clubs are making tactical mergers and acquisitions. Slowly, over the past decade, they have begun to consort and blend with Middle Eastern organized crime gangs. Allegiances open new markets and increase the pool of workers for motorcycle gangs. In turn, they offer Middle Eastern groups the legitimacy and street cred of a famous outlaw bikie 'brand'. The Comanchero, Nomads and Bandidos are recruiting in the Middle Eastern community, Whyte says. 'I can't help but feel that the edge has been blurred as to whether they're a bikie group that has Middle Eastern membership, or whether they are a Middle Eastern crime gang that's using the shield, the name and the aura of a bikie group'.
>
> (Baker 2008: 9, quoted in Morgan et al. 2010: 584)

At the same time, former South Australian Premier, Mike Rann, said legislation akin to counterterrorism laws was required to tackle 'organized crime gangs', such as bikies, 'because these people are terrorists within our community' (Martin 2012: 210). As we have already seen, similar justifications for draconian asylum seeker policies have also been used in Australia, and elsewhere, drawing on constructions of the Muslim-terrorist-refugee as transnational folk devil (Martin 2015b). Significantly, though, Garland (2008: 16) says it is important to disentangle panics from 'rational reactions to underlying problems'. Thus, in some instances, the initial moral panic may serve to attract public attention and force the problem onto the political agenda. We saw a good example of this in Chapter 1, when we referred briefly to Greer's (2003) research, which found increased media coverage of sex crime had the positive effect of bringing the problem of sexual violence to public attention; making it less privatized or 'hidden' behind social awkwardness and cultural taboos in the process.

Finally, one of the more contentious points Garland makes is his observation there has been a general shift away from moral panics to *culture wars* (or moral crusades and symbolic politics). He says that nowadays, 'the meaning and value of the conduct in question will tend to be much more contested, and the power balances between contending groups much less asymmetrical' (Garland 2008: 17). For example:

> Recent conflicts involving same-sex couples and the question of gay marriage, or illegal immigrants and law reform, or Muslim women and the wearing of the *hijab* in school, have sometimes begun as moral panics and ended up as politically contested culture wars.
>
> (Garland 2008: 17, original emphasis)

In large part this has to do with the fragmentation and heterogeneity of contemporary society, the successes of various forms of identity politics, as well as media proliferation, including diffusion via social media, which now enables far more alternative sites of resistance to be set up to contest dominant definitions of a situation (see Chapter 8). However, contrary to what Garland says about conflicts over illegal immigrants fitting into his model, and notwithstanding some points of disruption and resistance (noted above), Martin (2015b: 318–319) argues moral panics over refugees appear to refute Garland's idea that media proliferation and political fragmentation provide for a shift from *consensual* moral panics to *conflictual* culture wars. As he shows, moral panics over asylum seekers, of which the Australian case is but one example, have many of the hallmarks of a classic moral panic, including a strong moral dimension, and a broadly held set of societal values shared by a majority of people (i.e. a consensus), which are disturbed by the conduct of a supposedly 'deviant' group (cp. Hamm 1995). The social reaction, Martin contends, also demonstrates the enduring influence of traditional political actors, such as the state, as well as the mainstream mass media, to act as powerful agents or moral entrepreneurs when it comes to labeling refugees and asylum seekers as folk devils.

TRIAL BY MEDIA

It is somewhat unusual to include material about media trials alongside material about folk devils and moral panics. However, there are some significant similarities between these concepts. Arguably, the whole idea of a trial by media involves the creation of some folk devil/s. While this often entails the demonization of an individual rather than a group or category of people, the process of vilification in the mainstream media resembles very much the process of labeling certain people or groups as deviant and as representing an affront to 'decent' values.

In this section of the chapter we will examine two case studies that have applied the trial-by-media concept. The first concerns the disappearance of 3-year-old Madeleine McCann from her hotel room one night in May 2007, while her parents were dining at a restaurant in the hotel complex in the Algarve, South Portugal. In this case, there was some controversy over blood traces found in the McCann's apartment, and in a car the family had hired, which, according to some sections of the media, pointed suspicion at Madeleine's parents. The McCanns, who threatened the media with lawsuits, eventually received financial compensation and front-page apologies for the accusations made against them (see also Greer and McLaughlin 2012a). Nevertheless, given the mystery surrounding the disappearance of Madeleine has never been resolved, it continues even now to be an inherently newsworthy example, being as it is about a white, middle-upper-class child, suspected of being taken by a child predator or international pedophile ring.

Machado and Santos (2009) analyze two Portuguese newspapers, *Público* and *Correio da Manhã*, which adopted very different approaches when reporting on Madeleine's disappearance. On the one hand, *Público* provided a distanced, neutral and reflexive stance, balancing the provision of factually correct information with an ethic of quality journalism. On the other hand, *Correio da Manhã* offered a 'popular' and more sensationalistic perspective, which sought to construct a crime narrative, and, as such, was closer to entertainment or 'infotainment' rather than seeking to provide the right information. Hence, Machado and Santos (2009: 146) argue the sensationalist narrative of the Portuguese popular press, 'provided the audience with a daily dose of vicarious participation in a criminal drama which developed into a trial by media, sustained by a rhetoric that encourages the audience to "take sides"'.

The socio-economic status of each newspaper's readership mattered too. Readers of *Público* tend to be more highly educated and professionally specialized individuals, whereas readers of *Correio da Manhã* are more likely to be professionals who are less educated and less skilled. Moreover, social class differences, argue Machado and Santos (2009: 153), have an implicit affect on the way emotions are used in journalistic style, language and vocabulary: 'while the quality press's literary and careful use of language translates into efforts of objectivity and impartiality which serve informative and explanatory purposes, the popular press's colloquial use of vocabulary emphasizes more emotional and implicit understandings'.

The divergent reporting styles of the newspapers also reflected their different journalistic angles and editorial policy. For instance, the sensationalistic approach of *Correio da Manhã* privileged the immediacy of events, and provided readers with a daily dose of 'vicarious participation' in the police investigation. As Machado and Santos (2009: 155) state, '[s]uch news generates experiences in individual readers that one might assume are shared by many others, thus producing an emotional collective consensus that can actively contribute to the public construction of visions of crime and disorder'.

To the extent that the role of scientific evidence also impacted strongly on the media trial, *Público*'s coverage tended to reflect its 'quality' status. Hence, by addressing a more educated audience, the newspaper highlighted the probabilistic rather than categorical nature of DNA evidence, and discussed the complexities regarding its interpretation. On the other hand, *Correio da Manhã* adopted a more populist perspective, which drew on fictional representations of forensic science – such as those depicted in television shows like *CSI* – to build an image and narrative of an efficiently organized crime justice system premised on the certainty of scientific evidence.

For Machado and Santos (2009: 147), then, the story surrounding the disappearance of Madeleine McCann represents a classic example of trial by media whereby 'the media sometimes exercise parallel functions of justice, potentially fulfilling in the eyes of the public a role that lies beyond the capacity of institutional justice'. Additionally, they argue, the case can be thought of in terms of the construction of a 'public drama', or 'the commodified production of an emotional collective consensus', which is rendered visible by the empirical evidence extracted from the content analysis of the two Portuguese newspapers in question (Machado and Santos 2009: 147). Hence, as Machado and Santos conceive of them, public dramas are comparable to moral panics (see also Wright 2015). Indeed, like moral panics, they also tend to focus on exceptional and high-profile cases, produce negative and distorted public perceptions of the criminal justice system, discharge and invoke intense emotional and moral feelings, and can produce significant social, political and legal outcomes.

One of Machado and Santos's key arguments is that the sensationalist narratives presented in the popular press function to invoke empathy by creating what Peelo (2006) terms, 'mediated witnesses', who are invited to take sides. In this way, readers are called upon to identify personally and emotionally with the victims by, for instance, being asked to 'experience the child's parents' feeling of victimhood, as well as disgust and moral condemnation towards them when suspicions of their involvement in their daughter's disappearance were raised in the media' (Machado and Santos 2009: 150–151).

According to Machado and Santos (2009: 148), a trial by media should be thought of as more than simply 'the media frenzy following the discovery of a crime and which precedes the court trial'. That is because the media do not simply act in the public interest by engaging in a search for the 'truth', since 'public interest can be transmuted into audience interests, which can affect the news-making process's standards and priorities' (Machado and Santos 2009: 148). Again, we can apply a criminogenic perspective by considering the money-motive that underlies the way the media hijacks and dramatizes real-life criminal cases when creating media trials, which Surette (2015: 23) defines as, 'the co-optation of a regional or national crime or justice event by the media, which are developed and marketed along entertainment style storylines as a source of drama, entertainment, and profit'. He continues:

> Media trials are distinguished from typical news coverage by the massive and intensive coverage that begins either with the discovery of the crime or the

> arrest of the accused. In a media trial, the media cover all aspects of a case, often highlighting extralegal aspects. Judges, lawyers, police, witnesses, jurors, and defendants are interviewed, photographed, and frequently raised to celebrity status. Personalities, personal relationships, physical appearances, and idiosyncrasies are commented on regardless of legal relevance. Coverage is live whenever possible, pictures are preferred over text, and text is characterized by conjecture and sensationalism. A media trial is, in effect, a dramatic mini-series developed around a real criminal case.
>
> (Surette 2015: 23)

Implicit in what Surette says here is the idea there is a degree of artistic license being employed in the generation of media trials, and that itself implies there is some blurring of crime-fact and crime-fiction, which is a recurrent theme of this book. Moreover, as Surette states, the principal driver for the dramatization of real crime is moneymaking, which, as already said, reflects the criminogenic view of the mainstream commercial media operating in the pursuit of profit (Chapter 1). And, inasmuch as that is intensified in the highly competitive 24–7 news mediasphere of contemporary capitalist societies, it fuels the production of ever more sensationalist and dramatic storylines.

Another case of trial by media involved former Metropolitan Police Service Commissioner, Sir Ian Blair, which, according to Greer and McLaughlin (2011: 24), highlights how the power of the police to define crime and justice news has given way to the 24–7 news media. This begs the question: is the Blair case a one-off? Greer and McLaughlin (2011: 43) think not, since Blair's media trial 'laid down a clear symbolic marker about what "type" of Commissioner and policing philosophy is acceptable in contemporary Britain'. Conservative and tabloid commentators were antagonistic to the 'PC policing' they thought Blair stood for, and made demands for more 'law and order' initiatives.

Greer and McLaughlin's analysis is set within the context of what they perceive to be important transformations that have occurred in the status of the police in contemporary society. First, they note the elite and privileged position of the police in the 'hierarchy of credibility' is changing. Here, the hierarchy of credibility has a normative or moral quality, which makes the role of police analogous to that of 'moral entrepreneurs' in moral panic theory, i.e. those with the power to define what counts as 'deviance' or moral/immoral behavior and so on. Secondly, and related to the first point is the changing position of an 'elite police voice', which, according to Greer and McLaughlin (2011: 26), has to do with a number of factors, including:

- proliferating news platforms and heightened competition, which has threatened the established hierarchy of credibility;
- multiple sources of 'police news' (including internal diverse 'police voices'), which now make it easier to challenge the 'official' line; and
- the expansion of a new *commentariat*, each expressing their own opinions, with Greer and McLaughlin (2011: 27, original emphasis) commenting that today,

'the news media *commentariat* cast themselves as moral arbiters of the "public interest" in a climate of ambiguity and uncertainty'.

According to Greer and McLaughlin (2011: 27), a trial by media is, '[a] dynamic, impact-driven, news media-led process by which individuals – who may or may not be publicly known – are tried and sentenced in the "court of public opinion"'. Both the processes and targets of trials by media can be diverse, ranging from pre-judging formal criminal proceedings against 'unknowns' to those involving high-profile celebrity personalities. Despite their diversity, however, Greer and McLaughlin identify a number of core characteristics of such 'trials', which, they say, differentiate them from other ways of conceiving of news media reactions, such as moral panics. It is worth noting, too, that all of these elements are 'quasi-legal' in nature (see Box 3.2).

For Greer and McLaughlin, the British media's characterization of Sir Ian Blair had many of the hallmarks of a trial by media. To begin with, Blair was seen as a politicized Police Commissioner: he was regarded as *politically correct* (reforming, progressive, etc.) and *politically aligned* to New Labour in supporting its counter-terrorism agenda, and in its proposal to introduce compulsory ID cards.

In accordance with the idea that the news media exercises a parallel 'justice' function extending beyond the interests or capabilities of the formal justice system, the trial by media of Commissioner Blair depicted him, and the institution he represented, as essentially incompetent, and ultimately corrupt. Examples included a number of blunders and gaffes the press thought typified Blair's time as

BOX 3.2 KEY FEATURES OF MEDIA TRIALS

Greer and McLaughlin (2011: 27) provide this useful summary outlining what they see to be the key characteristics of media trials:

- News media act as a proxy for 'public opinion', seeking to perform parallel 'justice' functions in the perceived absence of competent and/or willing formal legal institutions.
- Due process and journalistic objectivity are ceded to sensationalist, moralizing speculation about the motives and actions of accused persons.
- The judicial scrutiny of 'hard evidence' is substituted for 'real-time' dissemination of disclosures garnered from paid informants, hearsay and speculation from 'well-placed sources'.
- Given that news media effectively become a substitute for the prosecution, judge and jury, targets find themselves 'defenseless', and 'guilty until proven innocent'; they can also be subject to processes of 'naming and shaming', which, among other things, can be deeply damaging to the reputation of those accused.
- The 'mediatized punishment' is characterized by the 'relentless savagery' of 'attack journalism', and amounts to public execution as spectacle.

Commissioner. These included cover-up and mistimed media releases relating to the fatal shooting in July 2005 of Jean Charles de Menezes, the Brazilian national who was executed at Stockwell underground station, London, by police officers suspecting him to be a terrorist (Figure 3.3).

Following Blair's admission de Menezes was in fact innocent and had been shot dead in tragic circumstances, the media's initially sympathetic response gave way to a public relations disaster for the Metropolitan Police Service, after it became apparent from a number of sources, including police whistle-blowers, that Scotland Yard's version of events was flawed, and intended deliberately to mislead the public. Accordingly, Blair's media trial was accompanied by the collapse of the Metropolitan Police Service's place in the hierarchy of credibility: prime-time TV news coverage led with stories of leaked documents appearing to confirm the positive identification and subsequent shooting of de Menezes was the result of a series of blunders; newspapers maximized the visual impact of the story, publishing front-page headlines with a leaked color photograph of de Menezes in a pool of blood on the floor of the train; and journalists gave high-profile coverage to the *Justice4Jean* campaign, which called for murder charges to be laid against the police officers, and for Sir Ian Blair's resignation.

The beginning of the decisive stage in Blair's media trial occurred in January 2006, after he attacked the news media's selectivity in reporting murder cases. Following coverage of the murder of a 31-year-old, Cambridge-educated City lawyer after a street robbery – which was set within the wider context of public

© PA Images/Alamy Stock Photo

Figure 3.3 Sir Ian Blair talking to the press at the Jean Charles de Menezes Stockwell shooting trial

concern over increased violence in London – Blair accused the mainstream media of 'institutional racism' for under-reporting murder in ethnic minority communities. At the same time, he expressed consternation at the widespread attention the media had given in August 2002 to the abduction and killing in Soham, Cambridgeshire, of two 10-year-old schoolgirls, Holly Wells and Jessica Chapman, by school caretaker, Ian Huntley (discussed further in Chapter 6). While both stories featured in media reports, it was Blair's 'Soham slur' that dominated the headlines.

Shortly afterwards, Sir Ian apologized for his comments about the Soham murders, but by then the damage was done. He was labeled the 'gaffe-prone' Commissioner, whose credibility was shredded by his handling of the Stockwell shooting, his institutional racism remarks, the Soham comments and his political connections with Prime Minister, Tony Blair, and New Labour. Moreover, in contrast to the McCann case, all sections of the press – liberal and conservative, tabloid and broadsheet – became aggravated by Sir Ian Blair, such that they 'were firmly in control of the news agenda, and were speaking with an increasingly coherent and consensual voice' (Greer and McLaughlin 2011: 36).

The dénouement came when Conservative party candidate, Boris Johnson, was elected Mayor of London in 2008. After this, Sir Ian Blair's position became untenable. Not only had Johnson stated publicly that Blair should be removed, but he was now also able to use newly granted legislative powers, as Mayor, to assume the chairmanship of the Metropolitan Police Authority and remove Blair, although the media's relentless attacks, over a two-year period, on a variety of public relations and operational 'gaffes', also played their part. Thus, when he eventually resigned on 2 October 2008:

> There was a palpable sense of triumphalism among certain journalists, who applauded the Mayor for ousting Blair. Their conclusion was that he had brought his downfall upon himself: this was a serial offender who was incapable of learning from his mistakes but, thanks to a critical and free press, justice had finally been done.
>
> (Greer and McLaughlin 2011: 39)

In later chapters we will draw on the concept of trial by media, examining, for instance, the case of Lindy Chamberlain, who was found guilty of murdering her nine-week-old baby daughter, Azaria, at Uluru (formerly known as Ayers Rock) in Australia in 1980. As we shall see in Chapter 6, Chamberlain's 1982 conviction was quashed in 1986, and in 2012 her version of events was confirmed when the Northern Territory coroner officially amended Azaria's death certificate, stating the cause of death was a result of being attacked and taken by a dingo. Among other things, we will look at the media-orchestrated witch-hunt against Lindy Chamberlain, in which the media and Australian public pre-judged her criminality and guilt, and consequently, it was argued, negated her ability to receive a fair trial. In particular, the male-dominated media were enraged as well as perplexed at Chamberlain's apparent refusal to play the role of a properly gendered woman exhibiting stereotypically 'natural' signs of a grief-stricken mother.

Later in the book we will also consider how the media, and especially new media networking platforms, such as YouTube and Facebook, increasingly allow individuals and groups to intervene in formal justice processes, much in the way the media performed a *parallel justice function* in the case of Sir Ian Blair. In this way, social media and digital technologies, such as mobile phones equipped with video cameras, pose a threat not only to the police's position in the hierarchy of credibility, but also, as we saw in Chapter 2, can challenge the position of professional journalists and the mainstream media in an age of 'post-journalism' (Altheide and Snow 1991). In Chapter 8, we will see how developments in new media and digital technologies provide greater scope than ever before for police accountability, increasing the visibility of the police, whereby they have now to be more attentive to the public image they project, especially at high-profile events involving social protest and mass demonstration.

CONCLUSION

The idea that moral panics are productive and have a legacy is often talked about negatively as diminishing civil liberties and human rights, undermining the rule of law, and increasing state surveillance. However, activism and resistance to moral panics, as discussed earlier, raise the prospect they might also have positive effects where, for instance, 'we approve the values beyond the "panic" but not the label itself' (Cohen 2011: 241). That, in turn, heightens the potential for stirring up 'approved crusades', or 'good' moral panics, where cultural workers might set about 'constructing social problems, making claims and setting public agendas' (Cohen 1972/2002: xxxiii; see also Cohen 2011: 238–239).

Cohen himself recognized that 'an expanding range of moral entrepreneurs have been successful in gaining media attention for new sets of issues and concerns' (David et al. 2011: 219), including high crimes of state (e.g. Hamm 2007), corporate crime, environmental concerns (such as pollution and climate change), mass atrocities and political suffering (David et al. 2011: 219; see also Cohen 1972/2002: xxxiii, Cohen 2011: 240). To this list can be added awareness raising around the treatment of refugees and asylum seekers (Martin 2015b, 2018; Martin and Tazreiter 2017). Here, the advent of 'citizen journalism' and growing use of social media, highlighted above, increases possibilities for protest and resistance: expanding the means by which alternative collective voices are heard and their messages disseminated (Martin 2015a).

An example of a potentially good or positive moral panic can be found in responses to the 2008 global financial crisis (or GFC), although opinion has been divided as to whether 'greedy bankers' responsible for the crisis should be accorded the status of 'elite folk devils' (David et al. 2011: 218). On the one hand, it is argued they are essentially corporate criminals who, along with expenses-fiddling politicians, should join the rogues' gallery of usual folk devil suspects, such as pedophiles and drug takers (Cohen 2011: 240; David et al. 2011: 218; Jenks 2011: 235). By contrast, others have argued white-collar criminals, such as bankers, are never likely to become folk devils, 'even when they jeopardize the entire financial system', as 'white-collar crime is perhaps not seen as threatening the moral order of society and white-collar criminals are too powerful to be cast as villains' (Critcher 2011: 261; see also Levi 2009). Moreover, whether corporate crime is a legitimate subject for moral panic research is questionable. For example, it is said the banking crisis should not be regarded a moral panic in the proper sense of the term, as the fallout from the crisis addressed 'a "real" issue that is of serious public and indeed global import and is therefore outside the scope of moral panic research because concerned and anxious responses are not in the least "disproportionate"' (David et al. 2011: 219).

As we have seen, the distorted and disproportionate reporting of crime in the mainstream media is a function of commercial imperatives. Specifically in relation to moral panics, it has been argued heightened market competition increasingly informs shock-oriented news framing, which has had the effect of feeding a widespread 'culture of fear', resulting in 'an endless stream of fear-framed stories . . . reinforcing a general feeling of distrust and anxiety' (David et al. 2011: 224–225; see also Altheide 2009). Hence, Chas Critcher (2011) talks about the *political economy of moral panics*, offering a Marxist reading of a criminogenic mass media, which, as result of focusing disproportionately on 'newsworthy' crime stories, creates the impression crime and disorder is everywhere; thus contributing to what, as we will see in Chapter 5, Valverde (2006: 105) calls a 'law and order effect'.

Although Cohen has dismissed it as an oxymoron, some have proposed that as a consequence of these processes we are now living in a period of *permanent panic*: given the generalized feelings of fear, distrust and anxiety, including those induced by moral panics, we are subject to a *normalized state of exception* (Martin 2010, 2012, 2015b), accustomed to the idea that extreme times call for extreme measures (Morgan et al. 2010: 596). In the next chapter, we develop some of these ideas further, examining, for example, the pervasiveness of *crime fear*, and exploring some of the effects of that on peoples' perceptions of crime in society, as well as their behavior and conduct in everyday life.

SUGGESTED FURTHER READING

The study of moral panics is now a huge area and there are numerous books and articles on the topic. A couple of key texts that have made important contributions by extending the original conception of folk devils/moral panics are:

Garland, D. (2008) 'On the concept of moral panic' *Crime Media Culture* 4(1): 9–30.

Goode, E. and Ben-Yehuda, N. (1994) *Moral Panics: The Social Construction of Deviance*. Oxford: Blackwell Publishing.

Stanley Cohen's (1972/2002) classic study is still essential reading, and since its publication in 1972 two subsequent editions have appeared, each with updated introductions. The introduction to the 2nd edition (published in 1980) deals with developments in subcultural theories of delinquency (i.e. the action/folk devils side of the equation), while the introduction to the 3rd edition (published in 2002) deals with the reaction or moral panic side, reviewing the uses and criticisms of the moral panic concept in the 30-year period since Cohen's book was first published. Other developments have been considered in journal special issues, including a 2009 edition of the *British Journal of Criminology* (49(1)) and a 2011 issue of *Crime Media Culture* (7(3)).

Further reflections on trial by media can be found here:

Greer, C. and McLaughlin, E. (2012b) 'Trial by media: Phone-hacking, riots, looting, gangs and police chiefs' in J. Peay and T. Newburn (eds) *Policing, Politics, Culture and Control: Essays in Honour of Robert Reiner*. Oxford: Hart Publishing, pp. 135–154.

CHAPTER 4

Crime fear and the media

INTRODUCTION

As we saw in Chapter 1, crime features regularly in mainstream media reporting. Moreover, news media tend to sensationalize stories about crime, as well as focus disproportionately on sex and violent crimes. Having said that, it is difficult to reach any firm conclusions about crime reporting in the mass media from content analysis studies. For example, while Dominick (1978: 108) found 'a typical metropolitan newspaper probably devotes around 5–10 per cent of its available space to crime news', as we saw in Chapter 1, Marsh (1991: 73) reviewed approximately 36 studies, suggesting between 1.6 and 33.5 percent of newspaper coverage relates to crime news. Variation in findings can also be attributed to the deployment of different methods. Hence, in Chapter 1, we saw how quantitative studies have the advantage of helping us understand the *extent* of media reporting on crime, while qualitative studies help us understand the *nature* of crime reporting. We know too that many people have only a partial understanding of crime, and that few have firsthand experience as crime victims, for instance. It is not surprising therefore that most people's experience of crime is mediated through radio, television and newspaper reporting, and increasingly via digital means, such as the Internet:

> In brief, then, most people do not have any direct experience of crime, but they read about it in newspapers, hear about it on the radio, and see it on television. Crime drama is typically violent, but even when apparently factually reporting events, crime 'news' tends to be selective and distorted with a general overemphasis on crimes involving sex and violence.
>
> (Chadee and Ditton 2005: 324)

To this we can add that people tend also to experience crime through cultural representations and fictional depictions, which, as we have already seen in the book, often overlap with factual accounts and real-world stories. All of this leads to the conclusion that, notwithstanding the flaws of 'media effects' theories, which were discussed in Chapter 1, audiences will be affected in some way or other by mediated representations of crime, although those will be interpreted differently depending on such things as whether people have direct experience of crime or have come into contact with the criminal justice system, as well as structural-demographic factors, like race, gender, social class and geographical location.

In this chapter, we build on the ideas presented in Chapter 1, when we considered, among other things, the centrality of 'newsworthiness' and 'news values' in media reporting on crime. It will be recalled that market competition and the commercial imperative to make profit require mainstream media institutions to produce 'good stories' that will appeal to the general public. Often that means news stories will be sensationalized, thus presenting a distorted picture of the 'crime problem', rather than providing a true account of crime in society. In the last chapter, we saw how the same drivers might contribute to the generation of moral panics and foster a generalized 'culture of fear' across societies. Indeed, according to David Altheide (1997: 648, original emphasis) it is 'the interaction of commercial media, entertainment formats and programming' that has produced and promoted a '*discourse of fear that may be defined as the pervasive communication, symbolic awareness and expectation that danger and risk are a central feature of the effective environment*'.

Here then we are interested in the notion of 'media effects' as a means of comprehending the impact of both news media reporting and fictional portrayals on people's perceptions and purported 'fear' of crime, and how those perceptions and fears, might, in turn, affect behavior and conduct in daily life. As with audiences' other mediated experiences of crime and criminal justice processes, we will see how these perceptions (possibly amounting to fear) will also be influenced by such things as neighborhood, age and gender, as well as any direct experience people may have of crime, either as victims, perpetrators or bystanders. Moreover, just as findings from content analysis studies vary according to which methods are used, so we will see how the results from fear of crime research are also influenced by method and approach, such as the way survey questions are phrased. We begin by looking at a variant of the media effects model that remains controversial insofar as it posits heavy exposure to television violence and cultivates a view of the world as 'mean and violent', and therefore instills widespread fear of crime.

CULTIVATION ANALYSIS AND ITS CRITICS

Cultivation analysis is a variant of the media effects model insofar as it is a macro-system approach that sees meaning located in messages disseminated across the entire mass media environment, the effect of which is to *cultivate* certain public beliefs. To discern patterns of meaning, cultivation theorists use content analyses, which, they say, 'should look for patterns of meaning across the total media landscape and therefore make no distinction between information versus entertainment, fact versus fiction, high culture versus low culture, good versus bad, images versus words, or levels of artistic excellence' (Potter 2014: 1017).

Despite this stress on the *total* media landscape, cultivation theorists have narrowed their attention to look only at television, focusing further on primetime and children's weekend morning programs across three dominant commercial television networks, reasoning that would provide the largest viewership, 'and if there were particular meanings widespread across the entire media landscape, those meanings should be in evidence in their sample' (Potter 2014: 1018). Examining only entertainment programs narrows the focus further. *Frequency of viewing* was pivotal, too, with researchers asking respondents about viewing habits that would indicate whether they were light, moderate or heavy viewers.

Early on, Gerbner and Gross (1976: 182) defined 'cultivation analysis' as being based on 'inquiries into the assumption television cultivates about the facts, norms and values of society'. Drawing on results from content analysis, Gerbner et al. (1977, 1980) found people who watch television for more than four hours per day (i.e. 'heavy' television users) develop a view of the television world as 'mean and violent', and are therefore more fearful of crime. They did not claim exposure to televised violence causes real-life violent crime; rather heavy television viewing *cultivates* a misleading and exaggerated perception of real-world violence, and heavy viewers are more likely than light viewers to distrust others and develop a 'mean world view' of the society in which they live (see also Gerbner et al. 1994). Put another way, Signorielli (1990: 96–102) argue that when *reel-world* violence is compared to *real-world* crime (via official statistics) it seems the media exaggerates the incidence and severity of danger, thus 'cultivating' a misleading view of the world based on unnecessary anxiety about the risks of victimization from violent crime (see Reiner 2007: 321).

Earlier versions of cultivation analysis came to be modified by Gerbner et al. (1980), who amended their initial hypothesis of 'worldview cultivation', or the idea that *all* media viewers are affected, to the notion of 'mainstreaming', or the belief that:

> the media affect some viewers more than others regardless of exposure level. They now argue that the media are homogenizing society, influencing those heavy television consumers who are currently not in the mainstream to move towards it, while not affecting those already in the mainstream.
>
> (Surette 2015: 215)

To cultivation theorists, the damaging effects of violence-laden television are not limited to the breakdown of trust and erosion of social relationships, but extend to threats to democracy, such that, crime fear can be used by politicians as a rationale to introduce harsher and more punitive 'law and order' measures. We will look at this more closely later in the chapter when we consider the productivity (or consequences) of fear of crime. For now, it is useful to see what cultivation analysts perceive to be the deeper problems posed by televised violence:

> This unequal sense of danger, vulnerability, and general malaise cultivated by what is called 'entertainment' invites not only aggression but also exploitation and repression. Fearful people are more dependent, more easily manipulated and controlled, more susceptible to deceptively simple, strong, tough measures and hardline postures – both political and religious.
>
> (Signorielli 1990: 102)

Subsequent developments in cultivation analysis have moved away from looking at the locus of meaning as being in media messages, and towards a view that sees the locus of meaning as residing in the ways audience members receive and interpret media-produced meanings and messages. Connected to that is a move from macro-level analyses toward an appreciation of micro measures of exposure. For example, some studies suggest a view of the world as mean and violent is 'attributable to exposure to violent programming more than to total TV exposure', with empirical tests finding 'genre level exposures (crime drama and news) . . . to be stronger predictors of cultivation than total TV viewing exposure' (Potter 2014: 1021, citing Grabe and Drew 2007; Hawkins and Pingree 1980; Potter 1988). Indeed, it has been questioned whether these 'genre-specific effects' should in fact be termed cultivation at all, given the effect is based on *selective exposure* rather than some overarching and widespread process of cultivation (Morgan and Shanahan 2010: 340–341; see also Sparks 1992a: 95).

Assumptions about the passivity of audiences and the universality of cultivation effects are then among the key criticisms of the cultivation thesis (Banks 2005: 171). Another that is raised by Reiner (2007: 322) taps into the fundamental question as to whether any association between viewing and fearfulness results in a causal process opposite to the one posited. In other words, might scared people simply watch more television than less fearful viewers? One answer, provided by Gunter (1987: 270), indicates the relationship between media and public perceptions is circular rather than causal, since '[g]reater fear of potential danger in the social environment may encourage people to stay indoors, where they watch more television, and are exposed to programmes which tell them things which in turn reinforce their anxieties'. Notwithstanding that, Ditton et al. (2004: 598, citing Heath and Petraitis 1987: 122; O'Keefe and Reid-Nash 1987) contend, 'it is now accepted, from consideration of non-locally generated fear and from longitudinal study, that it is the media which cause whatever fear is discovered'.

Moreover, asks Reiner (2007: 321–322), does exposure to violence via the media survive the introduction of controls such as class, race, gender, locality and actual experience of crime? That question, in particular, points to limitations arising out of cultivation theory's reliance on content analysis, which is unable to account for various contextual factors. For example, it is like comparing apples and oranges to equate representations of violence in Disney cartoons, and slapstick comedy shows, such as Laurel and Hardy, with realist drama or horror movies (Carter and Weaver 2003: 11). Another contextual factor concerns the relationship of crime fear and television viewing to social location (e.g. age, class, ethnicity, gender), as well as geographical place and proximity to criminal activity. Some have linked this to 'broken windows theory' (discussed in Chapter 2), finding levels of fear are 'driven, at least in part, by individual perceptions of the extent of low-level disorder in the area, with increases in the extent of disorder that people witness resulting in higher levels of fear' (Brunton-Smith 2011: 896). Accordingly, it has been claimed those living in high crime areas tend to be more fearful of crime, and hence more likely to stay at home watching television (Doob and MacDonald 1979). Indeed, as Greer (2005: 172, citing Chiricos et al. 2000; Eschholz et al. 2003) notes, US studies have shown coverage of local crime might increase levels of fear, especially when those surveyed have been crime victims and thus perceive television content as realistic.

Also in the US, Romer et al. (2003) have tested the hypothesis that fear of crime is partly a byproduct of exposure to crime-saturated local television news. Their findings provide strong support for the television-exposure hypothesis, which 'predicts that viewers of local television news should experience heightened perceptions of crime risk on both a personal and societal level' (Romer et al. 2003: 99). This was verified at national, regional and local levels. By contrast, a UK study suggests local crime reporting has no relation to crime fear, and is simply perceived as 'background noise', having little impact on people's daily lives (Roberts 2001: 12). Moreover, it was observed that national coverage could reduce or alleviate people's feelings of fear, as it tends to describe a 'crime problem' that is geographically far away from the relatively safe (and more knowable) local community. This study reinforces findings from previous studies that show how newspaper coverage of serious crimes occurring in places other than places where respondents live provides *reassurance* they are safe by comparison (Heath 1984; Liska and Baccaglini 1990).

Hence, geographic locality and place of residence are important contextual factors, especially when considered in relationship to the kinds of behavior we might expect to accompany fear. For example, in answer to the proposition of Gerbner and Gross (1976) that heavy television viewers are more likely to believe they could become victims of violent crime, Hughes (1980) found heavy television watchers are less likely to be afraid to walk alone at night *in their own neighborhood* – a finding that confirms an earlier study by Doob and MacDonald (1979), which revealed correlations between television viewing and fear of crime to be contingent upon place of residence.

More recently, *sense of community attachment* has been seen to have a 'moderating effect' on fear of crime in local contexts, helped by people using local newspapers to source information about community and social activities rather than stories about crime (Banks 2005). Williams and Dickinson's (1993) investigation into newspaper reading and fear of crime proffers similarly surprising results, finding a significant relationship between reading newspapers with more violent crime content and fearfulness, yet the relationship was not found with associated behavior, such as going out after dark. That is to say, it did not stop people doing that, nor did the study rule out the possibility that fear led to heavier reading of newspapers with more crime content (see Reiner 2007: 322).

More generally, it has been demonstrated that rather than increasing fear, watching television may actually alleviate anxiety about crime and disorder, whereby more television watching could have the effect of reducing crime fear, rather than producing it. In this way, Richard Sparks (1992a: 148–150) has shown how the consumption of televised crime drama may provide a positive *reassurance function* by portraying a just and safe world rather than a frightening and dangerous one. Indeed, Weaver and Wakshlag (1986: 154) extend that argument to suggest anxious people may actually seek out violent television drama to relieve their anxiety. Positing a view of media audiences as *actively engaged* in choosing to watch television shows about crime that produce a 'just' resolution (Wakshlag et al. 1983), this perspective stands in contrast to a strong version of cultivation analysis, or what we identified in Chapter 1 as a 'pure media effect' model, which likens the mass media to a hypodermic syringe that injects noxious emotions and values into an audience of passive cultural dopes (Allen et al. 1998: 55).

As Greer (2005: 172, original emphasis) shows, while earlier studies tended to de-contextualize violent acts, 'recent work considers the complete scene, in which the consequences of violence are also shown, or the entire programme, in which the *overall* message may be one of restored order and reassurance, rather than dread and fear' (see also Potter et al. 1995, 1997). In Chapter 5, we will revisit this type of argument when we consider different television shows, such as *CSI* and *Law & Order*, where it has been suggested the latter might perform more of a resolution/ reassurance function, since it provides viewers with a story about the *entire* criminal justice process (from police investigation to court proceedings), whereas the former concentrates on the initial police investigation, offering no legal resolution.

Hence, particularly for viewers who have been or have known victims of crime, watching crime drama may be a strategy they employ that enables them to cope with or assuage anxiety (Wakshlag et al. 1983: 229; Zillman and Wakshlag 1987: 13). Thus, Sparks (1992a: 95) argues it is important to recognize the 'selective exposure' of viewers who 'are not passive "dopes", and that the uses viewers make of crime drama are contingent on their relation to social experience'. That is why many scholars have criticized cultivation theory's reliance on content analysis and quantitative methods, arguing qualitative methods (e.g. diaries) are better able to capture the subtleties and complexities of understanding and meaning audience members attach to media texts and imagery (see Greer 2005: 172–173; Reiner 2007: 322). Such an approach is endorsed by Jewkes (2015: 104, original emphasis) who states that most contemporary media research is audience-centered, rather than media-centered work, since the 'emphasis is very much on what people do *with* the media as opposed to what the media do *to* people'. That is to say, agency/action is privileged over structure/passivity.

In their study, Ditton et al. (2004) adopt a mixed method approach consisting of quantitative *and* qualitative components. While the quantitative data they gathered reveal some fear of crime (though that was not necessarily related to media consumption), the qualitative data reveal as important, 'the interpretation of media content as relevant to and by the consumer' (Ditton et al. 2004: 607). This approach has been referred to as 'reception' research, which conceives of audiences as 'interpretive communities'. Accordingly, 'the qualitative material indicates respondents' perceptions and interpretations are more important than the frequency of media consumption and/or any objective characteristics of media material' (Ditton et al. 2004: 595). Drawing on both their quantitative and qualitative data, Ditton et al. (2004: 602) discovered the existence of what they describe as 'three worry groups':

1 *Low worriers* – the ubiquity of media coverage of crime allows some people in this group to dismiss its relevance. They rely on their own local knowledge and experience to overrule media portrayals of crime, and they believe actual risk is not randomly distributed. Moreover, respondents in this group said media representations cause one to *think* not *worry*, which might have the positive effect of people seeking to take precautions against victimization, such as not going out at night.
2 *Medium worriers* – this group begin to reverse the relationship between local experience and media portrayal of crime, e.g. distance from offending increases worry in the same way as it reduces worry for low worriers. People in this group worry greatly when they are confronted with crime stories in newspapers or on television, and are concerned more if it happens near them, but less so if it occurs elsewhere.
3 *High worriers* – while medium worriers seem not to know what to think, high worriers do. People in this group feel they are surrounded by ever-increasing amounts of general and specific nastiness. These people act on mediated rather than lived/real experience (highlighting the need to get out more, as a low worrier put it): their relationship is 'realer' than life itself. The location of crime is irrelevant; all that matters is that it happened. While those who worry less believe the media increases fear of crime, some high worriers believe, conversely, that the media increases crime itself.

Notwithstanding the foregoing criticisms of cultivation analysis, most studies support the proposition that the mass media causes whatever fear of crime is uncovered in research and surveys, no matter how significant or insignificant that connection might be. Of course, as will be apparent from what we have discussed so far, crucial here is the approach adopted and methodological techniques used when studying crime fear, which is the subject of the next section.

BOX 4.1 *BOWLING FOR COLUMBINE* – CULTURE OF FEAR IN AMERICA

As we saw in Chapter 2, the power of documentary films lies in their ability to use moving images to 'make a case' (Pauwels 2017: 69). In this vein, Michael Moore's 2002 documentary, *Bowling for Columbine*, attempts to make sense of the 1999 massacre at Columbine

High School in Colorado, which it places within the wider context of gun violence in the US. The film addresses a number of themes that are of particular relevance to us in this chapter. First, is the notion, related to the 'media effects' model, that exposure to graphic violence on television and videogames for instance, causes violent behavior. As will be discussed in Chapter 6, in the case of James Bulger it was believed – wrongly as it transpired – the killers had watched a horror movie, *Child's Play 3*, and that had contributed to them committing their heinous crime. In the Columbine case, along with attending a school bowling class on the morning of the attack – a detail later found to be baseless – listening to the music of controversial figure, Marilyn Manson, was apparently the last thing killers Eric Harris and Dylan Klebold did before the massacre.

A second theme raised in Moore's documentary film is the idea, succinctly summed up by Altheide (1997: 648), that 'fear is pervasive in American society and that it has been produced through the interaction of commercial media, entertainment formats and programming'. Hence, Moore states, '[t]he media, the corporations, the politicians have all done such a good job of scaring the American public'. Subsequently, he is filmed walking down a boulevard in South Central, Los Angeles, with Barry Glassner (Figure 4.1), author of the book (published in 1999), *The Culture of Fear: Why Americans Are Afraid of the Wrong Things*. As they walk, Glassner and Moore talk about white America's fear of the black man: the anonymous urban black male who does bad things. As Glassner says, when we turn on the news, what do we hear about: 'dangerous black guys'. The film then cuts to Arthur Busch, County Prosecutor – Flint, Michigan, who continues:

> Quite frankly, the black community has become entertainment for the rest of the community. The entertainment being that the crime of the day – you know, if it

Figure 4.1 Michael Moore (R) walks with Barry Glassner (L) in South Central, Los Angeles in the 2002 documentary film *Bowling for Columbine*

> bleeds, it leads – gets to be the front story. And then that becomes the perception and the image of an entire people, which couldn't be further from the truth, in my opinion. In fact, you'll find, I think most African-Americans are quite averse to gun possession.
>
> In suburbia, I think there's some notion that there's going to be an invading horde come from either the city or from some place unknown to savage their suburban community. To me, not only is it bizarre, but it's totally unfounded. . . . We've never really had many problems with the guns in the city. Not to say that we haven't; we've had some. But that's never been the biggest problem. The biggest problem has been the gun possession by these adolescents in suburbia.

The camera tracks back to Glassner, who says: 'My favourite statistic in all the research I did discovered that the murder rate had gone down by 20 per cent. The coverage – that is, how many murders are on the evening news – went up by 600 per cent'. In fiction too that has been the case, with Lichter et al. (1994: 275–276) finding that from 1965–1975 the FBI-calculated rate for violent crimes doubled to three incidents per 1,000 inhabitants, while the television rate was more than 30 times greater, at 114 incidents per 1,000 inhabitants.

Accordingly, as Country Prosecutor Busch opines, '[t]he American people are conditioned by network TV, by local news, to believe that their communities are a lot more dangerous than they actually are. For example, here in this community, crime has decreased every year for the past eight years. Yet gun ownership, and particularly handgun ownership, is on the increase', he says. Similarly, Glassner tell us that: 'Crime rates have been dropping; dropping, dropping. Fear of crime has been going up, up, up. How is that possible? It doesn't make any sense! But it makes perfect sense when you see what we're hearing from politicians and seeing in the news media'.

Cutting back to the street on South Central, Michael Moore observes they have reached the corner of Florence and Normandie, which, he says, is 'kinda ground zero for the LA riots'. Glassner responds, saying,

> [y]ou know, a couple of white guys go down and walk around South Central are going to get killed, which, I can tell you, is a common perception. The odds that something's going happen to us are really, really slight – miniscule.

A little later in the film, Moore interviews Dick Hurlin, former producer of the reality TV show, *COPS*, which we discuss in Chapter 5. What Moore's questioning reveals is why mainstream commercial media focus on 'newsworthy' street-level crime, rather than faceless and supposedly victimless crimes like corporate and state crime. Moore asks: 'Why not be compelled to do a show on what's causing the crime, as opposed to just chasing criminals down?' To that, Hurlin responds:

> Because it's harder to do that show. I don't know what that show would be. Anger does well. Hate does well. Violence does well. Tolerance and understanding and trying to learn to be a little different than you were last year, does less well.

RESEARCHING CRIME FEAR

In Chapter 1, we looked generally at some of the ways the relationship between crime and media is studied and researched. The field of crime fear research is no different, where, as we saw in the last section, questions of method, approach and emphasis are key. And, like other areas, researching fear of crime is not a straightforward task, but throws up a series of issues and problems from the outset. Not least there are methodological issues related to the problem of 'measuring' fear of crime. First, there are definitional issues. Should we be looking at *fear* or can we include feelings of *worry* and *concern* too? Secondly, do we look specifically at 'concrete fear' (i.e. actually being a victim of crime), or should we also be looking at 'formless fear', where the fear is of some vague threat to one's security (see Box 4.2)?

BOX 4.2 FEAR OF CRIME SURVEYS

In his review of the crime fear literature, Hale (1996) shows how the distinction between 'concrete fear' and 'formless fear' has become relatively widespread in studies, citing Canadian data from Keene (1992), which uses questions like the following for formless fear:

> How safe do you feel or would you feel walking alone in your neighborhood . . . (a) during the day? (b) How about after dark?

Concrete fear, on the other hand, is measured by responses to the question:

> We would like you to rate on a scale of zero to ten the chances of the following events happening to you in the future. A zero means that you think it will never happen and a ten means that you think the event will almost certainly happen to you. Rate the chances of
>
> (a) Deliberate damage to household or personal belongings.
> (b) Theft of household or personal belongings.
> (c) Assault or threat of assault.

(Hale 1996: 88)

These questions throw up a number of issues. For example, by making a distinction between 'during the day' and 'after dark', the first question implies to respondents that walking alone at night is more dangerous/unsafe than walking alone in the daytime. So, respondents will be inclined to say they feel less safe when walking alone after dark because of the way the question is worded. People will also interpret the term 'neighborhood' differently. As we have seen, people's fear of crime and concern they may become crime victims can bear a strongly relationship to how they feel about their place of residence, locality or neighborhood, as well as to their social identity and own experiences, if any, of crime. This goes to what Rachel Pain (2000: 379) has identified as the *situatedness* of crime fear, or 'the ways in which place, as a site where historical and contemporary economic changes interplay with social identities and relations, has an influence upon the fear of crime of people living locally'. Other studies have similarly stressed the need to situate people's fears in specific contexts:

> people's responses to crime (in its association with other matters of concern to them) are both informed by, and in turn inform, their *sense of place*; their sense, that is, of both *the place* they inhabit (its histories, divisions, trajectories and so forth), and *their place* within a wider world of hierarchies, troubles, opportunities and insecurities.
>
> (Girling et al. 2000: 17, original emphasis)

The second question in Keene's (1992) questionnaire may be seen as problematic for different reasons. For instance, rating probability on a scale of zero to ten will differ from person to person. It is largely a subjective measure, which will be influenced by things like people's direct experience as crime victims or their perception of crime that may have been gleaned from media reports. Moreover, the question is a measure of risk assessment, there is no mention of fear, which has been a source of controversy associated with the risk/fear debate, wherein some have challenged research that seeks to compare objective risk and subjective fear (Sparks 1992b).

Thirdly, are we trying to understand a person's mental state (e.g. anxiety), or are we attempting to discern fear that is related to actual events? Fourthly, are we trying to make actual or hypothetical assessments, such as the difference in asking, '*Do* you feel unsafe when walking alone at night?' or '*Would* you feel unsafe when walking alone at night?' While some studies mix actual and hypothetical questions, asking purely hypothetical questions to certain classes of people can produce questionable results. For instance, going out alone at night is a rare activity for many women, so asking whether or not they feel safe in relation to what is essentially a non-existent activity or an event lying well outside their normal experiences has raised questions about the validity of some studies. The same might be said for the elderly who, somewhat surprisingly states Hale (1996: 86), 'have been a major focus for much of the work on fear of crime', even though, as we shall see shortly, they are less likely to be victims of crime.

Lastly, it is important to ask questions about *frequency* and *intensity* of fear, e.g. 'all the time', 'some of the time', or 'very fearful', 'quite fearful'. Accordingly, Stephen Farrall (2004a: 163, emphasis added) is concerned to explore 'the *frequency* with which people *actually* feel these emotions in the course of their lives, and the frequency with which people *report* feeling these emotions', concluding that the matrix formed by people's lived experience of crime and crime fear does not easily fit current research questioning styles, which tend often to conflate frequency and severity of emotional responses. Farrall therefore argues that surveys have grossly overestimated worry about crime, and that survey designers need to refocus questions about fear, anger or concern about crime to include the frequency with which people experience these emotions (see Box 4.2).

FEAR-VICTIM PARADOX

A key area for researchers interested in fear of crime is the potential effect crime fear has on people's behavior and activities in their daily lives. In terms of crime and media relations, a central hypothesis is that the more crime is reported in the media, the greater its effect on behavior and everyday conduct. Hence, people who read about crime or watch more crime-related news and fiction are likely to be more fearful of crime, and will modify their behavior accordingly by, for instance, not going out alone after dark, or avoiding certain parts of town designated 'trouble spots' or 'crime hotspots' in the media. Although this suggests a version of the media effects model is at play here, the relationship between media exposure and behavior is not straightforward, since researchers have identified an apparent paradox: people who are more likely to fear crime tend to be less likely victims of crime. Much of this inquiry goes to the issue of *vulnerability*, i.e. those more vulnerable groups in society (e.g. women, the elderly, the poor) might be expected to be more fearful of crime.

In the case of women, the key question is why, given crime statistics and victimization surveys suggesting women are less likely than men to be victimized, do women appear to fear crime more than men? Hale sets out two broad responses to that question. First, statistics and victim surveys fail to capture fully the nature and extent of women's victimization: 'Once the full extent of their victimization is taken into account their fear is not inappropriate' (Hale 1996: 97). On that basis, fear of crime among the female population should not be regarded as inappropriate or disproportionate. Indeed, many crimes committed against women are perpetrated in private, behind closed doors, and so feminist criminologists in particular have argued that even though they may not report victimization, women's actual lived experience as crime victims is quite proportionate to their fear.

The second response to the victimization-fear paradox in respect of women distinguishes between perception of risk and fear, 'and maintains that the explanation for women's greater levels of fear lies in their heightened perceptions of personal vulnerability' (Hale 1996: 97). In a sense, this also relates to the first point, where a resolution to the paradox lies in understanding that women may be more afraid because they are more likely to confront threatening situations, and because they experience a wide range of hidden violence, sexual assaults and sub-legal harassment, which do not appear in official statistics and crime victim surveys. All of this 'sensitizes women to the fact that their environment is unsafe and to the need to adopt precautionary lifestyles in order to protect themselves from it' (Hale 1996: 98).

The focus of this type of research is on social relations (or, as we discussed in relation to cultivation analysis, social location), and, with particular respect to women and fear of crime, the experience of sexual oppression in patriarchal society. Thus, according to Valentine (1989), much of women's fear in certain places (i.e. situated fear) is in fact simply fear of men (see Box 4.2). So, in her Finnish study, Koskela (1999) debunks the myth of a 'safe' countryside and 'dangerous' city, as well as the idea that 'natural' hazards, such as darkness, explain fear among women, who,

> tended to perceive summer and winter nights as equally dangerous, despite the differences in the amount of light: in winter because of fears that attackers might be hiding in the darkness; in summer because the warmer temperatures mean that more men are around in parks and forests.
>
> (Pain 2000: 372)

Feminist scholars, such as Sandra Walklate (1997: 40), have countered the idea that the fear-victim paradox is a problem for women by questioning as irrational men's apparent lack of fear, arguing that, 'it is (young) men who behave irrationally given their greater exposure to risk from crime and their reported lower levels of fear of crime'. However, Sacco's (1990) arguments about differential socialization to risk among girls and boys might provide some explication as to the spurious relationship between victimization and fear. According to Sacco, unlike girls, boys are encouraged to take risks so as to anticipate their involvement in the public sphere of production. And that helps explain 'the reverse anomaly of why men, who have high objective risks of violent criminal victimization, express relatively low levels of concern for their personal safety' (Hale 1996: 99). On the other hand, some studies question the stereotype of fearless men, showing fear may lead to constraints on behavior just as much for men as for women (see, for instance, Gilchrist et al. 1998; Goodey 1997; Stanko and Hobdell 1993).

The elderly are also a vulnerable group, which, while statistically less likely than the young to be victims of crime, seem to be more fearful (Miethe and Lee 1984). That is why some suggest fear of crime rather than crime itself is the real problem for the elderly (Baumer 1978; Cook et al. 1981). However, as with women, although the fear-victimization paradox may seem irrational, some, like Warr (1984), have attempted to explain it in terms of 'perceptually contemporaneous offenses', which refers to the association of certain crimes with others that are potentially more serious. Hence, people under the age of 65 may not be afraid of begging, whereas the elderly may be fearful of it because they might view being approached by a beggar 'as a prelude to other more serious offences (e.g. assault or robbery)' (Warr 1984: 695).

Other researchers have found variations in the elderly's level of fear across different environments. For example, the elderly are more fearful in high crime neighborhoods (Jaycox 1978), the effect of age is more pronounced in inner city areas than in small towns and rural communities (Clemente and Kleinman 1976) and the elderly are more likely than young people to be fearful in low-income areas than in high-income areas (Lebowitz 1975). All of this demonstrates that, like fear in the female population, crime fear among the elderly is not irrational and disproportionate to their risk of victimization. Indeed, the elderly's fear may be congruent with the actual level of threat, as 'urban and low income areas tend to be more dangerous than rural and higher income areas' (Hale 1996: 101).

The poor have also been identified as a vulnerable group, which is expected to be more fearful of crime than others. Hale (1996: 103) argues that is because '[p]eople in lower socio-economic groups are less able to protect themselves or their property or to avoid situations which might produce anxiety'. Moreover, lack of material and social resources means the poor are likely less able to cope with individual victimization, just as poor communities are ill-equipped to deal with victimization, since they tend to lack contacts, organizational ability and political networks as compared to neighborhoods of higher status.

Ethnic minorities also tend to be more fearful due to a combination of factors, including living in poorer inner city areas that tend to have higher crime rates, increased likelihood of racially inspired attacks, and lack of confidence in the police and others in positions of power to protect non-white populations and alleviate their sense of vulnerability. These themes are also reflected in research on other vulnerable groups who can be victims of 'hate crime', such as trans women, who, as Perry and Dyck (2014: 58) show, 'do not necessarily have to be victims themselves to fear for their safety'.

In their study, Perry and Dyck (2014: 58) found that, regardless of context, trans women live in constant fear of assault, stating that: 'because of the fear that is perpetuated by the looming threat of homo/transphobic speech and action, many participants admitted that they were always on the watch for cues that suggested potential for harassment or violence'. And, as with ethnic minor communities, the problem is exacerbated by the failure of law enforcement agencies to intervene, which, ironically, also propagates 'widespread distrust if not fear of police among trans women' (Perry and Dyck 2014: 57). In another piece of research, Perry and Alvi (2011: 68–69) show how participants believed that just as hate is learned via a combination of the education system, home environment and media culture, so it can be challenged by the likes of activist groups providing factual media coverage to shed light on issues related to hate crimes, such as homophobia/gay bashing.

Disability is another vulnerability that may impact upon victimization and fear of victimization. In her study of women's fear of sexual violence, Pain (1997) discovered those women with a physical disability felt they were more susceptible to attack as well as less able to respond to it. Accordingly, 'they are more likely to employ avoidance behavior, bypassing certain places, people and situations altogether in response to their fear of attack' (Pain 1997: 241).

BOX 4.3 FEAR OF CRIME FEEDBACK LOOP

Interestingly, Farrall (2004a: 165) 'raises the possibility that the very act of being surveyed about their feelings concerning crime, if not "creating" these feelings, certainly appears to be exaggerating them'. Accordingly, he has asserted that 'the results of fear of crime surveys appear to be a function of the way the topic is researched, rather than the way it is', which has led to a situation whereby 'levels of fear of crime and, to a lesser extent, of victimization itself, have been hugely overestimated' (Farrall et al. 1997: 676). It has even been argued that 'there was no "fear of crime" in Britain until it was discovered in 1982' (Ditton et al. 1998: 10).

Thus, in a debate with Mike Hough (2004), Farrall argues that rather having little real significance, reported fear levels and the measurement of crime fear actually means a lot. Not only does it matter to citizens, but also to policymakers, police, community safety partnerships and to local councils. And, Farrall (2004b: 178) argues, that relates to what has been described as the 'fear of crime feedback loop', or a recursive process relating partly at least to the small academic industry that has grown up around fear of crime research, which operates:

> symbiotically to produce and intensify crime fear and the research related to it; that research into victims produces and maintains the criminological concept of 'fear of crime' quantitatively and discursively; that this information operates to identify fear as a legitimate object of governance or governmental regulation; that the techniques of regulation imagine particular types of citizens – *fearing subjects*; that these attempts to govern 'fear of crime' actually inform the citizenry that they are indeed fearful; that this sensitizes the citizenry to 'fear of crime'; that the law and order lobby and populist politicians use this supposed fearing population to justify a tougher approach on crime, a point on which they grandstand, and in doing so sensitize citizens to fear once again; and that this spurs more research into 'fear of crime' and so on.
>
> (Lee 2001: 480–481, original emphasis)

The argument here is that research into crime fear may not only increase fear among citizens, but it can also lead to the imposition of harsher penalties, which, 'given that harsher penalties have not been demonstrated to reduce offending', Farrall (2004b: 179) argues, 'probably leads to a secondary feedback loop whereby more crime is actually committed'. The idea that fear of crime matters in political and policy terms is an important one. As we saw in Chapter 3, fears and anxieties associated with *episodic* moral panics can lead to the introduction of *permanent* 'law and order' measures. Crime fear, and attendant fear of crime research, can have similarly significant effects on the criminal justice system, as evident in the example of responses to 'anti-social behavior'.

PRODUCTIVITY OF CRIME FEAR: THE CASE OF ANTI-SOCIAL BEHAVIOR

In Chapter 3, we considered the productivity of moral panics; that is, some of the ways moral panics produce legacies, or have lasting effects/outcomes, which we said was an interesting point given Cohen's (1972/2002) original idea about moral panics being transitory and episodic. In that chapter, we saw how some of the lasting effects of moral panics include increasingly coercive and punitive measures introduced by the state, which have been accompanied by the erosion of rights and freedoms, and an undermining of the rule of law. Many of these arguments might also apply to links between fear of crime, crime fear research and punitive 'law and order' politics (see Box 4.3). Indeed, as we saw in Chapter 3, the creation of *fear* and *anxiety* about particular groups in society (folk devils) is a key element of moral panics. That is no less so in the case of state responses to anti-social behavior, which, in Britain especially, have been framed in a media context consisting of diatribes against young 'hoodies', and street corner socializing (Martin 2009: 236; Figure 4.2), tabloid sensationalism over 'neighbours from hell' living in social housing (Field 2003), and moral panic over the 'hen party menace' (Skeggs 2005: 966).

In fact, as Bev Skeggs suggests, it could be argued the media-induced societal reaction to anti-social behavior in Britain has amounted to a moral panic, not least because the response to young 'hoodies' (or 'chavs' as they are know colloquially) has assumed a normative element, which, according to Lawler (2005: 800), is just one manifestation of a widespread disparagement of the poor and dispossessed that claims not to be about class yet 'invokes class distinctions at every turn' (see also Tyler 2008). Likewise, Squires (2006) argues the anxiety over youth as rude, loutish, intolerant, selfish, disrespectful, drunken and violent has moral roots based on longstanding 'respectable' middle-class fears. Furthermore, politicians tap into these sentiments to effectively reposition the criminal justice

Figure 4.2 Anti-social behavior or young people hanging about on a street corner?

system, which 'is more explicitly becoming a criminal law service working for victims and the "moral majority"' (Squires 2006: 151).

On the other hand, Stuart Waiton (2008) has argued it is better to talk of the reaction to anti-social behavior as an *amoral* panic, since the panic is not driven by moral concerns so much as by an anxious preoccupation with risk, safety and security. Either way, the rationale for introducing measures to tackle anti-social behavior is founded on people's *perceptions* and *fears* rather than on actual behavior or the commission of crimes, which is a rationale enshrined in the legal definition of anti-social behavior. Hence, section 1(1)(a) of the *Anti-social Behaviour Act 2003* (UK) provides for the creation of 'anti-social behaviour orders', or ASBOs, if it appears that any person aged 10 or over has acted 'in a manner that caused or was likely to cause harassment, alarm or distress to one or more persons not of the same household as himself' (see Martin 2011a: 382).

Thinking about this in terms of the productivity or legacy of fear of crime, and maybe crime fear research too, that way of conceiving of anti-social behavior as not being limited to acts causing harassment, alarm or distress but including those that are *likely* to cause harassment, alarm or distress, effectively reverses the presumption of innocence. Accordingly, Alison Brown (2004: 205, original emphasis) argues that in issuing an ASBO, '[a] case goes to court not to prove someone is a perpetrator of anti-social behavior; but to authorize a sanction against one who is *already* a perpetrator'. Thus, someone's fear, apprehension or perception of crime/anti-social behavior, while possibly unfounded, could nevertheless have very real consequences for people who otherwise may not be subject to criminal sanctions.

Moreover, to Brown (2004: 208), the inclusion of 'sub-criminal' activity, such as hanging around on street corners (Figure 4.2), within the scope of anti-social behavior leads to a scenario where 'new categories of people and behavior are brought into the control system', which is an instance of Cohen's (1985) prediction that deviancy control measures will increasingly entail 'widening the net' and 'thinning the mesh' of social control. An important facet of this process is that it blurs boundaries, which, in the case of anti-social behavior measures in Britain, means breaching the fundamental boundary between criminal and civil law by such things as conflating criminality and incivility, introducing a lower standard of proof, and substituting 'a rule so vague almost anything could break it' (Brown 2004: 205).

In some cases too the rules of evidence are ignored where, for instance, hearsay evidence has been admitted into court when people have been reluctant to appear as witnesses who 'grass' on their neighbors for fear of retaliation (Martin 2011a: 383). Indeed, when discussing some of the consequences of fear of crime, Hale (1996: 82) makes a similar point about the fear associated with suspicion of neighbors and behavior, which tends to operate according to 'a downward spiral in which fear causes people to constrain their behavior and this behavioral response in turn heightens their fear' (see also Liska et al. 1988). And it has been argued this phenomenon applies not only to high crime areas but also supposedly safer 'gated communities', which, ironically tend to create more rather than less fear, isolation and social exclusion (Davis 1998).

Finally, it is important to place the approach to anti-social behavior outlined above within the context of a broader set of developments associated with what Lucia Zedner (2007: 262) calls 'pre-crime', which 'shifts the temporal perspective to anticipate and forestall that which has not yet occurred and may never do so'. In the emergent 'pre-crime society', pre-emptive measures are increasingly sought to avert risk, meaning people may be charged and prosecuted (and thereby criminalized) on the basis of fear or anticipation of crime rather than on the basis of something that has actually occurred or been done, which is how the criminal justice system has tended traditionally to operate.

CONCLUSION

To the extent the emergence of a pre-crime society entails a coupling of fear and risk, it is indicative of developments highlighted towards the end of the last chapter and beginning of this one, whereby attempts to manage, control or stave off risk can be seen as responses to a pervasive 'culture of fear'. However, just as the universality of cultivation analysis has been challenged on the ground crime fear research ought to consider contextual factors such as sense of place, location and community attachment, so responses to the perceived ubiquity of crime and disorder, 'vary according to social position, material advantage and experience of place' (Carrabine 2008: 52). Hence, the affluent middle classes might retreat into fortified communities while the less affluent are left to manage their daily lives in 'high crime' urban areas.

Nevertheless, argues Carrabine (2008: 52), studies attempting to understand fear of crime as locally and socially situated 'do not directly address media consumption, audience interpretation and collective representations in any great detail'. In part that is because there is a lack of in-depth research into the ways media representations of crime are interpreted within 'domestically rooted and geographically located' contexts and places (Banks 2005: 170). What we do know, however, is that the mainstream mass media does have *some* effect not only on audiences, but also more broadly on crime policy, which becomes more punitive in response to increasing levels of fear, as evident in what has been described above in terms of a 'fear of crime feedback loop'.

Hence, the example of anti-social behavior demonstrates how laws with real consequences can be formulated on the basis of what may, in fact, be imagined fears and anxieties. This then connects to the idea presented in Chapter 3 about the productivity or lasting legacies of what are often ephemeral moral panics, which like apprehension associated with anti-social behavior, are founded on fears and anxieties that are largely illusory. It also links to the notion in cultural criminology, discussed in Chapter 2, about the importance of examining loops and spirals between mass media formats and individual experience as 'mediated understandings of crime and crime control are . . . more likely than ever to penetrate everyday social settings' (Ferrell 2015: 298). We take this up in the next chapter, where, among other things, we consider the impact on audiences of popular dramatizations about crime and law enforcement, which can sometimes affect legal outcomes, thus highlighting the slippage between fiction and reality.

SUGGESTED FURTHER READING

Although now a little dated, the following article reviewing the fear of crime literature remains a very useful starting point:

Hale, C. (1996) 'Fear of crime: A review of the literature' *International Review of Victimology* 4(2): 79–150.

Several of the issues canvassed in this chapter are addressed in the following book, which is written from a broadly Foucauldian perspective:

Lee, M. (2007) *Inventing Fear of Crime: Criminology and the Politics of Anxiety*. Cullompton: Willan Publishing.

The debate between Farrall and Hough is interesting for providing divergent views on fear of crime and crime fear research:

Farrall, S. (2004a) 'Revisiting crime surveys: Emotional responses without emotions? Or look back at anger' *International Journal of Social Research Methodology* 7(2): 157–171.

Farrall, S. (2004b) '*Can* we believe our eyes? A response to Mike Hough' *International Journal of Social Research Methodology* 7(2): 177–179.

Hough, M. (2004) 'Worry about crime: Mental events and mental states' *International Journal of Social Research Methodology* 7(2): 173–176.

CHAPTER 5

Law, crime and popular culture

INTRODUCTION

In the last chapter we saw how insofar as it might impact government policy, fear of crime research can have lasting effects on criminal law and crime justice processes. Similarly, in Chapter 3, we saw how although they are manufactured, moral panics, such as those over asylum seekers, can be productive, having real effects and legacies, such as influencing crime policy and law. Importantly, part of that manufacturing process can involve portrayals in popular culture, as demonstrated by Kinney (2015), who has shown how fictional media representations of human trafficking as 'crimmigration' has shaped not only people's beliefs about trafficking but also impacted on the practices of legal institutions responding to it.

This type of argument represents an articulation of a broad reading or interpretation of the media effects model, examined in Chapter 1, which, to reiterate, posits both non-fictional and fictional media representations of crime and disorder can affect audiences, as well as bring about transformations in government policy, legislation and criminal procedure. Although, as explained in Chapter 2, cultural criminologists consider scholarship on media effects part of a 'formulaic' and 'static' body of knowledge (Hayward 2010: 5), in this chapter, and indeed throughout the book, we will see how this relatively simplistic view might cause us to overlook some subtle and varied media effects on audiences, and on legal and political processes to boot. In this chapter, for instance, we will see how it has been proposed that forensic television dramas, like *Crime Scene Investigation* (*CSI*), can have multiple effects on audiences, possibility also having an impact on court proceedings, with juries being cautioned by judges as to the probable disjunction between what they have viewed on television and what they can expect to experience in court in terms of the quantity and quality of available scientific evidence.

Inasmuch as any media effect is itself a function of the increased blurring of fiction and reality, which like media effects, is also something canvassed in this book, Richard Sherwin (2004: 95) has argued there is two-way traffic between law and popular culture, in that '[r]eal legal issues and controversies give rise to popular legal representations just as popular legal representations help to inform and shape real legal issues and case outcomes'. Two very different examples can be used to illustrate that point. The first demonstrates how popular television shows can influence people's career choice. It is the example of Sadiq Khan, the former Labour politician and subsequent Mayor of London, who, when asked how he became a human rights lawyer replied: '*LA Law*', in reference to the hit US television series of the 1980s. Among others, it starred the Hispanic actor, Jimmy Smits, as the dashing young attorney, Victor Sifuentes, who Khan cites as an inspiration. Khan continued:

> Don't underestimate the power of TV. In *LA Law*, you had these lawyers acting for underdogs, doing these great cases, and I was reading in the newspapers about the Guildford Four, the Birmingham Six and all those miscarriages of justice. Those were my formative years.
>
> (Hasan 2011: 32)

Another television series, this time a British courtroom drama, also continued to affect Khan in adulthood. When asked whether he was surprised by Ed Miliband's victory in the Labour leadership contest of September 2010, he said the night before the result he told Miliband to 'prepare for defeat', adding, 'I learned this from *Rumpole of the Bailey*. . . . Always tell your client he's going to lose because, if he loses, he's expecting it; if he wins, you're the fantastic lawyer who got the victory' (Hasan 2011: 33).

A second example concerns the banning of the Australian gangland crime drama, *Underbelly*. In February 2008, Justice Betty King imposed a suppression order prohibiting the broadcast of the first series of *Underbelly* in the state of Victoria during the trial of one of the show's protagonists, Carl Williams (Hunter and Tyson 2017: 778). Justice King imposed the ban believing the portrayal of the 'gangland killings' would prejudice a fair trial, which was also the view of the court when Channel 9 appealed King's decision because, the court held, 'what was seen on television by any juror would contemporaneously put colour and drama into the evidence led by the prosecution' (King 2009: 18).

While the first example provides a biographical account pertaining to some kind of media effect, the second is illustrative of systemic issues arising from media depictions that, it is believed, might impact negatively on legal processes and court proceedings. In that case, the presiding judge (and appeal court) was worried media coverage that dramatized real events would influence jurors in ways that would be prejudicial to the defendant. That is not to say all media coverage impacts negatively on processes of law and crime policy. In this chapter, we will look at cases of positive influence too, which also appear throughout the book. For instance, towards the end of Chapter 2, we saw how podcasts and documentary films and series about what are sometimes controversial cases have led to a re-examination of judicial findings or review of legislation. And, later in the book, in Chapter 8, we will look at the ways video activism and 'citizen journalism' might intervene in allegations of police misconduct, as well as engage more generally with crime and justice issues.

Issues regarding both positive and negative media effects are brought into sharp relief in what has become known as the '*CSI* effect', which now has many facets but essentially posits jurors who have watched *CSI*, and similar shows, are more likely to acquit defendants on account of the mismatch between the quantity, quality and availability of scientific evidence in the real courtroom as compared to forensic television shows. Because the forensic evidence in real criminal trials does not match high juror expectations created by watching shows like *CSI*, some studies reveal juries are more likely to doubt the guilt of accused persons, which means they are less likely to convict. However, that proposition is by no means settled, and in the chapter we will explore various accounts that have argued for and against the existence of a *CSI* effect.

Although we look at some fictional literature, the main focus in this chapter is on movies and television shows, including law films, courtroom dramas, cop shows and forensic-themed television. In this way, the chapter fits within the ambit of cultural criminology not only because of its focus on the visual and imaginary of crime, but also because, following Rafter (2007: 416–417), it is premised on a view that film, television and other visual media are sources of 'cultural information', and thereby primary means through which people get ideas about crime. Put another way, and also flagged in Chapter 2, Katz (2016: 235) has observed that 'a great bulk of cultural criminology' is made up of studies of culture *about* crime, including both visual *and* textual representations in popular culture. Accordingly, this chapter explores popular media representations of what may be regarded the triumvirate of crime justice processes: (i) cops; (ii) courts; and (iii) criminals. We begin by looking at depictions of the highly masculine world of 'hard-boiled' private detectives in US film noir during the 1940s, which, as we shall see, have provided a prototype for subsequent portrayals of both male and female detectives.

HARD-BOILED DETECTIVES AND FILM NOIR

In her analysis of hard-boiled detective stories and the related genre of film noir, Mariana Valverde (2006) provides a contrast with the early English detective mysteries of the 1930s, like Agatha Christie's fiction, which generally uphold conventional bourgeois morality (see also Young 1996: 98), and end in restoring the world (often in a small village community) to its pre-crime condition. Hard-boiled detective stories, by contrast, are thoroughly pessimistic. Stories end having revealed the truth about a crime but the city remains a place of greed, alienation and meaninglessness. In fact, Valverde (2006: 96) says, 'the truth about a particular crime always turns out to also be a truth about the essential selfishness of the alienated individuals shown wandering aesthetically but without moral purpose through a menacing urban landscape'.

Partly born of movie budget restrictions combined with the practice of rationing after the Second World War, and partly an aesthetic choice, the stark and spartan style of film noir 'provided the ideal format for bringing hard-boiled detective stories to the screen' (Valverde 2006: 93). In both the stories and movies, hard-boiled detectives are portrayed as hyper-masculine and showing few emotions. They are also amoral, and not motivated by a search for the truth about the crimes they are employed to solve, or by the pleasure involved in unravelling mysteries. Rather, they are in business to make money.

The depiction of these hard-boiled private detectives not only reveals corruption at the heart of conventional society on what novelist Raymond Chandler called the detectives' 'mean streets', but also the corruption in the hearts of the detectives themselves. Cheating on people, seducing women and acts of violence are all done in the pursuit of the detectives' self-interest, not in seeking the truth. The fact that hard-boiled detectives are private eyes employed by private individuals bypassing the police, also represents an implied critique of the criminal justice system. In this way, telling audiences that only the private sector, including insurance companies, is concerned with discovering the truth and restoring order, sends a subtle message about the incompetence of government law enforcement agencies. In the 1941 movie, *The Maltese Falcon*, for instance, Sam Spade, played by Humphrey Bogart, is employed to solve a real (i.e. legal) crime – the theft of the statue of the Templars' falcon – though the police are not called; the offense is portrayed as a crime against the private owners who employ private personnel to recover this unique and ancient artefact (Figure 5.1).

Just as hard-boiled detectives are depicted as amoral, so a signature of the film noir genre is the archetype of the *femme fatale*: women who use their beauty for immoral ends. In the 1944 movie, *Double Indemnity*, for example, Barbara Stanwyck's character, Phyllis Dietrichson, uses 'her sexual wiles to inveigle a not overly moral insurance salesman into helping her to fraudulently take out a life insurance policy on her husband and to then kill him, in a complicated, "perfect crime" scenario' (Valverde 2006: 93).

According to Alison Young (1996: 102), hard-boiled fiction is one of a number of sub-genres that adhere to 'the laws of crime which govern the genre of detective fiction'. In film noir, for instance, the formulaic structure provides for misogynistic representations of women, which is particularly evident in the detective novels of Chandler, for whom Philip Marlowe's heroism hinges on the counterpoint of amoral femininity. Hence, for Marlowe to be law, Young (1996: 97) argues, 'a woman must be sacrificed'. That is exemplified by his failed marriage to Linda, which, once dissolved, allows him 'to resume his independent, masculine life. Femininity is thus deadly or suffocating and emasculating for Marlowe. Pleasure and danger are inextricably linked and located in the feminine body' (Young 1996: 98).

Figure 5.1 Poster for the classic American film noir movie *The Maltese Falcon*, 1941

By contrast, in Sir Arthur Conan Doyle's classical detective stories about Sherlock Holmes, women are more or less evacuated, giving rise to a form of 'sexual apartheid' (Young 1996: 100). For instance, after Dr Watson marries Miss Morstan, she appears as a protagonist in *The Sign of Four*, but never again: 'she exists in shadow, a constant absence whose function is to tend to the home that awaits Watson at the end of each adventure with Holmes' (Young 1996: 100). The role of the woman here 'is to *be* absent, to be unadventurous' (Young 1996: 100, original emphasis), which enables Watson and Holmes to continue their homosocial relationship unaffected by the former's marriage. Thus, as Young (1996: 100) says, while 'Chandler wrote women into his stories as the embodiment of fatality, Doyle's texts exclude women, lest they threaten either the peaceful co-existence of men or the execution of the detective method'.

BOX 5.1 FEMALE HARD-BOILED DETECTIVES

In response to Chandler's construction of femininity, a strand of feminist detective fiction emerged portraying 'the female hard-boiled detective' (Umphrey and Shuker-Haines 1991), as exemplified by Sara Paretsky's V. I. Warshawski and Sue Grafton's Kinsey Millhone. These female detectives are very different to the women of Chandler's texts, and actually exhibit many of the characteristics of male hard-boiled loners: 'independent (financially and emotionally), physically strong, often heroic in action' (Young 1996: 100). Indeed, Young (1996: 100) suggests 'this is one of the many attractions offered to the contemporary feminist reader: liberating the woman from confinement in her home, circumventing the female fear of attack in the dark urban streets'. Hence, Warshawski is as solitary as Marlowe, and 'she blames the urban decay of Chicago as much as he mourns the decline of Los Angeles' (Young 1996: 101).

Walton and Jones (1999) argue female detective fiction draws on the hard-boiled tradition not only as a formal but also as a political gesture. Establishing a distinctive feminine voice and empowered female subject 'is literally what puts them in business, making them saleable to what appears to have been a previously untapped readership' (Walton and Jones 1999: 5). However, although female hard-boiled detectives can be distinguished from their male counterparts by anti-sexist and anti-racist politics, the genre has been criticized because 'the feminist detective's "successes" in terms of solving crimes often mean a restoring of order to the patriarchal world that oppresses them' (Young 1996: 100). Moreover, when physical threat and violence are visited upon the female detective, as they often are, 'the price of detection is literalized on her body', which registers 'the costs of curiosity, of unconfined circulation around the city space' (Young 1996: 100).

The reproduction of a dominant patriarchal order is something Ruth Penfold-Mounce (2016) intimates when commenting on television crime drama, *The Fall*. Although focused on the activities of serial killer Paul Spector (Jamie Dornan), the portrayal of a strong, empowered female lead, DCI Stella Gibson (Gillian Anderson), has led some to classify *The Fall* a feminist show, even the most feminist show on television (Sullivan 2015). However, Penfold-Mounce (2016) says *The Fall* is in many ways an example of 'the continuing use of women as victims of violence in the crime drama genre'. Hence, even though the body count is relatively low, 'the content and imagery of the drama suggests a fetishism of lethal violence against women'. For instance, Spector's careful and often artistic positioning of his dead victims has the effect of stylizing the female corpse 'in a manner almost reminiscent of pornography' (Penfold-Mounce 2016).

Such portrayals normalize women as being vulnerable to male violence, reinforcing the view of them as what Nils Christie (1986) terms, 'the ideal victim'; that is, they 'rely on the construct of ideal victimology, as the sadistic serial killer seeks out idealized targets as victims, and they are almost invariably unsuspecting, Caucasian and female' (Houlihan 2012: 445). According to Penfold-Mounce (2016), this allows 'murderous cruelty to become pleasurable entertainment'. On the other hand, just as feminist detective fiction has created its own hard-boiled detectives, so Penfold-Mounce (2016) says the new era of strong female leads has also given them 'greater opportunity to become aggressors', as well as 'purveyors of violence rather than simply the victim'.

In an even more devastating critique of *The Fall*, Deborah Jermyn (2017) has argued the show tells us much of what it takes in the postfeminist media landscape for women cops to stay on screen. In contrast to feminist themes in the earlier series, *Prime Suspect*, she says *The Fall* 'spoke to a media culture where ratings can be won via a superficial but glossily packaged nod to postfeminist "gains", despite the fact that these dress up a deeply regressive impulse' (Jermyn 2017: 266), namely relishing misogynistic violence and eroticization of dead women, who, according to Clarke Dillman (2014: 2), 'need to be dead before an exploration of their lives, subjectivities and experiences is authorized in mainstream representations'. Indeed, the nod to the female detective's postfeminist 'progress' is quite literally dressed up; evident in the power-dressing credentials of the series that focus on Stella Gibson's blouses. Ultimately, though, the series delivers 'postfeminist lip-service to feminist issues, as a disguise for pre-feminist scorn', which draws most overtly on the *femme fatale* archetype: 'highly fetishized through [Gibson's] constricting pencil skirts and stilettoes, through the textures of her long loose hair and her tactile silky blouses, and her mastery of the gun/phallus on the shooting range' (Jermyn 2017: 217).

NORDIC NOIR

In recent times there has emerged another version of noir: Nordic noir. Examples include book series that have become televised, such as *The Killing*, *The Bridge* and *Wallander*. Nordic noir is so called because it incorporates elements of the American hard-boiled private detective stories of film noir in a Scandinavian context. However, it also has things in common with the British crime tradition of Agatha Christie, such as the use of rural settings (Creeber 2015: 21–22; Waade and Jensen 2013: 191).

Creeber (2015: 22) writes that Nordic noir is 'typified by a dimly-lit aesthetic (hence its implicit reference to film noir) that is matched by a slow and melancholic pace, multi-layered storylines and an interest in uncovering the dark underbelly of contemporary society'. The slow pace, including long scenes, gives the impression of 'temporal deceleration' (Creeber 2015: 25). Melodic and ethereal music and soundtracks evoking a sense of quiet meditation also add to the slowed down mood of Nordic noir dramas. Setting is important too. Sense of place, location and landscape all symbolize remoteness, isolation and loneliness, which is echoed in the inner mood and feelings of characters, such as Kurt Wallander, who, like so many protagonists, is depicted as a troubled detective, 'a man who drinks too much, rarely exercises, battles with depression and has few close friends' (Creeber 2015: 26; see also Gray 2014: 76). In combination, these ingredients follow in a tradition of 'Nordic melancholy', which 'is expressed in the main characters' inner psychological and personal conditions and conflicts, but also in terms of external conditions such as landscape, nature, climate and general atmosphere' (Waade and Jensen 2013: 192).

Central to the narrative structure of Nordic noir crime drama is the notion of 'double-storytelling' (Creeber 2015: 23), which alludes to having two detectives work on a case. However, unlike the Holmes/Watson scenario (i.e. genius detective with less smart sidekick), the dynamic in Nordic noir is two police officers of the same or similar rank, who bring different skills to an investigation, provide contrasting sides of policing and possess different kinds of moral or ethical codes. Unlike film noir, however, male detectives can be less hard-boiled than their female counterparts. Indeed, as Gray (2014: 77) argues, there is a *gender reversal* in Nordic noir, with 'male detectives (re)imagined and represented as emotionally dependent on women'. For example, Kurt Wallander relies on his daughter, Linda, for emotional support, and later turns to his boss and neighbor, Katarina.

Similarly, in *The Bridge*, Danish detective, Martin Rohde, undoes the trope of male noir hero: early on it is revealed he has had a vasectomy (a dent to his masculinity) after fathering five children; he is distressed when his wife ejects him from the family home after discovering he has had an affair with a witness; and he becomes distressed when his son is kidnapped by the Bridge Killer/trust Terrorist. By contrast, Sweden's female detective, Saga Norén, is emotionally composed and ends up solving the case, which she does in spite of being shot several times, showing she is also physically invulnerable. In this way, like the detectives of feminist fiction, discussed earlier, Saga 'offers a particularly interesting version of the hard-boiled noir hero(ine)' (Gray 2014: 79).

Creeber (2015: 32) states that while '[t]he two detectives provide a love story of sorts, the murders represent social problems and the criminals symbolize the evils that threaten to destroy society'. Hence, another theme in Nordic noir concerns the malaise that arises from a loss of belief in the creation of a utopian society, and attendant disillusionment over the decline of the welfare state and undermining of liberal democracy (Gray 2014: 75; McCabe 2017: 60). Preoccupations in Henning Mankell's *Wallander* stories include immigration and racism, inequality and hierarchy, the breakdown of community and inclusion/exclusion; and the crimes Wallander is called upon to investigate include sex trafficking, transnational cyberterrorism and trade in human organs (McCabe 2017: 60). That is, global problems generating local anxiety. As Kenneth Branagh, who plays Wallander, has put it, '[t]he *Wallander* novels are a sort of requiem for a lost utopia, for the lost innocence of Sweden' (Stasio 2009). Indeed, it is well known that Mankell started writing *The Kurt Wallander Mysteries* after spending several years working in Africa. Upon his return, he found Sweden to be very different: more xenophobic, and a more troubled country (McCabe 2017: 59). This sentiment is reflected in the character of Wallander who, according to Bergmann (2014: 56), 'feels lost and alienated in a Sweden he perceives as changing. He repeatedly claims to feel like a stranger, or perhaps rather obsolete: like a dinosaur in the present version of his home country'.

To Creeber (2015: 24), what makes Nordic noir distinctive is its stark sense of realism, and it is the 'aesthetic blending of social realism and film noir that is at the heart of its moral, political and philosophical critique'. Indeed, to the surprise of Danish tourist agencies, it is the sombre, noir-inspired image of Copenhagen portrayed in *The Bridge*, not the typical historic image, that attracts foreign visitors to the city (Agger 2013: 236). Nordic noir is also appealing to viewers because of the socio-political insights it affords, providing 'a complex picture of Scandinavian society – in particular, the cracks that have appeared in the social democratic ideal, an ideal which has been cherished for so long by observers in America, Britain and the rest of Europe' (Forshaw 2012: 2).

For these reasons, Nordic noir has global reach, which has seen its formula adapted and applied in other countries. This is especially so in respect of the philosophical and moral aspects of its narrative structure. While it mourns the loss of a utopian ideal and demise of the welfare state, Nordic noir nevertheless attempts to resurrect cornerstones of Scandinavian social democracy – e.g. tolerance, inclusiveness, cooperation and equality – but does so in the context of increasing complexity, diversity and division (cp. Schclarek Mulinari 2017). In *The Bridge*, that is symbolized by two detectives from different countries, with distinct personal and professional styles, working together. As Creeber (2015: 24) puts it: 'The moral of the story appears abundantly clear; everyone must work together for their mutual benefit, even two nations like Denmark and Sweden. In short, bridges have to be built'.

The feeling that the liberal democratic ideal has somehow been lost is felt beyond Scandinavia, as evident in the way the Nordic noir formula has been exported. For instance, the UK television show, *Broadchurch*, also provides an example of 'double-storytelling', portraying two diametrically opposed female-male detectives who make a formidable team: 'her closeness to the community enabling them to gain access to places and people he may have missed, while his distance from the community gives a much needed injection of objectivity' (Creeber 2015: 28). The storyline also provides a moral tale underpinned by a philosophy that is hinted at in the first few second of the first series, when the camera rests on a poster by the local church, which reads: 'Love Thy Neighbour As Thyself'.

> a simple Christian message of respect and interconnectedness, but one that will resonate through the entire narrative. Every community is, after all, a 'broad church' and it must learn to accept, understand and eventually forgive all of its diverse and often fallible inhabitants if it is to survive.
>
> (Creeber 2015: 29)

COPS, LAWYERS AND COURTROOMS

Following the film noir and hard-boiled detective era, Valverde (2006) observes two types of film emerging in America from the late 1950s to the 1970s: (i) cop films; and (ii) lawyer films/courtroom dramas. Rather than focusing on individual criminal behavior and individual prowess in detecting crimes, cop films focus on the criminal justice *system* as protagonist and source of narrative interest. Drawing on the lineage of Westerns where the figure of the sheriff is depicted traversing the lines between law and lawlessness, order and arbitrariness, so

> US police films and television programmes blur the public-private line . . . by showing cops who act as if they were private eyes, that is, without much regard either for superior officers, or the letter of the law, or the usual procedures of police work.
>
> (Valverde 2006: 97)

Cops are portrayed as mavericks or loose cannons, but nevertheless honest and at odds with a corrupt or malfunctioning system. And if they break the law or take the law into their own hands, they do so only to observe and uphold the spirit of the law. In this way, cop films serve to 'reassure Americans that an honest and courageous individual can bring about justice, even if the system remains essentially ill-designed or even corrupt' (Valverde 2006: 97). Similarly, in the British context, it has been argued that from 1970 an upswing in films portraying crime as ubiquitous corresponded to:

> the increasing predominance of police heroes rather than amateur sleuths. As crime is increasingly portrayed as endemic to society, it justifies the employment of a large bureaucracy, with police heroes leading the narrative, but also with increasing prominence accorded to the organizational pressures and problems which lie behind their activities.
>
> (Allen et al. 1998: 66)

The popularity of police films waned from the 1980s, and from the late 1990s the television format became a means for audiences to 'imaginatively explore the small-scale dramas of real life, be it the life of the family explored in soap operas or the life of the city explored in police series' (Valverde 2006: 102). The police television series *COPS* provides an example of a form of reality TV whereby the audience can experience the 'real' world of police; what it is 'really' like for police to patrol the streets of the urban/suburban jungle, though the story is told from the largely white police perspective. Most of the action in *COPS* consists of

> disconnected bits, through which respectable viewers sitting at home not only see life 'in the projects', among the underclasses, but are actually thrown

> into a semiotically confusing succession of badly lit video clips with noisy soundtracks that rarely amount to a coherent narrative.
>
> (Valverde 2006: 103–104)

Police-centered television series like *COPS*, which show police traveling across the social divides of class and race, therefore enable 'middle class and respectable working class viewers to explore, from the safety of the armchair, the seamy side of urban life' (Valverde 2006: 102). In other terms, they allow 'Americans to engage in some vicarious slum travel' (Valverde 2006: 107). In *COPS*, for example, the interiors of houses appear as disorderly (beer bottles are strewn over floor); family life is dysfunctional (children are up late); there is a focus on the poor neighborhoods of ethic minorities; and women are impliedly depicted as 'white trash' (scantily clad in bright polyester, and usually overweight). By contrast, the representation of police is unambiguous, and although drinking is not alien to cop culture, 'since their leisure time is not represented on the show, what we see is that the disorderly classes are often drunk and incoherent, whereas the cops are always rational and sober' (Valverde 2006: 105). Similarly, the show creates the impression drugs are ubiquitous, which has a 'law and order' effect, 'because people who are caught having just consumed mind-altering substances don't look very rational when filmed', says Valverde (2006: 105). Importantly, rather than being an artless (and off-the-cuff) form, the reality TV genre of a show like *COPS* has its own formal conventions and technical features, which, in turn, has important political effects:

> Imagining that 'tricks' are only used in film and in professionally made television shows, [viewers] do not see that the fact that the camera goes with the cop from the cruiser into the apartment or house under investigation has the effect of presenting the 'underworld' as the cop sees it, that is, as a space of constant risk and potential danger . . . the 'reality' soundtrack, full of unintelligible sounds, conveys a certain message about the world of crime precisely through the lack of coherent meaning.
>
> (Valverde 2006: 104)

Needless to say, states Valverde (2006: 106), 'no microphone stays behind to record what the hapless inhabitants of the underworld think or say'. A distinctive feature of *COPS*, then, is that each episode focuses on the escapades of a 'star' police officer whose story is 'personalized and rendered sympathetic' (Valverde 2006: 104). Like other reality TV police shows, *COPS* focuses solely on officers who work on the streets as upholders of law and order in the face of the uncivilized hordes inhabiting the urban/suburban jungle: 'rational, well-dressed, sober white men with well-trimmed haircuts trying to make sense of an inherently unintelligible world' (Valverde 2006: 105). Earlier cop films also present a one-dimensional view of good, honest cops, though the emphasis here is on the ways these police officers are impeded by the criminal justice system and actors therein, such as judges and prosecutors undoing the investigative work involved in apprehending someone who, in the eyes of police, is clearly culpable. There are parallels here with reality TV shows about judges, such as *Judge Judy*, which, like shows about their police counterparts, provide a partial and often distorted view of the 'reality' they purport to represent, tending to

> blur the lines between judging and entertaining so that viewers might think they have watched a case and now think they have some inkling about what takes place in a courtroom, when in fact they have watched entertainment on a stage set that just happens to have some of the trappings of a courtroom.
>
> (Marder 2012: 230)

Lawyer films and courtrooms dramas also tend to offer one perspective or viewpoint, and do so from a location that pays little or no attention to police work, or otherwise sees it as an obstacle (e.g. the botched investigation). By contrast, the long-running television show, *Law & Order*, has a split-format structure, providing the police side of the story in the first half, and the legal side in the second half. The show always begins with a crime scene, where the police find clues, interview witnesses and suspects, and send off physical evidence for forensic analysis. The half-half format relies on confidence in the police having found a plausible suspect; otherwise the second half of the show cannot proceed. However, the prosecutors are always victorious. Nevertheless, the second half allows for more complexity to be introduced where, for instance:

> failure arises from the conflict between moral guilt and legal guilt. In one episode, the cops gathered evidence from the trash contained in a garbage bag left on the curb by a suspect, only to have the prosecutors inform them that since they only had a search warrant for the house, not the sidewalk or the garbage bag, this evidence was legally inadmissible.
>
> (Valverde 2006: 99)

Although the format of *Law & Order* does provide for a more complex appreciation of criminal justice processes than cop films, it still largely omits the vital third segment told from the defense's perspective, which, according to Valverde, is symptomatic of a broader trend towards representations of crime in the US having politically conservative effects. Echoing what Brunsdon (1998: 223) says about British television crime fiction speaking 'very directly to the concerns of a Great Britain in decline under a radical Conservative government with a strong rhetoric of law and order', Valverde (2006: 99) argues it is no coincidence that from the Reagan years to the second Bush administration a 'huge increase in harsh treatments and prison populations' coexisted alongside televisual dramas romanticizing the capture and prosecution of villains but 'almost wholly from the point of view of victims, cops and prosecutors'. Problematic too are the nationalistic references evident in the sprouting of US flag in the 2003 season of *Law & Order*, which was shot in 2002, immediately following the terror attacks of 11 September 2001. To Valverde, this is indicative of the links between *Law & Order* and rising tide of American conservatism. However, it also gives viewers the false impression that murder is a national or federal matter, rather than, as is actually the case, a concern of individual US states:

> But the literal flag-waving has the effect of undermining this longstanding legal doctrine and suggesting to readers that local homicide detectives are paid out of local property taxes labour not for their municipality but for the nation. Prosecutors, while less likely to sport flag lapel pins, rarely mention the criminal code of the State of New York, and are shown as all-purpose, national crime fighters.
> (Valerde 2006: 100)

Accordingly, just as we saw in Chapter 4 how Sparks (1992a: 148–150) argues televised crime drama might reassure audiences rather than instill fear, so representations of crime and justice in *Law & Order*, post-9/11, have acted as a source of reassurance. Indeed, Valverde (2006: 101) argues that, although the normalization of police brutality and violence in the show may be seen to reflect the fact that this is simply part of the job of police work nowadays, the depiction of a black cop beating up suspects for no reason, and with no consequences for either him or the system, 'is perhaps not unrelated to the official US Government's response to the Iraqi war prisoner torture scandals', such as occurred at Abu Ghraib (see Chapter 9). White characters, by contrast, appear completely 'reasonable' when compared to violence-prone racial minorities, even though they have evident flaws of their own, including failed relationships and substance abuse.

Shannon Mader (2009: 127) provides a slightly different take on *Law & Order*, arguing first that although the focus is on prosecutors, which acts as a means of 'legitimizing law and order as an appropriate issue for liberals', defense lawyers are some of the most memorable characters in the show. Secondly, he argues, to define *Law & Order* as a championing of conservative politics is a little too simplistic. Instead, he contends a variety of political (and legal) viewpoints are portrayed resulting in 'a political synthesis of sorts – a melding of the generally conservative politics of the cop show with the more liberal politics of the legal drama' (Mader 2009: 119).

Importantly, Mader points to the evolution of the show as reflecting wider transformations in American society. In the first two seasons, 'New York City frequently plays the role of 1960s America in a microcosm – a city constantly on the edge, with racial and ethnic tensions threatening to boil over at any time' (Mader 2009: 120). Moreover, the character of Ben Stone epitomizes the coolly intellectual prosecutor with an unemotional courtroom manner. By the fifth season, Stone has departed and been replaced by Jack McCoy, who, in contrast, is driven by moral indignation, outrage and emotion, and 'will employ whatever legal theory he has to in order to prosecute offenders' (Mader 2009: 123). For Mader (2009: 122), this shift in the style and tone of the show echoed broader developments:

> With the election of Bill Clinton as president and Rudy Giuliani as mayor of New York City, a new centrist consensus on crime seemed to be emerging that rendered the first two seasons' stark racial and ethnic polarization and boiling-cauldron image of New York City less relevant.

BOX 5.2 LAW'S FICTIVE VOICE

Even though *Law & Order* tends to focus on prosecutors, it still provides a reasonably realistic (and relatively complex) depiction of crime and justice processes as compared to cop films. In this way, the show bolsters Sheila Brown's (2003: 82) argument that, 'fictive texts are reading crime', meaning crime fiction can be used as 'a tool for reading the culture' and history of a society, which is why they are important for criminology. Hence, in relation to detective fiction's ability to provide a critique of state crime, for instance, Brown (2003: 83) says, crime fiction of this kind can often be 'far richer in its range of perspectives and accounts of corporate crime and state crime than is "official" criminology', which, as we saw in Chapter 2, and will pick up again in Chapter 9, 'has traditionally neglected the subject for various reasons'.

Just as crime fiction can act as a means of understanding crime, culture and history, so too can reading law via fictive forms like film. The subtext of Brown's argument – as well as a recurring theme of this book – is that films about lawyers and lawyering frequently involve the elision of fact and fiction, such that in their quest for legal realism they might use actual cases, or parts thereof, as the basis for their dramatizations. This relates to what Sherwin (2004: 101, original emphasis) refers to as the 'culture-shaping role of law', which entails popular legal meanings infiltrating '*upward* into the highest echelons of legal power'. It also involves the spirit of law infiltrating 'through society right down to the lowest ranks' (Sherwin 2004: 103). Consequently, 'official and unofficial legal meanings, sometimes unmixed, other times intermingled, routinely circulate through the mass media of popular culture' (Sherwin 2004: 101).

A well-known example illustrating how we might learn about law through the medium of film is the 1993 movie, *In the Name of the Father*. Based on the autobiography of Gerry Conlon (1990), the film charts the journey of four men falsely convicted of killing four off-duty British soldiers and a civilian in the 'Guildford pub bombings' carried out by the Irish Republican Army (IRA) in 1975. In 1989, the convictions of the 'Guildford Four' were quashed after it emerged there were serious irregularities in original police records, statements and interview notes, and that at trial the prosecution had not disclosed vital alibi evidence to the defense. Hence, the film provides a dramatic and emotive backdrop to a case involving real legal issues: a miscarriage of justice resulting from police corruption, and the Crown's deliberate failure to disclose exculpatory evidence.

Brown (2003: 90–91) argues the 'suitability' of law and justice for dramatic representation operates on a number of levels. First, metaphysically speaking, and as a matter of 'first principles', stories involving 'natural justice' continue to be 'an enduring source of human endeavour'. Secondly, insofar as they embody 'principles on which the legitimacy of authority depends', Western systems of justice are 'de facto legitimate and desirable focuses of public debate'. Thirdly, law simply makes for good viewing, which is a version of what we have already seen at various points in the book, namely that crime stories are newsworthy and have public appeal. In short, Brown (2003: 91) states, 'all films that address issues of legality and justice appeal to a strong and vocal "popular legal imagination" ', and therefore,

> just as 'everyone' has a view on crime (what it is, its causes, and its consequences for victims) so 'everyone' has a view on the law . . . what the law is, what it is for, and what it should be.

Brown (2003: 91–92) draws on Foucault's (1977/1991) ideas to show how the law is both a site of power and a site of resistance, which means, importantly, that 'popular culture is as valid a source for reading law as are formal legal texts'. To illustrate that point, she uses the example of the 1962 film adaptation of Harper Lee's (1960) novel, *To Kill a Mocking Bird*. In this 'story of law', white liberal attorney, Atticus Finch, 'struggles to utilize the discourses of supposedly in the defence of a poor black man accused of raping a "white trash" woman' (Brown 2003: 92). The problem, however, is that Mayella Ewell 'encouraged' him, and although he politely refused her 'attentions', the Southern code required her reputation be vindicated, and the black man be tried. Hence, the story:

> unfolds as an ideological battleground for the structural and cultural tensions of race, gender and class in the American South. . . . The discourse of the law is shown to be precisely that, a text in which all the principal actors refuse to follow the script, for the strictly legal and technical applications of the legal code mean nothing in the face of the entrenched visions of moral and racialized justice embraced in the face of the Southern code. . . . In the end, what counted were the divisions of white-dominated America, a racialized fear and loathing so deep and so institutionalized that any liberal notion of justice must fall before it.
>
> (Brown 2003: 92)

While Valverde (2006: 99) laments the absence of defense attorneys like Atticus Finch in what are mainly politically conservative representations of crime on US television, Brown (2003: 93) believes, '[p]opular cultural forms such as the cinema are both informed by and transformative of discourses of law', which means 'the cinema by definition provides us with powerful readings of outlaws, and thereby of legal critique'. She uses as another example to illustrate that point; the film, *Thelma and Louise*. Often acclaimed as the first feminist road movie, it portrays Thelma and Louise as 'relentlessly executing natural justice against the men who stand in their way and attempt to subordinate them' (Brown 2003: 94). Ultimately, though, the movie highlights 'the sheer impossibility of legal justice from a feminist perspective' (Brown 2003: 94), and ends in a tragic dénouement:

> Knowing that there will be no recourse to justice for them in a male-dominated legal culture, they make a choice at the end of the film. In a burst of exhilarating freedom they join hands and drive their T-bird into the Grand Canyon – better the jaws of death than the arms of the law.
>
> (Brown 2003: 94)

TELEVISION JUDGES

As we have seen, Nancy Marder (2012: 244) argues possibly the greatest cause for concern with reality TV judge shows is that they 'offer a blend of entertainment and judging that could leave viewers confused as to how much is real and how much is fake'. Another associated concern is that even though nearly all have served as actual judges, 'television judges do not act like judges' (Marder 2012: 243). For instance, they lack the essential attributes of fairness and impartiality, with Judge Judy being the worst offender: 'She is rude and insulting to parties and interrupts them constantly. She uses body language, such as rolling her eyes, finger-pointing, and dramatic pauses, to reveal her biases, which most judges try assiduously to avoid' (Marder 2012: 243).

Huws (2015: 150) see this as a function of the neoliberal assumptions underpinning shows like *Judge Judy* and the UK equivalent, *Judge Rinder*, where 'the voice of an intervening authority encourages us as viewers to dissociate from any identification with or empathy for the participants and give rein to our curiosity and disgust'. The voyeurism is justified on the basis that victims are antithetical to the deserving neoliberal worker, that is they are presented as greedy, lazy, self-indulgent and ignorant – because they are voluntary participants they are seen either as showing off or being in it for the money – and are therefore deserving of scorn, ridicule and punishment.

On a more positive note, Marder (2012: 242) suggests daytime television judges perform a 'translator' function by taking the specialized ideas and language of the law, such as 'hearsay' or 'credibility', and explaining them in ways viewers can comprehend. In addition, fictional representations of lawyers and courtroom procedures may perform a similar 'infotainment' function that, ironically, may be more realistic than depictions of judges and judging on reality TV, given they are not so driven by the 'entertainment' imperative. However, the media's drive to newsworthiness through its preference for emotionally charged and visually compelling stories (as outlined in Chapter 1) can just as equally mean law dramas get things wrong by providing inaccurate representations (Sherwin 2004: 102). That can in turn produce content adhering to 'backwards law', which 'states that the media's crime and justice portraits will be the opposite of what is true' (Surette and Gardiner-Bess 2014: 374).

By contrast, *Judge John Deed* might be thought of as an example of 'law in context' or 'law in action' – a realistic version of a courtroom drama incorporating pertinent issues, albeit novel in that it is told from the perspective of a trial judge. Running for five seasons from 2001 to 2007, *Judge John Deed* was created by G. F. Newman, who previously wrote and produced the British series of *Law & Order*. Putting the legal system under the microscope, each of the four episodes of *Law & Order* presents a somewhat jaundiced view of the justice system: 'Nobody does their job honestly. People betray their colleagues and the ethos of their profession, whether they be police, lawyers, or thieves. The police fabricate evidence and invent confessions to secure convictions' (Greenfield et al. 2009: 208).

Perhaps unsurprisingly, given the focus on police misconduct, Newman's *Law & Order* has been credited with helping to bring about major changes in the way police officers conduct interviews, including the requirement interviews be tape-recorded, as provided for in the *Police and Criminal Evidence Act 1984* (UK) (Greenfield et al. 2009: 208). This reinforces a point made by Sherwin (2004: 97), namely that popular culture portrayals, both real and in fiction, may have the effect of changing laws and government policies. In *Judge John Deed*, Newman again addresses the theme of systemic corruption in legal institutions, providing a quite believable blend of realism and dramatization, where 'political critique is enfolded in the life of a sympathetic, charismatic lawyer with an interesting private life and a commitment to his version of justice' (Greenfield et al. 2009: 208).

In doing all this, the show dispels a number of myths (though it reinforces others), including presuppositions about the neutral operation of law: for instance, John Deed dispenses justice as *he* sees it. Newman also refuses to tick the 'political correctness' boxes, presenting 'a male-dominated, white, stridently heterosexual world', which 'is both ironic and a challenge to those dramas that would lead us to believe that major changes have occurred in the distribution of power' (Greenfield et al. 2009: 215); something we will turn to consider later in the chapter when we discuss the show, *Life on Mars*.

Hence, much like those hard-boiled private eyes we looked at earlier, Deed is portrayed as thoroughly masculine, though unlike the hard-boiled type, he is not unemotional. Also like them, he is a maverick, both suspicious and somewhat disrespectful of authority. Unlike them, though, he is far from amoral and unconcerned with discovering the truth or revealing corruption in a dysfunctional system. Rather, he is portrayed as a heroic fighter for justice. However, what is distinctive about Deed is that he is not an outsider, but 'is fighting from a relatively unpromising position within the system' (Greenfield et al. 2009: 210); a status reinforced by his working-class roots, which makes him an outsider of sorts.

Another way the neutral operation of law myth is dispelled is in the characterization of Deed as *judicial activist*. Most significantly, he provides an additional counsel in the courtroom. For example, 'he asks the questions he thinks the barristers should have asked', and he 'twists arms to discourage certain actions and has a much more active role than any trial judge of modern times in the British justice system' (Greenfield et al. 2009: 211). The final way *Judge John Deed* dispels the myth of law's neutrality – in this case via the doctrine of the separation of powers – is in its portrayal of Deed as someone who resists the political interference of those acting on behalf of the state. There is a degree of legal realism in the show here, which recognizes that beneath the courtroom setting there are deeper (and real) forces at work, none of which would be mentioned in the syllabi of conventional laws schools. Thus, Deed's daily legal life is beset by struggles with politicians and other actors who attempt to exert pressure on him and his decision-making. He also recognizes the absurdities that may result when adhering blindly to formal applications of legal procedure. Among those Deed locks heads with are actors and institutions of the British establishment, including the Lord Chancellor's Department, Foreign Office, Home Office and the Prime

Minister's Office. Other forces that are brought to bear on his work include the media, big money and foreign influence.

Especially in the post-9/11 context, Deed's struggles with the British establishment are loaded in the sense state actors regard their actions as being in the national interest, and when 'complex' cases arise they need to be 'dealt with by a "sound" judge who can be counted on to make the right decision' (Greenfield et al. 2009: 212). Accordingly, the Lord Chancellor's Department is contacted immediately by the court's List Manager if Deed does anything unusual or attempts to take a case from another judge lined up to hear it. Deed, then, is prepared to enter the fray, and battles constantly with those who assign cases. And since the idea of the 'national interest' has no formal status or recognition in law, 'he is able to fight for the alternative principle of "Deed's justice" by seeking to retain cases or get them assigned to him' (Greenfield et al. 2009: 212). Deed's approach to the way he believes the law ought to operate is evident in a scene of the episode, 'Defence of the Realm'. In it, Deed is shown lecturing a group of trainee judges to whom he makes clear that it is incumbent on judges to resist state interference in judicial decision-making, pronouncing:

> As the criminal justice system comes under increasing pressure from government, the most contentious issue you will ever have to deal with as judges is separation of powers. The purpose of the criminal law courts is to determine whether a defendant is guilty as charged; politicians should not and must not play any part in that process. And it's up to judges to resist them when they try.

Although the series dispels a number of myths about the neutral operation of law, *Judge John Deed* is also uncompromisingly masculine, heterosexual and even misogynistic. As stated, it presents Deed very much as a product of his background and of his time: a working-class boy done good who, despite being educated in the 1960s, has radical politics that do not incorporate the second wave of feminism. Indeed, not unlike those classic hard-boiled detectives discussed earlier, he has a somewhat cavalier attitude towards his treatment of women, who frequently take a hit so he can continue to fight the system from within. Ultimately, however, women provide only a vent for his class envy and frustration at being unable to change anything at all: 'As a working-class lad made good, he is confronted by a wave of rich, available women on whom he can release his frustration at the unchanging nature of the system of power' (Greenfield et al. 2009: 214).

CRIME SCENE INVESTIGATION AND THE *CSI* EFFECT

As we have seen, a key concern in crime and media research relates to questions about the effect on audiences of media exposure. An area that has attracted a great deal of attention in this respect has been the so-called '*CSI* effect'. As we shall see, like other studies into media effects, research in this area also provides no definitive answers or conclusions as to the existence of the *CSI* effect, nor to its extent and exact nature. What we can say, however, is that like research into crime fear, including cultivation analysis (Chapter 4), audiences are affected by mediated representations of crime, and that the effects of media exposure will depend on an array of factors, like age, gender, class, race, as well as lived experiences, such as whether people have been or have known victims of crime or have come into contact with the criminal justice system in other ways.

Narrowly defined, the *CSI* effect refers to the perception – mainly emanating from the anecdotes and personal impressions of police, prosecutors and judges, but also journalists – that jurors who have watched *CSI* and *CSI*-type shows, are more likely to 'wrongfully' acquit defendants when the prosecution does not present scientific evidence to support its case. A prominent example concerns the acquittal of American real estate heir, Robert Durst, who was accused of murdering and dismembering a neighbor, which one news report attributed to the *CSI* effect, because watching the show apparently 'raised jurors' expectations of what prosecutors should produce at trial' (Willing 2004: 1A). Essentially, the argument is that 'watching *CSI* causes jurors to have unrealistic expectations about the quantity, quality and availability of scientific evidence' (Smith et al. 2011: 4). Put another way, the proposition is that:

> when potential jurors watch crime dramas on television, there are key positive yet unrealistic conclusions that they draw from the information presented in the show regarding the quality, availability, and accessibility of forensic evidence at a crime scene. Specifically, these perceptions involve the belief that forensic evidence is infallible, is found at every crime scene and subsequently tested, and that testing forensic evidence is a quick process.
>
> (Schanz and Salfati 2016: 63)

In an early appraisal, Tyler (2006: 1052) couches it in similar terms, stating that 'the millions of people who watch the series develop unreasonable expectations about the type of evidence typically available at trials, which, in turn, increases the likelihood that they will have "reasonable doubt" about the defendant's guilt'. However, against this narrow view, which, like the notion of a 'pure media effect' (discussed in Chapter 1), posits a direct causal link between viewing shows like *CSI* and juror decision-making, studies have tended to show that although there are 'significant expectations and demands for scientific evidence, there was little or no indication of a link between those inclinations and watching particular television shows' (Shelton et al. 2006: 333).

For example, Podlas's (2007) survey of the beliefs and experiences of assistant district attorneys disproves the existence of any *CSI* effect on the basis the majority of their own prosecutions resulted in convictions not acquittals. Similarly, Cole and Dioso-Villa (2009: 1343) provide 'acquittal rate data that show only equivocal evidence of an increase in acquittals actually following the debut of *CSI* and its spinoffs and imitators'. In their earlier assessment of a survey conducted in 2005 by the Maricopa County Attorney's Office, which claimed *CSI* did influence juries, Cole and Dioso-Villa (2007: 458) found there was insufficient data to support the claim, stating, 'their own respondents reported that they had not perceived any rise in acquittals following the advent of *CSI*'. Indeed, rather than supporting the belief that television crime dramas disadvantage prosecutions, they propose the opposite may be true, namely that 'forensic-themed police procedural dramas may actually advantage the prosecution in criminal cases' (Cole and Dioso-Villa 2009: 1342). Hence, they say, 'jurors may come to trial with the counterfactual preconception that the prosecution is disadvantaged, and some of these jurors may unconsciously compensate for that perceived disadvantage' (Cole and Dioso-Villa 2009: 1342–1343).

While the *CSI* effect may be described as a 'self-fulfilling prophecy', Cole and Dioso-Villa (2009: 1372) argue it might just as easily be referred to as a 'self-denying prophecy' on the part of prosecutors, whereby in 'disseminating through the media the notion that the *CSI* effect is occurring, prosecutors may be preventing the strong prosecutor's effect from occurring'. And if that is in fact what is happening, then a new effect may be created, which advantages rather than disadvantages prosecutors. Hence, Cole and Dioso-Villa (2009: 1371) identify what they say is a second-order media effect on juries in criminal trials, which negates the strong prosecutor's effect and regards the *CSI* effect as essentially an inappropriate prosecution bias:

> We might call this the '*CSI* effect effect': juries that have become convinced through media that there is a strong prosecutor's effect that disadvantages prosecutors and has led antecedent juries to acquit inappropriately might tend to sympathize with the prosecution and enact a seemingly 'corrective' pro-prosecution bias.
>
> (Cole and Dioso-Villa 2009: 1371)

In another study, Podlas (2006) surveyed 306 US college students, concluding there was no *CSI* effect against prosecutors: 'frequent viewers of *CSI* were no more likely to cite the lack of forensic evidence for their not guilty verdicts as compared to infrequent viewers' (Smith et al. 2011: 5). However, Podlas's study has been criticized on the ground it has limited application to real-world situations. First, the small sample size of university students means it has limits on generalizability, and, secondly, there are limits resulting from student jurors being asked to make verdict decisions when considering only one type of hypothetical crime scenario (in this case, a rape) rather than being asked 'to determine the existence or not of the *CSI* effect on a diversity of criminal trial scenarios' (Kim et al. 2009: 454).

In their study, Shelton et al. (2006: 332) attempted to resolve these methodological limitations by producing the first empirical survey of 1,027 prospective jurors 'who had been called for jury duty in a Michigan state court during a nine-week period in June, July and August, 2006'. The survey included information on jurors' demographic characteristics – such as age, race, gender, education and political views – as well as their television-viewing habits to assess whether jurors expect prosecutors to adduce scientific evidence, and to determine whether they would demand scientific evidence as a condition of delivering a guilty verdict. It also examined respondents' potential verdicts across several crime scenarios, finding jurors do indeed expect and even demand that prosecutors utilize the advantages of modern science and technology to meet the burden of proving criminal guilt beyond reasonable doubt. However, watching *CSI* only increases marginally expectations that scientific evidence will be presented in certain types of cases:

> *CSI* watchers were slightly more likely to expect scientific evidence of some kind in cases charging murder or attempted murder, rape or other criminal sexual conduct, breaking and entering, and cases involving a gun. They were also slightly more likely to expect DNA evidence in cases charging physical assault and rape or other criminal sexual conduct. *CSI* watchers were also slightly more likely to expect fingerprint evidence in cases charging breaking and entering, theft, or cases involving a gun. Finally, *CSI* watchers were slightly more likely to expect ballistics evidence in gun cases than those who did not watch *CSI*.
>
> (Shelton et al. 2006: 358)

BOX 5.3 EDUCATIVE EFFECTS OF *CSI*

The idea particularly apparent in the research of Shelton et al. (2006), that *CSI* viewing educates audiences, goes to something we identified earlier in the chapter in respect of the 'translator' function of reality television shows like *Judge Judy*, which, according to Marder (2012), educate audiences in the specialized ideas and language of law. Known as the 'educator's effect' there is indeed a line of argument claiming television crime dramas, such as *CSI*, *Law & Order*, *LA Law*, might increase the quantity and perhaps the quality of applicants to law schools and forensic science degree programs (Cole and Dioso-Villa 2009: 1344, 1346; see also Stinson et al. 2007: 125–126). On the other hand, it has been found that misconceived questioning of crime scene procedures might afford investigative personnel opportunities to educate the public about the realities of police work (Huey 2010). Moreover, Chan (2013) has shown that, although watching forensic-themed television dramas may reinforce misconceptions about criminal investigations, it can equally serve as an educational tool, by providing the public with realistic and factual information.

Conversely, these educative effects could have less positive consequences. Called the 'police chief's effect', one view 'holds that *CSI* has educated criminals on how to avoid detection', examples of which 'include wearing gloves and dousing crime scenes with bleach' (Cole and Dioso-Villa 2009: 1344; see also Stinson et al. 2007: 126). A few respondents in Stinson et al.'s (2007: 127) study, for instance, indicated *CSI* shows were 'educating the bad boys'. If the police chief's effect does exist, it would be particularly significant for criminologists, since, argue Cole and Dioso-Villa (2009: 1345), it 'could mean that *CSI* is both increasing crime and decreasing detection of those crimes'.

While Shelton et al. (2006: 358) say the reasons for the trends they discover are unclear, they conjecture that it may be 'those who watch crime shows on television simply have been better educated about criminal justice investigative procedures than those who do not watch such shows'. Along with gender and political view, education is identified by Shelton et al. (2006: 348) as a key demographic variable significantly related to *CSI* watching, i.e. respondents with less education tended to watch *CSI* more frequently than those with more education. Moreover, confirming the view that watching *CSI* and shows like it performs an educative function (see Box 5.3), they show how in cases involving a gun, for example, 'the *CSI* watchers appear to better understand that tests for fingerprints and ballistics evidence would be a normal part of the police investigation' (Shelton et al. 2006: 358). This type of conclusion is echoed in Schweitzer and Saks's (2007) study, which found *CSI* viewers were more critical of forensic evidence presented at trial, as reflected in the respective likelihood of delivering a guilty verdict: 29 percent of non-*CSI* viewers stated they would convict as compared to 18 percent of *CSI* viewers. Though this difference is by no means statistically significant, Schweitzer and Saks (2007: 357) also found forensic viewers were more confident in their verdicts than non-viewers, 'suggesting that scepticism toward the forensic science testimony was specific to those whose diet consisted of heavy doses of forensic science television programs'.

In a parallel study to Schweitzer and Saks (2007), Maeder and Corbett (2015) examined the conjunction between perceived realism of programs like *CSI* and frequency of viewing. Focusing on DNA evidence, they hypothesized that even among frequent watchers of crime television there may be important differences between those who believe crime dramas are realistic and accurate and those who do not. Their findings in respect of this hypothesis were mixed. On the one hand, they found 'those who perceived crime television as more realistic had more positive attitudes toward DNA evidence and were more influenced by its presentation in the trial' (Maeder and Corbett 2015: 102). On the other hand, they found 'continuous frequency of watching crime television was also directly related to guilt certainty in this case involving DNA evidence presented by the prosecution' (Maeder and Corbett 2015: 102). Their findings here support Schweitzer and Saks' (2007) results about *CSI* viewers being more critical and skeptical of forensic evidence than non-viewers. However, whereas Schweitzer and Saks (2007) found forensic viewers were more confident in their verdicts than non-viewers, Maeder and Corbett's (2015: 102) results reveal 'those who watch more crime television were actually less certain of the defendant's guilt'.

Specifically, Maeder and Corbett (2015: 85) are interested in discovering whether there are significant differences between viewers of crime television shows who think they constitute accurate portrayals of criminal justice processes, and those who watch them simply for their entertainment value, understanding they are not realistic in nature. The results of their study suggest *frequency of consumption* and *perceived realism* should be considered alongside one another when assessing any possible *CSI* effect on jurors:

> A potential juror who watches a great deal of crime television and believes it to be a realistic depiction of the criminal justice system may have a completely

> different set of attitudes toward forensic scientific evidence than one who watches no crime television or watches strictly for entertainment purposes.
> (Maeder and Corbett 2015: 103)

More generally, Shelton et al. (2006) argue findings such as these reflect the fact that, ordinary people, like jurors, are now able to learn more than ever before about science and technology from the media, whether that be from online sources, such as the Internet, 'factual' news stories or fictional crime dramas. Indeed, they state that instead of complaining about the *CSI* effect, and the expectations of jurors, who they try to convince to 'ignore everything they have "learned" about the courts and modern science', prosecutors and other actors in the legal system ought to try to keep pace with wider societal change (Shelton et al. 2006: 366). Given the 'technology and information revolutions are now thoroughly integrated into popular culture', Shelton et al. (2006: 366) say, we must acknowledge 'popular culture in turn is directly reflected in the courts, which is as it should be in a system that puts its faith in the people to decide the outcome of cases'. Accordingly, prosecutors might find ways to convey to jurors that in some cases it has been impossible to obtain scientific evidence, or that such evidence is irrelevant, or even that in certain cases it is not reasonable to demand scientific evidence.

To Shelton et al. (2006), the key problem is that the use of the term '*CSI* effect' is too crude, and the statement of the issue too narrow. Hence, the results of their survey demonstrate no statistical relationship between *CSI* watching and demand for scientific evidence to prove guilt. Moreover, although they found frequent *CSI* watchers had higher expectations for all kinds of evidence – including scientific and non-scientific categories of evidence – than non-*CSI* watchers (Shelton et al. 2006: 353), their survey results provide no evidence that watching crime-related television programs like *CSI* will have an effect on jurors, such that they are more likely to acquit defendants. Indeed, while they do not deny jurors have significant expectations and demands for scientific evidence, they propose 'those predispositions may have more to do with a broader "tech effect" in popular culture rather than any particular "*CSI* effect"' (Shelton et al. 2006: 333). That is to say, 'these increased expectations of and demands for scientific evidence [are] more likely the result of much broader cultural influences related to modern technological advances' (Shelton et al. 2006: 362). Hence, they state, 'if there is a media effect on juror expectations, it is an "indirect" effect and part of a larger transformation occurring in popular and technological culture' (Shelton et al. 2006: 333). In this way, media representations of criminal justice, in particular, in both fiction and non-fiction, have brought about 'a cultural awareness of adversarial justice that transcends or is bigger than any alleged "*CSI* effect"' (Shelton et al. 2006: 333).

Another version of the idea that the *CSI* effect is essentially a cultural phenomenon is presented by Cole and Dioso-Villa (2009: 1343), who remark on the rising status and authority of science in society, and the corresponding decline of law as a truth-producer and institution that is effective in resolving disputes. To Cavender and Deutsch (2007: 68), this accounts for the popularity of *CSI*, which, in accordance with what Sparks (1992a: 148–150) says about the reassurance provided by some televised crime drama, 'offers surety and certainty' at a time when 'the moral authority of policing and science seems to be lacking'. Similarly, Cole and Dioso-Villa (2009: 1373) argue the *CSI* effect embodies anxiety about the threat posed by science to law's legitimacy as a truth-generating institution in society, evident in the fact that 'discourse among legal actors about the supposed *CSI* effect is rife with lamentations of the law's purported inability to provide proof with the strength that jurors supposedly desire'.

While the arguments of Shelton et al. (2006) especially suggest there is a degree of slippage between fiction and non-fiction, which impacts on real-life court settings, some parts of the literature discount any *CSI* effect on the basis of discrepancies that exist between reality and fiction. For instance, Smith et al. (2011: 6) conducted a content analysis of the first seasons of *CSI* and *CSI: Miami*, finding there was a clear difference between actual forensic investigations and popular portrayals whereby, in contrast to real-life investigations, crime scene investigators on the shows 'conducted 72 per cent of the scientific tests', whereas in 'actual investigations, specialized laboratory technicians conduct the majority of tests'. To Kim et al. (2009: 459), this has real implications for law enforcement agencies and prosecutors who cannot reasonably 'collect the type of scientific evidence or perform the types of forensic examinations depicted in some crime show dramas, either because the technology does not exist or because it is only available to national defence agencies'. While this means police officers and prosecutors may in these cases have to rely on eyewitnesses or circumstantial evidence, from the defense perspective, this has inherent dangers, which have been well documented when, for example, eyewitness testimony has resulted in wrongful conviction.

To that end, Smith et al. (2011: 4–5) show how not only has the *CSI* effect been subject to judicial consideration in actual courts cases, but also how it has been incorporated into trial strategies of both prosecutors and defense attorneys (see also Stinson et al. 2007: 125). From this perspective, it is recognized there is a *CSI* effect on the legal community as well as on juror behavior. According to Cole and Dioso-Villa (2007: 447, 2009: 1343), the 'strong prosecutor's effect' is the canonical effect, which claims television viewing alters juror behavior, such that, '[w]hen the scientific evidence presented at trial fails to meet jurors' television-enhanced expectations, they are more likely to acquit the defendant' (Smith et al. 2011: 4). Podlas (2006: 453) calls this the 'anti-prosecution "*CSI*-effect"', because unreasonable juror expectations, formed by watching shows like *CSI*, make it harder for prosecutors to secure convictions. Assuming juries are over-acquitting, some prosecutors adopt remedial measures in response to *CSI* and similar shows. Cole and Dioso-Villa (2007: 448, 2009: 1343–1344) call this the 'weak prosecutor's effect', which alters prosecutor, not juror, behavior. Measures adopted by prosecutors include, 'questioning jurors about the show during voir dire, explaining the absence of forensic evidence in opening and closing arguments, and calling on experts to explain why evidence was not found or why results may have been found inconclusive' (Cole and Dioso-Villa 2007: 448).

An opposite effect is proffered by defense attorneys, which Cole and Dioso-Villa (2009: 1344) call the 'defendant's effect', positing '*CSI* and similar television programming, through their positive and heroic portrayals of state-employed forensic scientists, enhance the perceived credibility of the government's forensic witnesses, thus advantaging the prosecution'. In other words, the 'favourable portrayal of forensic scientists in the media increases their credibility, making their testimony highly compelling and influential in verdicts' (Smith et al. 2011: 4). To Cole and Dioso-Villa (2009: 1348), the defendant's effect would seem the most intuitive, while the prosecutor's effect appears counter-intuitive. That is because scientists are generally esteemed by the general public, so positive portrayals of them should advantage the prosecution: 'the popularity of television programs that portray scientists as hardworking, virtuous, honest, truthful, heroic, skilled, and attractive should benefit those litigants who employ forensic scientists as expert witnesses' (Cole and Dioso-Villa 2009: 1348).

A final effect has been documented by Stinson et al. (2007), who conducted the first study to measure the opinions of police officers regarding the existence of the *CSI* effect. They discovered the public's skewed and distorted perceptions of police and forensic investigations can, in fact, have positive effects, allowing police investigators to justify collecting more evidence at a crime scene, as well as increasing their accountability in court by having them spend time explaining issues like the technical aspects of investigations. Alternatively, Wise (2010) has shown how, in the Australian state of New South Wales, criminal justice practitioners have changed their practices to accommodate the *CSI* effect, and how those changes might impact negatively on both victims and offenders. For example, increasing prosecutor requests for additional DNA testing can put pressure on already stretched forensic laboratories, leading to backlogs, which can postpone court proceedings, as well as increase the likelihood of laboratory errors, all of which could affect adversely accused persons and victims. For the accused, delays could mean they are unfairly detained in custody while awaiting trial; for victims (e.g. of sexual assault), delays could mean prolonging closure on traumatic experiences.

BOX 5.4 PSYCHOLOGY OF THE *CSI* EFFECT

Writing from a psychological perspective, Tyler (2006) has interrogated the fundamental premise of the *CSI* effect – increased leniency – asking why it might be that jurors impose higher standards of proof and acquit more frequently. First, if jurors are more lenient, it may be due to *sympathy for the defendant*. For example, 'there is considerable evidence juries are increasingly willing to accept a variety of excusing conditions, from post-traumatic stress disorder to battered wife syndrome' (Tyler 2006: 1077). Secondly, there is the issue of *differing thresholds for conviction*. Hence, the *CSI* effect is a fiction created by prosecutors who have an unreasonably inflated belief in the strength of their cases. Jurors might not share this and have a more realistic assessment as well as having some degree of empathy or sympathy for the defendant.

Thirdly, increasing jury acquittals might be explained by *declining trust and confidence in legal authorities*. In other words, 'juries are less likely to convict because they increasingly lack trust in the legal authorities who are responsible for investigating and prosecuting cases' (Tyler 2006: 1081). Tyler suggests legal authorities might re-establish credibility by drawing on the reliability associated with scientific evidence. In this way, his argument is reminiscent of Cole and Dioso-Villa's (2009) point about the threat posed to law by science, and, like them, Tyler proposes science might save law's declining authority in accordance with the 'defendant's effect':

> From this perspective, the *CSI* effect is two sided. *CSI* may raise the standards of assessing guilt, but the use of scientific evidence may also increase the credibility of the state. At least, the scientific community seems to have higher credibility than does the state, suggesting that the association of the prosecution with science ought to increase trust and confidence in the state. As noted above, the investigators in *CSI* always get the perpetrator, conveying an image of competence that may influence juror views of authority. Hence, *CSI* may counter increasing distrust and scepticism regarding the law and legal actors.
>
> (Tyler 2006: 1081–1082)

Tyler also uses these kinds of argument to show how *CSI* might produce the opposite tendency to leniency, in that *CSI* viewing potentially lowers the standards used by jurors, making conviction more likely, not less likely. He argues jurors motivated by a desire to resolve tensions about an uncorrected injustice might do so by seeking to convict. However, they need to find plausible and legitimate reasons for conviction, and 'the general credibility of scientific evidence is one such legitimating tool', although jurors might find legitimacy in other kinds of evidence, such as those that 'enhance the perceived credibility of eyewitness testimony as a way of justifying a conviction' (Tyler 2006: 1063).

Another possible *CSI* effect that might lead to more not fewer convictions is that *CSI* watching *promotes the need for closure*. Indeed, Tyler (2006: 1068) says, 'if people are motivated by watching *CSI* to hold higher standards of reasonable doubt, this outcome would fly in the face of the typically strong desire to see wrongdoers punished'. While truth is never certain, Tyler (2006: 1065) proposes *CSI* is popular because it simplifies the messiness of crimes committed in the real world, as well as providing viewers with the reassurance assailants will get their just deserts. There is also an emotional need to achieve justice for the victim. And if viewers respond by raising the bar and acquitting wrongdoers, then there is no closure, no sense that justice has been done.

Another reason why there might be a tendency to convict rather than acquit is that jurors might have an *overbelief in the probative value of evidence*, which occurs 'when people are more highly motivated to resolve a crime and provide justice for the victim' (Tyler 2006: 1070). The general message of *CSI* is one of scientific credibility: scientific methods and evidence are legitimate and reliable. Moreover, *CSI* 'encourages a myth of forensic and scientific infallibility [and] aura of certainty' (Tyler 2006: 1072). The quality of the evidence is not at issue, because even where errors exist, jurors can make adjustments that fit with their desire to convict and thereby achieve justice for the victim.

A final explanation for more convictions than acquittals is that *CSI* viewing *creates a one-sided view of the law*, which 'potentially assists prosecutors by showing only the investigation and leaving the impression that the trial is a mere formality' (Tyler 2006: 1073). By focusing almost exclusively on the investigation, *CSI* leads its viewers to believe that finding the perpetrator is the only thing that matters, even though it is one step in a long process:

> By focusing on investigations, rather than trials, *CSI* understates the importance of both defenses and justifications, reinforcing the focus on the victim rather than the defendant. If the focus were on the trial, we might hear about the defendant's lousy childhood, her temporary insanity, or her sincere remorse. In a real courtroom, these factors force us to address what is just for the defendant. The focus on investigation, however, draws attention to the victim of the crime.
>
> (Tyler 2006: 1076)

By contrast, as we have seen, the split format of *Law & Order* enables it to show both investigations *and* trials, including the dramatization of potential defenses, even though according to some (Valverde 2006: 99), but not everyone (Mader 2009: 127), that aspect of criminal proceedings is often omitted. Moreover, evidence is not presented in such a definitive manner to the extent it is in *CSI*. Accordingly, Tyler argues that while it too contains inaccuracies as to the workings of the criminal justice system, *Law & Order* nevertheless provides a more realistic representation than *CSI* on two counts: (i) it stresses uncertainty about the truth; and (ii) it portrays the criminal trial as a search for truth, and the courtroom as an arena in which justice for both victim and defendant are at issue. As that 'often brings a criminal's state of mind into play. . . . *Law & Order* questions whether the person is factually guilty as well as what legal responsibility she bears' and, accordingly, 'suggests that audiences can grapple with criminal justice issues in a more complete way' (Tyler 2006: 1076).

LIFE ON MARS – A CONTEMPORARY COP SHOW?

Having focused in some depth on shows about court proceedings and forensic-themed television, in this section we return to examine cop shows, focusing on Garland and Bilby's (2011) treatment of British television series, *Life on Mars*, which first aired on the BBC in January 2006. At first glance, it appears to be a 'retro' police procedural set in 1973, which follows officers DCI Gene Hunt, DI Sam Tyler and their colleagues DS Ray Carling, DC Chris Skelton and WPCs Annie Cartwright and Phyllis Dobbs as they set about solving crimes (see Figure 5.2). However, it becomes apparent quite quickly that the series is

Figure 5.2 Cast of British television series *Life on Mars* (L–R): DS Ray Carling, DC Chris Skelton, WPC Annie Cartwright, DCI Gene Hunt and DI Sam Tyler

more than a simple cop show when, in the first episode, DCI Tyler is shown being hit by a car in present-day Manchester and is transported to 1973 (being demoted to DI in the process). Given this twist, the show thus becomes a blend of police procedural and science-fiction, psychological thriller and light dramatic comedy. Echoing a key theme of the book regarding the blurring of non-fiction and fictional depictions of criminal justice processes, the essential premise of Garland and Bilby's analysis is that:

> Police dramas, just like portrayals of other institutions, reflect current dominant cultural paradigms of how we conceptualize the criminal justice system and the law and order debate, as well as representing establishment beliefs about society's norms. . . . Audiences both make sense of the criminal justice system through watching fictionalized accounts of the police and other agencies and have their expectations shaped by the images which are broadcast.
>
> (Garland and Bilby 2011: 116)

Part of the appeal of *Life on Mars*, argue Garland and Bilby, is that it relies on nostalgia (and some amnesia) about policing in a bygone era. The character of Gene Hunt compares to *The Sweeney's* Jack Regan (Figure 5.3). Like Regan,

Figure 5.3 Dennis Waterman (L) as DS George Carter and John Thaw (R) as DI Jack Regan in *The Sweeney*

Hunt is tough on crime and criminals, and is unconcerned with social issues that may have contributed to the commission of a crime. He sees his role as cleaning the streets of villains, and keeping the ungovernable and chaotic society of 1970s Britain in order; rarely is he unsure of his actions, and he does not question his policing method, which is uncomplicated in a world that is becoming more complex. In terms of professional methods, Hunt also fights bureaucratic police systems, as well as the informal rules and fraternal bonds of his superiors and the establishment, and asserts a more intuitive approach to policing.

Similarly, Brunsdon (1998: 223, 226) shows how, in staging the trauma associated with the dismantling of the post-war settlement, *Inspector Morse* is nostalgic for a pre-Thatcherite age. That is evident in the 'heritage' programming of the show (e.g. narratively unnecessary shots of Oxford colleges, spires and green), as well as Morse's grumpiness, which betrays 'his sense of being out of sorts with the times' (Brunsdon 1998: 230). Like other fictional police officers we have looked at in this chapter, including Gene Hunt, Morse is skeptical about the apparatuses of the criminal justice system and is guided by his own moral sense, integrity and intuition. Having no recourse to the law and order rhetoric and 'prison works' philosophy of Thatcherism, his world is 'instead a melancholy place in which often the death of the offender by their own hand is the best solution' (Brunsdon

1998: 230). However, unlike Gene Hunt's world, the police culture of *Inspector Morse* is one that has been shaken by corruption and scandals over miscarriages of justice, as well as allegations of brutish drunkenness, sexism and misogyny. Therefore, although less evident in Colin Dexter's novels than in the television series, *Inspector Morse* demonstrates the impact of equal opportunities discourse with, for instance, 'Morse's predatory attitudes towards women replaced with a romantic yearning' (Brunsdon 1998: 228).

Like *Inspector Morse*, *Life on Mars* is more than simply a nostalgic show about a less complicated time when senior police and minority groups were put in their place. Rather, it presents a pastiche of policing corruption and change over the past 30 years. Accordingly, it requires the audience to have a sophisticated appreciation about when humor is being used, as well as to differentiate the fine line between reality and fiction when representing police images. Indeed, humor is a very real aspect of police occupational culture, which 'consolidates teamwork, relieves pressure from anxious situations and exaggerates the excitement of the routines activities of everyday policing' (Garland and Bilby 2011: 119).

While the character of Ray Carling is a vehicle for expressing a humorless social commentary of British society and policing in the 1970s, Hunt's unacceptable one-liners are meant to be interpreted by audiences as pastiche; funny for the social embarrassment they might cause in the twenty-first century, but socially acceptable in the 1970s. As Garland and Bilby (2011: 119) put it, '[w]ith jokes, we cannot react negatively to things which we find socially unacceptable'. Hunt is therefore a caricature whose unacceptable jokes and jibes should be taken lightly. Moreover, the audience's positive sentimental nostalgia for the 1970s is evident in the support we are asked to show for the hero and maverick, Gene Hunt, 'who is the embodiment of illiberal, populist anti-intellectualism, in the fight against crime and disorder', in contrast to 'the liberal, managerial elitism offered by Sam [Tyler]' (Garland and Bilby 2011: 120).

The sympathetic portrayal of Gene Hunt has parallels with the appeal of Judge John Deed, who, as we saw earlier, is a working-class lad done good, operating within the system, but often against the establishment, who ultimately seeks to deliver justice as he sees fit. Similarly, Hunt appeals because he

> puts away baddies, does not mind bending the rules as long as it is for the right cause, does not break the ethical code of being a police officer, and is ultimately a working-class hero who represents the anti-establishment challenges of bureaucracy, form-filling and managerialism.
>
> (Garland and Bilby 2011: 120)

Hunt's willingness to turn a blind eye to 'noble cause corruption' also contrasts with Sam Tyler's view that policing should be done 'by the book', which, in part, reflects the culture of policing in the years following police involvement in the wrongful convictions and miscarriages of justice in high-profile cases, like those of the Guildford Four and Birmingham Six (Garland and Bilby 2011: 127). As we saw earlier, police misconduct in those cases led to reforms contained in the *Police and Criminal Evidence Act 1984* (UK), such as the requirement police interviews be recorded to protect the rights of suspects in custody. In many ways, then, 'Tyler is the personification of our anxiety about modern society – about our safety and security, our attitudes towards people who share the streets and our concerns about how efficiently we deal with "others"' (Garland and Bilby 2011: 121). By contrast, 'Gene Hunt shows us that the lines between good and bad are blurred, and sometimes morally and ethically ambiguous, but we must also understand that it is acceptable to laugh at sophisticated social niceties, especially when they are portrayed through the mediated lens of the police procedural' (Garland and Bilby 2011: 121).

Sam Tyler's liberal, bureaucratic, managerialist approach to police work is used as a device so viewers can connect their own attitudes and anxieties about interpersonal relations and identity politics in contemporary society. In many episodes of *Life on Mars*, Tyler's progressive and liberal policing philosophies reinforce his estrangement from his 1970s colleagues whose occupational culture is male-dominated, sexist and characterized by 'horseplay' and heavy drinking. Sam's alienation is perhaps most pronounced in respect of the portrayal of police racism in the series. He is transported back in time to an era before two watershed moments in the troubled history of relations between police and minority ethnic communities. First, the Scarman Report into the 1981 Brixton riots, which identified racism among London's junior police officers, and, secondly, the Macpherson Report, following the botched police investigation into the murder of black teenager, Stephen Lawrence, in 1993, which described the Metropolitan Police Service as 'institutionally racist' (Garland and Bilby 2011: 122).

Both of these reports recommended a number of measures be taken to encourage people from ethnic minorities to join the police force, as well as suggesting steps to challenge police racism within the force. Given Tyler travels back in time to a period before publication of the reports by Scarman and Macpherson, it is unsurprising he clashes frequently with his 1970s colleagues over their racist attitudes. One example is when Ray describes a 'Paki' running from a crime scene, which, to Sam's astonishment, Hunt does not conceive as a racially motivated attack or 'hate crime' (Garland and Bilby 2011: 122–133). And while humor is used to make the attitudes of 1970s officers more palatable for a contemporary audience, according to Garland and Bilby (2011: 123), the differences between police cultures of the 1970s and the current day should not be overstated, since '[t]he present still has some of the cruder, more unpleasant aspects of the cultures and behaviours of 30 years ago while the past was not entirely characterized by brutality, racism and corruption'.

In contrast to the portrayal of racism as rather subtle in *Life on Mars*, the coverage of homophobia as a part of cop culture is more explicit. With the exception of Sam, the use of homophobic language is commonplace among all of the main male characters. An example of typical attitudes towards gay people is contained in the following exchange between Hunt and Tyler about the sexual orientation of a gangland boss:

GH:	[The club owner is] a bum bandit. . . . A poof. A fairy. A queer. A queen. Fudge packer. Uphill gardener. Fruit-picking sodomite.
ST [astonished]:	He's gay?
GH:	As a bloody Christmas tree.

(Garland and Bilby 2011: 125)

The homophobic banter reflects the values of 1970s police officers, while the policing methods espoused by Sam (e.g. preservation of crime scenes, fingertip searches or use of forensic techniques) are regarded effeminate. This contrasts with the hard-boiled characterization of Gene Hunt, and his view of the inherently macho nature of police culture, and the 'action' side of policing, which typically involves employing techniques of 'brawn' over 'brain'. On the other hand, Tyler's anti-racist attitudes and general 'political correctness' contrast with the 1970s police workplace culture, where attitudes and behavior now considered unacceptable went unchallenged, with ethnic minority officers, women and gay officers being marginalized and often extremely vulnerable. An example of these prejudicial attitudes is provided by Ray Carling's reaction when a black junior officer appears in the offices. In an open display of hostility, Ray, who reacted badly to the recent appointment of a woman (Annie) to the team, refuses to shake the officer's hand, and goes on to say: 'First women, then a coloured. What's coming next, dwarves? . . . You here to do the spadework then? Only it can get a bit cold round here. It's not like being back home' (Garland and Bilby 2011: 124).

Hunt sees his physical and aggressive approach to policing as more manly that Sam's 'touchy feely' approach, which is why he could not consider the prospect that, after being caught in a bomb blast, Ray might be suffering from what has become known as 'post-traumatic stress disorder'. Instead, Hunt reinforces the manly nature of carrying out proper police work when he says: 'The man's a bloody hero and you're accusing him of having the clap. . . . He's a police officer, not a fairy' (Garland and Bilby 2011: 125). This type of horseplay and banter, practiced by male officers, reflects a broader sexist culture typified by archaic attitudes towards women, including depictions of sexual harassment as a routine part of daily working life for female characters like Annie.

In conclusion, Garland and Bilby propose *Life on Mars* represents a challenge to post-Macpherson, New Labour policing in Britain, which is embodied in the figure of Sam Tyler who is cast as a humorless, left-liberal bureaucrat, obsessed with formal rules and committed to the kind of new managerialism that impedes 'proper' police work, as personified by Hunt's character. Tyler is also used as 'the tool through which we can play out our own anxieties about what we should believe in and how we should behave in a post-industrial and post-modern society' (Garland and Bilby 2011: 129). By contrast, Gene Hunt is clearly depicted as a hero, 'whose working-class voice has been lost in the liberal chattering of new policing methods in post-Blair British society' (Garland and Bilby 2011: 130). He is the force capable of dealing with the chaos of 1970s Britain and, if he can deal with the scum of the 1970s, we can all rest assured he will be able to assuage our twenty-first-century anxieties associated with anti-social behavior, crime and disorder.

REVERSING COP-CRIMINAL STEREOTYPES IN *THE WIRE*

The final example we will look at is another cop show of sorts, although creator of HBO's *The Wire*, David Simon, has described it as 'the greatest ever cop show that isn't actually a cop show' (quoted in Wilde 2009: 5). That is because, like *Life on Mars*, it is not a regular police procedural simply portraying good heroic cops apprehending bad villains. Rather, it is 'a subversion of the network cop show', which 'depicts police bureaucracy as "amoral" and "dysfunctional" and criminality [in the form of the drug culture] as bureaucratic' (Ramshaw 2012: 361). Indeed, as Penfold-Mounce et al. (2011: 156) observe, criminals in *The Wire* sometimes possess more morality than the actors in authority, which, as we shall see in Chapter 9, is also an argument that has been applied to the values of honor, loyalty and commitment, and the moral code of Mafia gangsters.

Insofar as it challenges, and even reverses, stereotypical perceptions of criminals, some of the themes addressed in *The Wire* are reminiscent of those raised in the early ethnographic works of the Chicago School of Sociology (see Chapter 2). Indeed, in some quarters the show has been heralded as the best ethnography of contemporary American society (Penfold-Mounce et al. 2011: 156). Also like the early Chicagoan researchers, who drew on journalistic techniques, Penfold-Mounce et al. (2011: 156) describe it as a form of social science-fiction, because it 'takes materials from good journalism and the social sciences and presents it in a compelling fictional form'. By doing so, *The Wire*, like the work of the Chicago School, confounds images of life on Baltimore's streets as socially disorganized. Instead, what emerges is a view of street life as highly organized and structured. Nowhere is that more apparent than in a now classic scene in season 1, episode 3, in which D'Angelo, a medium-level drug dealer articulates drug organizational structures using chess pieces as metaphors for the drug hierarchy:

> Beginning with the central piece the King, D'Angelo describes it as 'the King Pin' who can move in any direction he wants (but only one square at time) and the other pieces have to 'hustle' and watch his back. Capture the King you win the game, just as Avon Barksdale, the head of the drug ring and D'Angelo's uncle, is 'King' in West Baltimore. A second crucial piece is used to embody Barksdale's right-hand man, Stringer Bell, as the Queen or rather the 'go get shit done piece' and 'ain't no bitch, she got all the moves'. Meanwhile the Castle or Rook is the drug 'stash', which is regularly moved and protected by the 'muscle' of other pieces. The most expendable pieces are pawns. These are the soldiers, the front line who don't get to become king as

> 'The King stay the King'. In 'the game' (life in the drug scene in Baltimore) they get 'capped quick' (D'Angelo) and leave the game early 'unless they some smartass pawns' (Bodie).
>
> (Penfold-Mounce 2011: 158)

The similarities with *Life of Mars* also extend to similarities between Gene Hunt's character and, in *The Wire*, Detective Jimmy McNulty, who is also a stereotypically hard-drinking, working-class, rakish hero. Like Hunt, McNulty has a certain hard-boiled quality too: a maverick cop with a disastrous personal life, who always promises – though almost never delivers – to reform the 'right' woman (Ramshaw 2012: 367). According to Ramshaw, the introduction of McNulty in season 1 as a clichéd authority-bucking, maverick Irish-American cop is done purposely, so as to orient viewers, providing them with a recognizable and familiar cop show character. By season 4 McNulty appears less – no longer needed to hold the viewer's hand.

Simon's intent in creating *The Wire* was 'to tell a good story that matters to myself and the other writers – to tell the best story we can about what it feels like to live in an American city' (Walker 2004). In a move similar to attempts to deglamorize the study of crime from a cultural criminological perspective (Webber 2007), the storytelling focus of *The Wire* aims to present an authentic account of inner city life, which 'deglamourizes crime fighting by emphasizing the banal administrative duties involved and the sheer overwhelming hopelessness of the battle against crimes rooted in flawed social institutions' (Penfold-Mounce et al. 2011: 154). Indeed, part of the reason 'authenticity bleeds through the screen' is because of 'the deliberate blurring of fact and fiction that the creators have inscribed into the casting and the characters of the series' (Marshall and Potter 2009: 10). Hence, the show has employed largely unknown as well as non-professional actors and Baltimore residents, including prominent political and law enforcement figures (Penfold-Mounce et al. 2011: 159–160).

On the other hand, storytelling also allows the audience to relate emotionally to the show and its characters in ways that *are* comparable to cultural criminology, although, in this respect, Penfold-Mounce et al. (2011: 162) propose *The Wire* can be thought of as an example of 'lyrical sociology', which 'looks at a social situation, feels its overpowering excitement and its deeply affecting human complexity, and then writes . . . trying to awaken those feelings in the minds – and even the hearts – of . . . readers' (Abbott 2007: 70). This focus on emotion and affect indicates *The Wire* fits the remit of cultural criminology. More specifically, considering it 'a kind of visual novel that presents an ideal type of American social decay' (Penfold-Mounce 2011: 157), we might think it an example of the intersection between visual and narrative criminology (discussed in Chapter 2).

Indeed, Stephen Wakeman (2014: 230) argues that in its the depiction of 'Hamsterdam' – a experimental urban space introduced by Mayor Colvin in which the sale of heroin and crack cocaine is permitted in 'free-zones' ignored by Baltimore police – *The Wire* should be considered a 'cultural text', or 'cultural reference point from within which an alternative future direction of drug policy becomes discernible'. Following in the footsteps of Philippe Bourgois (2003: 321), who suggests decriminalizing drugs to destroy the profitability of narcotic trafficking, Wakeman shows how the Hamsterdam experiment succeeds, as violent crime and anti-social behavior associated with the drug trade is drastically reduced. Ultimately, however, the scheme is abandoned, after the Chief of Police discovers Hamsterdam. To Wakeman (2014: 231), that signals the strong adherence to neoliberal doctrines of individual responsibility and risk management in societies like the US (and UK), which, in contrast to more tolerant attitudes towards drug control in many European countries (e.g. Holland, Portugal, Sweden), manifests in aggressively prohibitive drug policies. This then explains why, when faced with an alternative system, in which marginalized and excluded populations are able to play a significant role in improving their own governance, neoliberal politicians revert to 'a failed and harmful system of regulatory governance (the prohibition of drugs)' (Wakeman 2014: 235), relying on 'tougher law and order policies, more people in prison, for longer, under harsher conditions' (Wakeman 2014: 229).

The focus on authenticity in *The Wire* represents a new take on reality TV that differentiates it from reality shows like *COPS*, which, as we saw earlier, is one-dimensional, formulaic and partially staged. Hence, Penfold-Mounce et al. (2011: 159) say *The Wire* can be thought of as 'authentic television' rather than reality TV. To Ramshaw (2012: 366), part of the authenticity and realism of the show derives from the improvisational quality of the dialogue. However, against this purported realism, critics, including viewers, have seen some of McNulty's behavior, for example, as too far-fetched, including his creation of a fictional serial killer to obtain more funding for police investigations, 'faking evidence, messing with crime scenes and lying to fellow police officers and medical examiners' (Ramshaw 2012: 374). According to Ramshaw (2012: 372, 374), this goes beyond the 'improvised legality' we have come to associate with maverick yet heroic cops to become 'blatant and scripted illegality'. It thus depicts police officers as corrupt rather than upholders of the law – betraying the 'horror of police' in providing an example of 'the contradictory figure that breaks the law to uphold the law' (Linnemann 2017). Omar Little is a similarly schizoid character: an '"honourable thief", the man who holds up drug dealers with a shotgun, yet takes his aunt to church every Sunday morning' (Wakeman 2014: 232).

A key argument of Penfold-Mounce et al. (2011: 155, original emphasis) is that *The Wire* constitutes a prime exemplar of C. Wright Mills's (1959) the 'sociological imagination', in that it strives to connect 'private troubles' to 'public issues' – it is, in other terms, 'the sociological imagination *as* popular culture'. As with the chess scene described above, the character of Felicia 'Snoop' Pearson highlights Mills's idea that individual biographies intersect with social circumstances. Indeed, true to the authentic realism of *The Wire*, Pearson plays a character with her own name, whose fictionalized representation has echoes with her real-life experiences of working as a child drug dealer, and eight years imprisonment for killing someone in self-defense. According to Marshall and Potter (2009: 11), this 'doubled awareness of actor and character serves to reinforce the emotional impact of the character as she moves through the violence that surrounds her'.

In accordance with Mills's arguments, Pearson also embodies a range of sociological issues. First, and much like classic depictions of Mafia and other forms of organized crime (Chapter 9), Pearson's character illuminates the social bonds and sense of belonging that are often believed to exist within drug gangs. Secondly, there is the issue of gender: she is the only female 'soldier' in the show, participating in a male-dominated world and responding to a masculine organizational hierarchy. Lastly, the character of Pearson provides insights into labor processes, alienation and the broader anomic conditions of contemporary society, such as the precariousness of drug dealing, which has analogies with other forms of newly precarious work.

Indeed, it has been argued that, to the extent *The Wire* is a drama about the nature of work, it has parallels with the neoliberalization of universities and research practices in contemporary higher education (M. Wood 2014). Especially pertinent to what Ramshaw (2012) says about the character of McNulty (i.e. an authority-bucking, maverick cop), university researchers increasingly face numerous threats (e.g. funding tied to external partners) to their independence, autonomy and professional judgment. In a similar extension of themes addressed by *The Wire*, part of the next chapter resonates with the portrayal of 'Snoop' Pearson, as it focuses on media representations of female criminality, which often portray women criminals as 'bad girls' who are 'doubly deviant', having transgressed not only criminal law but especially in the case of female killers the laws of nature and gender stereotypes.

CONCLUSION

The way *The Wire* and some representations of gangsters in movies like *Goodfellas* and the TV series *The Sopranos* portray 'self-conflicted gangsters' (Katz 2016: 236), against stereotypical depictions (which we will consider in Chapter 9), has a certain Shakespearean quality. This parallel has not gone unnoticed, with Wilson (2014) juxtaposing the Holmesian account of crime and justice that is relatively simplistic and scientifically driven, with the Shakespearean model, which is skeptical and more complex. In the Shakespearean version, 'crime is particular and situational, evidence is not statistical but anecdotal, and analysis is not quantitative but qualitative' (Wilson 2014: 99). To recall what we discussed in Chapter 2, Wilson's (2014: 108) account here chimes with cultural criminology's antagonism to quantitative forms of 'administrative criminology', as well as complementing *narrative criminology*, in that, he shows how Shakespeare allows his criminals to speak for themselves about their thoughts, feelings and actions.

The key, here, lies in William Shakespeare not reifying criminals, as well as not seeing the law as always good, and criminal acts as being committed always by bad men and women guilty of bad decision-making. In contrast to the world of Sherlock Holmes, where the term 'criminal' refers to an identity rather than an act, Shakespearean tragedies recognize the messiness of the social world. Accordingly any character, whether a cop or a criminal, a victim or a villain, is capable of good and bad actions. That is because 'these identities are not essential elements of our existence but roles that we play depending on the circumstances of the situations in which we find ourselves' (Wilson 2014: 104). In this sense, Shakespeare's humanism provides a valuable counterbalance to the 'leaky scientism' of some criminology, recognizing 'there is a criminal justice system, but it is humans who run the system, and since humans are prone to error and inadequacy, the system will never run perfectly, which means that justice is an ideal that, as a rule, cannot be attained' (Wilson 2014: 106; see also Ferrell 2015: 307).

Hence, Wilson (2014: 104–108) argues we should not so readily dismiss Shakespeare's works of fiction as mere drama, especially when we know 'real' issues of crime and justice are frequently dramatized in news and entertainment media (see also Katz 2016: 235; Presser 2016: 139). We must therefore embrace the blurring of fact and fiction, acknowledging also a role for *dramaturgical criminology*, which, influenced by Goffman (1959), takes seriously 'the scene of the crime', as well as the theatricality of crime and justice (Wilson 2014: 104). Of course, as we saw in Chapter 2, those concerns are central to cultural criminology, but they have also occupied other critical criminologists interested in some of the ways things like the theatrical architecture and spatial layout of a courtroom (e.g. judge elevated above the court; accused raised up in the dock and surrounded by rails, symbolizing captive state and thus guilt) might skew the administration of justice unfairly against defendants (Carlen 1976).

As we have seen in this chapter, and at other points in the book, mediated representations of crime, whether factual or fictional, or a blend of the two, can have real effects on audiences. In the case of a great many dramatized depictions, some of which we have looked at here, that can be because they possess a degree of realism, and are not so far-fetched as to be pure fantasy. We have seen, for example, how the perceived demise of a social democratic ideal in Scandinavian countries is reflected in the narrative style and structure of Nordic noir. In the next chapter, however, we will consider the proposition that, in real-life crime, that ideal seems to be alive and well, when we look at David Green's (2008a) comparative analysis of the child-on-child killing cases of Jamie Bulgar in England and Silje Redergård in Norway. As will be recalled from Chapters 1 and 2, while the Bulger killers were treated as criminals, the Redergård killers were regarded innocent victims of a tragic accident. Among other things, Green shows how the treatment of the child killers in each country can be considered an outcome of differing political cultures, whereby, in England, the highly adversarial majoritarian political culture is more likely to politicize criminal events, such as the Bulger killing, while Norway's consensus model gave rise to a kinder and gentler child welfare approach to Silje Redergård's killers.

SUGGESTED FURTHER READING

Initially engaging with the media effects model, the following article then traces a three-stage periodization of representations of crime and law enforcement in British cinema from 1945 to 1991:

Allen, J., Livingstone, S. and Reiner, R. (1998) 'True lies: Changing images of crime in British postwar cinema' *European Journal of Communication* 13(1): 53–75.

The following book is a little dated though remains useful for its analyses of televised crime drama, as well as its coverage of perspectives on the media's role in cultivating crime fear, which we considered in Chapter 4:

Sparks, R. (1992a) *Television and the Drama of Crime: Moral Tales and the Place of Crime in Public Life*. Buckingham: Open University Press.

On Nordic noir see:

Bergmann, K. (2014) *Swedish Crime Fiction: The Making of Nordic Noir*. London: Mimessis International.

Forshaw, B. (2012) *Death in a Cold Climate: A Guide to Scandinavian Crime Fiction*. London: Palgrave Macmillan.

The edited book by Asimow listed below is specifically focused on television shows about law, lawyers and courtroom dramas, while the Robson and Silbey collection looks at bit more broadly at law and justice, including chapters on reality TV judging, police dramas and serial killers.

Asimow, M. (ed.) (2009) *Lawyers in Your Living Room!: Law on Television*. Chicago, IL: ABA Publishing.

Robson, P. and Silbey, J. (eds) (2012) *Law and Justice on the Small Screen*. Oxford: Hart Publishing.

For a more theoretical exposition on the intersections of law and popular culture see Sherwin, and for a similarly theoretically driven approach, though with more detailed empirical analysis, see Valverde:

Sherwin, R. K. (2004) 'Law and popular culture' in A. Sarat (ed.) *The Blackwell Companion to Law and Society*. Oxford: Blackwell Publishing, pp. 95–112.

Valverde, M. (2006) *Law and Order: Images, Meanings, Myths*. New Brunswick, NJ: Rutgers University Press.

CHAPTER 6

Bad girls and evil little monsters

INTRODUCTION

In this chapter, we consider female criminality, including adult women who have killed children. Towards the end of the chapter, we will also look at children who have killed other children to compare the responses of the mainstream media, politicians and criminal justice actors in different cultural contexts. While violent male offenders are generally seen to conform to well-understood patterns of male behavior, violent female offenders are regarded 'doubly deviant and doubly damned' (Lloyd 1995), because, as Jewkes (2015: 133) puts it, '[w]omen who commit serious offences are judged to have transgressed two sets of laws: criminal laws and the laws of nature'. This is especially so when women harm or kill children. Not only have those women transgressed the norms and expectations associated with 'appropriate' feminine behavior, but they are seen as exceptional and 'unnatural' because what they have done indicates they lack the maternal, nurturing and caring qualities associated with the stereotypical, metaphoric woman. As we shall see, in such cases, the media response will tend to be more exaggerated than that for men, 'with female deviance often polarized between representations of the Madonna/whore, the gentler sex or the more deadly species' (Clifford 2014: 504).

Women who do not appear to conform to what the media and society regard as stereotypically appropriate female behavior come in for particularly harsh treatment, although women who do conform, in the sense of being conventionally attractive, can also be cast in the role of *femme fatale*, whereby the veneer of physical beauty is believed to conceal an evil essence. All of this is not say male gender is insignificant when looking at media representations of female criminality. Indeed, as Berrington and Honkatukia (2002) show, media portrayals of Rosemary West, which focused on her evil and deviant sexuality were highly gendered because they simultaneously ignored the role her husband, Fred West, played in the crimes, and thus failed to consider connections between male heterosexuality and violence. Similarly, in her analysis of the Lindy Chamberlain case, Middleweek (2017) states that media portrayals of male criminals tend to be gendered. In the case of Lindy's husband, Michael Chamberlain, he was frequently represented in stereotypically feminized ways, seen as effete, emotional and so forth, which, according to Middleweek, is an archetype amplifying the deviance of male offenders, who are depicted in feminized terms as Other.

Finally, in respect of thinking about cultural readings of female criminality and transgression, as we have seen throughout the book, media representations tend increasingly to blur fiction and reality, so much so that 'the construction of "real" crime is deeply entangled with constructions of fictional crime' (Wright Monod 2017: 350). To the extent narratives of women's behavior are no different, we should seek to understand these accounts in cultural terms, as being a version of events that 'lies somewhere between reality and representation' (Wright and Myers 1996: xii). And it is at this confluence of fact and fiction where peoples' imagination about female transgression is excited in a morbid combination of horrified fascination, titillation and damning judgment.

MEDIA REPRESENTATIONS OF FEMALE CRIMINALITY AS 'BACKLASH JOURNALISM'

Chesney-Lind and Eliason (2006) explore media representation of violent and mean girls ('bad girls'), and the ways popular culture and scholarly works have contributed to the demonization of two largely invisible groups: (i) adolescent girls; and (ii) adult lesbians. Drawing on the work of Faludi (1991), Chesney-Lind and Eliason (2006: 30) show how the 'bad girl' theme in journalism stems from a backlash against feminism that hypothesizes, 'the women's movement has a "dark" side, encouraging girls and women to seek equality in the illicit world of crime as well as the licit labour market'. Implicit in this fascination with 'bad girls' is a 'masculinization' theory of female violence, which 'assumes that the same forces that propel men into violence will increasingly produce violence in girls and women once they are freed from the constraints of their gender' (Chesney-Lind and Eliason 2006: 31). Accordingly, it is a theory of violence that extends women's claims to equality to crime by proposing not to consider gender as an important variable. By simply adding women to the mix in this way, Chesney-Lind and Eliason (2006: 34) argue this perspective fails, among other things, to consider the idea that the relational, hidden or indirect nature of much female aggression reflects women's powerlessness in patriarchal society; in short, these alternative forms of aggression are essentially 'weapons of the weak'.

The masculinization theory of female violence also assumes that 'if women begin to question traditional femininity, they run the risk of becoming like men, that is more violent, sexually "loose" (often conflated with interest and involvement in lesbian activities, particularly in prison settings)' (Chesney-Lind and Eliason 2006: 31). It must be noted, however, that, as with all representations of crime, media fascination with 'bad girls' does not reflect the real nature and extent of female criminality, which means news media frequently provide disproportionate coverage on trends in girls' crimes rates, while ignoring, for example, the more rapid rise in crime rates for boys. Notwithstanding this, Chesney-Lind and Eliason (2006: 35) argue that by the 1990s, trends in criminal justice responses to girls' violence entered the stage of being a self-fulfilling prophecy in ways that echo much of the research on crime fear, which we considered in Chapter 4.

For instance, in the US from the early 1980s through to the early 2000s, arrest rates for girls increased faster than boys' arrest rates, although more crime was being committed by boys and men: between 1992 and 2003 the arrest of girls 'increased by 6.4 per cent while arrests of boys actually decreased by 16.4 per cent' (Chesney-Lind and Eliason 2006: 36). Increases in arrest rates also reflected an intensification of policing of very minor forms of girls' violence (e.g. school fighting), as well as mandatory arrest for domestic violence disturbances, both of which illustrate the disjunction between actual behavior and arrest rates. Race and ethnicity were also factors, such that there was increased detention and judicial processing of girls of color. Unsurprisingly, the media latched onto the supposed increase in female violence, promoting the view that good girls had gone bad, and were becoming like boys. To Chesney-Lind and Eliason (2006: 36), these media constructions of female criminality need to be seen within the context of patriarchy, which leads them to suggest they may serve three functions.

First, such imagery provides *cautionary tales* to girls and women, whereby demands for equality might have adverse consequences. In another study, which we consider later in the chapter, Berrington and Honkatukia (2002: 59) argue similarly that the harsh treatment meted out to women often serves 'as both an example and warning'. Moreover, in relation to women whose victimhood may be attributed to them deviating from traditional feminine norms and expectations, they add that one of the underlying messages is clearly that 'young women should remain within patriarchal and familial control to minimize their chance of victimization' (Berrington and Honkatukia 2002: 69).

Secondly, Chesney-Lind and Eliason argue constructions of African American girls and women as 'bad' resonate with racism that is at the core of US history and culture. Thirdly, media representations of female criminality serve to demonize lesbian women, thereby celebrating 'good', white, heterosexual passive women as a cultural ideal. And this goes to one of their main points, namely 'that both the media and the criminal justice system play crucial and complementary roles in the control of women' (Chesney-Lind and Eliason 2006: 43). Hence, in cases where lesbian 'criminals' are on trial for crimes attracting the death penalty, the more 'manly' their sexuality, demeanor and dress, the more likely a jury will be to forget they are women. Indeed, prosecutors often stress the 'masculinity' of these women to make a case for the death penalty. Streib (1994) suggests in such cases prosecutors *defeminize* and *dehumanize* defendants to convince juries of the need for the death penalty; jurors are 'left with a gender-neutral monster deserving of little or no human compassion' (Chesney-Lind and Eliason 2006: 38).

In conclusion, then, Chesney-Lind and Eliason argue that while white, heterosexual women have gained some power as a result of advances in feminism, the backlash against feminism has been felt most strongly by women of color, poor women and lesbian/bisexual women:

> Recall, there is scant evidence that girls and women are actually committing more violence; indeed most of the evidence that exists is to the contrary. There is, though, very strong evidence that certain women, particularly girls of colour and lesbian girls and women, are being constructed by the press and popular culture as both masculine and violent. The function of such construction is clear: increasing imprisonment for these groups of girls and women, as well as the larger cultural message to all women – a cautionary tale that if they raise any challenge to the present sex/gender system, they risk arrest and incarceration.
>
> (Chesney-Lind and Eliason 2006: 43)

MONSTROUS VISIONS: THE CASE OF MAXINE CARR

Like Chesney-Lind and Eliason, Jones and Wardle (2008) draw on theories about portrayals of female criminals in their analysis of the *visual press coverage* of Maxine Carr, who was the girlfriend of Ian Huntley, a school caretaker found guilty and sentenced to life imprisonment in December 2003 for the abduction and murder of schoolgirls Jessica Chapman and Holly Wells in 2002 in Soham, England. They draw on a study by Grabe et al. (2006: 137) that aims to test the 'chivalry hypothesis', which 'posits that female criminals receive more lenient treatment in the criminal justice system and in news coverage of their crimes than their male counterparts'. While the study provides some evidence to support the chivalry hypothesis, Grabe et al. show how a more nuanced version tends to prevail, which recognizes the ways both the criminal justice system and the media engage in a form of 'patriarchal chivalry' that reinforces stereotypical female sex roles. Under this system, say Grabe et al. (2006: 143), 'women who commit crimes that can be explained in a way that does not threaten patriarchal ideology receive so-called lenient media treatment [whereas] women who commit crimes that challenge gender expectations might receive unforgiving media treatment'.

Accordingly, women who commit violent crimes or crimes against children will likely receive the harshest treatment, since those crimes break deep-seated cultural taboos around women and mothers. Grabe et al. (2006: 151) also discovered the existence of what they termed the *Bonnie-and-Clyde effect*, whereby '[s]tories about men and women collaborating in crime are often associated with harsher journalistic treatment than stories about men and women acting without each other's support in committing crime'. Jones and Wardle apply some of these ideas to the case of Maxine Carr who, despite being charged with the lesser offense of perjury (supplying a false alibi), was portrayed with the same degree of interest as Huntley who was charged with more serious offenses. Indeed, visual representations of Carr were more numerous than those of Huntley.

In December 2003, Carr was found guilty of perverting the course of justice, and was sentenced to three-and-a-half-years imprisonment, but was released on license in May 2004, and supplied with indefinite anonymity. It is noteworthy that Carr is one of only four people in the UK who have been granted indefinite anonymity, and is the only one who has not committed murder; the others were Mary Bell, who was 11 years of age when convicted in 1968 of the manslaughter of a 3-year-old and a 4-year-old, and Robert Thompson and Jon Venables, who, as discussed later in the chapter, were both 10 years old when they abducted and killed 2-year-old James Bulger in 1993.

Jones and Wardle's assessment of the Soham trial chimes with the idea it resembled a trial by media, which was defined in Chapter 3 as: 'A dynamic, impact-driven, news media-led process by which individuals – who may or may not be publicly known – are tried and sentenced in the "court of public opinion"' (Greer and McLaughlin 2011: 27). Hence, to Jones and Wardle, the media were instrumental in fostering an extreme reaction towards Huntley and Carr, with stories written in highly emotional, sensationalist and lurid language (see also Box 6.1). Indeed, such was the concern that amidst the media trial both Huntley and Carr would not receive a fair trial, trial judge, Justice Moses, issued a warning to the media that highly colored and inflammatory reportage would constitute a breach of the *Contempt of Court Act 1981* (UK), the object of which is to avoid trial by media.

To be convicted of contempt, the legislation calls for strict liability, which guarantees that 'where a publication creates a substantial risk of serious prejudice to proceedings . . . it will be no defence that such an affect was not intended' (Crone 2002: 142). Moreover, any reporting that portrays a defendant as 'the type of person who would commit the crime with which he is charged or which suggests that he should not be believed is likely to attract a charge of contempt' (Crone 2002: 148). Just as serious, intimated Justice Moses, would be any breach of the media's wider responsibility to the community and general public and, in particular, to those most acutely involved, namely the parents, friends and relatives of the deceased.

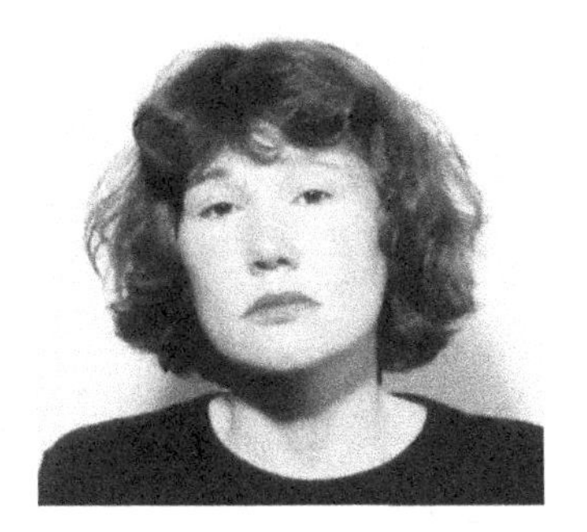

Figure 6.1 Maxine Carr photographed by Cambridgeshire Police following her arrest in August 2002

BOX 6.1 MEDIA TRIAL EFFECTS

In accordance with a broad reading of media effects (Chapter 1), including ideas previously discussed regarding the productivity of media-induced processes, such as moral panics (Chapter 3), media trials can also have consequences for the people that are their focus as well as for legal procedures. They can, for instance, affect sentencing, as highlighted in the case of the daughter of a prominent former Australian politician, Harriet Wran, who was subject to 'a sustained and unpleasant campaign' in the tabloid newspapers for her role as an accessory after the fact to murder and robbery in company (Brown 2016: 275). Finding the press' treatment of Wran amounted to 'extra-curial punishment' and was therefore a ground for mitigation, New South Wales Supreme Court justice, Ian Harrison, said in sentencing her that:

> In my opinion the publication of these egregious articles warrants the imposition of a sentence that takes account of Ms Wran's continuing exposure to risk of custodial retribution, the unavoidable spectre of enduring damage to her reputation and an impeded recovery from her ongoing mental health and drug-related problems.
>
> (Justice Ian Harrison, quoted in Brown 2016: 275)

Crucially, Jones and Wardle argue gender played a key role in the public's negative view of Maxine Carr. Newspaper reporting drew on stereotypical depictions of female criminals, and especially iconic imagery of Myra Hindley (Figure 6.2), who, along with accomplice, Ian Brady, was responsible for the torture, sexual assault and killing of five children in Greater Manchester in the mid-1960s, in what came to be known as the 'Moors Murders' because two of the victims were discovered in graves on Saddleworth Moor. Juxtaposing newspaper images of Hindley therefore 'encouraged a dominant reading of Carr's guilt as Huntley's accomplice' (Jones and Wardle 2008: 56). Importantly, Carr was portrayed with the same level of interest and put on an equal footing with Huntley, despite being up for a far lesser charge: 'She was not portrayed as a perjurer: she was portrayed as an accomplice to a murder, connoted as the next Myra Hindley' (Jones and Wardle 2008: 67). In this way, although not committing any violent crime, Carr 'suffered guilt through association, not just from Ian Huntley, but also from Myra herself' (Jones and Wardle 2010: 59). However, 'visual images "told" a very different story to the accompanying newspaper articles, whose detailed texts spelled out the differences in their crimes', such that 'there were no such qualifications in their visual representation, with Carr in fact featuring more frequently than Huntley' (Jones and Wardle 2008: 56).

Jones and Wardle (2008: 58) argue women who commit violent acts often fall into three distinct categories: (i) *lunatic* – hysterical, suffering from pre-menstrual tension or battered woman syndrome; (ii) *monster* – the inadequate mother, the lesbian, the just plain evil; or (iii) *idiot* – the dupe, the tool carrier, the confidante.

Figure 6.2 Portrait of Myra Hindley taken during her trial in 1966

Applying the relevant categories to media constructions of Maxine Carr, they show how lunacy was evident in a double page spread in the *Sun* newspaper: 'the full page headline shrieks "Carr scrubbed tiles so hard she said paint was coming off" with an accompanying large image of Carr, defiant, cold and outwardly calm' (Jones and Wardle 2008: 62). Monstrosity was also depicted in the *Sun*, where a full front page spread:

> showed Carr, in half profile looking to her right, staring blankly into space. Although she is facing forward she does not look directly at the reader, but drops her eyes slightly. This is a photograph of Carr [Figure 6.1] associated with the iconic mugshot of Hindley from 1965. . . . Along this image a banner headline presented in block capitals, coloured red and outlined in white, screams, 'MYRA MK II'.
>
> (Jones and Wardle 2008: 62)

LINDY CHAMBERLAIN'S MEDIA TRIAL

Like Maxine Carr, Lindy Chamberlain was also subject to a media trial following the disappearance of her 9-week old baby daughter, Azaria, while camping at Uluru (formerly Ayers Rock) in Australia in 1980. Chamberlain was subsequently convicted of murder in 1982, though that conviction was eventually quashed in 1986. Adrian Howe (1995) has suggested Chamberlain's trial by media negated her ability to receive a fair trial. The media trial was evident in the fact that the prosecution did not seek to prove any motive for the killing, nor indeed did it seek to invite speculation as to motive. However, according to Howe, there was clear a motive in the case against the media, which was to foster a perception of Lindy Chamberlain as a dangerous woman:

> a dangerous, provoking counter-stereotypical woman who refused to play her assigned gender role; who spoke out on her behalf and on behalf of all women, demanding her right to tell her story, her dreadful story of the death of her child, in her own way, her own defiant, nonpassive way, a right which was denied her be a male-dominated media which was angered and terrified by her refusal to play the role of a properly gendered woman.
>
> (Howe 1995: 175–176)

This quotation sums up many of the key elements of Howe's argument, namely that in lieu of a motive, a body and a murder weapon, Chamberlain was subject to a media-orchestrated witch-hunt whereby the question of her criminality and guilt was pre-judged by both the media and the Australian people. Central to that witch-hunt was the media's near obsession with Chamberlain's appearance, her body and her sexuality. She was seen as a figure embodying the power and threat of female sexuality, being variously described as 'the pert brunette', 'striking', or wearing a 'filmy apricot dress . . . she was braless beneath' (Howe 1995: 176). Innumerable male journalists also depicted her body as having a witch-like ability to change shape. For example, on one day she was described as looking like a schoolgirl, while on another day she was said to look like a film star (Howe 1995: 176).

Chamberlain was also condemned in the media because she did not display any recognizable signs of grief. Her reaction to the loss of her child did not fit the stereotype of a distraught mother because, at times, she came across as too composed and poised. Accordingly, her 'unnatural' impassiveness (e.g. she didn't cry), and weird, non-stereotypical behavior reinforced the image of Lindy the Witch, such that:

> By the time of her trial in September 1982, she had been found guilty, in the media, of more than child murder: she stood condemned for violating the stereotypes and sanctity of motherhood, of transgressing the boundaries of normal, passive motherhood. Moreover, by raising the possibility of having killed her child, she became transformed into an unnatural mother and a witch.
>
> (Howe 1995: 177)

Figure 6.3 Lindy Chamberlain with her husband Michael leaving court in Alice Springs, 2 February 1982

The role of experts and scientific evidence was crucial to this media trial too. Expert evidence was presented as scientific fact in the media, whereas other knowledges were submerged and repressed, such as the testimony of the people of Uluru, and especially that of black trackers who said they had traced dingo tracks around the Chamberlain's tent, leading to the theory a dingo had taken and killed Azaria. Subsequently, much of the 'expert' evidence of scientists was discredited at the 1986 Morling Inquiry into the Chamberlains' convictions, where

Aboriginal tracker Barbara Tjikadu was also finally permitted to give evidence 'that she had identified tracks of a dingo carrying a baby and the places where it put the child down on the sand' (Howe 1995: 179). The media's failure to report the testimony of Aboriginal trackers and their criminal construction of Chamberlain was, according to Howe (1995: 179), 'profoundly racist'. Moreover, he says, the case 'exemplified the tyranny of expert knowledge; the tyranny which obliterated the knowledge of ordinary people' (Howe 1995: 179). And, by presenting expert opinion as scientific fact, the media also supplied the evidentiary grounds for the witch story whereby 'Lindy Chamberlain became, thanks to the media, a scientifically-proven witch' (Howe 1995: 179).

Howe argues the police were also part of the process of the criminalization of Lindy Chamberlain, providing the press with incriminating information and false facts, including gossip about Lindy dressing her baby in black, about her not caring for her child, and that Azaria meant 'sacrifice to the wilderness'. To Howe (1995: 179), then, the question of a police conspiracy to subvert the course of justice is something to be taken seriously, because '[t]hese well-documented "special" connections between journalists and the police constituted a material factor in the miscarriage of justice that was the Chamberlain trial'.

Lindy Chamberlain was released from prison in February 1986. At that point, the media started to deconstruct the witch image, decriminalize her and reclaim her as a normal, natural woman. Appearing for an interview on national television, she cried throughout, now showing appropriate emotion, where previously she had shown no emotion at all, which, for many, had implied her guilt. And she was now allowed a voice, explaining that it was her lawyers who had previously instructed her to remain expressionless. However, throughout this 'reclamation process', the media continued to be preoccupied with her body, which now was seen to conform to norms of femininity, with Lindy being described as 'tiny', 'bird-like', 'sharp-featured' and having a 'trim waist', 'shapely legs' and 'beaming smile' (Howe 1995: 180).

In June 1987, Lindy Chamberlain was pardoned by the Northern Territory government following the Morling Inquiry, which found the new 'truth' about her, 'namely that she was a "normal, healthy caring mother" who loved her normal healthy baby girl right until the time she disappeared' (Howe 1995: 181). And, finally, on 12 June 2012 the Chamberlains' version of events was confirmed when the coroner of the Northern Territory officially amended Azaria's death certificate, stating the cause of death was a result of being attacked and taken by a dingo (Rourke 2012).

BOX 6.2 DEVIANT DIVAS: CHAMBERLAIN AND CORBY COMPARED

Belinda Middleweek (2017) looks at the cases of Lindy Chamberlain and Schapelle Corby to redress what she sees as a lack of attention given to 'celebrified criminals' and, in particular, to links between gender and criminality in the construction of celebrity types. The facts of the Chamberlain case have been outlined already. In the case of Schapelle Corby, she was found guilty in May 2005 of importing cannabis into Bali on 8 October 2004. Subsequently, she was sentenced to 20 years in jail but in February 2014 was released on parole on condition she remain in Indonesia until July 2017, upon the expiration of her parole period.

Although the two cases can be distinguished on the basis Lindy Chamberlain was ultimately exonerated of her daughter's murder while Corby was convicted of drug smuggling (despite her claims of innocence), both were subject to similar patterns of media representation. Hence, Middleweek (2017: 95) argues, notwithstanding the very different mediascapes of the 1980s and 2000s, and especially the role of social media in the latter period, 'in alternative media such as blogs and cartoons about the Corby case the Chamberlain event is interpellated'. For example:

> On claims made by Corby's defence team that a corrupt baggage handler smuggled the marijuana into the surf-board case or 'boogie board bag', *The Punch* blog site headlined its news item with 'Schapelle Corby: The drongo did it, maybe'. The 'drongo', aside from being Australian slang for an incompetent person, is part of a cultural slogan that alludes to the Chamberlains' defence caseline, 'The dingo did it' which, in 1980s common parlance was also shorthand for a scapegoat or dupe (namely, the baggage handler).
>
> (Middleweek 2017: 95, original emphasis)

Middleweek argues further that both cases also provide examples of the *consumptive value of celebrity*. Both, for instance, were subject to extensive media investment, which capitalized on the cases through live streaming of court proceedings, books, films and TV interviews, and the production of 'celebrity merchandise', such as tee shirts and caps and even, in the case of Corby, G-strings and dog collars (Middleweek 2017: 93). Thus, considering the inattention given to gender in research on celebrity, Middleweek (2017: 100) argues for a new category of celebrity: the *deviant diva* – a concept similar to the term *femme fatale*, which is itself a cultural construct tending 'to provoke a particularly conflicted tangle of emotions, including horrified fascination, titillation, stern reproach and damning judgment' (Simkin 2013: 36).

In developing this idea, Middleweek draws on Jewkes (2015: 133) to show how women who commit serious crimes (and especially those accused of killing children) are *doubly deviant*, in that they are regarded as transgressing criminal laws as well as the laws of nature. Indeed, we saw this in the example of the media trial of Lindy Chamberlain, who was portrayed as an 'unnatural' mother. Moreover, Middleweek (2017: 98) argues, media representations of female criminals reflect the treatment of women in the wider society where sexuality, sexual history, physical appearance and attractiveness are all subject to intense scrutiny. Again, this was very much evident in the Chamberlain case, with the media focus on Lindy's body and sexuality.

While both the Chamberlain and Corby cases demonstrate the prevalence in media representations of stereotypically gendered assumptions about female criminality, arguably one of Middleweek's most insightful points relates to her proposition that representations of male criminals and crime celebrities are gendered too. Here, she looks at the example of Lindy Chamberlain's husband, Michael Chamberlain (see Figure 6.3), showing how although much of the scholarly focus has been on the sexualization of Lindy Chamberlain in news media discourse, Michael Chamberlain was also the subject of media commentary, which 'often depicted him in stereotypically feminized terms' (Middleweek 2017: 99).

For instance, he was periodically framed in news reports as an emotional effete, or a 'weeping woman', which, according to Middleweek (2017: 100), is an archetype amplifying the deviance of male perpetrators, whereby 'the male offender is represented in feminized terms as the "Other"'. This, in turn, gives credence to feminist criminology which argues that, 'the media tap into, and magnify, deep-seated public fears about deviant women, while paying much less attention to equally serious male offenders whose profile does not meet the *psychosocial* criteria of *otherness*' (Jewkes 2015: 131, original emphasis). Indeed, this was precisely the process at work in the case of Maxine Carr who, as we saw earlier, was portrayed with the same level of interest and on an equal footing with boyfriend, Ian Huntley (who was accused of murder), despite being up for the much lesser charge of perjury. Berrington and Honkatukia (2002) adopt a similar theme in their examination of media reporting on Rosemary West, which is discussed later in the chapter.

AMANDA KNOX: TWENTY-FIRST-CENTURY *FEMME FATALE*

Like Lindy Chamberlain, the media focused in on both the appearance and behavior of American exchange student, Amanda Knox, who, on 5 December 2009, along with her Italian boyfriend, Raffaele Sollecito, was convicted for her role in the murder of British exchange student, Meredith Kercher, in November 2007. Kercher's body was discovered in the small house she, Knox and two Italian women shared, which was located just outside the city walls of Perugia, Italy. Prosecutors speculated Kercher had been the victim of a sex game that had turned violent. Earlier, Rudy Guede, originally from the Ivory Coast, has been tried and found guilty of Kercher's murder and sexual assault after requesting an expedited or 'fast-track' trial, separate from Knox and Sollecito. Knox and Sollecito appealed in December 2010 and were acquitted and cleared of murder charges on 3 October 2011. Not unlike other women accused of violent crimes that we examine in this chapter, Knox was the subject of intense media interest from the outset.

Stevie Simkin (2013) considers the representation of Knox in the UK tabloid newspaper, the *Daily Mail* to explore connections between celebrity, sex and violence, which, he says, reveal something about contemporary attitudes towards transgressive female sexuality. As in other cases of female criminality, Knox's appearance was a focal point for media attention. To Simkin (2013: 37, original emphasis), the way Knox was portrayed in the *Daily Mail*, until her acquittal, reflected the figure of the classic *femme fatale*, 'who is defined in part by a capacity for deceit, and a facility to take on different *personae* in order to mask her true intentions, feelings or identity'. Accordingly, Knox was seen to be 'hiding her true evil nature beneath the veneer of beauty' (Simkin 2013: 37). Hence, the *Daily Mail* frequently employed dichotomized ways of representing Knox:

> It habitually interpreted the radical disjunction between her appearance (fresh-faced innocent) and the supposed reality (deviant killer) either in terms of the *femme fatale* meme, or as evidence of a psychotic dissociation between the Catholic-educated, 'nice', middle-class girl and sex-crazed, drug-fuelled thrill-seeker.
>
> (Simkin 2013: 34, original emphasis)

Like other media representations of female criminality, Knox's behavior was also heavily scrutinized, and often regarded as inappropriate. Her courtroom appearances were of particular interest. For example, in her first courtroom speech, Knox spoke about how the sex toy she kept in a transparent beauty case, which had apparently made Kercher feel 'uncomfortable', was meant to be a joke. While this disastrous move 'compounded the impression that she had no idea of appropriate behaviour . . . the press used her spontaneous declaration to further enhance the sexualized image they had been constructing' (Simkin 2013: 39). Knox's PR company, by contrast, attempted to counter these impressions, presenting images of her as a desexualized, hard-working, sporty tomboy, and explaining away her courtroom behavior as quirkiness. However, nowhere was the media's preoccupation with the angel/devil construct more obvious than in what was probably a rather lucky shot of a twenty-first-century 'slipped halo', as the *Daily Mail* reported it (Figure 6.4).

As we shall see when we look at celebrity serial killers in Chapter 7, the creation of a nickname is of crucial importance in media constructions of celebrity criminals: it provides immediate newsworthiness and means their notoriety will be that much more memorable than those who have not been given a nickname. In the case of Amanda Knox, the media latched on to a nickname derived from her MySpace social networking webpage, 'Foxy Knoxy'. This was perfect for media purposes, 'putting her sexuality front and centre' (Simkin 2013: 36). It mattered not that this was a childhood nickname referring to her childhood footballing prowess, 'since the moniker was a media dream – a headline waiting to happen – which subsequently stuck in the popular imagination and effectively served to reinforce Knox's reputation as a "sinister temptress"' (Clifford 2014: 504).

While Knox herself used social media to counter these images and proclaim her innocence – tweeting a 'selfie' declaring, SIAMO INNOCENTI ('We Are Innocent') – others used social media as a vehicle to campaign to overturn the convictions of Knox and Sollecito. Drawing on data from in-depth semi-structured research interviews, Lieve Gies (2017) looks at the role of social media in raising public awareness of miscarriages of justice of this kind. Significantly, gender featured in two significant ways in the Knox-Sollecito innocence campaign. First, women tended to be reluctant to take part for fear of becoming

Figure 6.4 'Slipped halo' image of Amanda Knox illustrating her allegedly angelic-demonic split personality

victims of Internet trolling. Gies (2017: 732) adds this 'inhibiting effect' of women participating in online campaigns 'stands in marked contrast with the prominent role female campaigners (often female relatives of the victim) usually tend to play in miscarriage of justice campaigns' (Gies 2017: 732).

Secondly, and in contrast to much of the material presented in this chapter on negative media constructions of female offending, several of the innocence campaigners believed women, including Knox, were not capable of committing this type of offense precisely because of their gender. Such explanations rehearsed well-established gender scripts, with Knox being seen as

> a wholesome 'college kid' who may not have been perfect (there was acknowledgement of her use of soft drugs) but who was nevertheless a 'nice' young woman who was simply incapable of committing the kind of crime the prosecution alleged to have taken place.
>
> (Gies 2017: 737)

Interviewees involved in the innocence campaign tended to be convinced Rudy Guede had acted alone, but claimed race was not the motivation for this belief. Equally, US-based innocence campaigners denied their criticism of the Italian justice system was xenophobic, pointing to examples of wrongful convictions in the US criminal justice system, sometimes leading tragically to the imposition of the death penalty. This last point is significant because it relates to other research highlighting the ways the Italian legal system was represented by the media in the US and elsewhere. For instance, Annunziato (2011) shows how numerous American journalists believed negative coverage of Knox in the Italian media could have contributed to her conviction. Her portrayal as a cold-hearted American beauty who failed to behave in accordance with accepted cultural norms (e.g. flirting, kissing and laughing with her boyfriend while waiting at the police station to give a statement to authorities) was regarded by many in the American media as proof of the malicious prosecution of Knox.

Accordingly, in the days following her conviction, American journalists tended to be sympathetic to her plight. Indeed, as Annunziato (2011: 67–68) shows, the American media were often one-sided in their coverage, providing information on points of law or forensic evidence from experts seeking to discredit the case against Knox, with no experts interviewed to provide opposing viewpoints. The Italian legal system was also criticized with some saying the prosecution's case would not have been admissible in an American law court. Moreover, in coverage where forensic experts appeared, Italy was said to be 'the poor man of Europe' when it comes to the administration of justice. The Italian judiciary was criticized too, as was the Italian jury system, which does not require judges to sequester jurors, 'theoretically leaving them to read and watch media coverage of any case in which they deliberate' (Annunziato 2011: 71). Interestingly, Annunziato shows how the American media's coverage of the Knox case also reflected criticisms of Italy and its justice system made by friends and family of Knox. Thus, in an instance of 'litigation journalism', where one side attempts to influence the outcome of proceedings via the media (Manheim 1998), she says some reporters appeared to have 'traded journalistic objectivity for access to interviews with Knox supporters by presenting only favourable coverage of the American student and depicting the country that prosecuted her as villainous' (Annunziato 2011: 75).

Boyd (2013: 45) has argued these criticisms of the Italian legal system are essentially unwarranted not least because sequestration is rarely used these days in the US, even in high-profile cases (Mirabella 2012). What this demonstrates to Boyd, among other things, is unfamiliarity not only with the US legal system, but also the Italian system. He uses data from the *Guardian* and the *New York Times* newspapers to show how media depictions of the Knox case were often premised on fundamental misunderstandings of the Italian legal system, which led to 'a rather one-sided and generally erroneous picture of the Italian criminal justice system' (Boyd 2013: 46).

In contrast to the common law systems of the UK and US, the system of civil law in Italy proceeds on the basis of an inquisitorial process where the judge is permitted, for instance, to question witnesses. Moreover, civil law does not usually have a jury, but a hybrid system for the determination of serious crimes, which comprises two professional judges and six lay judges, who discuss matters of fact and law, and who have only to arrive at a majority verdict rather than decide a case unanimously. Notwithstanding these significant differences, UK and US journalists *recontextualized* legal terms and concepts, leading to a *misrepresentation* of the Italian legal system. For example, newspaper reports would frequently use words and phrases to frame proceedings as if they were occurring in a UK or US courtroom, thereby obscuring their true nature, such as referring to the 'judge and jury', or the 'prosecution', and, in one case, describing the lay judges as 'civilians', which is a term connoting a military context.

PRESS REACTIONS TO FEMALE KILLERS IN ENGLAND AND FINLAND

As in the case of Myra Hindley, Berrington and Honkatukia (2002) show how media coverage of female serial killer, Rose West, focused on images of evil and deviant sexuality. Totally missing from these gendered portrayals, however, was any consideration of male heterosexuality and violence and how that may have impacted on events. Accordingly, by 'focusing on Rose as "a willing partner" the press ignored Fred's equally "willing" participation' (Berrington and Honkatukia 2002: 62). Like Middleweek (2017), Berrington and Honkatukia (2002) compare two cases of female criminality, but they do so to draw out the very different media and societal responses to female violence in England and Finland. They first examine the case of Rosemary West who, with husband, Fred West, abducted, abused, tortured and killed several women over 20 years at 25 Cromwell Street, Gloucester, England. Victims included Fred West's first wife and stepdaughter, lodgers and strangers, and in two cases the bones of a late-term fetus were interred with the mother – West being the alleged father of both babies.

Fred West committed suicide prior to trial, but Rose West was convicted of ten counts of murder in 1995. Upon examination of newspaper reports in England, Berrington and Honkatukia (2002) show how Rose West was portrayed in the media as an evil monster who 'was effectively on trial for "lack of womanhood" and deviation from prescribed and expected maternal, nurturing roles' (Berrington and Honkatukia 2002: 51). Moreover, the demonization of her in the British press has assured her a place in history, alongside Myra Hindley, as a 'bad killer woman' (Berrington and Honkatukia 2002: 50), or 'icon of "evil womanhood"' (Berrington and Honkatukia 2002: 70).

The press largely ignored Fred West's involvement in the crimes, 'because he was dead, and therefore not on trial', and so 'male physical and/or sexual violence was not "in the frame"' (Berrington and Honkatukia 2002: 62). By contrast, the tone, style and content of media representations of Rose West provided 'deeply disturbing sensationalized, sexualized and misogynistic material' (Berrington and Honkatukia 2002: 60). As often happens in serial killer cases (see Chapter 7), the media focused on family background – Rose was allegedly abused by a brutal and sadistic father – and on 'personalization and individual pathology used to "explain" the crime' (Berrington and Honkatukia 2002: 61).

Media reporting of the case of Sanna Sillanpää in Finland differed remarkably from the Rose West case. Sillanpää walked into a gun club in Helsinki in 1999 and opened fire, killing three men, and injuring a fourth. Rather than being portrayed in the media as 'bad', however, Sillanpää was regarded 'mad', and her case treated as sad and tragic. She was constructed in the press as sick rather than evil, and, indeed, at the final court ruling in 2000, she was found to be suffering from paranoid schizophrenia, and thus not responsible for her actions. Instead of being sentenced to a prison term, she was ordered to a hospital for the mentally ill.

Like in the cases of Lindy Chamberlain and Amanda Knox, discussed earlier, the media focused on Sanna Sillanpää's physical appearance, but did so in a way that portrayed her as a 'poor thing'. For instance, far from presenting as a 'violent woman' who did not adhere to female stereotypes, she was described as 'shy', 'quiet', 'ordinary' and 'mousy', and, in court, wore an anorak. Her appearance was also used to explain a sudden change in her both mentally and physically in 1996, when it was alleged by her sister that she had been raped. It was believed, therefore, that male hatred following this sexual assault could have provided a motive for her crime, which resulted in her being portrayed as a victim by the media.

It was hard to determine motive, though, as Sanna refused to talk, either to the police or in court. Indeed, while in some cases silence of this kind can be construed as an indicator of cold-heartedness, in Sanna's case it was seen as indicative of her mental illness, as was her tranquility at the shooting range while she carried out the killings (Berrington and Honkatukia 2002: 67–68). Regardless of the differences with the Rose West case, however, the labeling of this as a 'sad case', especially in the tabloid press was, according to Berrington and Honkatukia (2002: 66), still connected to gender, with stories referring to her as a 'killer woman', a 'shooter woman', as well as 'a woman suffering from mental problems', or simply just a 'girl'. However, unlike Rose West, Sanna Sillanpää is unlikely to be remembered precisely because she was seen as 'sad' rather than 'bad'. So, thanks to the lack of demonography, the case 'has been buried in the archives as an individual pathology or "human tragedy"' (Berrington and Honkatukia 2002: 70).

While Rosemary West and Sanna Sillanpää reveal what Berrington and Honkatukia (2002: 52) see as two contrasting dominant discourses of female criminal violence – i.e. 'bad' and 'mad' respectively – it could be said their comparison of West's truly heinous crimes and Sillanpää's arguably less grave, or, at least, less repugnant crimes is to compare apples and oranges. Having said that, they propose that beyond the limits of the case studies themselves, their study highlights the differences between England and Finland, and the contrasting media traditions of both countries. On the one hand, competition in a crowded media marketplace drives sensational news reporting in the United Kingdom, and that is compounded by the fact that there is a significant constituency of 'floating' readers beyond each newspaper's core readership. In Finland, on the other hand, there is 'less variety and diversity and a greater level of "brand loyalty", including subscription-based sales' (Berrington and Honkatukia 2002: 55).

Ultimately, then, Berrington and Honkatukia emphasize the importance of developing a political-economic interpretation of crime and media representations. Particularly in an age when news and information can be delivered to audiences quickly and cheaply, and there is even more pressure on newspapers to maximize profits, they say, 'it remains deeply significant that the press operates in a highly competitive environment where, for some newspapers at least, there is a constant struggle to remain economically viable within a dwindling market' (Berrington and Honkatukia 2002: 56). While this theoretical framing of media reporting on crime chimes with arguments made previously in this book about the criminogenic nature of the mass media, which has an institutional predisposition – born of the commercial imperative to make profit – to generate newsworthy and/or sensationalized stories, including those fueling crime fear and feeding moral panics (e.g. Altheide 2009; David et al. 2011: 224–225; Critcher 2011; Young 1971: 37), a cross-cultural analysis very similar to that of Berrington and Honkatukia is also provided by Green (2008a) in his study of child-on-child killing in two countries, which is the subject of the next section.

WHEN CHILDREN KILL CHILDREN: COMPARING THE BULGER AND REDERGÅRD CASES

So far in this chapter we have focused on media representations of female criminality, including those involving women who have, or have allegedly, killed children. In these last parts of the chapter we will take a slightly different tack by looking at the media's treatment of children who have killed other children. The main focus here will be on David Green's (2008a) comparison of the Bulger and Redergård cases in Britain and Norway respectively, which, as we shall see, has many parallels with Berrington and Honkatukia's (2002) comparative analysis of the West and Sillanpää cases.

On 12 February 1993, two 10-year-old boys, Robert Thompson and Jon Venables, abducted 2-year-old James Bulger from a shopping center in Bootle on the outskirts of Liverpool, England. They walked him some two and a half miles away to a railway line and murdered him. Stan Cohen's (1972/2002: ix) assessment of the Bulger story is that it 'triggered off an immediate and ferocious moral panic' (see also Scraton 2003), a hallmark of which, as we saw in Chapter 3, is *disproportionality*, whereby the threat or conduct posing a threat is highly exaggerated. Indeed, the number of children who kill children is tiny and not increasing, and so it was precisely the rarity of the event – a 'news value' discussed in Chapter 1 – and its context (grainy CCTV footage showing the toddler being led away by the two older boys) that made it so abhorrent; yet inherently newsworthy.

Long before the trial of Thompson and Venables began, the Bulger story was portrayed in the news media as a potent symbol for all that had gone wrong with Britain, including the 'breeding' of violent children; feckless fathers (and mothers) and dysfunctional underclass families; and the exploitation of children by violence on television and 'video nasties'. Indeed, the *Sun* newspaper called for 'a crusade to rescue a sick society', and even the more serious *Economist* magazine described a situation where Britain was 'examining the dark corners of its soul' (cited in Cohen 1972/2002: ix). Amid claims by the trial judge that a probable cause of the boys' heinous crime was exposure to violent videos (i.e. some kind of 'media effects' theory), it quickly became a 'factoid' that the last video rented by the father of one of the boys was *Child's Play 3* (where a child kills a manic doll), although subsequent evidence revealed this to be a baseless claim (Cohen 1972/2002: x).

The Bulger case, then, was seen as symptomatic of a moral crisis; it was 'a meaningful omen and accurate barometer of societal moral health' (Green 2008a: 198). However, in accordance with the idea presented in Chapter 3 that moral panics can have lasting effects, the case was also a seminal, watershed moment in the context of criminal justice in Britain. Following the case, Tony Blair adopted the slogan while in opposition, 'tough on crime, tough on the causes of crime', which became a crucial aspect of New Labour's landslide victory in the 1997 election. According to MORI (Market & Opinion Research International Limited), concern about crime immediately doubled after the Bulger case was reported, and in subsequent years the adult prison population in England and Wales rose inexorably, with the imprisonment of young people aged 15–17 rising from 769 to 2089 between 1993 and 2002 (Green 2008a: 197–198).

Green (2008a: 200) conducted a 'comparative media analysis' of the Bulger case in Britain and the Redergård case in Norway where his express purpose was

> to assess the tenor of the times, the prevailing cultural sensibilities, specifically in relation to two particular acts of homicide, and to expose the bounded discursive limits imposed upon debates sparked in the wake of the two killings of children by children.

Unlike Jones and Wardle's (2008) approach, which analyzes both text *and* visual imagery in the case of Maxine Carr, Green (2008a: 201) adopts a 'text-only approach', comparing tabloid and broadsheet newspaper reporting; although both approaches involve to some degree or other a 'politics of representation' (see Box 6.2).

BOX 6.3 OFFENDING IMAGERY, ETHICS AND JUSTICE

There is some similarity between the way female criminals and young offenders can be demonized in news media. Earlier in the chapter we saw how most of the news coverage about the Soham murders focused on Maxine Carr, even though she was charged with a lesser offense than Ian Huntley. Likewise, Wright Monod (2017) shows how, in the New Zealand case of Bailey Kurariki – the 13-year-old convicted of manslaughter in relation to the death of pizza delivery man, Michael Choy in Auckland in 2002 – press coverage was dominated by his photograph simply because he was the youngest of the group of young offenders responsible for the killing. Although his name was suppressed and the media denied permission to take photographs in court during the trial, once Bailey was convicted the press were permitted to take pictures and name offenders. While virtually all pre-trial reports mentioned each of the offenders, post-trial reporting focused disproportionately on Bailey. And despite being released to a secret address after serving his sentence, the press tracked him down, paparazzi style, and ran stories about him seemingly living a new lavish life and enjoying himself.

The post-trial treatment of Bailey especially by the press, but also by criminal justice agents, has been described as 'obsessive' as well as being tantamount to harassment. Indeed, Wright Monod (2017: 348) highlights the impact that treatment had on Bailey's future; resulting, for instance, in him having few friends and difficulty finding employment. All the more reason, she argues, to consider granting anonymity through permanent name suppression, particularly in young offender cases (Wright Monod 2017: 345). Moreover, she says, the Bailey case highlights the need to examine the 'ethics of representation', as part of a 'critical visual criminology' (Wright Monod 2017: 344–345). That is, intervening in practices of crime control to consider 'the politics of representation' of deviant acts and persons, and 'to imagine the most just response for those depicted in them' (Wright Monod 2017: 353).

As often happens in cases like Bailey in New Zealand, and Bulger in the UK, campaign and lobbying groups emerge calling for harsher sentences and so forth. However, referring to Ferrell (2013), Wright Monod suggests critical criminological activism and intervention may take the form of interrogating some of the unjust practices that can stem from us looking at news images of convicted criminals. That, in turn, may cause us to consider people who have the 'right to look' at such images

> are those who are privy to the context and details of each case, those who are capable to respond in ways that will protect the human rights of the person who has transcended [our laws], whose encounters with such images will be ethically cognisant.
>
> (Wright Monod 2017: 352)

To Green, the Bulger and Redergård cases are quite distinct. In the former case, Venables and Thompson were arrested, interrogated and charged; they were held in pre-trial custody with no psychiatric treatment; and they were tried in a modified adult court, and ultimately given the equivalent of a life sentence – detained 'during Her Majesty's pleasure' (Green 2008a: 199). Meanwhile, in Norway, 12 months after the Bulger murder, when three 6-year-old boys killed 5-year-old Silje Marie Redergård, they were swiftly identified and questioned only briefly; when their parents withdrew consent for the questioning, child welfare agencies became responsible for the case. And the boys were not punished but offered places in kindergarten, so teachers and psychiatrists could monitor them and assist them in coming to terms with what they had done.

Green compares what he identifies as *dominant frames* and *themes* (both of which can be *diagnostic* and *prognostic*) as presented in the press in Britain and Norway that attempt to account for the homicides in each country, and then considers some possible explanations for the sharply divergent themes constructed by the press in each jurisdiction. The dominant frame in the Bulger case was criminal, where the Redergård case was not. The press coverage of the Bulger case focused on the kidnapping and brutal and willful murder, while, in Norway, coverage concerned the death of an innocent by innocents. Hence, the Bulger case was conceptualized within a 'criminal justice' frame, whereas the Redergård case was given a 'child welfare' frame.

The themes or angles adopted in the press in each country also differed markedly. The Bulger murder was regarded as indicative of a deeper moral malaise and societal anomie afflicting British society; epitomized by an editorial in the *Daily Mirror* declaring, 'There is something rotten at the heart of Britain'. By contrast, the Redergård homicide was depicted as a tragic accident, along the lines of the 'all victims' theme. That is, the perpetrators were also constructed as victims of their own innocence – innocent of the knowledge of the damage their violence could do and innocent victims of televised violence. In short, the killing 'was not interpreted as a typical act to be expected from anomalous children, but instead as an anomalous act committed by normal children' (Green 2008a: 204).

Interestingly, a similar attitude was displayed by Norwegian Prime Minister, Jens Stoltenberg, who, in the wake of Anders Behring Breivik's murderous rampage on 22 July 2011 promised, 'more democracy, more openness, and more humanity, but never naivety' (quoted in Reid-Henry 2011). This example has been used to argue that parliamentarians in Western democratic states should be less cavalier when enacting punitive crime control measures, and instead ought adopt more considered responses to the management of risk and social control (Martin 2012: 230). However, if Green's arguments are to be heeded, we also need to consider the effects of cultural differences *between* Western democracies, and the various social and political institutions contained therein.

Indeed, his findings show how none of the themes in the Norwegian press contended Silje's death was a consequence of moral decay, or intrinsically evil children or a belief that criminality among young people is out of control, all of which were dominant themes in the English press (both tabloid and broadsheet). In fact, the only point of convergence related to a concern about the effects of media violence and the need for censorship. Moreover, while the remedies advocated by the English press included punishment, moral reaffirmation, condemnation and exclusion, all of the prognostic or prescriptive elements of the frames employed in press coverage of the Redergård case were forward-looking and not condemnatory or retributive, stressing reintegration, healing, expert-guided treatment and inclusion (Green 2008a: 204). Green shows how these quite divergent reporting styles may be explained by reference to what are essentially cultural differences between Britain and Norway.

First, the two countries differ in terms of *the way childhood is constructed*. For instance, in the criminal justice context in England and Wales, the age of criminal responsibility, before 1998 at least, was between 10 and 14, whereas now it is 10 years of age, since the abolition of the *doli incapax* ('incapable of doing wrong') presumption under the *Crime and Disorder Act 1998* (UK). In Norway, by contrast, criminal responsibility is 15 years old, which means children there could not be constructed (in the press) as criminally culpable, punishable, moral entities as the Bulger killers were in England.

Secondly, Green discusses *the importance of legitimate claims makers*, saying that comparing the Redergård and Bulger cases there was a higher prevalence of expert claims makers in the Norwegian press than in the English press; and that is partly because the views of experts are not valued by reporters and editors in the English press as they are in the Norwegian press. In Chapter 3, we saw similar arguments made by Machado and Santos (2009) in respect of the trial by media and public drama associated with the disappearance of Madeleine McCann. It will be recalled how the role of expert evidence (DNA evidence in that case) played a crucial role in the media trial, with the more serious newspaper, *Público*, discussing the complexities of such evidence, while the tabloid, *Correio da Manhã*, adopted a more populist view – likely drawn from fictional representations in television shows such as *CSI* – which relied on a belief in the certainty of scientific evidence.

However, Green does not differentiate tabloid and broadsheet reporting, which, he claims, in the case of both Redergård and Bulger, were quite similar. Rather, he suggests there are very different 'press cultures' in Britain and Norway. Indeed, echoing Berrington and Honkatukia's (2002: 55–56) point about the significance of providing a political-economic analysis of media representations of crime, and the fact that media traditions in England and Finland are quite distinct, Green shows how, even with the growth of online newsfeeds, newspaper markets in Britain and Norway remain very different. In the highly competitive English market, where ten national daily newspapers vie for readers, editors and journalists are tempted endlessly to feed off political conflict and scandal to sell copy. In Norway, by contrast, there are only two national daily newspapers with large circulations. Moreover, Green says, the stress on sensationalizing news reporting is likely intensified in Britain where most newspapers continue to be sold from newsstands and not, as is the case in Norway, through subscription, which probably decreases the need to create sensationalized headlines, since most readers receive newspapers on their doorsteps regardless of whether headlines are provocative or not. In short, he states, '[b]oth of these tendencies – the political and commercial capitalization on the public's distrust – appear to perpetuate the notion that citizens ought to be distrustful' (Green 2008a: 213).

The third factor Green says may explain the divergent themes constructed by the press in Britain and Norway concerns *the legitimacy of societal institutions and elite expertise*. At the time of the Bulger case, Britain was undergoing a recession: there was disillusionment with political leadership, almost half of Britons wanted to emigrate, and law and order was second only to employment as a worry for the public. Thus, '[t]he Bulger case only crystallized more generalized anxieties and broader concerns that had been accumulating, providing an opportunity for people to express them' (Green 2008a: 211). By contrast, the Redergård case occurred at a time when the Norwegian public's confidence in their press and parliament was nearly twice the level of Britain's.

Fourthly, Green states there is a key role for *political culture and incentives to penal populism*. Not only is there competition between newspapers in Britain, but also between politicians. So, while 'English majoritarian political culture is highly adversarial . . . Norwegian political culture is based on a consensus model and is thus characterized by "inclusiveness, bargaining, and compromise"' (Lijphart 1999: 2, cited in Green 2008a: 213). This suggests incentives are much stronger in majoritarian democracies to politicize criminal events like the Bulger case than they are in consensus democracies like Norway. Indeed, in adversarial countries the opportunity to exploit apparent crises is quite hard to resist. By contrast, Lijphart (1998, 1999) has shown how consensus democracies tend to be 'kinder and gentler' than majoritarian systems: 'Their incarceration rates are lower than those of majoritarian democracies, they use the death penalty less, are more protective of the environment, more generous with foreign aid and are committed welfare states' (Green 2008a: 213).

Furthermore, different types of *political economy* can also explain the contrasting societal responses in the Bulger and Redergård cases. As we saw in our analysis of *The Wire* in Chapter 5, and, in particular, the role of 'Hamsterdam' as a means of subverting dominant approaches to drug control, which, in places like the US and UK, incorporate neoliberal doctrines of individual responsibility and risk management (Wakeman 2014: 231), so Green shows how the reaction to the Bulger murder also evinces the influence of *neoliberalism*, and especially its stress on individual responsibility, which has prevailed in Britain since the 1980s:

> Appetites for punitive responses to crime are highest in those countries where neoliberalism dominates. Neoliberalism arrived in Britain in the 1980s with the New Public Management movement under Margaret Thatcher and has continued under New Labour. It is premised on the belief that a large and interventionist public sector is inefficient and undermines the autonomy of the individual.
>
> (Green 2008a: 214)

In contrast to neoliberal countries, and as we know from our discussion of Nordic noir (Chapter 5), Norway and other Scandinavian countries have at their heart a *social democratic corporatist* ideal, meaning they 'generally tend be more egalitarian, have narrower income disparities, broad and strong welfare systems, low levels of social exclusion and left-wing political ideologies' (Green 2008a: 214). These traits are reflected in the criminal justice systems of Scandinavian countries, which, accordingly, 'have lower cultural appetites for punishment, inclusionary penal intervention and low imprisonment rates'. (Green 2008a: 214).

CONCLUSION

As we have seen throughout this chapter, the media frequently treat with suspicion women who do not adhere to stereotypical female behavior. For instance, Amanda Knox was treated as a classic *femme fatale* whose physical beauty masked her evil nature. Her behavior was also scrutinized and regarded inappropriate, given the circumstances surrounding her detention and trial. Similarly, Lindy Chamberlain was condemned and regarded 'unnatural' for not displaying the requisite signs of grief upon losing her baby daughter. Her physical appearance was similarly scrutinized and her body assumed to have a witch-like ability to shapeshift. The sexuality of both Knox and Chamberlain was also a central element of media portrayals. Some years later, parallels were drawn between Chamberlain and Joanna Lees, the English backpacker who escaped after being held captive in Australia's Northern Territory by Bradley Murdoch, who had earlier killed her boyfriend, Peter Falconio. Lees was portrayed enigmatically: she was seen either as the 'perfect victim' who managed to evade her attacker, or 'as a capricious femme fatale whose incomprehensible desires caused her to dispose of her boyfriend and then to make up an extraordinary tale of assault and escape from which she emerges the heroine' (Davis and Morrissey 2003: 393).

We have also seen how, according to Middleweek (2017), the image of the *femme fatale* can be wrapped up in a kind of celebrity, which provokes a set of conflicting emotions, including morbid fascination, titillation and reproach (Simkin 2013: 36). Moreover, part of the process of 'celebrification' involves the designation of nicknames, such as 'Foxy Knoxy' in the Amanda Knox case, but also some degree of demonization, as with the examples of Rosemary West and Myra Hindley, both of whom are remembered as monstrous icons of 'evil womanhood' – although Hindley remains 'the archetypal violent "monstrous" woman' (Jones and Wardle 2010: 59). Indeed, for Penfold-Mounce (2009: 74), female criminals like Hindley and West encapsulate Brophy's (1986) monstrous Other as well as reinforce the 'metaphoric woman', which stands for 'an array of qualities, values and meanings of femaleness, namely an innate maternal and caring womankind'. In a sense, this is a recapitulation of the idea raised earlier in this chapter, that women who commit serious violent crimes, and especially those who harm or kill children, are regarded 'doubly deviant', because they breach criminal laws and laws of nature that dictate the bounds of acceptable female behavior.

Indeed, Rose West's involvement in sexual violence and murder with husband Fred West demonstrated her failure to live up to the female maternal role that society presumes natural, but the apparent lack of maternal feeling was reinforced by the fact her victims included her own daughter and stepdaughter. Accordingly,

Penfold-Mounce (2009: 74) argues, 'she is the monstrous Other combined with the "Otherness" of women; she has double the allure of a typical male serial killer and so is a more prominent target for public disgust, fear and loathing'. Mediated images, often blurring reality and unreality, enable the formation and consumption of the well-known monstrous Other, and provide an important component in Kooistra's (1989) psychological explanation for the development of narratives about criminal celebrities, namely that they allow members of the public to live vicariously through celebrated criminality. We will continue this theme in the next chapter when we consider the public's fascination with understanding the psychology of serial killers, like Rosemary West, although, as we shall see, this is only one way of making sense of serial killing, which should also be analyzed by reference to the role the mass media plays in modern society, the emergence of consumer capitalism and rise of celebrity culture.

SUGGESTED FURTHER READING

To further explore some of the issues raised in this chapter regarding media representations of woman and female criminality see:

Chesney-Lind, M. (2007) 'Beyond bad girls: Feminist perspectives on female offending' in C. Sumner (ed.) *The Blackwell Companion to Criminology*. Malden, MA: Blackwell Publishing, pp. 255–267.

Lloyd, A. (1995) *Doubly Deviant, Doubly Damned: Society's Treatment of Deviant Women*. London: Penguin.

In his review of recent developments in cultural criminology, Hayward (2016: 306–307) responds to criticisms that it is fixated on prototypically masculine forms of transgression and ignores feminist criminologies by citing various feminist influences on cultural criminology, including feminist works within cultural criminology itself, such as: a four-chapter section on the construction of gender and crime in Ferrell and Websdale's (1999) collection, *Making Trouble* (i.e. Cavender 1999; Chesney-Lind 1999; Howe 1999; Wedsdale 1999); a section on sex and gender work in Ferrell and Hamm's (1998) *Ethnography at the Edge* (i.e. Kane 1998; Mattley 1998); and Cyndi Banks's (2000) monograph, *Developing Cultural Criminology*.

A more detail and expanded account of David Green's (2008a) study of child-on-child killing can be found in his book:

Green, D. A. (2008b) *When Children Kill Children: Penal Populism and Political Culture*. Oxford: Oxford University Press.

In the chapter listed below, Phil Scraton (2003: 21) examines the moral panic surrounding the James Bulger case, which, in accordance with the arguments made in this chapter and elsewhere (e.g. Chapter 3), he says is important for exemplifying the point that 'the moral panic [had] real consequences for social policy, law reform and professional intervention'.

Scraton, P. (2003) 'The demonization, exclusion and regulation of children: From moral panic to moral renewal' in A. Boran (ed.) *Crime: Fear or Fascination?* Chester: Chester Academic Press, pp. 9–39.

CHAPTER 7

Serial killers

INTRODUCTION

There has been a tendency in the scholarly literature to search for psychological and even biological explanations for serial killing. Often these accounts stress dysfunctional family background or childhood trauma as a cause of psychopathy leading to the type of predatory violence that is characteristic of serial killing. While these accounts produce fascinating case studies, as with other topics examined in this book, we are less interested in individualized explanations than with exploring the relationship between crime and media by reference to wider social and cultural contexts and structures. A key concern here, as it is throughout the book, relates to the observation of many that increasingly there is a blurring of the lines between factual and fictional depictions of crime and criminality, and that, in combination, those representations can tell us much about the nature of the society we live in.

In respect of serial murder, Alexandra Warwick (2006: 553) argues the obscuring of fiction and reality indicates '[t]he figure of the serial killer is being used in ways that go beyond entertainment and police work, having more to do with ways of understanding ourselves and modern society'. Similarly, it has been suggested the true crime case of Britain's most prolific serial killer, Dr Harold Shipman (see Box 7.4), resonated with the general public because 'Shipman embodied some of society's deepest fears of authority: of trust being abused and the vulnerable being preyed upon' (Penfold-Mounce 2009: 73). To be sure, while televised crime drama can act to allay people's fears about crime, providing what Sparks (1992a: 148–150) refers to as a positive *reassurance function* (see Chapter 4), as Penfold-Mounce (2009: 73) proposes, some crimes, such as those of Shipman, can be a source of 'twisted entertainment', resonating with 'negative emotions and topics' to become 'a form of perverted pleasure, founded upon gratification based on tension, fear, anxiety and revulsion'. Indeed, when we consider the case of Shipman later in this chapter we will see how despite lacking the modus operandi seen as emblematic of serial killing (i.e. not engaging in violence or sexual assault), media accounts nevertheless emphasized the centrality of transgression, reimagining Shipman's crimes so that they adhered to the dominant ideal of the serial killer.

In this chapter, then, we consider serial killing in the context of broader social, cultural as well as historical processes. We begin by picking up where we left off in the last chapter, looking at cases of female serial killing, including analyses that locate the root of psychopathic tendencies in serial killer biographies. Also considered here, and elsewhere in the chapter, is the idea that there is a symbiotic relationship between factual and fictional portrayals of serial killing. For example, serial killers have been known to revel in their own celebrity status and have sometimes emulated fictional serial killers. Moreover, we will see how the interests of crime-fiction writers, journalists and those involved in the 'business' of law enforcement (i.e. politicians, police, professional profilers) are entwined to such an extent that it has been argued a highly profitable 'serial killer industry' has developed, which taps into people's fears about this sort of crime (Soothill 1993: 341). These ideas tend to gainsay the view that serial killers are naturally bad or born evil, or indeed that their activities can be understood by examining individual pathology, biography or family history. Thus, instead of seeing the serial killer as a natural category, it is proposed the serial killer, as a criminal type, is essentially a discursive construct; that is, a product of social, cultural and historical processes.

This view is reinforced by Haggerty (2009: 176) who shows how prior to the 1970s, when police embraced the concept of the 'serial killer', this type of crime was known simply as 'stranger killing'. Jenkins (2002: 1) argues likewise that creating and perpetuating the figure of the serial killer – as a uniquely dangerous predatory villain – has served the interests and 'law and order' ambitions of conservative politicians, as well as agencies such as the Federal Bureau of Investigation (FBI), which sought to expand its jurisdiction in the late 1980s. Indeed, drawing on Jenkins, Valverde (2006) shows how, with the decline of communism, the FBI was an organization in crisis. That caused it to reinvent itself as a crime-fighting force, combating a new national threat in the shape of the serial killer: a new supralocal criminal type that 'seemed naturally to demand the expensive expertise that only a national high-tech institution with the latest crime-fighting weapons could provide' (Valverde 2006: 116). Hence, the FBI's Behavioral Sciences Unit was born, as featured (and glorified) in the film, *Silence of the Lambs*, and more recently popularized in the Netflix show, *Mindhunter* (Tallerico 2017).

It is important to note here that the FBI's invention of the serial killer also had a racial dimension. In profiling serial killers as white males, black serial killers have been absent in media portrayals, including those from American popular culture. Branson (2013: 1, 6) shows how the FBI's unquestioned ethnocentric profile of white serial killers has influenced media portrayals, which, while apt to show black males as low-level criminals, are seemingly reluctant to consider the notoriety and celebrity of black serial killers alongside their white counterparts, even though some 90 black serial killers have been identified in the US since 1945.

The idea of examining serial killing as a social and historical construct also enables Haggerty (2009: 170) to show how rather than being enigmatic and exceptional, serial killing reflects taken-for-granted and quite normal processes of modernization, such that, 'serial killing is patterned in modernity's own self-image'. Indeed, academic treatments of serial murderers often emphasize 'the terrifying normality of the murderer' (Jarvis 2007: 329), though these killers are seen 'as the dark doubles of the normals in society', and their behavior 'interpreted as an over-conformity of sorts to modernist and capitalist meta-narratives' (Force 2010: 330). Hence, the fact that many serial killers in both reality and fiction regard their activities as performing some kind of community service, by cleaning the streets and ridding society of disparaged groups, such as homosexuals and prostitutes, chimes with Enlightenment and modernist notions of progress and social betterment.

Similarly, as we shall see later in the chapter, because of his attempts to blend in by adhering to the conventions of normativity, and because he selects victims he believes deserve to die (in his case, confirmed murderers), fictional serial killer Dexter Morgan (Box 7.3) has been regarded 'as the ruthless embodiment of modernity' (Force 2010: 341). Moreover, like those maverick cops disillusioned with the corrupt and dysfunctional workings of the modern system of criminal justice that we considered in Chapter 5, Dexter is regarded a 'vigilante anti-hero', who, frustrated by a failed justice system, applies his own specific code of justice (Nurse 2012). As a law enforcement officer, however, he drifts in and out of delinquency, as David Matza (1964) might put it: accepting a moral obligation to be bound by the law and the norms of society, yet 'developing a special set of justifications for his behaviour which allows him to rationalize the violence that violates social norms' (Nurse 2012: 412).

While these accounts emphasize the ways serial killers and serial killing conforms, albeit in extremis, to the values and norms of modernity, Anthony King (2006) argues the serial killing self actually constitutes a postmodern inversion of the unified, stable and centered modern self (see also Biressi 2001: 193–194). To King, rather than reflecting modernity, the serial killing self reacts against the boredom, routine, control, regulation and anonymity characteristic of modern living. In this way, serial killing is a release from the mundanity and normalcy of everyday life, as exemplified in fictional depictions of Dexter, as well as Patrick Bateman, who is the protagonist in Bret Easton Ellis's (1991) novel, *American Psycho*. And this is also where, towards the end of the chapter, serial killing is linked to consumption and consumer culture, which, although a key feature of modern societies, has contributed to the emergence of a new kind of self quite distinct from the modern self: a postmodern consumer self, who, freed from the repressive routines of modern forms of institutionalization, is submerged in the immediate gratification and euphoria of consumptive acts. The serial killer, according to King, at least, represents an extreme version of this new kind of self, which is no longer a citizen subject to the disciplinary controls of the state, but a consumer beholden to multinational capitalism.

NATURAL BORN SERIAL KILLERS?

Given the last chapter was mostly about female criminality, it is perhaps apposite we begin this chapter by considering why women may murder sequentially. Statistically, female serial killers (and killers, in general, for that matter) are far less numerous than male serial killers. Moreover, as Hale and Bolin (1998) point out, women who commit multicide have tended not to figure in accounts of serial killing because they tend not conform to the stranger-on-stranger dynamic, which is contained in the conventional definition of a serial killer as 'someone who has killed three or more people who were previously unknown to him [sic]' (Haggerty 2009: 169). Instead, they are likely to target 'latent victims' (i.e. people unable to defend themselves, or who have limited ability to defend themselves, such as children, the old or sick), and people with whom they are familiar or intimate with, including their own children, spouses or, in the case of nurses, their patients (Hale and Bolin 1998: 42; see also Holmes et al. 1998b: 62).

Indeed, research on female murderers concentrates overwhelmingly on crimes motivated by 'justified homicide' or repeated victimization, which are crimes perpetrated by those experiencing 'battered woman syndrome'. Arrigo and Griffin (2004) redress this by examining the case of Aileen Wuornos: a woman who between 1989 and 1990 killed seven men, and was executed at Broward Correctional Institution, Pembroke Pines, Florida, on 9 October 2002. Sometimes referred to as 'the first predatory female serial killer' (Arrigo and Griffin 2004: 383), Wuornos's modus operandi was to linger on a Florida highway until someone would stop and offer to give her a lift:

> While in the car, Aileen would openly admit that she was a prostitute and that she needed help making money. Alcohol, marijuana, and other stimulants were frequently used during these exchanges. While the victim parked the car in a secluded area, Aileen would peel off her clothes and discuss prices. Some hugging and kissing occurred until Aileen encouraged her companions to undress. Then, while these men took off their clothes, Aileen exited the car's passenger side, taking her belongings with her. When the victims sensed danger, Aileen would shoot and kill them.
>
> (Arrigo and Griffin 2004: 386)

One justification she would provide for the murders was that she was trying to protect herself from being raped, and, indeed, prior to killing her victims she would typically scream at them: 'I knew you were going to rape me!' (Arrigo and Griffin 2004: 386). Arrigo and Griffin (2004: 389) show how Wuornos characterized each of these men as evil rapists who deserved to be killed. Accordingly, she showed no emotion in the acts of killing, nor remorse or guilt after the murders, which were 'rational, planned and goal directed' (Arrigo and Griffin 2004: 389); her victims 'ragefully devalued' objects (Meloy 1992: 232). As we will discover, like other serial killers, Wuornos was fascinated with fame, comparing herself and homosexual partner, Tyria Moore, to Bonnie and Clyde, and saying one day a book would be written about her. Indeed, soon after her execution, the movie *Monster* (2003) was released, chronicling Wuornos' story from childhood to her first conviction for murder.

Wuornos also said she would be 'doing society a favour' (Arrigo and Griffin 2004: 385). As we shall see, the self-perception of providing a community service by ridding society of its detritus is not unusual among 'mission-oriented' or 'visionary' serial killers, including female serialists like Priscilla Ford, who heard the voice of God telling her to 'kill people she crossed on the street because they were "bad people" and deserved to die' (Holmes et al. 1998b: 66). Likewise, the fascination with fame, notoriety and media attention is not uncommon. To be sure, Arrigo and Griffin (2004: 382) say that if it benefits from media attention, predatory violence receiving public fascination and instilling fear will only serve to reinforce the psychopathic offender's view of themself as omnipotent, and, in some cases, 'psychopathic individuals may believe that being mythologized in the media is their only opportunity to achieve notoriety'.

Arrigo and Griffin's study aims at uncovering the psychological roots of Wuornos's serial killing with recourse to attachment theory and research on psychopathy, although they do not discount the possibility that Wuornos may have 'beg[u]n with a biological predisposition for psychopathy' (Arrigo and Griffin 2004: 389), because her 'fits of rage . . . reflect those of her biological father' (Arrigo and Griffin 2004: 387). However, their analysis has far more to do with attempting to explain Wuornos's predatory aggression as a direct result of environmental factors and, in particular, her childhood experiences of abuse, abandonment and isolation, which led in adulthood to coping mechanisms that 'included prostitution, alcohol abuse, violence, and crime, resulting in material gain' (Arrigo and Griffin 2004: 388).

Although experts say we may never know or understand the exact motivation behind serial killing (Holmes et al. 1998a: 121), the quest to 'get inside the mind of the serial killer', to search for the psychological or even physiological/biological causes of serial killing, is nevertheless a source of great intrigue for scholars and students alike. Often this search will be guided by a desire to develop an understanding of the dynamics of serial killers' behavior to arrive at early diagnoses and identification of 'warnings signs' so as to prevent psychopathy leading to predatory homicide, as well as provide possibilities for rehabilitation (Arrigo and Griffin 2004: 390; Holmes et al. 1998a: 121). Sometimes too serial killers themselves have provided insights, including thoughts on inner turmoil:

> deep inside of himself, each serial killer does have an acknowledged awareness of the fact that his future victims are innocent beings deserving nothing of his wrath. Yet to admit this fact directly, he would also have to openly admit that he – and the violence he intends to inflict – is altogether unjust and wrong.

> And, for a man grown accustomed to the goodness and the pleasure it provides, any such admission of actual wrong is intolerable. Not only intolerable, but impossible.
>
> (Anonymous 1998: 129)

Arguably, one problem with psychological explanations is that they cannot account for the behavior of people who, seemingly like many serial killers, experience neglect, abuse and abandonment in childhood, but unlike those killers do not go on to murder sequentially. Having said that, Arrigo and Griffin (2004: 380) provide some insight here, noting the abundance of research correlating psychopathy and serious crimes other than serial killing, including Gaconò's (2000: xix) observation that 'psychopaths . . . are involved in many of today's most serious problems: war, drugs, murder, and political corruption'.

The location of psychopathic tendencies in early childhood trauma is a clearly discernible theme running through many accounts of serial killers, including those in fiction, such as Dexter Morgan who in the eponymously named television series, *Dexter*, is orphaned at a young age after witnessing a massacre in which his mother was killed, only to be discovered days later in a blood-filled crime scene with his mother's corpse (Force 2010: 329). However, rather than focus on the psychological cause of Dexter's predilection to kill sequentially, William Ryan Force (2010) uses Dexter's attempt to be 'normal' and blend in as a means to understand the ways 'normal' and mundane identities are achieved, performed and managed by each and every one of us on a daily basis. Similarly, in this chapter, as with the book in general, we are inclined to explore sociological and cultural accounts of serial killing, which highlight, among other things, the relationship between serial killers and media representations of them and their crimes. Therefore, we are not so much interested in whether serial killers are born or made bad, than with understanding and interpreting the various meanings that may be attributed to serial killers and serial killing in media portrayals, which increasingly involve the blurring of reality and fiction.

Indeed, that very point is made by Warwick (2006) who reports on the slippage of fictional and factual representations of serial killers and serial killing. One reason, she says, the boundary between the real and imagined is not secure is because of the vested interests of those involved in the 'business of law enforcement', including professional profilers, police, politicians, journalists and crime-fiction writers (Warwick 2006: 556). As Jenkins (1994: 81) writes, 'it is difficult to know whether the bureaucratic law enforcement attitudes toward serial murder preceded or followed changes in popular culture'; moreover, 'the investigative priorities of bureaucratic agencies are formed by public and legislative expectations, which are derived from popular culture and the news media' (Jenkins 1994: 223).

To illustrate the symbiotic relationship between factual and fictional portrayals of serial killing, Warwick quotes Simpson (2000: 79), who says, criminal profiling 'fits within a long literary and cultural tradition', and that 'the ontology of the entire hyperrational profiling process as canonized by the Federal Bureau of

Investigation lies in detective fiction'. Moreover, Simpson notes, 'their "veneration" of 19th century detective fiction, and indeed, books by British and American profilers are threaded with literary references' (Warwick 2006: 555). Serial killers also read biographies and other accounts of those preceding them, as well as fiction, academic psychology and criminology. Warwick (2006: 556–557) cites the example of British serial murderer, Colin Ireland, who during his time in solitary confinement wrote:

> I decided it would be fun to carry out something I labelled 'reinforcing the stereotype'. I had my radio with me . . . on hearing [the staff] I would leap up and change the station to a classical one. I would be on my bed before the door opened, my book or paper open, and as the door opened I would glance in a superior fashion around the edge of the reading material. 'Yes, officers?' I would enquire in my best Hannibal Lecter cold, distant, but polite tone.
>
> (Gekoski 1998: 9)

The idea that there is a 'looping effect' at work here is present in the work of Seltzer (1998: 107), who describes the way '[t]he killer's experience of his own identity is directly absorbed in an identification with the personality type called "the serial killer": absorbed in the case-likeness of his own case'. A further idea is that fiction may be more realistic than reality, which is conveyed by Holmes and Holmes (1998a: vii) when they say, '[s]ome works of fiction, such as Thomas Harris' *Red Dragon* and *The Silence of the Lambs* are often more realistic – and more accurate – than true-crime books'.

While fear and indeed intrigue about serial killers generates large profits in the culture industry, politicians and government agencies can also draw on those sentiments to pursue punitive 'law and order' initiatives in ways similar to those set out in other parts of the book when we have considered the productivity/legacies of moral panics (Chapter 3) and fear of crime research (Chapter 4). In this way, professional profilers and politicians have shared an investment in creating and perpetuating the figure of the serial killer, which, as Jenkins (2002: 1) shows, fulfilled a distinct purpose in the US at least, with the FBI wanting to expand its jurisdiction, and conservative politicians feeling it 'rhetorically and politically necessary during the early 1980s to posit the existence of uniquely dangerous predatory villains, against whom no counter-measures were too strong'.

Indeed, this goes to Warwick's (2006: 554) argument that the figure of the serial killer is in fact a social construction; it is not a natural category but instead 'a discursive construct through which certain acts are made intelligible and meaningful to us' (Cameron 1994: 151). Moreover, while that construct may have served very particular interests, such as those relating to offender profiling and law enforcement, its invention is not singularly deliberate, but the result of 'a complex process of accumulation of ideas and representations' (Warwick 2006: 554). To Warwick, the Whitechapel murders in Victorian England mark the origin of serial killing, and Jack the Ripper – the figure regarded as responsible for the murders – was the first example of this criminal type. The idea of serial killing as a social or discursive construct is also evident in this example:

> we can say that the Whitechapel murderer and Jack the Ripper are two distinct entities. The Whitechapel murderer is simply the person who committed the crimes, whereas Jack the Ripper is the title of a far more complicated accretion: the discursive construct arising from those killings.
>
> (Warwick 2006: 554)

Although this distinction might hold true only because the perpetrator was never caught, Warwick (2006: 566) argues the legacy of the Whitechapel murders and Jack the Ripper nevertheless 'have contributed a mythical origin to a constructed identity – "the serial killer", and that identity goes forward, supported by an increasing panoply of descriptive material'. Accordingly, the original type has been divided and sub-divided whereby 'killers are categorized as organized, disorganized, assertive, reassuring, commuters, marauders, missionaries, hunters, each with their particular features' (Warwick 2006: 566). However, far from illuminating the common characteristics of the serial killer, these attempts at classification suggest no such species exists:

> What appears instead is a highly variegated collection of very different crimes and perpetrators spilled across fiction and documentary. What holds them together is not coherence but confusion, the confusion of the inside and the outside, of person and place, that is enacted in all representations of serial murder, whether forensic, factual or fictional.
>
> (Warwick 2006: 566)

Another important legacy of Jack the Ripper is that, even though he was not by any means the first serial killer, he can be seen as the inaugurator of a particular form of modern identity, in that he provides a means of understanding the peculiarly modern experience of living in industrialized urban spaces, with their densely populated streets, which enabled his escape and invisibility. He is thus regarded 'as the inevitable product of urban anonymity, a figure of the brutalized working-class mass and as the technologized "killing machine" that is a logical outcome of industrialization' (Warwick 2006: 560).

More specifically, it is argued the Whitechapel murders ushered in a modern age of sex crime. In accordance with Foucault's (1976/1990) assertions, sexuality becomes a core element of people's identity and their experiences in modern societies, whereby sexual acts are not simply acts carried out by a person, but are fundamental aspects of personality. In this context, the serial killer is not merely a murderer of strangers, since 'sexuality is somehow and often indefinably implicated in the killing' (Warwick 2006: 558). And, according to Warwick (2006: 558), that 'linkage of sexuality and murder in the figure of Jack the Ripper has proved to be one of the most persistent and complex of the legacies of 1888'.

MODERN SERIAL KILLERS

Although he does not make the express connection between sexuality, serial killing and modernity in the way Warwick does, Kevin Haggerty's (2009) work on serial killers similarly posits that the phenomenon of serial killing must be seen within the context of modernizing processes. This view of serial killers stands in stark contrast to other themes in the literature, which tend to downplay the sociological origins of serial killing (see also Soothill 2001; Soothill and Wilson 2005). Accordingly, as noted earlier, the literature on serial homicide has been dominated by a search for the cause or etiology of such behavior, where the focus is on the pathological characteristics of serial killers, or socio-psychological factors, or the biography of particular offenders, such as dysfunctional family background. By arguing that serial killing is a distinctively modern phenomenon, Haggerty is critical of theories that focus on the individual and pathologized etiology of serial killing, since, he says, such accounts ignore the broader social, cultural and historical context in which serial killers operate:

> Serial killing is contextual, and any biological predispositions, individual desires or personal pathologies that might play a role in motivating killers or shaping their actions are conditioned by larger structural factors. Most of the characteristic attributes related to the dynamics of serial killing are unique to modern societies.
>
> (Haggerty 2009: 171)

What Haggerty is articulating in this statement is a version of the structure-agency dilemma, which is a key idea in sociological theory. The issue here is whether, and to what extent, people are able to act of their own free will and make decisions independently of broader social structures, such as socio-economic class, gender or race. French sociologist Emile Durkheim (1897/1970) sought to provide some answers to this problem in his study of suicide, where he set out to explain the social origins of that most individual of all acts. Durkheim's argument, like Haggerty's, was that suicide could be explained by reference to what he called 'social facts', which, for his purposes, were statistics on suicide rates. Using those data, Durkheim showed how certain types of suicide may be the result of sociological factors (i.e. degrees of social integration and social regulation), and could not therefore be explained exclusively with recourse to individual psychology. Looking at different suicide rates by religion, for instance, Durkheim showed how because Protestants tend to be free thinkers, or, as he put, '[t]he Protestant is far more the author of his faith' (Durkheim 1897/1970: 158), they are more likely to commit *egoistic suicide* than Catholics on account of Protestantism 'being a less strongly integrated church than the Catholic Church' (Durkheim 1897/1970: 159).

Likewise, Haggerty is interested in discovering the social origins of individual acts of serial killing, arguing there are six factors or preconditions that can explain serial killing as a distinctively modern phenomenon. First, there is the existence in modern societies of the *mass media and attendant rise of a celebrity culture*. Serial killing, says Haggerty, is predominantly a media event. And, while it is statistically the rarest form of crime, it is nevertheless a staple in true crime and popular fiction. However, there is not a simple 'media effect' at play here, whereby people become serial killers because they are exposed to violent television (see Chapter 1). Indeed, some serial killers use the media to communicate with the public and taunt the police, while some collect newspaper clippings of their crimes, which, according to Dietz (1996: 11), help them 'complete an identity transformation in the same way that reading their press does for athletes and entertainers'.

In short, Haggerty (2009: 175, original emphasis) says, 'whereas in pre-modern societies killing sequentially might have been something that someone *did*, today a serial killer is something that someone can *be*'. Thus, in pre-modern times those who killed sequentially largely worked in the dark when creating an identity based on killing others, while the enduring media prominence of serial killers in modern societies means, '[t]roubled individuals now have readily at hand a host of serial killer exemplars as a point of reference that would have been unavailable prior to the development of the mass media' (Haggerty 2009: 175). Moreover, the mass media fosters a culture of celebrity, which 'promises to liberate people from a powerless anonymity and make them known beyond the limitations of class and family . . . fame also offers citizens the prospect of surviving beyond death' (Haggerty 2009: 174).

Reveling in his celebrity, Ted Bundy basked in the media's fascination with his crimes, and maintained constant contact with the global press even after the judge sought to limit that contact. John Wayne Gacy also 'took pride in his sinister celebrity, bragging that he had been the subject of 11 hardback books, 31 paperbacks, two screenplays, one movie [Figure 7.1], one off-Broadway play, five

Figure 7.1 Brian Dennehy as John Wayne Gacy in *To Catch a Killer*, 1992

songs, and over 5,000 articles' (Schechter 2003: 198). Thus, to reiterate a point made earlier, and one that is made throughout this book, there is no straightforward media effect at work here. Rather, there is a symbiotic relationship that seems to exist between the media and serial killers, that is, a relationship of mutual benefit or advantage.

BOX 7.1 WHO WAS TREVOR JOSEPH HARDY?

While they do not wish to contradict Haggerty's claims about the relationship between serial killing and modernity, and the crucial role played by the mass media in that relationship, Wilson et al. (2010: 165) argue, 'this relationship might be more complex and is dependent on a range of case-specific variables that might, or might not, engender the circumstances which would allow any particular serial killer to have "newsworthiness" and thus become "prime time" '. To that end, they consider the case of British serial killer, Trevor Joseph Hardy – who killed three women in Manchester, England between 1974 and 1976 – as a counterexample to the view that serial killers are inherently newsworthy, and that the rise of mass media has turned serial killing into a 'media event'. To all intents and purposes, the Hardy case 'had all the hallmarks of a "newsworthy" crime – a serial killer who preyed on young women' (Wilson et al. 2010: 156). Indeed, even the four Manchester-based journalists Wilson et al. (2010: 160) interview, 'expressed disbelief at the limited amount of reporting of these events and were surprised that the Hardy case was not well known'. Why then did the case disappear from public view?

First, and most saliently, was the issue of time scale: Hardy was not identified publicly as a serial killer prior to his trial, which precluded any build-up of publicity. Probably in an effort to avoid fear and panic in the area, police ruled out any link between the murders, with one officer even claiming that it 'looks like a one-off job' (Wilson et al. 2010: 163). Furthermore, 'by the time the murders did come to be linked, the case was sub judice, and strict reporting restrictions were implemented', since '[a]ny careless reporting could be deemed to prejudice a jury and lead to the trial being ruled unsafe' (Wilson et al. 2010: 163). Secondly, there was the issue of the north/south divide, which meant the case received very little coverage in the south as compared to the north of England. Location was also a factor in the third theme identified by Wilson et al. (2010: 165), who say, perhaps because the murders occurred in an area of low socio-economic status, where violence would have been regarded unexceptional, it 'was thus of less interest to the police, and thereafter, to the media'.

Fourthly, the fact that Hardy had no clear motive may have contributed to the underreporting of the case. Fifthly, unlike many other serial killers, Hardy was not given a catchy nickname to ignite the public's imagination. Sixthly, if Hardy's girlfriend, who provided him with a false alibi, had given her version of events, that would have increased media exposure of the case, as the presence of a female accomplice did earlier with the Moors murders, where Myra Hindley was the accomplice to Ian Brady, and later the Soham murders, where Maxine Carr provided boyfriend, Ian Huntley, with an alibi (see Chapter 6). Here the analysis of Wilson et al. is similar to Berrington and Honkatukia's (2002) study, discussed in Chapter 6, which considers the principal reason the Sanna Sillanpää case will be forgotten is because it lacked demonization in the press and iconography of 'evil womanhood', both of which have made cases like Hindley and Rosemary West intrinsically newsworthy and memorable.

The second precondition for serial killing that is distinctly modern is the existence of a *society of strangers*. The rise of urbanization and mass migration established the interpersonal context for the emergence of serial killers, and especially the social anonymity upon which they rely. Hence, '[d]ense urban environments represent ideal settings for the routinized impersonal encounters that are the hallmark of serial killing' (Haggerty 2009: 176). Indeed, a defining attribute of serial killers is that they prey on strangers, such that, '[p]rior to embracing the phrase "serial killers" in the 1970s, the police categorized such behaviors as "stranger killing"' (Haggerty 2009: 176).

In pre-modern times, by contrast, individuals typically lived in a local environment where they encountered approximately 100 people throughout their entire lives (Braudy 1986), they knew each other by name 'and often had deep subjective knowledge of their neighbor's family history and personal predilections' (Haggerty 2009: 175). Hence, Haggerty's argument is that modern notions of privacy also function to shield the activities of serial killers. For instance, neighbors will often justify their failure to investigate suspicious behavior, smells and so on by appealing to their own as well as their neighbor's 'right to privacy'. Indeed, Haggerty's arguments about how the operation of privacy might mask the activities of serial killers has been applied to the case of Josef Fritzl, the 73-year-old man from the small Austrian town of Amstetten who, it was discovered in 2008, had imprisoned his daughter in a cellar under his family home for 24 years, subjecting her to abuse of various kinds and fathering her seven children. Martin and Scott Bray (2015: 261–262) show how Austria's preoccupation with privacy and culture of secrecy, which have their roots in the Nazi-era when neighbors turned a blind eye to collaboration, fraternization and compromise, might explain how and why Fritzl was able to get away with his crimes for so long.

The third modern precondition for serial killing is the emergence of a *mean/ends rationality that is largely divorced from value considerations*. The dispassionate style of rational thought that ideally characterizes scientific modes of thinking associated with the Enlightenment from the eighteenth century, also characterizes how serial killers approach their actions. The rationalistic (means/ends) framework associated with modernity is reproduced by serial killers, who use rational strategizing to plan killings, which can be one of the most integral (and pleasurable) aspects of the crimes, e.g. orchestrating abduction, torture, disposal, sexual fantasies. Moreover, serial killers tend to *instrumentalize social relationships*, treating individuals as means towards personal ends:

> Victims, for them, are reduced to a means towards a particular end – typically a means to fulfill a psychic desire for control and self-aggrandization. Their

> victims are only valued to the extent that they fulfill such purposes. Moral and emotional considerations are typically evacuated, allowing them to torture and kill others without considering the human dimensions of their actions.
>
> (Haggerty 2009: 178)

The instrumentalization of relationships leads, in turn, to narcissism (i.e. a fixation on and love of one's self), and it is, according to Haggerty (2009: 179), '[t]he self-absorption and lack of empathy displayed by serial killers [that] is the most stark manifestation of this modern psychic orientation'. We saw many of these traits in the example of Aileen Wuornos, discussed earlier, who became fascinated with her own fame and notoriety, who showed no emotion in carrying out murders that were, 'rational, planned and goal directed' (Arrigo and Griffin 2004: 389), and whose victims were 'ragefully devalued' objects (Meloy 1992: 232), evil rapists, deserving to die.

This goes to Haggerty's fourth precondition for serial killing, namely the existence of *cultural frameworks of denigration, which tend to implicitly single out some groups for greater predation.* Even if they appear so, serial killings are not random and victimhood not haphazard. Modern societies have fairly consistent markers of symbolic denigration evident in 'devalued populations' and 'disposable classes', such as the poor, homeless, homosexuals, women and ethnic minorities. Victims of serial killers, including female killers (Hale and Bolin 1998: 38), tend to be drawn disproportionately from these essentially powerless groups. However, rather than determine the classes of people serial killers tend to kill, it is easier (and arguably more revealing) to consider who they do *not* kill, namely wealthy Caucasian heterosexual males, which, says Haggerty (2009: 180), are 'the esteemed benchmark in western societies'. Accordingly, such a victimization pattern indicates serial killers embrace and reproduce wider cultural codes and markers in respect of stigmatized and marginalized groups. Little wonder, states Haggerty (2009: 180, quoting Holmes and DeBurger 1998: 12), 'that a serial killer responsible for the murder of a procession of female prostitutes "verbalized a sense of pride because of rendering the community such a great service"'.

A fifth and related precondition for serial killing is the existence of *particular opportunity structures for victimization.* Women comprise 60 percent of serial killers' victims, which is partly due to them assuming a place in the public sphere (a result of feminist advances) meaning they are now also more frequent targets for public forms of victimization, including serial killing. Accordingly, the relative accessibility of female street prostitutes helps explain why they constitute a large proportion of victims of serial killers. One estimate indicates 'that of all the prostitutes murdered in the United States, an astounding 35 per cent were killed by "serial perpetrators of prostitute homicide"' (Haggerty 2009: 181, quoting Brewer et al. 2006: 1106).

According to Wiest (2016: 338) this 'points to the cultural meanings associated with social status and occupational prestige'. In a US newspaper article about a case of serial murder that took years to uncover, largely because the victims were prostitutes, she quotes a female sex worker as saying, '[i]f it was in the better neighbourhoods, you could be sure somebody would be asking questions. But it was here, so nobody cared' (Wiest 2016: 338). As this case indicates, and is also revealed by Wilson et al. (2010: 165), when they explain lack of police and media interest in the Hardy case partly by reference to the economically deprived area where the killings occurred, members of dispossessed classes and devalued groups are also outside the system of 'effective guardianship' (e.g. police investigation and concern), which reduces the likelihood their victimization will be detected:

> A prominent Canadian case provides a telling example of this tendency. Starting in the 1990s women began to disappear from Vancouver's Downtown Eastside. It was only after more than 60 women had gone missing and in the face of intense pressure from the local community that the police began to seriously investigate these disappearances.
>
> (Haggerty 2009: 181–182)

The sixth and final precondition for serial killing that is quintessentially modern is the idea that *society can be engineered*. Earlier we saw how the victims of serial killers are drawn disproportionately from modernity's devalued populations, and that serial killers therefore see themselves as performing a community service by ridding the world of people they tend often to characterize as vermin, insects or as a plague on society (Haggerty 2009: 179). This connects to the idea of progress that is integral to Enlightenment and modernist thinking, and to which serial killers frequently subscribe, expressing utopian progressive ambitions and the uniquely modern ideals of social betterment or improvement (see Box 7.2).

BOX 7.2 *TAXI DRIVER* – A 'VISIONARY' KILLER

Ideas about exterminating modern society's devalued populations as a means of engineering social progress figure in the Martin Scorsese movie, *Taxi Driver*, where the protagonist, Travis Bickle (played by Robert De Niro) expresses precisely this sentiment when, prior to going on the rampage, he diarizes his disgust at New York City and some of its less savory inhabitants:

> May 10th. Thank God for the rain which has helped wash away the garbage and trash off the sidewalks. I'm workin' long hours now, six in the afternoon to six in the morning. Sometimes even eight in the morning, six days a week. Sometimes seven days a week. It's a long hustle but it keeps me real busy. I can take in three, three fifty a week. Sometimes even more when I do it off the meter. All the animals come out at night – whores, skunk pussies, buggers, queens, fairies, dopers, junkies, sick, venal. Someday a real rain will come and wash all this scum off the streets.

© AF archive/Alamy Stock Photo

Figure 7.2 Robert De Niro as Travis Bickle in the 1976 movie *Taxi Driver*

As a sub-category of serial killers, 'mission-oriented' killers see it their calling to rid society of particular types of people, where 'the murder of members of the disposable classes is explicitly connected with progressive social objectives' (Haggerty 2009: 183). That is why many serial killers, like Travis Bickle in *Taxi Driver* (Box 7.2), liken their activities to cleaning the streets of rubbish:

> Expressions of these ambitions can be found throughout the literature, and in a single textbook Egger (2002) documents numerous instances. Russian serial

> killer, Ilshat Susikov, for example, claimed that 'I am a nurse of society. I am cleaning up all the rubbish. At work, I swept streets. Now I'm cleaning up a different kind of rubbish' (p. 15). Yorkshire Ripper, Peter Sutcliffe, reproduces this sentiment almost exactly when he noted that 'I were just cleaning up the streets' (p. 83). Charles Sobhraj, who killed at least eight travelers on the drug trails running through Thailand, Turkey, and India also called his acts 'cleaning'. After his capture John Wayne Gacy suggested that he was just ridding the world of some bad kids and that 'all the police are going to get me for is running a funeral parlor without a license' (p. 120).
>
> (Haggerty 2009: 183)

These 'visionary' killers, then, self-consciously kill people on behalf of 'society'. Indeed, the notion of doing acts in the service of some greater social good, and actions being in the service of 'society', are themselves distinctively modern notions that would have been inconceivable in pre-modern times, where allegiances were to family, clan or village and not to some amorphous idea of 'society' (itself a concept that only arrived in Europe during the formation of modernity from the eighteenth century).

BOX 7.3 *DEXTER* – PORTRAIT OF AN EXCEPTIONALLY 'NORMAL' SERIAL KILLER

William Ryan Force's (2010) analysis of fictional serial killer, Dexter Morgan, in the US television series, *Dexter*, has some similarities with the work of both Warwick and Haggerty. Like Warwick, Force shows how Dexter's identity is socially constructed. Dexter learns a very regimented set of principles or codes from his adopted father, Harry, to which he must adhere to blend in (not stand out), and appear as a 'normal' guy. Force draws on the ethnomethodology of Harold Garfinkel (1967) and interactionist sociology of Erving Goffman (1959, 1963) to reveal the identity work involved in Dexter's efforts to present as a 'normal', and therefore hide his dark, sinister inside, which, as is common in serial killer narratives, Dexter himself sees as emotionally 'empty' or 'hollow' (Force 2010: 334). In this way, Force argues, Dexter is a 'practical sociologist' because he 'reveals the social order's constructedness by demonstrating its mundane accomplishment' (Force 2010: 333), which encourages 'us to recognize the concerted efforts human actors undertake to arrive at what would be socially regarded as a mundane, unexceptional person' (Force 2010: 343).

Accordingly, people do not acquire normative scripts intuitively, rather 'hegemonic identity incitements are merely so ubiquitous and diffuse they appear to be effortless' (Force 2010: 340). Force's analysis of Dexter's performance of normativity thus reveals the technologies people employ in 'doing' normal. Key in identity management of this sort is the *adoption of markers of unmarkedness*, which, for social deviants, like Dexter, means the 'accumulation and appropriate display of mundane auxiliary characteristics becomes a primary technology for presenting a normal person' (Force 2010: 340). Hence, 'Dexter purposefully communicates normativity by incorporating the presentation of several auxiliary traits that render one mundane: markers of heterosexuality (Rita [his blonde, white auxiliary marker girlfriend]), niceness or decency (smiling), and law abidingness (job with Miami PD)' (Force 2010: 340). While having a job in law enforcement is probably his most brilliant auxiliary characteristic:

> Niceness, politeness, and decency are communicated interactively in a variety of ways: making a 'Thank You' card for a blood transfusion as a young boy, forcing a smile in photos, playing well with children, performing household chores at Rita's home, maintaining a close relationship with his sister, making small talk with and knowing all his coworkers' names, and bringing donuts to work.
>
> (Force 2010: 341)

Like Haggerty, Force (2010: 341) argues 'Dexter can be viewed as the ruthless embodiment of modernity and its adherence to conventions of normativity', part of which involves the *instrumentalization of social relationships*, evident for instance in his adoption of auxiliary characteristics that will enable him to pass as a normal, regular guy. Choosing prey from disparaged groups is also part of this whereby 'he must confirm his victims "deserve" it by being lawless killers themselves' (Force 2010: 336). Accordingly, Dexter fits the profile of a 'mission-oriented' or 'visionary' killer whose killing of dispensable classes connects to modern notions of social progress and the idea that the killing provides a social service. However, Force's analysis diverges from Haggerty's in his choice not to treat Dexter 'as a synecdoche for the social order or some unsavory aspect of it', but instead to see him as 'simply useful in revealing the mundanity of reproducing that order' (Force 2010: 333).

SERIAL KILLING AND THE POSTMODERN SELF

While Haggerty is interested in looking at modernity as creating the conditions for the emergence of serial killing, Anthony King (2006) considers the serial killing self as a reaction *against* those conditions. Hence, Haggerty is looking at the phenomenon of serial killing as *modern*, whereas King is looking at the serial killing self as *postmodern*. In order to determine whether there is such a thing as a postmodern self, King first considers the 'civilizing processes' – detailed by people like Freud (1949, 1961, 2001) and Elias (1982, 1987) – that have contributed to the formation of the modern self. Essentially, these historical processes have resulted in the suppression of individual internal drives and desires by wider social, political and cultural structures:

> As the modern state monopolized violence and colonized lifeworlds, individuals simultaneously developed internal mechanisms of self-control and discipline. Sexuality and violence, in particular, were repressed and controlled.

> Through its internalization of norms and routines, the modern self was constituted as a unified, centred and rational entity.
>
> King (2006: 110)

King (2006: 110) notes that, over the past few decades, social scientists have attempted to understand the emergence of a new kind of self, where the self is regarded as a reflexive project, which, unlike the modern self, 'is no longer the mechanical product of its background but an agent who is capable of reconstituting itself through a diversity of cultural expressions'. And it is in this context that he hopes his 'analysis of serial killing may be able to offer some provisional accounts of the self and its mutation in contemporary society' (King 2006: 112). Accordingly, he argues the personality complex of serial killers is almost an inversion of the modern self whereby the killer murders '[t]o overcome the institutionalized anonymity of rationalized society', and where '[v]iolence is not a means of cleansing the self but a desirable end in itself' (King 2006: 112).

The perspective of cultural criminology, which we looked at in Chapter 2, is of relevance here because, on this reading, serial killing is considered a form of transgression, edgework or thrill-seeking in the face of the boredom and monotony people experience in everyday life. King's example of the fictional serial killer, Hannibal Lecter, in the book by Thomas Harris (1997), and subsequent movie, *The Silence of Lambs*, illustrates this point, showing also how the release through violence that is central to the serial killing self is quite different from the repressed core of the modern self:

> Lecter's true identity is realized in these moments of transgression. Lecter's self is not the product of a unifying super-ego and ego whereby the external controls of the state are internalized. On the contrary, Lecter struggles against the institutionalization which threatens him with anonymity, with a mass in his own person. His self is formed through ecstatic moments of violence in which he penetrates the bodies of others. Only then is he able to assert his autonomous selfhood, constantly denied and repressed by the disciplinary institutions of the state.
>
> (King 2006: 115)

King also illustrates his point about sexual and violent (ecstatic) transgression being hallmarks of serial killers by reference to Bret Easton Ellis's (1991) novel, *American Psycho*. Similar to the movie, *Fight Club*, which, as we saw in Chapter 2, ends up 'reproducing the very problems [it] attempts to address' (Giroux 2000: 38), the message of *American Psycho* is ambiguous. Hence, although like *Fight Club*, it 'is intended as a critical commentary on multinational consumer capitalism', which it does via 'the autobiography of a "yuppie" serial killer, Patrick Bateman . . . it is uncertain whether Easton Ellis's satire is successful since the text descends into misogynist and pornographic fantasies' (King 2006: 116). Nevertheless, as with the portrayal of Lecter's crimes in *The Silence of the Lambs*, King (2006: 116) argues, 'the extreme descriptions of sexual violence which punctuate the novel do highlight a distinctive self'. Hence, during transgressive climaxes, Bateman loses control, and 'is no longer a ego but has submitted himself to his drives which flood out to mix with others' (King 2006: 116). Moreover, 'away from these moments of ecstasy, Easton Ellis stresses the stultification of Bateman's shallow existence; in normal life, the mass threatens Bateman with boredom and anonymity' (King 2006: 116). So, to King, serial killers represent the modern self unleashed; breaking free from the routines and repression of modern forms of institutionalization:

> the serial killing self is in stark contrast to the modern self centred through disciplinary routine. With the serial killer, the mass in the self is ironically extirpated only by transgression when the individual transcends the institutional controls of the state. Unlike the modern self, serial killers cannot be sustained by repressing their internal drives. On the contrary, institutional identification and psychic repression threaten the very individuality of the killer.
>
> (King 2006: 116)

BOX 7.4 THE PUZZLE OF HAROLD SHIPMAN

The view presented by King (2006) of the serial killing self as constituting an inversion of the modern self is challenged by the case of Harold Shipman (Figure 7.3), who, in accordance with Haggerty's analysis, appears to be a distinctively modern serial killer. Shipman was a doctor working in Greater Manchester, who is believed to have killed as many as 260 of his mainly elderly female patients from 1974, when he started general practice in

Figure 7.3 Police handout photograph of Dr Harold Shipman

Todmorden – a West Yorkshire market town whose name, ironically, is reputed to derive from two words for death: *tod* and *mor* (as in *mort*), meaning 'death-death-wood' (Hughes 2006: 6). He was eventually arrested in 1998 after being caught in a bungled attempt to forge the will of his last victim. Indeed, so poorly was the will drafted that some suggested Shipman wanted to be caught (Soothill and Wilson 2005: 688). Others claim amending the wills of victims meant Shipman had a financial motive for his killings, indicating he lacked certain important characteristics, which have become emblematic of serial killing:

> By amending the wills of some of his victims, he gained some extrinsic material reward from his activities. More particularly, although Shipman seems to have gained some gratification from the power of life and death which he exercised over his victims, he engaged in no violence and there was never any sexual dimension to his activities. Shipman never engaged in mutilation and sexual abuse which has become a critical motif for serial killers.
>
> (King 2006: 114)

Moreover, as with Haggerty's theory about serial killers targeting devalued groups, it has been observed, 'Shipman overwhelmingly chose victims who were poor, elderly and female, and therefore vulnerable on three counts' (Wilson 2009: 265). Accordingly, in her book on Shipman, Carole Peters (2005: 226) concludes likewise that he targeted the elderly and infirm because they 'simply ceased to be as valuable as human beings and so there was no reason to keep them'. In this way, Shipman's killings can be seen to conform to the 'mission-oriented serial killer' identified by Haggerty (2009: 183), because he preyed on those 'perceived as living outside the moral order of a competitive capitalist society [and are] not seen as an asset to the community but as a socio-economic burden' (Wilson 2009: 265). On the other hand, his modus operandi fits that of female serial killers who, as we saw earlier, tend to target 'latent victims' who are unable to defend themselves as well as people familiar to them or with whom they are intimate.

We will never fully know or understand Shipman's motivations for murder partly because he refused to have anything to do with Dame Janet Smith's public inquiry into his killings, which meant her team of forensic psychiatrists could not interview him, and because Shipman committed suicide at HMP Wakefield in January 2004 while serving a sentence for the murder of 15 of his patients (Soothill and Wilson 2005: 686–688). However, King argues despite evidence to the contrary, Shipman's activities have been reinterpreted to accord with paradigmatic contemporary understandings of serial killing as a form of violent and sexual transgression. On this view:

> serial killing does not include all multiple killers but prioritizes a very specific type of violence: murder, mutilation and sexual defilement. Serial killing is an act of orgasmic bodily intercourse in which the parts and fluids of the killer and victim merge. Serial killing is an act of physical and moral transgression in which the institutionalized rules of modernity are breached as the murderer penetrates the body of the other.
>
> (King 2006: 113)

Although Shipman's modus operandi was quite different to that of other serial killers, or male killers, at least, the centrality of transgression to contemporary representations of serial killing meant his activities were reconfigured in the public imagination until they cohered with the dominant ideal. That is why some accounts focused 'on "the lethal injection of diamorphine" by Shipman and, in one case, the graphic image of the needle penetrating the skin of his elderly victims was central' (King 2006: 114). Shipman's preference for drug overdosing also makes him unusual, and again more like female serial killers, whose most popular method of murder is poisoning, with arsenic being a particular favorite (Hale and Bolin 1998: 38). Moreover, a relevant sub-category of female serial killer identified by Holmes et al. (1998b: 66–67) is the 'comfort serial killer', who usually kills people with whom they are acquainted, and stands to gain materially from killing, or has 'the promise of money such as insurance benefits, acquisition of business interests or real estate' (Holmes et al. 1998b: 66). A pertinent example of this type of female serialist is Amy Archer-Gilligan, who opened a rest home in Connecticut in 1901, and in the proceeding 14 years killed by poisoning at least 27 men and women; marrying five of the men she nursed, each of whom was insured for substantial amounts of money, and, in the cases of elderly women, killing them after she had helped them amend their wills (Holmes et al. 1998b: 66).

SERIAL KILLING AND CONSUMPTION

One distinctively modern phenomenon Haggerty (2009) does not consider in his analysis of serial killing is its connection to consumption and the rise of consumer culture. This is the focus of Jarvis (2007: 328), who argues the serial killer (as depicted in film and fiction) is a 'gothic double' of the serial consumer. So, for example, in *American Psycho*:

> the eponymous Patrick Bateman embodies a merger between ultra-violence and compulsive consumerism. A catalogue of obscene and barbaric atrocities (serial murder, rape and torture) is interwoven with endless shopping lists of designer clothes and fashionable furniture, beauty products and audiovisual equipment, videos and CDs alongside multiple purchases at restaurants, gyms, health spas, concerts and clubs.
>
> (Jarvis 2007: 330)

Indeed, as James Annesley (1998: 16) notes, '[i]n *American Psycho* the word "consume" is used in all of its possible meanings: purchasing, eating and destroying'. Moreover, Jarvis (2007: 330) states, '[e]ach brand of consumption is described in the same flat, affectless tone to underscore Bateman's perception of everything in the world as a series of consumables arranged for his delectation', and, in this way, Bateman 'represents a gothic projection of consumer pathology'.

King (2006: 117) also considers the intersections of serial killing and consumption, saying an important 'characteristic which separates contemporary representations of the serial killer from previous historical examples' is that '[t]he contemporary serial killer's transgressions are commodified', and '[t]he act of serial killing is mediated and framed by commodity consumption'. Accordingly, 'commodities are the medium of transgression' (King 2006: 117). Indeed, in its most literal expression, consumption is demonstrated by the act of cannibalism. For instance, Hannibal Lecter 'consumes his victims as he consumes other commodities' (King 2006: 118); thus, in a now famous line in the film, *The Silence of the Lambs*, Lecter says, 'I ate his liver with some fava beans and a big Chianti' (see Figure 7.4).

Automobiles also play a central role in the activities of many serial killers, transporting killers between victims while also being used to abduct victims or remove bodies, and 'in a number of cases the car itself becomes a critical space in which murder and abuse occur' (King 2006: 119). Hence, 'as a commodity, the car becomes the actual and metaphorical vehicle of transgression' (King 2006: 119). Serial killers Harvey Louis Carignan and Peter Sutcliffe were both arrested after their vehicles were identified (King 2006: 119), and Douglas Clark revealed he shot his young females in the head while they performed fellatio on him in the back seat of his car (Holmes and Holmes 2010: 158). In other cases, commodities figure in more unusual ways, such as in the account of Dennis Nilsen, who dismembered the bodies of his victims' bodies while listening to Aaron Copland's *Fanfare to the Common Man* on his Walkman (Seltzer 1998: 19), the music recorded on his personal stereo thus acting to frame his transgression (King 2006: 119). Drawing on each of these examples, King (2006: 118) is able to propose a

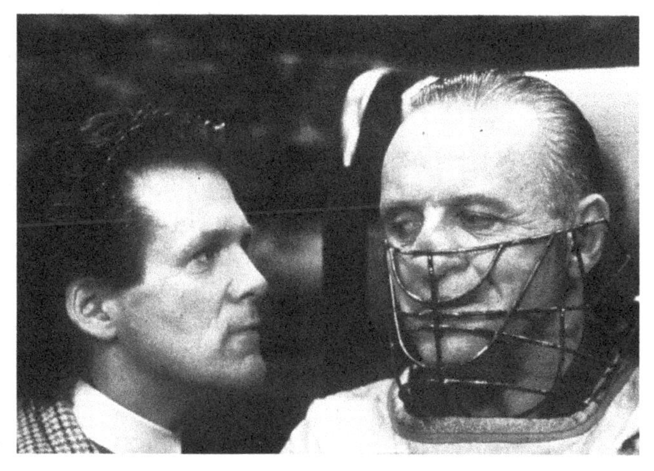

Figure 7.4 Anthony Hopkins (R) as cannibal serial killer Hannibal Lecter in *The Silence of the Lambs*, 1991

wider thesis, namely that 'commodification . . . becomes the medium of transgression', or that:

> Through transgressive commodity consumption, serial killers are able to transcend their routinized anonymity and to assert a novel form of self-identity. The serial killer stands as a totem of an emergent social order where relations between individuals are increasingly mediated by means of commodities.
>
> (King 2006: 119)

King (2006: 120) also returns to his analysis about the formation of the serial killing self as constituting a reaction against modern conditions, which 'points to an alienated Freudian self, living in a bleak industrialized world'. The upshot involves what Frederic Jameson (1991) describes as the emergence of a *flattened commodified self* that has a 'waning effect', resulting in a situation whereby 'the self has thinned, expressing itself through immediate acts of consumption' (King 2006: 120), which stimulates new emotions: 'The commodification of the self liberates the modern ego from existential angst, allowing the now flattened subject to experience the euphoria of consumption' (King 2006: 120).

In contrast to the modern self, which is incorporated into state institutions via regular disciplinary exercises that coalesce to form a super-ego, or social conscience, the postmodern consumer self is submerged repeatedly in acts of consumption. The decline of the state and emergence of multinational capitalism denotes a new institutional complex wherein both the act of consumption and associated feelings of euphoria occur. King (2006: 121) refers to this as a 'new social order', which 'facilitates the development of a new kind of self' that is no longer a citizen, but a consumer; and the serial killer is simply 'an extreme representation of this new form of social agency'.

Another kind of consumption linked to serial killing concerns the notion of 'murderabilia', or 'the sale of items associated with famous violent crimes' (Denham 2016: 230). According to Denham (2016: 242), 'murderabilia collecting is often reported as a wholly negative hobby, while murder and corpse invade all planes of popular culture'. However, he shows how, in death, 'the seductive qualities of the criminal celebrity are immortalized in the corpse, while the negative features of their myth are selectively forgotten' (Denham 2016: 233).

For Denham (2016: 230), the act of immortalizing criminals in this way leads to 'altered remembrance', such that 'all aspects of a criminal's behaviour, personality and lifespan are not remembered with equal diligence'. Indeed, he argues, '[r]epresentations of the criminal dead are extremely discriminating when it comes to who will be exhibited, and what parts of their lives they will be celebrated for – a central process of selective remembrance' (Denham 2016: 230). Hence, using a framework of 'selective memory', he highlights how the visceral qualities of the transgressive act of criminal celebrities – associated with violence, gore and blood – are 'selectively forgotten' posthumously. Through this commodification of the criminal corpse, and with the help of prudent marketization, gruesome histories are overpowered by brand-like qualities, which emphasize a serial killer's flattering 'assets', such as cunning, wily characteristics and intelligence in a mythologizing process, which means they 'frequently enjoy more positive representations than they did when alive' (Denham 2016: 233). What then is the essential notoriety and celebrity of serial killers is the subject of the next section of this chapter.

SERIAL KILLERS AS POSTMODERN CELEBRITIES/CULTURAL MONSTERS

We have noted previously in this chapter the symbiotic relationship that exists between the media/celebrity culture and serial killing, showing, for instance, how celebrity serial killers can revel in their infamy, which sometimes means they themselves become objects of consumption and commodification. For example, we have already seen how John Wayne Gacy was proud of his sinister celebrity, as evident in the production of numerous books, articles and songs, as well as a movie (see Figure 7.1), and a play about his crimes. Indeed, this taps into Middleweek's (2017) point, raised in Chapter 6, about the *consumptive value of celebrity*, where she considers female criminals like Lindy Chamberlain and Schapelle Corby, both of whom have been subject to media investment in their stories (e.g. documentary films, books), and various kinds of merchandizing (e.g. tee shirts, caps, G-strings).

Part of the process of the convergence of celebrity and serial killing involves the elision of fact and fiction, which, according to Chris Jenks (2003: 180–181), means 'the serial killer has become a postmodern celebrity', whereby the 'live circus of characters' like Jack the Ripper, John Wayne Gacy, Harold Shipman, Dennis Nilsen and Jeffrey Dahmer 'has drifted into entertainment through film and literature', which, to Biressi (2001: 169), has increased the public's general appetite for both true crime and fictional crime stories. Jenks uses the example of Patrick Bateman in Ellis's (1991) *American Psycho* to propose:

> Bateman's deep and sickening transgressions are provided with some fascination because they are attached to the vehicle of postmodern, unconstrained amorality – the serial killer. Ellis successfully ironizes this election by sustaining our excitement and interest while abandoning responsibility for his creation's actions or, indeed, his reality even within the narrative.
>
> (Jenks 2003: 183)

In accordance with this type of analysis, Ruth Penfold-Mounce (2009: 90) proposes serial killers can be classified as 'iniquitous celebrity-criminals' because they 'cross a cultural line that alienates them from the public; they are anti-celebrities just as heroes can be anti-heroes'. Unlike serial killers, however, celebrated cultural heroes, such the historic figure of Robin Hood, evoke widespread public resonance for reaffirming societal norms and values (e.g. freedom, equality, justice) in bad times. By stealing from the rich to give to the poor, Robin Hood 'encapsulates the "good", honourable and cunning individual who becomes a criminal in order to stand up for the public against an oppressive regime' (Penfold-Mounce 2009: 75). British gangsters Reggie and Ronnie Kray were later versions of Robin Hood, who 'possessed glamour, cunning and daring, and despite not fighting a specifically dictatorial state or giving all their gains to the poor, they resisted the law and were reputedly generous to charity and were self-professed protectors of their local community' (Penfold-Mounce 2009: 76).

From a historical-cultural perspective, then, gangsters and bandits who achieve celebrity status reflect the values and conflicts of a specific group of people at a certain time. For instance, gangsters and bank robbers in the US during the 1920s and 1930s represented the concerns and fears of many Americans in the Great Depression; a period that 'provided the cultural conditions for lawbreakers to become symbolic representatives of justice while the legal and political system seemed to be operating against the interest of the people' (Penfold-Mounce 2009: 76). Hence, characters like John Dillinger, who, as part of their robberies, would destroy mortgage records, were seen as latter-day Robin Hoods, attacking what the public saw as the source of their financial misery. Moreover, in a society oppressed by the Great Depression, displays of daring and ruthlessness were romanticized: 'gangsters were moulded figures of romance and ideological longing who battled against the state with automatic guns and fast cars' (Penfold-Mounce 2009: 77). Hence, 'fighting moral codes and repressive state institutions' made Bonnie and Clyde 'counterparts for the public's own personal and communal struggles' (Penfold-Mounce 2009: 77). As with other cases we have looked at in this chapter, Bonnie and Clyde also bought into and lived out their own gangster myth:

> Bonnie's letters to Clyde when he was in jail demonstrated her belief in the glamorous crime myth in which they were living by using language from movies, radio, magazines and pop songs . . . which was only reinforced by the pair indulging their mobster image by submitting poems and photographs of themselves in mock gangster poses with guns and cars to newspapers in order to further their self-aggrandizement.
>
> (Penfold-Mounce 2009: 78)

While criminal-celebrity cultural heroes, social bandits and underworld figures might all attain celebrity status because their activities resonate positively with wider norms and values, according to Penfold-Mounce (2009: 91), iniquitous celebrity criminals, such as serial killers, 'achieve celebrity through reverse heroization'. They are anti-heroes who embody 'the dark side of not only celebrity, but also criminal-celebrity' (Penfold-Mounce 2009: 91). The fascination attached to them resulting in their celebrity derives not from them being likeable or admirable but instead from them invoking disgust, revulsion, loathing, fear and horror.

The idea that celebrity images of serial killers register with wider cultural norms and values is also present in a study by Julie Wiest (2016). Similar to

Green's (2008a) comparative analysis of child-on-child killing cases in England and Norway, discussed in Chapter 6, Wiest compares media representations of serial killers across the US and UK to connect those portrayals and elements of culture in the two countries. Indeed, just as Green focuses on the contrasting cultures of England and Norway to explain the different ways the child killers were treated, Wiest (2016: 330) argues media portrayals are an important aspect of 'recorded culture', which reveal much about a country. Accordingly, her aim is 'to uncover the cultural messages in the US and UK news media representations of serial killers, with a particular focus on the presence of monster and celebrity imagery' (Wiest 2016: 329).

Employing a qualitative content analysis of print and online news sources, Wiest found UK print media tend to be more sensationalized in their reporting, and tend more than US articles to include serial killer nicknames. In addition, US articles tend to be killer-focused, while UK articles appear to devote more attention to victims. In terms of the use of monster imagery, Wiest (2016: 331) argues serial killers can be thought of as 'modern cultural monsters', because they indicate 'what members of a culture abhor'. Wiest (2016: 335) discovered the word *monster* is used with similar frequency in both countries, including 'descriptions of killers that evoke a sense of savagery or animalistic qualities'.

While monster imagery indicates what a culture abhors, celebrity imagery suggests 'what members of a culture celebrate, and media play an integral role in the creation of celebrity' (Wiest 2016: 331). Celebrity imagery is used in both UK and US articles, including stories pointing to the fame achieved by killers and records set by them, e.g. 'one of America's most prolific killers', or 'Britain's worst woman serial killer'. Other markers of celebrity status are that both sets of articles mention similarities with fictional serial killers, whereas only US articles refer to apparent special abilities and expertise, such as killers who have been hard to catch because they are 'exceptionally cunning', or others who may have 'forensic . . . and criminal sophistication' (Wiest 2016: 336). Accordingly, this media depiction of serial killers as possessing extraordinary traits and abilities appears contrary to Penfold-Mounce's (2009: 91) argument that iniquitous criminals, like serial killers, 'achieve celebrity status on the basis that the definition of celebrity declares anyone can be celebrated by simply becoming well known'.

Notwithstanding many of the similarities between depictions of serial killers in both article sets, Wiest proposes a major difference in how serial killers are described. UK sources use more sensationalized headlines, and more fear-invoking language as compared to US articles. While both sets of articles use monster imagery, they do so in different ways. In the UK, representations portray serial killers as more *traditional monsters* (i.e. savage, nameless animals prowling neighborhoods and preying on innocent victims), which, to Wiest (2016: 337),

> along with a greater focus on victims in the news stories, indicates a low value for the killers and may suggest a culture that values the group over the individual and in which only normative cultural ideals are celebrated (e.g. graduating with honours or running the best marathon time).

In the US, by contrast, serial killers are portrayed as *fantastic monsters* (i.e. advanced predators with exceptional abilities and expertise, much like the imagery of celebrity), which, to Wiest (2016: 337–338),

> along with an almost exclusive focus on killers in the news stories, indicates a high value for these killers and may suggest a culture that values individuals over the group and in which even deviant versions of cultural ideals may be celebrated (e.g. setting a record for murder victims or pulling off a daring prison escape).

Although elements of celebrity status are found more frequently in US articles – supporting Schmid's (2005) argument that serial killers are a type of modern celebrity – fictional serial killers, traditionally a mainstay of US entertainment media, have started to appear in UK television dramas, such as *Luther* (2010), *The Bletchley Circle* (2012) and *The Fall* (2013). And while the detectives tend to be the stars of those shows, the killers are nevertheless portrayed more as celebrities than traditional monsters. Finally, in line with what we have discussed previously in the book when considering the impact of media representations of crime on public perceptions and crime fear (Chapter 4), monster and celebrity imagery can resonate with broader anxieties associated with social, economic and political developments. In one US article, for instance, 'serial murder cases are linked to insecurities about immigration and urbanization in Mexico', while, in another, serial killing is connected to 'gang activity, drug abuse, police corruption, and changing gender roles there' (Wiest 2016: 338). Performing a diversionary function in a manner similar to the creation of folk devils and moral panics (Chapter 3), another US article redefines problems in hospitals and nursing homes as a problem with serial killers:

> The article's headline proclaims 'Hospital Serial Killers are Big Threat', yet the 2,100 patients worldwide it claims were murdered by doctors and nurses from 1970 to 2006 pales in comparison to the 98,000 deaths per year in the United States alone that the article attributes to medical mistakes. Given these numbers, it would seem the real problem is medical mistakes, not serial killers, in hospitals. But, because most US Americans would prefer to believe that the US healthcare system operates for the good and safety of patients, recognizing issues with the system would require an uncomfortable reconsideration of those beliefs.
>
> (Wiest 2016: 338)

CONCLUSION

Wiest's focus on the essential similarity between deviant values and cultural ideals, particularly in respect of US news sources depicting serial killers as fantastic monsters with exceptional abilities and special skills, brings to mind the work of

Matza and Sykes (1961), which we looked at in Chapter 2. It will be recalled how Matza and Sykes argue many supposedly deviant values are merely an inappropriate expression of dominant values. For instance, the search for adventure and excitement, which is characteristic of 'edgework' (Lyng 1990), is not a deviant value as such. Instead, it is a *subterranean value* – a deviant expression of a value that on other occasions is it acceptable to possess, such as being daring in sport and recreational activities.

As many accounts discussed in this chapter demonstrate, this way of thinking can be extended to encompass the idea that serial killers – including media representations of them – can conform to, rather than deviate from, societal norms and values. Indeed, by placing serial killing within wider social, cultural and historical contexts and structures, Haggerty (2009) is able to show how serial killers and serial killing are very much products of modernizing processes, rather than deviations from them. For example, the visionary orientation of some accords with modern notions of social progress that can be achieved partly by ridding society of devalued, marginalized and dispossessed groups (e.g. women, the poor, homosexuals, ethnic minorities), which are common targets of serial killers. Similarly, Force (2010) shows how fictional killer Dexter Morgan's adherence to modernist conventions of normativity, as well as his targeting of disparaged groups (in this case, fellow confirmed murderers), reveals the social processes all of us are involved in when performing and managing identities in daily life.

Even though the etiology of Dexter's homicidal tendencies appears rooted in childhood trauma (i.e. witnessing the violent death of his mother at a young age), explanations of serial killing by recourse to biography and family background, as in the case of Arrigo and Griffin's (2004) account, discussed above, are of limited value and applicability because their psychological/individual focus restricts our ability to generalize across cases. Equally, as Warwick (2006: 566) notes, attempts to discover common characteristics and classify serial killers have proved allusive, since what we are confronted with in reality are a highly diverse collection of very different crimes and perpetrators present in both documentary and fictional accounts. Notwithstanding that, we have seen how both factual and dramatized portrayals of serial killers often display common themes that are connected to wider structures and contexts.

One of the most prominent contextual factors is the existence in modern societies of a mass media, which, we have seen, has a symbiotic relation to serial killing, e.g. serial killers revel in their fame and notoriety, which, in turn, provides newsworthy media stories. Indeed, according to Haggerty, the role of the mass media in modern societies has been crucial in helping create celebrity serial killer identities. And here there is a link to consumer culture, another key feature of modernity, whereby celebrity has an inherently consumptive (i.e. profitable) appeal. However, rather than seeing consumers, including serial killers, as reflecting or in any way embodying a *modern* self-identity, King (2006) argues consumer capitalism transforms the unified, centered ego of the modern self – with its correspondingly stable super-ego, or conscience – into a fractured postmodern consumer self that is flattened and thinned via immediate and repeated acts of consumption. To King, therefore, serial killers constitute an extreme version of a new kind of self: an amoral *postmodern* self that is not constrained by the institutionalized rules, disciplinary routines and controls of modernity. One such control is surveillance, which, as we will see in the next chapter, has been enabled by modern institutions like the state, media and consumer culture, while simultaneously decreasing the anonymity and privacy Haggerty sees as modern preconditions for serial killing.

SUGGESTED FURTHER READING

Although examined in some depth in the chapter, it is still worth reading in their entirety the differing yet strangely complementary accounts of Haggerty and King; where the former considers the modern preconditions *for* serial killing, while the latter looks at the postmodern serial killing self as a reaction *against* modernity.

Haggerty, K. D. (2009) 'Modern serial killers' *Crime Media Culture* 5(2): 168–187.
King, A. (2006) 'Serial killing and the postmodern self' *History of the Human Sciences* 19(3): 109–125.

A variety of perspectives on serial killing are explored in this edited collection:

Holmes, R. M. and Holmes, S. T. (eds) (1998b) *Contemporary Perspectives on Serial Murder*. Thousand Oaks, CA: Sage.

The two books listed below place serial killing in a broader cultural context. Seltzer's (1998: 21) concept of 'wound culture' has been particularly influential for denoting the growing role of public violence in contemporary culture, evident, for example, in the 'spectacular public representation of violated bodies, across a burgeoning range of official, academic, and media accounts, in fiction and in film'.

Schmid, D. (2005) *Natural Born Celebrities: Serial Killers in American Culture*. Chicago, IL: University of Chicago Press.
Seltzer, M. (1998) *Serial Killers: Death and Life in America's Wound Culture*. New York, NY: Routledge.

On the invention of the serial killer category and the related symbiosis of law enforcement agencies, the media and popular culture, and serial killers see:

Simpson, P. L. (2000) *Psycho Paths: Tracking the Serial Killer Through Contemporary American Film and Fiction*. Edwardsville, IL: Southern Illinois University Press.
Soothill, K (1993) 'The serial killer industry' *The Journal of Forensic Psychiatry* 4(2): 341–354.
Warwick, A. (2006) 'The scene of the crime: Inventing the serial killer' *Social & Legal Studies* 15(4): 552–569.

CHAPTER 8

Surveillance, new media and protest policing

INTRODUCTION

In the last chapter, we saw how, according to Haggerty (2009), the anonymity afforded by living in a modern society of strangers is a precondition for serial killing. In pre-modern times, people lived in a highly circumscribed local area, had contact with a very limited number of people during the course of their lifetimes, and were intimately connected with family, friends and neighbors. Modernity, in contrast, is characterized by the emergence of dense urban environments with routinized impersonal social encounters, which are ideal hunting grounds for serial killers. Modern notions of privacy developed in tandem with increased social anonymity, and, as discussed in the last chapter, this can shield the activities of serial killers: for instance, neighbors may justify failing to investigate suspicious behavior, smells and such like on the basis of safeguarding both their own and their neighbors' 'right to privacy'.

A countervailing idea is present in Haggerty's writing with Richard Ericson, wherein they argue the extent of modern surveillance is such that we have witnessed the progressive 'disappearance of disappearance' (Haggerty and Ericson 2000: 619), meaning it is now almost impossible to escape the surveillant gaze of the state, as well as corporate and social media tracking and monitoring systems. One would think, therefore, that, under these conditions, serial killing becomes far more difficult to perpetrate, although, as we see later in the chapter, there still exists the phenomenon of 'missing persons', which goes against notion of the disappearance of disappearance. Like serial killing, however, contemporary surveillance has to a large degree been enabled by the existence of the modern mass media.

As we shall see, Michel Foucault (1977/1991) believed the omniscient style of state surveillance to which we are now accustomed could be regarded a blueprint for all forms of modern surveillance. He also saw it as standing more generally as a metaphor for the way power and control operates in modern society, which, in contrast to pre-modern society, he said, 'is one not of spectacle, but of surveillance' (Foucault 1977/1991: 217). Increasing surveillance is often premised on the idea of 'situational crime prevention', including measures that, as we saw in Chapter 2, are intended to *design out crime* by 'target hardening', such as installing closed circuit television (CCTV) cameras (Hayward 2004: 98–104). A rational choice theory of crime underpins the implementation of measures like these, which, it is assumed, will deter would-be offenders, as they decide consciously not to commit crimes on account of being under surveillance. Despite contention as to their efficacy, the presence of surveillance technologies, like CCTV cameras, is also justified on the basis they provide reassurance and allay people's fear about becoming crime victims (see Chapter 4). However, although they are quintessentially rationalistic (Freiberg 2001: 266), as we will discover later in the chapter, and as cultural criminology tells us, such crime prevention methods are infused with social meaning, which, in the case of CCTV, applies to operators and their targets alike.

Although it is widely acknowledged that Britain is the most surveilled society on the planet, with an estimated one camera for every 14 people (Surette 2015: 191, 296), surveillance has increased globally, and has intensified particularly since the terror attacks of 11 September 2001. In the US, for instance, the state has taken advantage of the 'surveillance effect', or the psychological effect of fearing you may be under observation, expanding surveillance programs and traditional police use of the stakeout and hidden cameras to encompass general public space applications (Surette 2015: 189). As we will see later in the chapter, these and other more sinister developments in policing methodology have increased in the post-9/11 era, as the state has mobilized narratives around the 'terrorist threat' to increase citizen surveillance, monitoring and control, and in the course of doing so, abrogate numerous civil liberties, legal safeguards and due process rights.

However, just as top-down modes of surveillance have increased, so various forms of resistance have emerged in response. Accordingly, we will consider a number of examples of what Monahan (2006: 515) calls, 'counter-surveillance', that is 'intentional, tactical uses, or disruptions of surveillance technologies to challenge institutional power asymmetries'. It is important to remember here too David Lyon's (2001: 2) definition of surveillance as 'any collection and processing of personal data, whether identifiable or not, for the purpose of influencing or managing those whose data have been garnered', since this indicates surveillance 'is relational, involving a power dynamic likely to unfold in complicated ways' (Fernandez and Huey 2009: 199). Gary Marx (2009: 296), another influential surveillance studies scholar, similarly says, 'surveillance needs to be viewed as a dynamic process involving emergent interaction and developments over time'.

In what follows, then, we examine not only those dominant forms of surveillance that are quite familiar to us, but also a variety of examples, including citizen and protestor use of social media and new digital technologies (e.g. miniaturized recording equipment), which reverse the surveillant gaze of the state and police especially, thereby posing a challenge to the axiom 'resistance is futile'. In this way, the material presented in the chapter resonates with a burgeoning body of work addressing the challenges posed not only to lawmakers and criminal justice personnel but also criminologists who are confronted increasingly with crime and justice issues born of transformations in social media and new technologies in the digital age. Examples include 'sexting' and other forms of online and image-based abuse (Powell, Henry and Flynn 2018; Salter 2017; Salter et al. 2013). Although, as we shall see, some issues have led to efficacious social media interventions and online justice campaigns, criminology is only just beginning to move beyond its conventional focus on computer and cyber crime to develop what has variously been called a 'digital criminology' (Powell, Stratton and Cameron 2018; Stratton et al. 2017) or 'virtual criminology' (Brown 2006a) to expand theoretical perspectives, concepts and empirical research when dealing with crime and justice matters as they emerge in contemporary digital age.

PANOPTIC OBSERVATION AND THE DISPERSAL OF CRIME CONTROL

The notion of Big Brother as an omniscient super-state was popularized in 1949 with the publication of George Orwell's *1984*. However, the idea behind this kind of state surveillance can be found in the earlier work of English philosopher, Jeremy Bentham, whose institutional reforms of prisons, schools, factories and workhouses featured 'panopticon' style architectural design, whereby inmates (pan) are observed (opticon) by a single watchman. Often characterized in terms of 'the few watching the many', as the image of Stateville Correctional Center – opened in 1925, but now closed – shows, this type of surveillance became a core element of modern prisons, and featured a circular cell layout with a central guard tower (Figure 8.1). The intent of the design is to act as a deterrent. Of course, it is impossible for a single watchman to observe all inmates at all times. However, such is the physical layout of the prison and its cells that inmates live under constant threat of being closely observed, which serves to 'encourage' conformity and good behavior.

As we saw earlier, Foucault (1977/1991) regarded state surveillance, and the panopticon in particular, as a metaphor for the operation of power and control in modern societies. Hence, as the panopticon fosters conformity, it constitutes a means of dispersing power and control, creating what Foucault (1977/1991: 136) calls, 'docile bodies', which 'may be subjected, used, transformed and improved'. Much like the 'fearing subjects' we examined in Chapter 4, who modify their behavior in light of what they know/hear about crime, citizens conform, and thus become docile, when they are, or imagine they are, under the gaze of an always watchful state, or subject to other forms of institutional regulation. According to Haggerty and Ericson (2000), then, Foucault extends Orwell's fears, although he

Figure 8.1 Stateville Correctional Center, Crest Hill, Illinois, 1928

departs from Orwell's analysis by proposing surveillance must be seen in terms of the operation of a distinct mode of power:

> This disciplinary aspect of panoptic observation involves a productive soul training, which encourages inmates to reflect upon the minutia of their own behaviour in subtle and ongoing efforts to transform their selves. Foucault proposed that the panopticon served as a diagram for a new model of power which extended beyond the prison to take hold in the other disciplinary institutions characteristic of this era, such as the factory, hospital, military, and school.
>
> (Haggerty and Ericson 2000: 607)

As we saw in Chapter 4, Stanley Cohen (1985) used similar ideas to show how deviancy control measures will increasingly involve two key processes: (i) *widening the net*; and (ii) *thinning the mesh*. Net widening involves 'an increase in the total number of deviants getting into the system in the first place and many of these are new deviants who would not have been processed previously' (Cohen 1985: 44). Mesh thinning occurs when 'there is an increase in the overall intensity of intervention, with old and new deviants being subject to levels of intervention (including traditional institutionalization) which they might not have previously' (Cohen 1985: 44). As we also saw in Chapter 4, this thinking has been applied to measures aimed at tackling 'anti-social behaviour' (Martin 2011a), which involve, among other things, the criminalization of behavior that previously would not have fallen under the purview of the criminal justice system (widening the net), as well as an erosion of the standard of proof (i.e. having to prove a civil offense according to the criminal standard of proof), abrogation of the rules of evidence (e.g. admission of hearsay evidence), reversal of the presumption of innocence, and the imposition of criminal sanctions following breach of a civil order, all of which involve thinning the mesh.

Consequently, anti-social behavior procedures *blur the boundaries* between criminal and civil law, which is another facet of the dispersal of social control identified by Cohen, who also discerns a third process at work, namely the creation of 'different nets', where 'new agencies and services are supplementing rather than replacing the original set of control mechanisms' (Cohen 1985: 44). Allied to the idea of boundary blurring, this process of producing different nets is key to what Haggerty and Ericson (2000: 606) observe as 'the convergence of what were once discrete surveillance systems to the point that we can now speak of an emerging "surveillant assemblage"'.

THE SURVEILLANT ASSEMBLAGE

To Haggerty and Ericson, the capacities of surveillance technologies have now surpassed Orwell's dystopian vision, such that we are seeing a growth not only of state surveillance but also the increased involvement of non-state actors, like corporations that use loyalty card schemes, and other means of monitoring customer spending habits. Moreover, these forms of surveillance now extend beyond their commercial utility to track lifestyle preferences, and develop consumer profiles that may contain extra information about 'a person's age, gender, political inclinations, religious preferences, reading habits, ethnicity, family size, income' (Haggerty and Ericson 2000: 617).

While Orwell failed to predict this extension and intensification of surveillance across society, Haggerty and Ericson argue Foucault's analysis is equally limited by its historical specificity, which is not able to account for the 'creep' of surveillance in contemporary societies that has led to the emergence of the 'surveillant assemblage', or a 'superpanopticon', as Poster (1990: 93) has named it. Although they talk of *the* surveillant assemblage, Haggerty and Ericson are clear that, as an assemblage, it operates as a multiplicity of heterogeneous technologies and practices working together as a functional entity. However, the surveillant assemblage is also emergent, unstable and lacking in discernible boundaries, and therefore cannot be located in a single bureaucracy or institution. This point is significant when thinking about attempts at attacking or resisting increased surveillance (see below), which, 'as important as they might be, are akin to efforts to keep the ocean's tide back with a broom – a frantic focus on a particular unpalatable technology or practice while the general tide of surveillance washes over us all' (Haggerty and Ericson 2000: 609).

As might be expected, a key feature of the surveillant assemblage is that it brings together different systems, and operates across state and extra-state institutions, as evident in the increased integration of systems and databases of police and corporate organizations, like insurance companies and financial institutions. For example, Haggerty and Ericson (2000: 616–617) cite research showing how police are now primary users of many systems originally intended for other (non-police) government purposes (Northrop et al. 1995), how there have been proposals to link the US National Crime Information Center police database to computers from Social Security, Internal Revenue, Passport, Securities and Exchange and the State Department (Gordon 1990), and how in some communities in South California, police now have direct access to digital school records (Davis 1998: 381).

As highlighted earlier by Cohen (1985), these processes almost inevitably lead to a blurring of criminal and non-criminal functions, whereby '[o]stensibly non-criminal justice institutions are being called upon to augment the surveillance capacities of the criminal justice surveillance system' (Haggerty and Ericson 2000: 617). So, in Canada, for instance, financial institutions have been compelled to monitor and report 'suspicious' transations in order to prevent money laundering:

> More recently, regulations have been introduced to require American banks to compare the financial holdings of their clients against an electronic list of parents who owe child support. Educators and medical practitioners are already legally compelled to report suspected instances of child abuse, and the police have started to request or confiscate media tapes of public disturbances in efforts to identify lawbreakers.
>
> (Haggerty and Ericson 2000: 617)

It is not only the police that have increased access to this kind of commercial and non-criminal government information. So too do the intelligence security services, which are also able to increase the amount of information they gather on individual citizens via computerized data matching. For example, Burnham (1997: 164–167) shows how:

> the FBI has employed commercial databases for undisclosed investigative purposes, and that the US Drug Enforcement Agency has developed its own in-house registry with information culled from mailing and telephone listings, direct marketers, voters records, and assorted commercial sources. Although cloaked in secrecy, this registry was expected to contain 135,000,000 records as of its inception in 1991 and would subsequently receive regular updates of corporate and residential data.
>
> (Haggerty and Ericson 2000: 617)

DATA DOUBLES

Just because the fucker's got a library card doesn't make him Yoda!

This line is taken from the 1995 movie, *Seven*, so titled because it is about a serial killer who, at each of his crime scenes, leaves clues leading police to believe his victims have all been guilty of one of the seven deadly sins. In the course of their investigation, Detective David Mills (Brad Pitt), who utters the words in the quotation, and Detective Lieutenant William Somerset (Morgan Freeman) discover a man named John Doe – who we later learn is the killer – has recently borrowed several library books about the deadly sins. The idea here is that reading habits can be used to 'profile' offenders, which pertains to a key feature of the surveillant assemblage, namely the emergence of our virtual alter egos or 'data doubles'.

Just as Foucault's work on panoptic surveillance shows how the dispersal of power and control impacts upon (docile) human bodies, so Haggerty and Ericson argue the surveillant assemblage gives rise to 'the formation and coalescence of a new type of body, a form of becoming which transcends human corporeality and reduces flesh to pure information' (Haggerty and Ericson 2000: 613). According to them, this new body, '[c]ulled from the tentacles of the surveillant assemblage' (Haggerty and Ericson 2000: 613), and found at the interface between technology and corporeality, is our 'data double'; a *hybrid* that

> can involve something as direct as tagging the human body so that its movements through space can be recorded, to the more refined reconstruction of a person's habits, preferences, and lifestyle from the trails of information which have become the detritus of contemporary life.
>
> (Haggerty and Ericson 2000: 611; see also Brown 2006b)

Not only are data doubles subject to increased government surveillance but they are also increasingly the object of marketing practices and other commercial enterprises, which attach a monetary value to constructing data doubles to create consumer profiles, refine services and target specific markets. Indeed, there is a growing trade in the corporate sale of this information, which governments are keen to profit from by on-selling data from official databases to corporate institutions, including license bureaus, personal income data and other information contained in employment records. Another version of this is captured by Stratton et al. (2017: 21) who say a feature of the 'social web' that emerged from the 2000s, 'is the increasingly "mobile web", with smartphones and wearable technology becoming ever-more ubiquitous and simultaneously collecting expansive "big data" about ourselves, our identities and our everyday lives'.

According to Haggerty and Ericson, no one is immune from these processes. Orwell and Foucault both focused on top-down monitoring and scrutiny, and surveillance studies has continued to focus on the ways surveillance is differentiated, tending not to touch on how the lives of the white mainstream are affected.

By contract, Haggerty and Ericson (2000: 617) argue, '[s]urveillance has become rhizomatic, it has transformed hierarchies of observation, and allows for the scrutiny of the powerful by both institutions and the general population'. Hence, while the poor may come into regular contact with a variety of surveillance systems related to social assistance or criminal justice, the middle and upper classes are also subject increasingly to forms of surveillance that include 'the regular monitoring of consumption habits, health profile, occupational performance, financial transactions, communication patterns, Internet use, credit history, transportation patterns, and physical access controls' (Haggerty and Ericson 2000: 618).

One point of distinction here, though, relates to possible ways of attacking or resisting surveillance, and the proposition that only certain groups, such as the middle classes, will have the capacity and resources (e.g. time and money) to resist and challenge contemporary forms of surveillance. In this context, it is useful to consider Karstedt and Farrall's (2006) work on the moral economy of everyday crime. What they call *crimes of everyday life* are essentially forms of white-collar crime positioned in a gray zone of legality and morality, and are the result of a syndrome of 'market anomie' (under neoliberalism) comprising distrust, fear/insecurity and cynical attitudes towards law, which has increased the willingness of 'respectable' (mostly middle-class) citizens to engage in illegal, sharp, shady or unfair practices in the marketplace.

In respect of our present discussion, crimes of everyday life may be considered a form of resistance to the 'forms of routine observation, documentation and analysis' to which 'the middle and upper classes are increasingly subject' (Haggerty and Ericson 2000: 618). Indeed, Karstedt and Farrall distinguish this type of 'protest' from historical peasant revolts against millers who sold corn or flour to them at inflated prices, stating the resistance of consumers and citizens these days tends to be more subtle and diverse:

> consumers are now exercised by 'value for money', mis-selling, hidden charges and inaccurate product descriptions. They resist and hit back by inflating insurance claims as a reaction towards small-print rules or overpriced premiums; they retreat into a shadow economy in which they pay cash-in-hand to circumvent tax and social security laws.
>
> (Karstedt and Farrall 2006: 1014)

Karstedt and Farrall (2006: 1014) add that subtle and diverse forms of resistance, like crimes of everyday life, will become more prevalent responses to unfair treatment in an unregulated market economy, and that 'consumer riots' are less likely to occur. However, while that may be true of middle-class resistance, the responses of less privileged and disenfranchised groups might still assume the form of collective action, as witnessed during the 2011 English riots, where social media played a crucial role not only in contributing to the rapid spread of the riots but also to the various modes of resistance and ad hoc surveillance strategies of ordinary citizens. For instance, Stephanie Baker (2012: 185) has shown how despite the police's failure to integrate social media services into their tactics for dealing with the riots, social media played a part in the informal policing of the riots, whereby

> social networking sites operated as public surveillance platforms to locate those responsible for the unrest. The blogging platform, Tumblr, for example, hosted an account called, 'Catch a Looter', which encouraged users to disseminate photos of looters and, thereby, expose their identities to the police.

On the one hand, it has been observed that the increased ubiquity of and access to small mobile surveillance technologies may encourage this type of 'mob activism' or 'virtual-vigilantism' (Dennis 2008: 348, 350–351, 355), including forms of public Internet humiliation, such as naming and shaming, reminiscent of community punishments meted out in medieval times. On the other hand, the use of miniature mobile surveillance devices can be used productively and positively for good purposes. For example, after the 2011 riots, 'Twitter operated as an extension of the public sphere', enabling the establishment of Riot Cleanup, which 'operated as a collective act of resistance against rioters with online social networks transpiring into an offline social movement' (Baker 2012: 182–183).

Baker's (2012: 176) key point is that the protests associated with the English riots did not give rise to amorphous 'digital mobs' (Dennis 2008: 353), but rather led to the formation of a *mediated crowd*, 'wherein the interactive online relationships enabled by social media connected aggrieved users into intense relationships that transpired offline'. Stressing both the online *and* offline aspects of crowd membership counteracts 'technological determinism', which, during the riots, allowed a common perception to form, among journalists, politicians and police, that social media alone was to blame for recruiting rioters and looters; instead of recognizing the human agency and emotionality of *people* that provided motivating forces to riot or not to riot (Baker 2012: 172–173). This more nuanced approach allows us to understand the role social media played in contributing to the speed and scale of the riots, as well as helping to appreciate how social media might have been used by those who chose not to participate, or was used as a means of orchestrating the clean-up in the immediate aftermath of the riots.

However, while citizen participation can be used for good, Gary Marx (2013: 58) points to the dangers of a *self-monitored society*, whereby in the face of government cutbacks, and especially since 9/11, the state relies increasingly on citizen involvement in surveillance programs, which can lead to individuals being 'asked to waive certain rights for the greater good or some benefit'. By relying on citizen responsibility and forging alliances with private entities, as we have seen happens in the surveillant assemblage, a morally ambiguous situation may arise, which Bob Hoogenboom (2010) refers to as 'gray policing', that is an unregulated area wherein 'police may delegate investigative tasks to private individuals, groups, and other countries not bound by the laws and policies that restrict state agents' (Marx 2013: 60). In this context, and to again invoke Cohen's (1985) ideas, the 'blurring of the lines between the public and the private may help control crime but [it] can also violate both the letter and spirit of laws intended to protect liberty' (Marx 2013: 60). Hence, there is a need to escalate independent checks on state and police power, which, as we will see later in the chapter, is a role that can be performed by citizen journalists using digital technologies and social media, either in partnership with or without the help of the mainstream media:

> We value nonprofits, social movements, whistle-blowers, and the investigative journalism of a free press precisely because of their potential independence from the state and other powerful organizations and their ability to ferret out abuse. . . . Citizens acting independently can serve as a check on, and alternative to, the state and other large organizations, through decentralized, crowd-sourced, and other uses of the Internet. We need to be vigilant of those with power, so this force can be a healthy corrective.
>
> (Marx 2013: 60)

BOX 8.1 THE DISAPPEARANCE OF DISAPPEARANCE

As we saw in Chapter 7 in relation to serial killing, modern living arrangements in urban environments have given people the freedom to be relatively anonymous and invisible. However, urban anonymity is also met with countervailing efforts by institutions seeking to gather 'discrete bits of information which break the individual down into flows for purposes of management, profit and entertainment' (Haggerty and Ericson 2000: 619). Insofar as such practices coalesce in the surveillant assemblage, Haggerty and Ericson (2000: 619) argue we now see the progressive *disappearance of disappearance*, which is 'a process whereby it is increasingly difficult for individuals to maintain their anonymity, or to escape the monitoring of social institutions'. While attempts to evade the gaze of surveillance systems can involve trading off social rights and benefits, such as not using the Internet to remain anonymous, as some privacy advocates advise, Haggerty and Ericson suggest the possibilities for disappearance have narrowed greatly. They provide two historical examples to illustrate that point.

The first example is that of the 'elusive activist' who was followed by secret service agents in the 1950s, but managed to evade them after taking a trip on an ocean liner, meaning she was out of reach, and the agents were not able to track her movements. Haggerty and Ericson (2000: 620) say that could not have happened today: 'Even on the ocean a person's whereabouts could still be discerned through the monitoring of credit card transactions, computer connections, travel arrangements and telephone calls'.

The second example they give is the 'invisible armada' – the greatest assembly of ships and boats ever gathered together during the allied invasion of Normandy in 1944. Although the Germans believed an invasion of France was imminent, they had no knowledge of it until the fog lifted on the morning of 6 June, revealing a fleet of over 5,000 vessels off the French coast:

> Again, the contrast between yesterday and today is telling. With advanced military sensing devices that now include globe-scanning satellites and submarines equipped

> with sensors that can detect the propeller of a ship traveling on the opposite side of the ocean, the surprise appearance of such a massive military grouping is simply inconceivable.
>
> (Haggerty and Ericson 2000: 620)

While there is a general inability to disappear these days as compared with times past, a couple of critical points are nevertheless worth noting. First, disappearance still happens. Missing persons cases are a prime example of this phenomenon, as highlighted in the tragic case of Madeleine McCann, discussed in Chapter 3. Secondly, privacy rights have been established in the face of increased surveillance, monitoring and tracking, as occurred in May 2014 when the European Court of Justice recognized the 'right to be forgotten', allowing people to request their removal from Internet search engine results (Kumar et al. 2015: 1).

SYNOPTICISM AND COUNTERVEILLANCE

Haggerty and Ericson's (2000: 617) observation that the rhizomatic or relatively flat, horizontal nature of contemporary surveillant forms now 'allows for the scrutiny of the powerful by both institutions and the general population' echoes what Thomas Mathiesen (1997) calls 'synopticism'. Essentially meaning 'that a large number of individuals are able to focus on something in common' (Haggerty and Ericson 2000: 618), synopticism appears to be the reverse of Foucault's notion of panopticism, though Mathiesen (1997: 231) argues, 'panopticon and synopticon reciprocally feed on each other'. Indeed, he says, 'the panoptical and the synoptical structures show several conspicuous parallels in development', which have been enabled by 'a common technology, the system of modern mass media', such that, '[i]ncreasingly, the few have been able to see the many, but also increasingly, the many have been enabled to see the few – to see the VIPs, the reporters, the stars, almost as a new class in the public sphere' (Mathiesen 1997: 219).

However, in what he calls the *viewer society*, Mathiesen (1997: 215) suggests there are some important ways panopticism ('where the few see the many') has been displaced by synopticism ('where the many see the few'), whereby

> the control and discipline of the 'soul', that is, the creation of human beings who control themselves through self-control and who thus fit neatly into a so-called democratic capitalist society, is a task which is actually fulfilled by modern synopticon, whereas Foucault saw it as a function of panopticon.

The synopticon, then, acts potentially as a democratic corrective to hierarchical forms of 'top-down' surveillance, allowing the general population to scrutinize the powerful, as a 'bottom-up' mode of observation. And, as such, it can be regarded as having a largely positive function, since although it does not represent 'a complete democratic leveling of the hierarchy of surveillance', it does 'cumulatively highlight a fractured rhizomatic criss-crossing of the gaze such that no major population groups stand irrefutably above or outside of the surveillant assemblage' (Haggerty and Ericson 2000: 618).

The role of social media and digital technologies is increasingly important in allowing the general public to monitor the powerful like never before, and we will return to explore the significance of these developments later in the chapter, when we look at the role of new media technologies (e.g. mobile phone video cameras) and 'citizen journalism' in scrutinizing and holding police to account in protest and public order settings. For now, it is sufficient to highlight some of the similarities that exist between the synopticon concept and Michael Welch's (2011) notion of 'counterveillance', which is itself an iteration of what Steve Mann (1998) calls 'sousveillance', to describe unmediated forms of bottom-up surveillance. Although Welch focuses expressly on prisons, as we shall see later in this chapter, the general principle of counterveillance as challenging the asymmetrical operation of state power has broad utility, which can be applied to a variety of contexts beyond the prison:

> counterveillance refers to a form of protest that reverses the visual field not only as a challenge to penal power but also toward institutional reform. It consists of two major inversions: (1) *turn the prison inside out*; and (2) *watch the watchers*. In the first inversion, counterveillance turns unwanted attention to inhumane conditions of imprisonment – which the state deliberately hides from public view. In so doing, prisoner neglect and abuses of state power are exposed to a wider audience; therefore, contributing to greater transparency of the state's penal operations.
>
> (Welch 2011: 304, original emphasis)

Welch states the second inversion (i.e. *watch the watchers*) shares with the 'synopticon' an important dynamic whereby the *many watch the few*. However, he distinguishes his idea of counterveillance from Mathiesen's analysis, which 'emphasizes that panopticism is actually coupled with synopticism, thereby producing a two-way – reciprocal – framework' (Welch 2011: 304). By contrast, he says, both Mathiesen and Foucault neglect the extent to which in modern societies:

> there are also instances in which those being watched also watch back. . . . By *watching the watchers*, key officials governing the penal apparatus themselves are monitored by a collective of prisoners, ex-cons, and activists. With that switch in attention, state officials are put on the defensive. That reduction of the symmetry of power has the capacity to enhance levels of official accountability.
>
> (Welch 2011: 304, original emphasis)

Others have also critiqued Mathiesen's observation that the panopticon and synopticon interact and work together, suggesting he does not provide very much detail about how these systems mutually reinforce one another (Doyle 2011: 296; Elmer 2003: 233). Moreover, echoing Welch, Doyle (2011) in particular argues Mathiesen's analysis of the role of the mass media in the viewer society, with its emphasis on celebrities and entertainment, pays little attention to the ways media of various sorts may act as sites of resistance, including resistance to surveillance at the stages of both production and audience reception. By focusing on the media's support for surveillance, Mathiesen ignores ideas that the media might be a contested space that allows openings for getting oppositional message across. In this way, Mathiesen's account is rather one-dimensional and provides little scope for exploring the complexity of media-surveillance relations, as well as thinking about the operation of media power in general. Not only does this approach ignore significant opposition in the news media to increased levels of surveillance but it also ignores the viewpoints and actions of oppositional groups that get into the news, such as Copwatch groups, which 'use video surveillance of police as a tool to resist police brutality and make such footage available on YouTube and to the news media' (Doyle 2011: 291–292). This idea that media can be used as a form of resistance and to hold to account those exercising state power, such as the police, is explored in more depth later in this chapter. Before looking at that, though, we will consider the somewhat more prosaic matter of citizen groups' resistance to speed cameras.

BOX 8.2 CCTV CAMERA OPERATORS: RULES OF ENGAGEMENT

The example of CCTV cameras is frequently cited to illustrate the escalating use of surveillance technologies in modern societies. Here, Britain is the world leader, with an estimated one camera for every 14 people (Surette 2015: 191, 296), meaning 'Britain now has more electronic eyes per head of population than any other country in the world, one-party states included' (Norris and Armstrong 1999: 39). There is a degree of mythology surrounding the operation of CCTV cameras, with some asking, who, if anyone, is watching? A sense of 'technological determinism' – also noted earlier in relation to the 2011 English riots – lies behind such questions, whereby the technology is treated as operating independently of any human influence. However, as Marx (2013: 57) reminds us, regardless of their level of sophistication, surveillance technologies still require human support. Accordingly, it is important to recognize that many CCTV cameras have human operators, and that CCTV should thus be treated as a *social medium*, 'facilitating interaction and socialization, the watched being both [passive] objects of information and [active] subjects of communication' (Smith 2007: 290). Moreover, as Norris and Armstrong (2009) reveal, CCTV operators import a variety of norms, values and attitudes into their work, such that they might broadly be seen to follow a number of tacit 'rules'.

Rule 1. *CCTV operators use prior knowledge to understand who is most likely to commit crimes.* Echoing their earlier observational study of three public space surveillance systems (Norris and Armstrong 1999), which found 93 percent of surveillance targets were males, 85 percent of whom were in their teens or twenties, the first rule of CCTV surveillance indicates operators target the young, black people, men and the working classes. Suspect youth, for instance, are identified by body language and cultural attire, with some operators making sardonic comments like: 'I wonder where he got those trainers from?' Racist comments are not uncommon among operators, and even though the language of black operators is not as venomous as that of white operators, they still tend to target young blacks rather than whites. These findings mirror those from McCahill's (2002) study of two shopping malls, which found males made up 71 percent of surveillance targets, 88 percent of whom were teenagers or young people in their twenties.

While women make up over half of the general population, they only account for 7 percent of those surveilled by CCTV operators. Importantly, being largely invisible as suspects also means women are unlikely to benefit from the 'protectional gaze' of CCTV cameras. Thus, Norris and Armstrong found the male gaze has little relevance for the security of women in urban settings, as the attitudes of operators are similar to those traditionally associated with the police when dealing with instances of domestic violence, namely that disputes between males and females in public settings are not regarded as worthy of surveillance by male operators who often consider them a private matter between the individuals involved. To Norris and Armstrong (2009: 528), the functionality of CCTV fosters a male gaze that is more voyeuristic than protective, showing how 'with its pan-tilt and zoom facilities the thighs and cleavages of the scantily clad are an easy target for those male operators so motivated'.

By way of a counterexample, in his study, Gavin Smith (2007: 302) found female operators – the majority of whom were older mothers – could initiate a caring observational gaze, reflecting their concern for a person's welfare or safety. Interestingly, he also shows how CCTV might serve to protect some of the most vulnerable urban dwellers, whereby 'many street beggars actually choose to sit in direct view of CCTV cameras, those spoken to in passing suggesting that knowing the cameras were watching over them made them "feel safer" as they tried to earn a living' (Smith 2007: 309).

Rule 2. *Some behavior warrants intensive surveillance because it is indicative of potential criminality (although appearances can be deceptive)*. Examples include fighting, horseplay, running and loitering with intent.

Rule 3. *CCTV operators target past offenders*. Notably, only 30 (i.e. 3 percent) cases of targeted surveillance were directly attributable to operators' personalized knowledge of a targeted person's criminal past. However, '[w]hen known offenders come into view they are targeted', although 'unless there are other features which indicate immediate dubious intent the surveillances tend to be short' (Norris and Armstrong 2009: 530). Similarly, Smith (2007: 297) found not only do operators target individuals known to them, but they also develop special relationships with what he calls the 'Stars of CCTV'; that is, characters that import color into the grayness of everyday life and bring entertainment to what is essentially an alienating job, making CCTV monitoring 'akin to watching a citywide soap opera'.

Rule 4. *Daily rhythms and different shifts are vitally important*. For instance, night shifts offer more opportunities for CCTV operators to generate arrests, especially in crime 'hot

Figure 8.2 CCTV control room

spots'. Thus, a typical workday pattern, such as the one outlined below by Norris and Armstrong (2009: 530–532), tends to influence whether a person is targeted or not:

- 7 am–2 pm: operators lapse into chat and drinking tea.
- 8:30 am–10 am: from 8:30 am operators focus on railways stations, and from 10 am they look for 'suspects' (young males) in pedestrian shopping malls.
- 5–6 pm: take breaks and wind down their state of alertness until post-8 pm.
- Post-8 pm: operators focus on the young and others who are dressed up arriving at pubs and nightclubs; the only early evening 'high alert' is *teen discos* on Saturdays, from 8–10:30 pm.
- 11 pm–2 am: target on male youths aged between 12 and 16, be they standing outside discos, fast-food outlets or transport termini.
- Post-2 am: surveillance is usually centered on red light areas.
- 4–7 am: tedious hours – operators snooze and watch for thefts of newspapers and bread and milk delivered to small stores before they open.

Rule 5. *Those who do not belong in certain areas are treated as Other*. This idea of 'otherness' is intimately connected to views about the appropriate use of social space and who has the 'right' to do things in towns and cities. Accordingly, CCTV operators will often focus on the homeless, vagrants and alcoholics, and people selling *The Big Issue*.

Rule 6. *People appearing lost, disorientated, and so forth are treated with suspicion*. Examples of such behavior include suddenly changing direction or wandering about aimlessly. Here, the attention of CCTV operators is drawn to incongruity, or 'those whose orientation to the locale through their interaction with both the social and physical environment is "out of place" ' (Norris and Armstrong 2009: 533). In this way, it is as if 'operators construct a map of the moral progress through the streets which is unidirectional', whereby '[p]eople of good moral character know where they are going and proceeded to their destination without signs of deviation' (Norris and Armstrong 2009: 533).

Rule 7. *Operators learn to see those who treat the presence of cameras as other than normal as other than normal themselves.* According to Norris and Armstrong (2009: 534), '[o]perators work with the absolute assumption that they have the right to surveille everyone on the street'. So, if anyone's behavior challenges that assumption they are immediately placed in a category of being morally suspect and thus worthy of surveillance. For example, if in the view of the operator, a person is directing their behavior to the presence of the camera, that awareness in and of itself demonstrates criminal intent, and therefore provides a strong basis for prolonged surveillance. Other examples of morally suspect behavior include things like abusive gestures to the camera, overt and theatrical forms of resistance, and token gestures of defiance, as in the following scenario:

> The operator resumes his surveillance of Santana's and sees half a dozen of the group board a bus and disappear leaving only four black males who walk across the road and down the High Street eventually disappearing from view. Before they are out of range, however, all four gesture abusively to the camera which angers the operator who says to his colleagues 'I'd love to go down there and run them all over'.
>
> (Norris and Armstrong 2009: 534)

Just as merely looking at a camera might compound suspicion, so activities deliberately intended to avoid cameras may be met with intensified observation. On the other hand, rather than trying to avoid surveillance, some might provoke it, as in the example of a group of young people given by Norris and Armstrong (2009: 535–536), who say that

> by demonstrating those behaviours they know will provoke surveillance, they indicate they are not merely passive objects of a disciplinary gaze. They too can have power, if merely by wasting the operator's time or by subverting the intentions of the system for their own entertainment.

This might also be thought of as a form of 'edgework', which, as we saw in Chapter 2, is a means of thrill-seeking and transgression to alleviate routine and boredom in contemporary society (Lyng 1990). Alternatively, these on-screen behaviors could be thought of as a form of 'playful resistance' (gamification-from-below) to the surveillance games CCTV operators are themselves engaged in (Woodcock and Johnson 2018).

RESISTING SURVEILLANCE: AGAINST SPEED CAMERAS

Although Haggerty and Ericson (2000: 618) argue there will never be a total democratic leveling of surveillance hierarchies, they do say that, due to its rhizomatic nature, no one will ever truly escape the gaze of the surveillant assemblage. That means powerless and powerful, rich and poor, black and white, female and male will all be subject to the control and monitoring of surveillance technologies, although it is also important to recognize new forms of inequality have emerged with the development of digital technologies. For instance, della Porta et al. (2006: 98) show how the Internet has created a 'digital divide', which reflects differences in Internet access across territories, social classes and groups with differing degrees of interest in politics (della Porta et al. 2006: 98). On the other hand, while it is most often already experienced activists who use the Internet and social media for political ends (Martin 2017b), less politically oriented citizens are also able increasingly to get involved in direct action and campaigning against surveillance.

One such group is the subject of a study by Wells and Wills (2009), who analyze the website discussion forums of organized anti-speed camera groups, including self-styled leaders of drivers' groups – e.g. Motorists Against Detection (Captain Gasto), and the Association of British Drivers – to explore the various 'narratives of resistance' to this type of surveillance. These narratives are used to justify 'acts of resistance', which include destroying speed cameras in innovative ways, such as pulling them down with tractors, setting fire to them with fuel-filled tires, or destroying them with shotguns and even dynamite. Wells and Wills identify three main narratives in discourses resisting speed cameras.

First, there is a narrative expressing skepticism about scientific expertise and government policy supposedly predicated on that expertise. This results in attempts by anti-speed camera groups to establish 'counter-knowledges' and 'alternate grounds for the right to participate in the debate', which are 'situated within an "experiential" expertise derived from direct, often daily, engagement with the risk issues which are used to legitimate surveillance by speed cameras' (Wells and Wills 2009: 263–264). In focus groups and online discussion forums, drivers recount their own stories to justify their right to comment and establish their own expert credentials. For example, they argue speed cameras are dangerous because they cause drivers to brake suddenly then accelerate furiously afterwards. Likewise, websites of the organized anti-camera groups demonstrate a preference for the 'real' expertise gleaned from experience: drivers are able to judge road conditions for themselves and make their own assessments as to the level of risk posed by speeding in certain circumstances; hence, their argument that speeding is not necessarily dangerous:

> The assumption of a flawed evidential basis allows both individual and group opponents of speed cameras to maintain that, if safety is not the motivation for the use of speed cameras, other motives such as revenue-raising must be paramount. By maintaining that their punishment results from such illegitimate aims, drivers are able to propose that their experiences of surveillance are, in fact, victimization.
>
> (Wells and Wills 2009: 265)

Secondly, Wells and Wills identify a narrative of the ordinary respectable citizen pitted against the oppressive state. Contained herein is a *narrative of oppression* about how the ordinary, respectable person who is opposed to an oppressive state is driven to unusual and extreme action. The emphasis here is on group members being 'respectable', 'decent', 'law-abiding', 'majority', in an attempt to maintain some semblance of credibility, as well as differentiating themselves from 'real' criminals. Accordingly, anti-speed camera activists go to great lengths to portray themselves as normal people by, for instance, making claims to be 'family men', 'ordinary blokes' or 'decent people'. The corollary is that they have been driven to extreme acts of vandalism out of desperation, and would not ordinarily be involved in criminal activity and conflict with the state. For example, Captain Gasto of the group, Motorists Against Detection, states: 'We are not criminals, just drivers going about our daily business and we are essentially law-abiding citizens' (quoted in Wells and Wills 2009: 267).

According to Wells and Wills (2009: 267), what is happening here is that anti-speed camera activists are attempting to distinguish themselves from other more 'political' activists, and that serves 'to depoliticize their activity, which is portrayed as non-ideological or non-political resistance'. Ironically, however, the language of being 'fed up', 'sick and tired', or 'driven to action' that is used by anti-speed camera activists, is also 'highly common in various activists discourses, ranging from environmentalists to anti-globalization' (Wells and Wills 2009: 267). Moreover, research supports the view that speeding is a majority activity, and that is used to legitimate drivers' respectable identity, as well as call into question 'the theoretical role of the police as defenders of a majority of respectable or law-abiding citizens from a minority of the criminally deviant' (Wells and Wills 2009: 268).

Thirdly, anti-speed camera activists articulate a narrative about how other groups and individuals are more deserving of surveillant attention than ordinary, 'law-abiding' drivers. This narrative stresses differences between the surveillance of worthy subjects versus the surveillance of undeserving subjects, and extends the narrative around 'respectability', discussed earlier, to the idea that by being inappropriately targeted, drivers are exposed to risks created by real criminals, 'who are left to continue their deviant behaviour unthreatened by a police force preoccupied with harassing motorists' (Wells and Wills 2009: 268). Furthermore, other types of driving behavior are constructed as far more risky, and thus more worthy of police attention, such as 'poorly-sighted, drunk, "dangerous", and uninsured drivers' (Wells and Wills 2009: 270).

Considering the implications of their study for theories of resistance to surveillance, Wells and Wills (2009: 271) say, first, that although many social movement protestors are motivated by having a sense of injustice, in the case of anti-speed camera activists, resistance is politically restricted and individualistic: 'restricted to a specific, visible and directly harmful surveillance technology, and promoted by social groups that previously occupied a privileged position'. That leads to a second point, also related to the notion of the 'digital divide' (discussed earlier), about how resistance to surveillance practices and technology may require a degree of technical or scientific expertise, or a type of 'critical literacy', which some communities are better able to develop than others. However, while critical literacy of surveillance technologies may occur more readily in relation to mass activities like driving, expertise is nevertheless limited experientially through the 'daily engagement with the processes and practices of this particular risk issue acquired through driving', and therefore 'is not practically possible in relation to many other risk issues such as global warming or the risks associated with nuclear power' (Wells and Wills 2009: 271). Thirdly, drivers' claims regarding their 'normality' (i.e. ordinary and respectable, law-abiding citizens) as compared to other deviant groups deemed more worthy of surveillant attention do little to foster solidarity and resistance across differing surveillance systems and subject populations. In short, the use of such claims:

> to legitimate political resistance to surveillance does nothing for the myriad populations that are 'abnormal' by these determinations but are still subject to surveillance which they may find oppressive or harmful. . . . Indeed, there is little evidence of objections to surveillance per se – close monitoring of the behaviour of deviant others is, by contrast, encouraged when it deflects attention from the activities of speeding drivers.
>
> (Wells and Wills 2009: 272)

The individualistic and depoliticized nature of anti-speed camera campaigns has implications for the formation of movements against other forms of surveillance, such as the introduction of identity cards, the development of automated number plate recognition technologies, or storing personal information on large databases. It also highlights problems associated with the *identity politics of surveillance*, which is unlikely to produce collective identities in the same ways as trade union politics or anti-racist activism (Rose 1999: 236). Indeed, as Wells and Wills argue, we ought not regard resistance to surveillance uncritically as having a necessarily positive or empowering purpose and effect. Distinctions can be drawn between resistance to surveillance based on wider social concerns, and resistance arising as a response to specific risks and costs caused to individuals, and where the latter prevails:

> increased exposure to surveillance is not opposed on the grounds that it is intrusive or contrary to any notion of human rights or social justice. It can, instead, be a further manifestation of existing processes of discrimination and 'othering' as surveilled populations' resistant efforts are focused only on redirecting the surveillant gaze from themselves and on to other traditionally suspect populations.
>
> (Wells and Wills 2009: 273)

VIDEO ACTIVISM AS COUNTER-SURVEILLANCE

Like Wells and Wills (2009), Wilson and Serisier (2010) have also examined the ways ordinary citizens might resist or even challenge state surveillance by looking at how protestors use video as a means of surveilling and hence turning the tables on the police. Notwithstanding certain inequalities that have arisen out of the development of digital technologies, as exemplified in the 'digital divide' (mentioned earlier), Wilson and Serisier (2010: 167) premise their arguments on the notion there has been a 'democratization and diffusion of image technologies', such that there is now greater equality of access to and use of surveillance, which 'opens up possibilities not only for resistance but also for more active empowerment'.

Wilson and Serisier (2010: 168) explore the perspectives of forest blockaders and anti-capitalist protestors in New South Wales, having conducting a number of semi-structured interviews with *video activists*, or 'people who use video as a tactical tool to deter police violence, document abuse and misconduct by police authorities, and in an effort to influence and set the political agenda'. Their findings confirm the three main functions of what Harding (2001: 65) terms 'witness video'. First, it can act as a pacifier of events (i.e. it can be used as a strategic tool to contain or diffuse nascent violence at protest events). Secondly, it can be used as a defense against false arrest or violent assault. Thirdly, it can act as a form of 'offense', that is, as a means of gathering what is called 'digital evidence' (Stratton et al. 2017: 25).

The pacifying and protective function of counter-surveillance was a persistent theme raised by video activists interviewed by Wilson and Serisier. Here, camcorders and visual imaging technologies are used as strategic tools to protect the public when dealing with the police, and as a means of containing potential police violence. Video recording police actions, however, is not without risk. Getting 'beaten up' by police was identified as the greatest hazard, with those interviewed reporting that 'individuals armed with video and digital cameras were commonly targeted by police at protest actions' (Wilson and Serisier 2010: 169).

Indeed, police draw on a range of actions aimed at neutralizing the counter-surveillance of protestors. One of the most common tactics is to render counter-surveillance inoperable by confiscating video recording equipment. Another is to use the power of legal statute to curtail filming with the threat of criminal proceedings – what is described below as a means of 'criminalizing dissent' – including threats to prosecute under counterterrorism laws. Neutralization techniques also extend to police failure to wear identifying badges at protest events, which means they are able to evade the gaze of video activists, and avoid official accountability for any other misconduct they perpetrate.

While these examples demonstrate some of the constraints activists face when using video as a means of holding police to account, video footage can still be used as an important tactical device in defending protestors against police accusations, especially if it captures police misconduct. Just as police mobilize legislation to neutralize counter-surveillance, so video activists also strategically engage the law as a means of providing evidentiary validation when filing complaints in respect of police misconduct. For instance, Wilson and Serisier (2010: 172) show how one protestor who was charged with assaulting a police officer used video evidence to reveal he had in fact been the victim of police brutality, having been put in a headlock and bashed in the face by a police officer, who, as often happens in these cases, was not subsequently charged with any offense himself. Ironically, though, protestors' own video footage can be used against them if it is subpoenaed in cases where activists are accused of committing offenses.

Hence, Wilson and Serisier's study demonstrates how the use of videographer footage is not straightforward, and can be double-edged, which also applies when we consider the mainstream media's interest in protest and dissent. For example, the involvement of commercial media may be useful in joining with activist footage to expose police misconduct, as happened during the APEC summit in Sydney in 2007 (see Box 8.3), when photos taken by one Sydney Copwatch observer revealed the widespread police (mal)practice of not wearing identification badges:

> during APEC I took just over 200 photographs of police officers not wearing badges, that had a very good outcome for us, it was a half page article in the *Sydney Morning Herald* on the anonymous police of APEC, highlighting the fact that many of the police officers either didn't put their badges on that day, or took them off.
>
> (Dale Mills, quoted in Wilson and Serisier 2010: 173, original emphasis)

Although media reporting may serve the interests of protestors, that is not necessarily done out of benevolence, but is rather an unintended consequence of the drive to make profit by producing sensationalized news, including coverage of potentially hostile clashes between police and protestors. In this way, the demands of newsworthiness, and especially in the case of reporting on the policing of protest, the media's preoccupation with news values around violence/conflict and predictability (see Chapter 1) can highlight the perils of engaging commercial mass media. Accordingly, as one of Wilson and Serisier's interviewees says, this may result in the de-contextualization of footage, which becomes freighted with meanings not originally intended by those filming:

> there are two issues. There's the issue around which the protest and the activism is happening and then there's the issue of police accountability and often we capture stuff which shows police behaving badly and the issue we're trying to get attention for gets ignored for the police stuff.
>
> (McEwan, quoted in Wilson and Serisier 2010: 174)

Wilson and Serisier's case study shows how police-protestor interactions constitute a series of moves and counter-moves, or how a 'tactical dance' is performed between police and protestors, where there is a 'coevolution' of tactics in what Marx (2009: 299) describes as a 'surveillance arms race'. Similarly, protest policing scholars have noted the existence of a relationship, such that 'repertoires of contention often interact with policing repertoires' (Martin 2011c: 28). Hence, in the mid- to late 1990s, the anti-globalization movement adopted decentralized, non-hierarchical, network-based forms of organizing (Fernandez 2008: 130, 137), along with developing more confrontational tactics, all of which culminated in 1999 in the so-called 'Battle of Seattle', when activists successfully disrupted the World Trade Organization ministerial meetings. Subsequently, and largely as a response to the evolving repertoire of anti-globalization activists, the tactics of police forces around the world adapted and changed.

The Battle of Seattle, then, is regarded as something of a watershed, with scholars identifying pre- and post-Seattle policing practices (Zajko and Béland 2008: 725), whereby, since 1999, law enforcement agencies have devised several strategies to deal with mass protest that involve things like securing physical space, building barricades, creating security (or frozen) zones and conducting mass pre-emptive arrests (Fernandez 2008: 92–93). So, instead of relying on negotiations and the issuing of 'protest permits' to engage protestors, as occurred previously, the state has now 'moved to control the physical landscape around protest, aiming to prevent another Battle of Seattle' (Fernandez 2008: 93). This *policing of space* requires increasingly sophisticated modes of social control that are neither purely repressive nor entirely negotiated, with Fernandez (2008: 15) observing that, 'the current mode is an effective mixture of hard- and soft-line tactics, including the use of new "non-lethal weapons" as well as laws, codes, regulations, and public relations strategies that attempt to control protest spaces directly and indirectly'.

Spatial strategies and soft-line tactics of social control are also identified as significant by Wilson and Serisier (2010: 169, 171), when both police and protestors mobilize law in their respective repertoires of surveillance and counter-surveillance. The use of soft-line strategies is of particular relevance in respect of what we examine in the next section, where we look at some recent developments in protest and public order policing which have been influenced by the use of surveillance practices, digital technologies and social media.

INTELLIGENT CONTROL: DEVELOPMENTS IN PROTEST AND PUBLIC ORDER POLICING

Many of the themes we have looked at so far in this chapter coalesce in what de Lint and Hall (2009) describe as 'intelligent control', which is a species of public order policing that places particular emphasis on intelligence and information gathering. Intelligence-led policing has a number of features that distinguish it from past policing approaches. First, intelligent control involves *exceptional consent*, which means, among other things, that 'a rights discourse is gradually evacuated as schedules of security become more pressing' (de Lint and Hall 2009: 266). Associated with this is the trend towards exceptionalism whereby the rule of law becomes subservient to a politics of privileging the rights of the state. After the terror attacks of 11 September 2001, that was evident in political discourse and introduction of legislation that eroded civil liberties enshrined in constitutional guarantees (e.g. freedom of speech, freedom of assembly and association) under the pretext of safeguarding national security. Reliance on secrecy has also become standard practice in intelligence control policing, which is itself part of a wider shift towards 'a more penetrating preventative police posture' (de Lint and Hall 2009: 267).

This leads to the second feature of intelligence-based policing: the increased use of *pre-emptive surveillance*. We have already seen how one of the most significant characteristics of the surveillant assemblage is the interoperability of police, security intelligence and commercial information systems and databases, which de Lint and Hall see as constituting new and exceptional practices of data collection and retention, including the use of biometrics that are now required in key citizen identity documents, like passports and driving licenses. For instance, the European Union now requires fingerprints and digital photographs (for facial recognition) for all its passport holders (Stach 2014: 44). Furthermore, as with many of the features identified by de Lint and Hall, the enhanced flow of intelligence between police and security agencies, which is exceptional but can also involve illegal data collecting and sharing practices, has expanded since 9/11, thus altering significantly the intelligence field. For example, after 9/11, 'Canadian officials developed more proactive measures to collect data and trigger alerts regarding the communication, travel, visa, and financial transactions of people' (de Lint and Hall 2009: 269).

Pre-emption is also tied to the third feature of intelligent control identified by de Lint and Hall, namely *boundary blurring and fusion*, which, as we saw earlier, is something Cohen (1985) also sees as crucial in contemporary forms of social control. In relation to intelligence-led policing the blurring refers to blending or fusion of police and security functions, whereby 'the harmonization of police and security protocols across distinct and differing national and political interests proceeds apace' (de Lint and Hall 2009: 270). It should also be noted here that not only is this occurring in protest and public order settings but increasingly forms part of everyday police practice, as attested to by de Lint and Hall (2009: 274), who state that, '[u]nder more recent police reforms, intelligence, secrecy, and knowledge exclusions have become the standard-bearing practices'. Hence, in the Australian state of New South Wales, for instance, police now have powers at their disposal that were formerly reserved for security intelligence services, such as the ability, when the commission of a serious crime is suspected, to perform clandestine 'warrantless searches' of premises using so-called 'sneak and peek' powers given them in legislation (Martin 2010, 2011c). Echoing Cohen's (1985: 44) conception of 'net widening', de Lint and Hall (2009: 271) say blurring and fusion result in interoperability between law enforcement agencies and security services, which brings 'a wide array of subjects into an expanded net'.

In the public order or protest context, interoperability now means 'demonstrators encounter a remarkable array of police and security officials' (de Lint and Hall 2009: 271). Fusion and boundary blurring here have also lead to the *militarization of policing*, 'particularly where the existential right of the nation-state itself is said to be threatened' (de Lint and Hall 2009: 271; see also L. J. Wood 2014). To the extent that such a threat or 'sovereignty spectacle' (de Lint and Hall 2009: 270) may occur at large-scale international events, like APEC, WTO and G20 meetings, militarization combines with the fourth feature of intelligent control: *reflexive dramatization*. This pertains to the need for governments to 'showcase security' at these events, and especially those held in global cities where the event provides a means of 'place promotion', advertising it as a safe, secure and attractive place for corporations to invest and tourists to visit (Martin 2011c). There is then a political-economic component to reflexive dramatization, with police and security work emphasizing 'the importance of public relations and the management of appearances, that control *must be seen to be done*' (de Lint and Hall 2009: 272, original emphasis). Indeed, Fernandez (2008: 100–101) describes the 'economy of protest' that has grown up around hosting large-scale events and training police officers, which can cost municipal and federal governments millions of dollars. For instance, the APEC meeting held in Sydney in 2007 cost an estimated $170 million (AUD), which is equivalent to the cost of a Hollywood movie (Martin 2011c: 33).

Increasingly, the management of so-called 'mega-events' (Boyle and Haggerty 2009) involves a 'performance art' (de Lint and Hall 2009: 272), such that the police themselves are aware of the need to provide a security spectacle. For instance, they might stage daily 'surges', whereby 'heavily armed officers congregate in massive numbers in self-described "shock and awe" intimidation displays' (de Lint and Hall 2009: 273). Similarly, they may put on 'random dramatizations of force at landmarks, critical infrastructures (banks, hotels, bridges, etc.), or targets of high symbolic value "to keep terrorists guessing and remind people to be vigilant"' (de Lint and Hall 2009: 273). All of this is intended to provide the public with reassurance, although in many respects intelligence-based policing is about simulating control and order through the management of appearances. That means there is, in essence, a triumph of spectacle over substance, which can lead to security breaches, such as the one that occurred at the Sydney APEC meeting in 2007, albeit only with farcically comic effect (see Box 8.3).

BOX 8.3 APEC 2007: POLICING PROTEST SYDNEY STYLE

Many of the elements of what de Lint and Hall (2009) term 'intelligent control', and, in particular, *reflexive dramatization* were on display at the APEC meeting that was held in Sydney in 2007. As at other such events, Sydney became fortified and militarized, with spaces around the meeting resembling a war zone (Fernandez 2008: 122–123). Like scenes from a James Bond movie, 'security measures at the meeting included a huge police presence, rooftop snipers, "ring of steel" fencing, water cannon, rolling prisons and police frogmen on jetskis' (Martin 2011c: 33, Figure 8.3). Accompanying these 'hard-line' tactics were 'soft-line' tactics (Fernandez 2008: 15), including the enactment of special legislation: the *APEC Meeting (Police Powers) Act 2007* (NSW) providing police with extraordinary powers in parts of the Sydney CBD for the duration of the APEC meeting. For example, within designated 'security areas' they could 'establish roadblocks, checkpoints and cordons; search people, vehicles and vessels; seize and detail prohibited items; give reasonable directions; exclude or remove people from APEC security areas' (Snell 2008: 5).

© Mandel Ngan/AFP/Getty Images

© epa European pressphoto agency b.v./Alamy Stock Photo

© Jewel Samad/AFP/Getty Images

© epa European pressphoto agency b.v./Alamy Stock Photo

Figure 8.3 Military style security operations in Sydney, Australia, during the 2007 APEC summit

One could be forgiven for thinking the approach to public order policing at the APEC summit was an example of what Alex Vitale (2005) calls 'command and control' style policing, which places particular emphasis on the strict micro-management of demonstrations. Indeed, certain areas of Sydney were micro-managed, with police officers telling restaurateurs to remove butter knives and forks from outdoor tables in case they were used as weapons (Martin 2011c: 42). Elsewhere, however, there was a huge security failure, which exposed policing at APEC for stressing spectacle over substance:

> On 6 September 2007, a team of satirical comedians from the Australian TV show, *The Chaser's War on Everything*, breached the security cordon by driving a fake motorcade displaying Canadian flags within 10 metres of the Intercontinental Hotel where the US president, George W. Bush, was staying. The police arrested 11 members of the cast and crew only after the motorcade was turned around by the show's executive producer and one of the comedians alighted a vehicle dressed as Osama bin Laden.
>
> (Martin 2011c: 35)

Although charges against the *Chaser* team were eventually dropped, the incident raised serious questions about police 'mismanagement' of the event (Gorringe and Rosie 2008), not to mention 'what might have happened had bone fide terrorists really managed to get away with such subterfuge' (Martin 2011c: 35). The hyper-security in Sydney was also criticized by international business leaders attending the APEC summit as delegates, who blamed it for hampering their ability to move about and mix with one another. The 'lockdown' also had negative effects on local businesses, some of which reported their worst days of business in years. And, contrary to the idea that showcasing security at high-profile events acts as a form of place promotion, there were concerns the security measures 'would tarnish Australia's image abroad, with tourism and hotel authorities fearing Sydney would be branded a hostile city because of APEC week' (Martin 2011c: 39). All of these points illustrate starkly the dangers of *overpolicing* or ' "tough" saturation policing', whereby in the process of preventing disorder, the events themselves are prevented (Jefferson 1993: 378). Indeed, Boyle and Haggerty (2009: 265) contend the security spectacle at 'mega-events' must not be *too* spectacular lest organizers 'frighten away the very people whom they are seeking to attract'.

While preventative action based on information is key to understanding intelligent control, as the phenomenon of reflexive dramatization illustrates, intelligence-led policing comprises a combination of what Fernandez (2008: 15) describes as soft-line tactics, such as pre-emptive surveillance, and hard-line tactics, such as 'shock and awe' surges. This goes to the fifth and final feature of intelligent control, that is, *hybrid policing*. Hence, public order policing is first and foremost about action on information, 'drawn as a result of pre-emptive or covert targeting, collection, analysis, and dissemination that is used to manage conditions of mass protest' (de Lint and Hall 2009: 275). However, intelligent control strategies often consist of a hybrid of 'liaison strategies' and 'intelligence-based coercion', which results in 'an overall approach that is measured, flexible, targeted (precise), and stage-managed' (de Lint and Hall 2009: 275).

Ultimately, say de Lint and Hall (2009: 277), the hybrid policing of intelligent control is about 'the co-existence of pre-emptive and informational policing and paramilitary and spectacular policing', behind which lies a political-democratic imperative requiring a dramaturgical dimension, such that when, as at protest events, coercion is visibly displayed, it is limited, managed and targeted, although, as we know, the police 'can change colour from black to blue'. The need for police to be attentive to forms of impression management, particularly at public order and protest events, where the use of video recording devices and other surveillance technologies are increasingly utilized by protestors and bystanders alike, is a subject addressed in the next section.

CITIZEN JOURNALISM AND POLICING'S NEW VISIBILITY

We have already seen how activists' video footage can be used tactically to record instances of police misconduct and abuse, and to deter police violence (Wilson and Serisier 2010; see also Bradshaw 2013). Another related form of counterveillance is the growth of 'participatory journalism' or 'citizen journalism', which Dennis (2008: 349) defines as a 'form of reportage that blends on-the-ground citizen news collecting, analysing, and disseminating, with a form of participatory surveillance'. As mentioned earlier in the chapter, the use of social media and digital technologies, such as mobile phone video cameras, are key developments in bottom-up forms of surveillance like this, which, as Haggerty and Ericson (2000: 618) recognize, do not represent 'a complete democratic levelling of the hierarchy of surveillance', but are nevertheless positive and productive components of the surveillant assemblage:

> the monitoring of the powerful has been eased by the proliferation of relatively inexpensive video cameras. These allow the general public to tape instances of police brutality, and have given rise to inner-city citizen response teams which monitor police radios and arrive at the scene camera-in-hand to record police behaviour.
>
> (Haggerty and Ericson 2000: 618)

Although maintaining silence and preserving secrecy can be legitimate police practices in lawful undercover operations, they can also be tactics employed defensively by police to avoid public embarrassment and formal accountability (Goldsmith 2010: 915). However, the advent of new digital and social media technologies now enables greater scope for police accountability, exposing alleged police misconduct to mass audiences, and providing opportunities for 'disruptive disclosure' and counter-surveillance, all of which means 'the tactics of maintaining secrecy, keeping silent and practising concealment are less available to police now' (Goldsmith 2010: 920). Accordingly, while police 'account ability' (i.e. keeping up normal appearances through forms of impression management that are within the scope of police control) has been greatly diminished, their accountability to the court of public opinion has increased markedly with the growing use of mobile phone cameras, video-sharing platforms like YouTube and social networking sites, such as Facebook. What Andrew Goldsmith (2010: 925–926) calls policing's 'new visibility' relates largely to police use of force and police brutality, which tends to be accentuated in protest and public order settings, where, by definition, those aspects of police behavior are more visible. The case of the death of Ian Tomlinson provides a powerful illustration of how citizen video recording of police action at protest events has the potential to affect real change by intervening in the administration of justice (Figure 8.4).

In April 2009, Ian Tomlinson was filmed walking past a police cordon at the Royal Exchange in the City of London amid the G20 summit protests. He was then struck with a baton and pushed to the ground by a police officer in the cordon. Not long after, he died. Tomlinson was not a protestor, but a newspaper vendor who had been walking home from work during the G20 protests. The video footage was taken not by an activist, but by American tourist Christopher La Jaunie, who had initially not realized the significance of the video he had taken, although when he did, he immediately sent it to the *Guardian* newspaper, which promptly released it on its website (Scott Bray 2013: 457, 468). In accordance with Wilson and Serisier's (2010) analysis, subsequent developments in the formal course of events reveal the power of citizen journalism, joined with commercial media, to expose police misconduct via 'witness video' (Harding 2001: 65).

© Kathy de Witt/Alamy Stock Photo

Figure 8.4 Ian Tomlinson memorial behind the Royal Exchange Buildings, City of London, UK

Prior to the *Guardian*'s publication of the footage taken by La Jaunie, the UK Home Office pathologist determined Tomlinson had died of natural causes; and at that time the death was not subject to review by the Independent Police Complaints Commission (IPCC). However, after the video's release, the IPCC assumed investigative control in the case, conducting an additional three independent investigations following complaints made by Tomlinson's family. The release of the video also sparked further autopsies, and ultimately led to a coronial verdict of 'unlawful killing' (Scott Bray 2013: 455). That, in turn, led the Crown Prosecution Service (CPS) to review its original decision not to prosecute PC Simon Harwood, who was the police officer shown striking and pushing Tomlinson. The CPS charged Harwood with manslaughter, but he was acquitted, which resulted in what has been described as an instance of 'paradoxical justice' (Scott Bray 2013: 471), where, on the one hand, a coroner delivered a verdict of unlawful killing, while, on the other hand, a criminal court acquitted the police officer involved of any wrongdoing.

On the face of it, citizen journalism implies there is now little need for professional journalists in an age of 'post-journalism' (Altheide and Snow 1991). Indeed, if citizen journalism is regarded a species of 'sousveillance', in line with Mann's (1998) analysis, it would, in its purest form, constitute a mode of *unmediated* of bottom-up surveillance. In reality, however, and as Wilson and Serisier (2010) note, the commercial media still play a role, incorporating stories about protest and dissent into news reporting (see also Dennis 2008: 349–350). The case of Ian Tomlinson provides a clear example of the melding of citizen journalism and mainstream media – a case of newer media setting the news agenda of older media (Yardley et al. 2017: 490; see also Jenkins 2006) – as attested to by the *Guardian*'s editor-in-chief, Alan Rusbridger, who described it as a situation where '"old-fashioned reporting was allied with the mass observation of people we wouldn't call reporters but who were, on the day, able to do acts of journalism"' (Wilby 2012: 37).

CRIMINALIZING DISSENT

As we have seen, the tactics of protestors and police tend to develop in tandem, interacting with one another in a series of moves and counter-moves. It is not surprising, then, that across Western democracies the state has introduced measures enabling police to counter the sousveillance tactics used by video activists and citizen journalists at protest events and in other public order settings. Many of these measures resemble the 'soft-line' tactics described by Fernandez (2008: 15), such as the enactment of new laws or regulations designed to control protest spaces, as happened at APEC in Sydney in 2007 (Box 8.3). However, these developments are part of a broader context in which the erosion of rights and freedoms has intensified since the terror attacks of 11 September 2001 when 'past conventions and practices that lead parliamentarians to exercise self-restraint with regard to democratic principles were put aside in the name of responding to the threat of terrorism' (Williams 2015).

Significantly, not only have laws infringing democratic freedoms increased in number – in Australia, George Williams (2015) has identified 350 examples, 209 (approximately 60 percent) having been introduced since September 2001 – but so has their severity. Hence, 'where legislation previously made conduct unlawful, and therefore had a low impact upon freedoms, more recent legislation criminalizes conduct, which can also be subject to long periods of imprisonment' (Martin 2017c: 103). Williams observes that the problem may well run much deeper, because the 350 instances of legislation infringing democratic rights and freedoms on the face of the law do not include infringements that could occur *indirectly*. Thus, he concludes, '[a] dynamic has been created whereby extraordinary anti-terrorism laws have created new understandings and precedents that have made possible an even broader range of rights infringing legislation' (Williams 2015).

The 'right to protest' – which 'is essentially an amalgam of the right to free speech, and the right to assemble peacefully in public' (Martin 2017d: 282) – has also been impacted by these developments. In the Australian state of Queensland, for example, protestors at the G20 summit held in Brisbane and Cairns, 15–16 November 2014, were subject directly to provisions of the *G20 Safety and Security Act 2013* (Qld). Most worryingly, however, protestors may have been affected indirectly by the *Vicious Lawless Association Disestablishment Act 2013* (Qld). Introduced to tackle the serious organized crime of outlaw motorcycles gangs (or 'bikies'), but now repealed, section 7(1) of that Act imposed

> mandatory sentences of 15 years' imprisonment in addition to the original sentence for a declared offence on a 'vicious lawless associate', such as a bikie club member, and an extra 10 years (i.e. 25 years on top of the original sentence) for a vicious lawless associate who was an office bearer of the relevant association at the time or during the commission of the offence.
>
> (Martin 2014: 535)

At the time of the Queensland G20 summit observers voiced concern at the prospect these two pieces of legislation could interact with one another:

> If for example an otherwise peaceful (and lawful) assembly turns violent, there is the possibility for people to be charged with affray, one of the offences listed as a trigger for operation of the *VLAD* [*Vicious Lawless Association Disestablishment*] *Act*. Carrying out such an act with three others deemed to be participants in a serious crime then renders the accused a participant in a criminal organization. This would attract the additional mandatory sentences.
>
> (Galloway and Ardill 2014: 6, original emphasis)

Although this is an extreme example of how protest may be criminalized inadvertently, across Australia dissent is gradually being criminalized (Martin 2017d). For instance, in New South Wales it has been claimed heavy-handed police tactics at anti-mining demonstrations have undermined the right to peaceful protest, and led the state government to consider new legislation to counteract 'illegal protest activity' and safeguard business interests (Gotsis 2015: 1), including up to seven years jail for protestors who lock onto mining equipment (Robertson 2016). Similarly, in Tasmania, legislation has been introduced 'to "rebalance the scales" between the right to protest and the rights of business to create economic opportunities and develop the economy' (Gotsis 2015: 35). Likewise, Western Australia has brought in laws 'to deter environmental protestors from locking on to equipment at mining and logging sites or taking other obstructionist action' (Gotsis 2015: 36).

What these examples highlight is that central to protest policing is an 'economy of protest' (Fernandez 2008: 100–101) or 'political economy of protest' (Martin 2017d: 286–288), which has become ever more apparent with the rise of the 'corporate state', as private and state interests increasingly converge – as evident also in the phenomenon of the 'surveillant assemblage'. However, while private corporations will tend to use civil litigation, such as Strategic Lawsuits Against Public Participation or SLAPPs, not to acquire damages but to silence protest, contain resistance and prevent criticism of corporate activities that threaten human rights and cause environmental damage, the state may act coercively, even criminalizing protest, or otherwise violating civil liberties and constitutionally protected rights (Martin 2017d: 287–288).

In Canada, for instance, although freedom of expression and freedom of peaceful assembly are protected under Section 2 of the Charter of Rights and Freedoms, research has revealed that protest policing involves, 'the systematic violation of constitutional protections against arbitrary arrest and detention . . . as well as protection against abusive searches' (Fortin et al. 2013: 41). In the US, the question of whether the First Amendment to the Constitution (guaranteeing freedom of speech and the right to peaceable assembly) extends to rights to surveil police was raised after a federal judge ruled the First Amendment does not protect a right to take photos or record videos of police, unless filming is done in the spirit of protest (Mock 2016). That decision is in line with proposals made previously in California to protect citizens recording or photographing police actions, as long as they do not prevent officers performing their duties; however, it is out of step with plans subsequently drafted in Arizona making it illegal to shoot close-up videos of police on the ground it would distract officers engaging with suspects, and thus put them in danger (Martin 2017d: 283).

In a more recent development, a group of 40 documentary filmmakers wrote an open letter to the US Department of Justice after it was revealed citizen journalists involved in the Black Lives Matter movement who filmed black people being shot by police were subsequently harassed and targeted by law enforcement agencies clearly intent on suppressing footage, intimidating witness, controlling stories and covering up police brutality and other forms of misconduct (Lartey 2016). By contrast, in New South Wales, Australia, where police are now issued with body-worn video cameras (Kidd 2015), authorities have apparently welcomed moves by Aboriginal groups involved in a Copwatch program in Broken Hill – a town in a remote part of the state – to learn rights and media skills around using mobile phones to safely document misconduct by government agents (Wainwright 2017).

This illustrates what Stratton et al. (2017: 26) identify as the role of social media and digital evidence not only in expanding the repertoire of law enforcement agencies (cp. Trottier 2015), but also in advancing the democratizing effect of digital technologies: that is, by increasing the ability of marginalized communities to 'watch the watchers', it enables the 'invigoration of social justice movements in a broader context of disenchantment'. These examples therefore stand as a rebuttal to the notion of the 'digital divide', showing how socially disadvantaged or marginalized groups are able to share information and images about police misconduct, for instance, by relatively cheap and simple means via social media and the Internet.

CONCLUSION

The Copwatch program in Broken Hill was sparked by stories of alleged racism, prejudice and harassment by government agencies, and particularly the police, in the town. Tips on how and when to film authorities, things to do before sharing the footage on social media, and ways to protect it, were also shared by lawyers involved in the case of Ms Dhu, a young Aboriginal woman who died in custody in Western Australia after being detained by police for unpaid fines totaling $3,622.00. A coronial inquest found Ms Dhu died of complications arising from septicemia, after suffering a catastrophic deterioration in her health during three days in police custody (Neuweiler 2017).

Similar circumstances have surrounded the emergence of the Black Lives Matter movement, which has also used social media as a key tool to confront state violence, racist patterns of policing, and extreme forms of surveillance targeting black communities (Carney 2016; Rickford 2016: 37–38). In essence, these are contemporary (post-segregation) means of enforcing racial hierarchy within a framework of white supremacy, which, according to Rickford (2016: 37), has been a central task of policing since the days of slavery, although today 'the criminal justice system performs social control tasks – the regulation of black bodies, the harnessing of black surplus labour in the name of corporate profit – once fulfilled by Jim Crow segregation and other overt forms of discrimination'. Likewise, Simone Browne (2015) places contemporary surveillance technologies and practices within the context of the long history of racial formation and methods of policing black life. Accordingly, to her, the conditions of blackness are a key site through which surveillance is practiced, narrated and resisted. Hence, it is not surprising to learn of a police backlash against Black Lives Matter protestors who are viewed as enemy combatants, and subject to extensive surveillance and acts of coercion, which the police discuss 'in precisely the terms of a colonial occupation' (Rickford 2016: 40).

This confirms what we have seen throughout this chapter, namely that surveillance is a dynamic, relational and interactive process, often involving a power struggle. And this is why it is important to consider state surveillance from above as well as resistance to it from below. While it remains to be seen what the long-term effects of the Black Lives Matter movement might be, an early empirical assessment examining how, to couch it in Doyle's (2011: 291) terms, the oppositional message of the movement has been incorporated in the mainstream media, suggests little has changed. Obasogie and Newman's (2016: 561) study shows how local news accounts of officer-involved civilian deaths remain strongly committed to color-blind reporting, have a focus on the police perspective and continue to use 'criminalizing language unrelated to the incident itself to characterize the victim's respectability'. On the other hand, one of the most successful recent examples of resistance to state surveillance has been Wikileaks, the main targets of which 'are national governments that try to censor and restrict Internet access and surveil people's traffic' (Martin 2017b).

As surveillance is a dynamic process, one would not expect the state to take Wikileaks's exposure of its criminal and politically corrupt activities lightly. Indeed, as the cases of whistle-blowers Chelsea Manning and Edward Snowden illustrate, when the state's legitimacy is threatened by such disclosure, it retaliates, hoping that will serve as a deterrent to other would-be whistle-blowers (Rothe and Steinmetz 2013: 287–289; see also de Zwart 2013: 254). The state acts in this way not for moral or ethical reasons, but out of rational self-interest, whereby the ends justify the means: 'the state pursue the goals of national security and stability regardless of the ethical or moral dubiousness of the means because the benefits of a stable and powerful country are of the upmost importance' (Rothe and Steinmetz 2013: 283).

When the state attempts to control potentially embarrassing or threatening behavior it will frequently mete out overly harsh and punitive treatments, including those violating due process and human rights guaranteed by constitutional law. In the case of Manning, this entailed, among other things, the illegal pre-trial punishment of subjecting her to a period of solitary confinement that lasted approximately 11 months, which was only terminated following political pressure from international non-government organizations and, in particular, the United Nations Special Rapporteur for Human Rights (Rothe and Steinmetz 2013: 286); thereby bringing an international political opportunity structure to bear on a nation-state's violation of human rights (Martin 2015a: 242–243). Ironically, then, although it was used to obscure the state's criminality, Manning's abuse actually suggests:

> [s]he has been victimized by the state, making another example of state harm and state crime that occurred through the state's efforts to maintain legitimacy, its power, and perhaps most importantly, the level of secrecy that enables it to practice realpolitik rather than the idealism and moral concerns the government espouses.
>
> (Rothe and Steinmetz 2013: 289)

In the next chapter, we will look at Mark Hamm's (2007) study of the exposé of prisoner torture and abuse by US military personnel and the Central Intelligence Agency (CIA) at the Abu Ghraib detention facility in Baghdad, following the invasion of Iraq in 2003. Although we noted earlier that Welch's notion of counterveillance has broad application beyond prisons, including applicability to the activities of Wikileaks (Martin 2015a: 206), the state crimes exposed at Abu

Ghraib provide a classic illustration of counterveillance as it applies strictly to prisons. Hamm's analysis also contributes to a small but growing body of work addressing what was discussed in Chapter 2 as cultural criminology's supposed failure to examine and critique harms caused by states and state agents; in this case, from the vantage point of visual criminology, with Hamm drawing specifically on photographic images of mistreatment perpetrated by American soldiers.

SUGGESTED FURTHER READING

The work of leading surveillance studies scholar, David Lyon, always proves a useful place to start for anyone interested in this area:

Lyon, D. (1994) *The Electronic Eye: The Rise of Surveillance Society*. Minneapolis, MN: University of Minnesota Press.

Lyon, D. (2001) *Surveillance Society: Monitoring Everyday Life*. Buckingham: Open University Press.

Lyon, D. (ed.) (2006) *Theorizing Surveillance: The Panopticon and Beyond*. Cullompton: Willan Publishing.

Lyon, D. (2007) *Surveillance Studies: An Overview*. Malden, MA: Polity Press.

Although they have been discussed in some depth in the chapter, it is still worth reading in full the following articles, both of which look at contemporary developments in surveillance beyond the relative confines of panopticism:

Haggerty, K. D. and Ericson, R. V. (2000) 'The surveillant assemblage' *British Journal of Sociology* 51(4): 605–622.

Mathiesen, T. (1997) 'The viewer society: Michel Foucault's "panopticon" revisited' *Theoretical Criminology* 1(2): 215–234.

To further explore the role of CCTV in contemporary society see:

Norris, C. and Armstrong, G. (1999) *The Maximum Surveillance Society: The Rise of CCTV*. New York, NY: Berg.

Smith, G. J. D. (2015) *Opening the Black Box: The Work of Watching*. London: Routledge.

The pages of *Surveillance & Society* (www.surveillance-and-society.org/) continue to produce cutting edge research on surveillance, and include a 2009 special issue on resistance (6(3)), and 2007 issues on criminal justice (4(3–4)). See also the 2011 special edition of *Theoretical Criminology* (15(3)) on surveillance in crime control.

The following book considers some of the challenges posed to criminology by the proliferation of digital communication technologies and new media:

Powell, A., Stratton, G. and Cameron, R. (2018) *Digital Criminology: Crime and Justice in Digital Society*. London: Routledge.

Although it is focused empirically on Canada, de Lint and Hall's study of contemporary developments in public order policing, including the role played by intelligence and surveillance in pre-emptive crime control strategies, has broad cross-jurisdictional application, and not only in relation to public order policing but also protest policing and everyday policing:

de Lint, W. and Hall, A. (2009) *Intelligent Control: Developments in Public Order Policing in Canada*. Toronto: University of Toronto Press.

CHAPTER 9

Organized crime, terrorism and high crimes of state

INTRODUCTION

We begin this chapter by exploring media representations of organized crime, which typically portray Mafia and other gangsters operating in a criminal underworld. From a popular culture perspective, narratives linking Italian American people to organized crime have been regarded problematic because they tend to depict 'hyper-reality . . . more than the concrete reality of daily life' (Beck 2000: 25). Accordingly, Beck (2000: 25) argues, 'the cultural role of the Italian American community and its identification with organized crime are dictated by literary even more than by sociological principles'. To criminologists, however, stereotypical portrayals of individuals and groups regarded as organized criminals are problematic because they provide a very limited way of conceiving of organized crime.

In that respect, some have stressed the similarities between legitimate and illegitimate business practices, arguing, for instance, there can be symbiotic relationships between organized crime, business, politics and even the media. This view 'discredits the alien-importation conventional history and emphasizes the coalition between business people, politicians, and crime groups in organizing and tolerating crime against the public interest' (Levi 2007: 778). One way of thinking about organized crime's symbiotic relationship with legitimate structures is captured by Rawlinson (1998: 353) who says it arises, 'whether by commission, as in the case of the legal profession, the financial world and politicians, or by omission, as in the case of law enforcement and administration'.

By inverting the conventional model, the symbiotic perspective attributes organized crime to business people, arguing crimes and other harms and injustices resulting from corporate activities are embedded in normal business practices in essentially two ways (see Haines 2017: 182–184). First, crimes or harms, such as environmental damage, are seen as normal and unavoidable byproducts of business activity, which can be protected or allowed in law. The idea that harms accrue from 'normal' business activity is also known as the 'business is business' model. Secondly, corporate offenders are seen as parasitical because they use the legitimate operations of a business as a shield for activities that might cause harm or injustice, even though they are not technically illegal. An example here would be how multinational corporations exploit child laborers working in sweatshops in countries with few, if any, labor standards or laws protecting worker rights. To the extent that governments in 'host' countries are complicit in these 'crimes', critical criminologists have proposed states can also perpetrate crimes.

Similarly, Charles Tilly (1985: 179) recognizes the symbiotic relationship that exists between the state, military and private industry, arguing there is an analogy between war making and state making and organized crime. Indeed, he says, 'war making and state making – quintessential protection rackets with the advantage of legitimacy – qualify as our largest examples of organized crime' (Tilly 1985: 169). His contention is that a government's monopoly on violence make its claims to be a legitimate protector more credible, or, at least, more difficult to resist. On this view, protection constitutes a core activity of states and state agents, and involves, among other things, '[e]liminating or neutralizing the enemies of their clients' (Tilly 1985: 181). By creating a threat and then charging for protection (e.g. via a system of taxation), Tilly claims, governments are no different to racketeers (though racketeers operate without government sanction):

> To the extent that the threats against which a given government protects its citizens are imaginary or are consequences of its own activities, the government has organized a protection racket. Since governments themselves commonly simulate, or even fabricate threats of external war and since the repressive and extractive activities of governments often constitute the largest current threats to livelihoods of their own citizens, many governments operate in essentially the same ways as racketeers.
>
> (Tilly 1985: 171)

Tilly's early contribution has remained relatively obscure in comparison to William Chambliss's 1988 America Society of Criminology Presidential Address, which inspired a generation of criminologists to study state crimes. In it, Chambliss outlined what he saw as the key causes of 'state-organized crime'. Although it seems somewhat contradictory that a state would violate its own laws, Chambliss explains this in terms of certain dilemmas states and state officials face in pursuing wholly legitimate goals, which they can only achieve realistically via illegitimate means. He illustrates this historically using the example of state complicity in piracy during the colonial period. At the time, the French, English and Dutch were not powerful enough to go to war with the Spanish and Portuguese, but still wanted to share in the wealth derived from Spain and Portugal's exploitation of labor and natural resources in the Americans and Asia. France, England and Holland therefore forged allegiances with pirates, who plundered Spanish and Portuguese ships on their behalf. While the cooperation with pirates violated their own laws and those of other countries, these nation-states 'organized criminality for their own ends without undermining their claim to legitimacy or their ability to condemn and punish piracy committed against them' (Chambliss 1989: 202).

Another more recent example provided by Chambliss concerns the dilemma between laws prohibiting arms smuggling, such as the Reagan administration's supply of arms to the Contras in Nicaragua during the 1980s, which contradicted the quite legitimate aim of fighting the global spread of communism. In this example, the *end* of fighting communism justified the *means* of arms smuggling, or as Chambliss (1989: 203) puts it, 'arms smuggling has been a price government agencies have been willing to pay "for other political goals"'. Similarly, government plots to carry out assassinations and perpetrate illegal acts against their own citizens to 'preserve democracy' are quite clearly contradictory because they support some of the most undemocratic institutions and activities imaginable.

Chambliss (1989: 204) accepted the limits of his study's focus on 'the conventional criminological definition of crime as acts that are in violation of criminal law'. In contrast, what is highlighted by the symbiotic model and 'business is business' perspective is the notion that to understand corporate crime and state-organized crime we must go beyond a narrow definition of crime to include activities and practices that while not illegal nevertheless result is harm and injustice: 'crime', that is, in a broad sense of the term. Stressing the broad view of crime also enables us to consider not only crimes of state but also their organized nature, which is another way of framing state-organized crime.

Later in the chapter, we apply this idea to Mark Hamm's (2007) analysis of the abuse and torture carried out by the US military at Abu Ghraib detention center following the invasion of Iraq in 2003 in the wake of the terror attacks of 11 September 2001. Like corporations that outsource manufacturing to countries with unprotected workforces, the US government's post-9/11 practice of 'extraordinary rendition' outsourced torture to countries with no human rights safeguards. Although the abuses that took place in those parts of the world were not criminal in the technical and narrow sense, they still violated international laws prohibiting torture and other forms of mistreatment. Comparable arguments have been made in respect of Australia's system for processing asylum seekers in detention centers run by private companies in overseas jurisdictions (Martin 2018).

Hamm's study not only demonstrates the criminal nature of what happened at Abu Ghraib, but also the deliberate, systematic and *organized* nature of those state crimes, which implicated the CIA, its director, and the US president. This leads to a final point we discuss later in the chapter, which concerns the view, flagged in Chapter 2, that from a critical cultural criminology perspective, we should seek to reverse the stereotypical view of terrorism and terrorists, regarding the state itself as an agent of terror and perpetrator of organized crimes. Here, again, we can apply Chambliss's idea about the contradictory origins of state-organized crime, which contends states are involved in organized crime often to achieve what are believed to be perfectly legitimate ends. Hence, the US government would no doubt look to justify the torture and abuse at Abu Ghraib, and other human rights violations that have been prosecuted in the 'war on terror', on utilitarian grounds, namely that they are a small price to pay to protect democracy and safeguard national security.

TONY SOPRANO – POSTMODERN GODFATHER

The definitional question of what is organized crime raised in the introduction to this chapter is crucial, especially when we consider that state crimes or high crimes of state, such as the systematic use of torture, ethnic cleansing and genocide, may be conceived of as a species of organized crime. Michael Levi (2007: 780–781) has defined organized crime as the commission of serious crimes over a long period. To him, the term denotes criminal *actors* as well as criminal *activities*. Examples of the latter include drug-trafficking, trafficking in people, extortion, kidnapping for profit, illegal toxic waste dumping (environmental crime), sophisticated credit card fraud, smuggling to avoid tax on alcohol and tobacco, and intellectual property theft, e.g. video and audio piracy and product counterfeiting (Levi 2007: 777). One problem arises, however, in confining these activities only to crimes committed by underworld-type figures, such as Mafia gangsters and mobsters, and so forth. Indeed, as we shall see, organized crime can also be a term applicable to the activities of corporations (corporate crime), as well as nation-states (state crime). There are connections to terrorism too, which we will explore later in this chapter. But for the time being we will look at the some of the ways typical views of underworld gangsters have been represented in the media. In this analysis, we concentrate on fictional representations, and here focus on Mafia-style mobsters, such as Tony Soprano.

Like *The Wire*, which has been described as 'a new take on reality TV' (Penfold-Mounce et al. 2011: 159), *The Sopranos* offers a realist portrayal of the everyday details of gang life at work and at home. Indeed, just as the producers of *The Wire* have used non-professional actors and real-life Baltimore people in the show (Chapter 5), so there is a similar elision in *The Sopranos*, e.g. 'the actor who plays Tony Soprano's son is arrested for robbery on the Upper East Side; and the actor who play Paulie Walnuts . . . was arrested 28 times and nearly became a made man before becoming an actor' (Parker 2012: 94). Moreover, as *The Wire's* authenticity lies partly in showing criminals contra stereotypical depictions – that is, as sometimes being more 'moral' than those in authority (Penfold-Mounce et al. 2011: 155–156) – so realism in *The Sopranos* is evident in the complex, ambiguous and nuanced account it provides, including its portrayal of Tony Soprano (Figure 9.1) as a 'self-conflicted' gangster (Katz 2016: 236); a mob boss with issues, who has panic attacks and depression and attends therapy. Accordingly, acts of brutal violence in the show are contrasted with moments of reflection. *The Sopranos* then combines the melodrama of the domestic with the traditions of the gangster genre. It is, as Jacobs (2005: 143) states, a show whereby, 'an epic canvas is combined with an intimate one'.

Figure 9.1 James Gandolfini as New Jersey-based Italian American mobster Tony Soprano with other members of the cast of *The Sopranos*

Jacobs's focus is to explore contemporary criminality and therapeutic culture, examining issues of personal responsibility, impulse control and criminality. He identifies two types of violence that are central in *The Sopranos*: (i) planned hits; and (ii) spontaneous (impulsive) outbursts of violence. The second kind of violence has implications for the modernization of the gangster genre. In *The Godfather*, for example, there are cases of planned murder but no instances of impulsive killing. And when violence and aggression are portrayed in movies like *Scarface* and *Goodfellas* it is variously interpreted by mobsters as pathological loss of control, a threat to the structure of organized crime, or as a self-destructive 'inability to place loyalty and solidarity to the Mafia family above personal hurt' (Jacobs 2005: 147). Like those errant figures in movies gone by, Tony Soprano's panic attacks are moments when he clearly loses control. However, even though he is forced to attend therapy as result, his violent and impulsive behavior has implications for group solidarity, which becomes an increasingly prominent issue in the later seasons of the show.

The gangster hierarchy is set up so there are rules against doing violence to guys who are higher up. This is a means of having some kind of structure for criminals with limited impulse control. However, in season 4, Tony's impulsive killing of a mob captain runs counter to the rules that ought to protect 'made mobsters' (i.e. officially inducted) from individual vendettas. Tony's impulsivity here not only threatens to destabilize the solidarity of the mob, but this example also demonstrates how instead of being opposed, therapy and violence are interlinked:

> Dramatically such instances of the failure to control one's temper allow for sudden and novel shifts in the narrative. But they are also part of a wider project of the show to understand the relationship between the therapeutic impulse to cultivate the Self, to express one's feelings, and the necessity of adult solidarity in the (mafia) group in order to maintain the system of organized crime.
>
> (Jacobs 2005: 151)

As with serial killing, it is tempting to apply psychological models to such behavior. Indeed, like depictions of serial killers, Tony Soprano possesses conflicting selves: on the one hand, he is an ordinary suburban husband and father; on the other hand, he is portrayed as a monster, who is expected, within the framework of the Mafia, to 'act upon his dark, primal urges' (Barretta 2000: 213). Moreover, like the hypermasculine characters in the movie *Fight Club*, which we analyzed in Chapter 2, Tony 'struggles with the redefinition of roles for contemporary men experiencing the trickle-down effects of feminism in the wake of the politically correct 1990s' (Barretta 2000: 213). This and other attempts he makes to control his multiple selves gives rise to Tony's panic attacks and requires him to undergo therapy.

Although the Mafia provides the perfect cover for Tony's behavior, 'within the norms of acceptable society, the ordinary person cannot act upon their darkest urges without suffering severe consequences' (Barretta 2000: 213). However, as Jacobs (2005: 146) points out, rather than being held responsible for a failure to control one's impulses and behavior, with the *medicalization of crime*, criminals can expect increasingly to receive a pathological label, which treats them as sick, and therefore diminishes their individual responsibility. In the case of mobsters like Tony Soprano, they may expect to be diagnosed as suffering an Anti-social Personality Disorder, having traits in common with serial killers, such as an inability to show remorse or disregard for violating the rights of others. Although these ideas are undoubtedly compelling, our interest and focus here, as with serial killers (Chapter 7), is on the socio-cultural dimensions of shows like *The Sopranos*. That is also an emphasis for Jacobs (2005: 144), who observes that, unlike *The Godfather* and *Goodfellas*, *The Sopranos* is grounded in the present day of New Jersey, which is a form of 'rooted contemporary realism [that] allows the show to incorporate into its narrative structures commentary on the contemporary world'.

A similar appraisal forms the basis of Hayward and Biro's (2002) political economy reading of *The Sopranos*. They are expressly concerned with contrasting the worlds of *The Godfather* and *The Sopranos*. Like Jacobs (2005: 146), they observe certain developments that have occurred in the American gangster genre. In the 1930s, for instance, the genre depicted gangsters as individual criminals, psychopaths or sick loners. After the Second World War, gangsters were still portrayed as loners but with tragic pathos about confusion over being war veterans, 'struggling with the unsympathetic rigidity of institutions and ultimately crushed by a petty and vindictive social order' (Jameson 1979: 145, quoted in Hayward and Biro 2002: 207). During the 'late capitalism' of the 1970s the emphasis shifted from gangsters as loners to gangsters as belonging to a criminal organization or 'family', as depicted classically in *The Godfather*.

Hayward and Biro (2002: 206) argue Tony Soprano inhabits a post-*Godfather* world 'in which the market is everywhere triumphant, and where loyalty (whether corporate or familial or, in the case of the Mafia, both of these at once) is increasingly treated as a commodity to be bought and sold'. Hence, they say, 'while *The Godfather* paints a picture of the Mafia as a community in which loyalty to the organization is the overriding value, in Tony Soprano's world, loyalty, like everything else, has its price' (Hayward and Biro 2002: 208). This shift in emphasis is evident in the trade in drugs, which the Mafia resisted for many years, fearing it would undermine bonds of loyalty vital to the organization's success. By contrast, '*The Sopranos* makes it clear that the only substance that is truly corrosive of familial-corporate bonds is not white but green' (Hayward and Biro 2002: 208). Accordingly, unlike the world Don Corleone inhabits in *The Godfather* (Figure 9.2), where certain things (e.g. honor, community, etc.) have intrinsic

Figure 9.2 From left to right: Salvatore Corsitto as Bonasera, James Caan as Santino 'Sonny' Corleone and Marlon Brando as Don Vito Corleone in *The Godfather*, 1972 – Bonasera asks Don Corleone to avenge the brutal rape of his daughter

worth, 'Tony Soprano is forced to inhabit a world in which dollar values are the only values that matter' (Hayward and Brio 2002: 208).

Employing Frederic Jameson's (1979) arguments, Hayward and Biro (2002: 209) propose that, 'films about gangsters have served as an index of much broader changes in social relations'. Thus, they contend the move from Scarface to Don Corleone to Tony Soprano represents:

> a shift from the 'rugged individualism' of early twentieth century laissez-faire capitalism, to the organizational imperative (with its corresponding 'organization man') of the Keynesian economy of the post-war period, to the flexibility and ephemerality of the post-Fordist New Economy, whose analogue at the individual level remains only vaguely defined.
>
> (Hayward and Biro 2002: 209)

Under these circumstances, it is hardly surprising Tony Soprano suffers debilitating panic attacks, since he is '[f]orced to inhabit a world in which the forces of commodification are such as to continually emphasize individualism and personal gratification at the expense of solidarity and communal pleasures' (Hayward and Biro 2002: 209). And this is why he is profoundly nostalgic; a sentiment expressed in his desire to return to the 1950s (the decade of *The Godfather*), as evident in an angry outburst, after feeling overwhelmed by his kids' demands for autonomy, when he bellows: 'In this house, it's 1954!' (Hayward and Biro 2002: 210).

Tony's longing for a time of perceived certainties – the 'solid ground' of an earlier era – not only brings about his definitional (or identity) crisis, but, according to Hayward and Biro (2002: 210), it also accounts for his racism, as manifest in his 'desire to reassert a particular form of racial segregation'. Here, there are clear parallels with the alienation felt by fictional detective, Kurt Wallander, who, as we saw in Chapter 5, also mourns the lose of a utopian dream, an innocent Sweden, unfettered by the complexities thrown up by neoliberal global capitalism. Similarly, Tony Soprano's problems are symptomatic of a more generalized cultural anxiety and insecurity produced by commodification and the decline of community.

Just as *The Wire* has been described as 'the best ethnography we have of contemporary American society . . . a kind of visual novel that presents an ideal type of American social decay' (Penfold-Mounce et al. 2011: 156–157), Hayward and Biro (2002: 211) suggest *The Sopranos* 'is a show about America, and anyone who watches with any degree of intelligence understands that right away'. In particular, the show demonstrates the limits of criminality as a response to contemporary problems, as evidenced by the fact Tony Soprano cannot solve his own problems using brute force, and requires therapeutic intervention. Hence, by highlighting the everyday anxieties of a Mob boss at the end of the twentieth century, the show demystifies the idea that criminality can provide an escape from the pressures of an economic system over which we have no control. Indeed, Hayward and Biro (2002: 212) argue, the gangster genre in general has repeatedly staged the contradictions of capitalism displayed in *The Sopranos*, that is, 'the tension between needs satisfied through communal living and the alienating effects of the division of labour enforced by the profit motive'.

STRICTLY BUSINESS? LEGITIMATE/ILLICIT SYMBIOSIS

Tony Soprano is not alone in displaying nostalgia. Drawing on Arlacchi (1988: 126) and Sterling (1991: 76), Martin Parker (2012: 108) shows how each generation of Mafia complains there were rules and respect in days gone by, how honor is a thing of the past and how everybody is into drugs nowadays. In this way, and as Hayward and Biro (2002) also observe, the contemporary approach is compared unfavorably to the former 'modern' way of doing things, which stressed loyalty and commitment, and was underpinned by a set of shared moral codes, a sense of duty, with attendant rights and responsibilities. This enables Parker (2012: 100–101) to propose the Mafia is, or was, as the case might by, an ethical business, which, allows him, in turn, to compare it to legitimate businesses, asking whether the latter are any more socially responsible when they trade in alcohol, cigarettes, semi-automatic weapons or burgers that cause heart disease?

The comparison between legitimate and illegitimate business often arises in discussions of organized crime. As Parker (2012: 95) notes, 'much Mafia business is just ordinary business', involving trade in products and services that are frequently the same as legitimate companies. Moreover, the Mafia's moral decline is often seen to reflect its involvement in businesses that are not only grubby but also rather dull. Being a mobster, then, is regarded as just another job, which, in reality, entails boring and repetitious work. However, the enduring attraction of mobsters, at least as they are depicted in popular culture, lies in the fantasy they present of escaping 'real' work. Hence, the Mafiosi becomes romanticized as an 'economic outlaw', or 'someone who is no longer shackled to the 9 to 5, and lives a life that evades power and celebrates freedom' (Parker 2012: 109).

A related idea is that organized crime can have a 'respectable' face. Levi (2007: 778) shows how research in Italy and the US, for example, has revealed 'the coalition between business people, politicians, and crime groups in organizing and tolerating crimes contrary to the public interest'. In fact, as Woodiwiss and Hobbs (2009: 108) point out, early US moral crusaders, such as the Reverend Charles Parkhurst, first used the term 'organized crime' to refer to 'gambling and prostitution operations that were protected by public officials', like politicians and police. Parker too argues both legitimate and illegitimate business operations generate money that is reinvested to buy off the state, thus ensuring business carries on as usual. Accordingly, he says, while outlaws are invisible, outside and far away, 'the gangster is hidden in plain sight' (Parker 2012: 104). Scholars working with that assumption, such as Woodiwiss (2005), invert the conventional model of organized crime to propose a radical view, which posits there is a symbiotic relationship between criminals and business. The underlying idea here is that capitalism itself is criminogenic and that organized crime is just a part of the way capitalist business is done. Corporate crime is not crime at all, on this view, which conceives of the harms and injustices that accrue from normal business activity as 'par for the course'.

It should be noted that the symbiotic model is not unproblematic and cannot, for instance, account for high-profile prosecutions, such as Enron, where it was revealed executives had misled the board of directors and audit committee about high-risk accounting issues, and put pressure on their accountants, Arthur Anderson, to turn a blind eye to those issues. In the fallout, former Enron President and CEO, Jeffrey Skilling, was sentenced to prison for 24 years and four months for conspiracy, fraud and insider trading (see Figure 9.3). This kind of corporate malfeasance is sometimes called 'willful blindness', which is a legal concept brought to public attention in July 2011 when the Murdochs appeared before the British Parliament's House of Commons select committee on Culture, Media and Sport to answer charges they had ignored what had been happening at News International during the phone-hacking scandal. The scandal involved employees of the *News of the World* newspaper (published by News International) who had sought 'good stories' by hacking the phones of celebrities, politicians and members of the royal family, and most controversially, the phones of murdered schoolgirl, Milly

© Mark Wilson/Getty Images

Figure 9.3 Former President and CEO of the Enron Corporation Jeffrey Skilling (M), Enron Vice President of corporate development Sherron Watkins (L) and President and Chief Operatin Officer of Enron Jeffrey McMahon (R) raise their right hand as they are sworn in before an investi gation into the collapse of the Enron Corporation by the Senate Committee on Commerce Scienc and Transportation, Washington, DC, 26 February 2002

Dowler, those of the relatives of deceased British soldiers and victims of the 7 July 2005 London bombings:

> Nowadays, this law is most commonly applied in money-laundering and drug-trafficking cases, but the behaviour it describes is all around us – in banks, the Catholic Church, at BP, in Abu Ghraib Prison, in most industrial accidents. The narratives nearly always follow the same trajectory: years of abuse involving a large number of participants, plenty of warning signs, and, when the problem finally explodes, howls of pain – how could we have been so blind?
>
> (Heffernan 2011: 33)

As the Leveson Inquiry later revealed, willful blindness was a cause of much secrecy, cover-up and corruption involving key British institutions spanning many years (see Whyte 2015; Martin 2017c). Moreover, what became quickly apparent during the Leveson hearings was the degree of collusion extant between senior politicians, police, journalists and news editors; evidence, if any more were needed, to support the symbiotic model. In reality, however, as with all forms of corporate crime, prosecutions such as Enron are a rarity, although the phone-hacking scandal also resulted in the prosecution and imprisonment of key personnel, including former *News of the World* editor and spin-doctor to the British Prime Minster, Andy Coulson, who was found guilty of conspiracy to intercept voicemails (i.e. phone-hacking), and sentenced to 18 months in prison (O'Carroll 2014). It is also questionable what 'real' changes inquiries like Leveson might effect. Indeed, when it comes to the crimes corporations commit, most are able to avoid prosecution and sanctions because they can afford the best legal resources and devise schemes that enable them to adhere to the letter of the law while defying its spirit, e.g. large firms pay minimal tax yet remain 'law-abiding' (Haines 2017: 183–186). Another why of thinking about this type of practice is in terms of 'creative compliance', which 'refers to the use of technical legal work to manage the legal packaging, structuring and definition of practices and transactions, such that they can claim to fall on the right side of the boundary between lawfulness and illegality' (McBarnet 2006: 1091).

BOX 9.1 MEDIA REPRESENTATIONS OF RUSSIAN ORGANIZED CRIME

Rawlinson's (1998) analysis of media representations of Russian organized crime provides a useful illustration of the symbiotic model in action. Just as dominant depictions of organized crime have equated it with underworld activities and actors, so orthodox conceptions of organized crime in Russia have tended to see it as being synonymous with the term 'Mafia', which Rawlinson (1998: 348) says, is due largely to the successful export of films like *The Godfather*; hence ensuring, even in the former Soviet Union, 'that the predominant image of organized crime was American-influenced'. However, Rawlinson (1998: 350) warns that transferring media representations of Mafia from the US to Russia is problematic, which, in Soviet times, before 1989 (when the Berlin Wall fell), meant Russian reporters imported 'specific cultural attributes (and numerous misconceptions) which did not reflect the unique and idiosyncratic nature of Russian organized crime'.

However, during the mid-1980s, Soviet media began to deconstruct the social reality of Russian organized crime. Rather than adopting the Western view of organized crime as an alien structure parasitic on an unwilling host, Russians saw it as an endemic part of the Soviet system, attributing the words 'organized crime' and 'Mafia' 'exclusively to the jungles of capitalist business' (Rawlinson 1998: 349). In the run up to the fall of communism, two camps emerged: on the one hand, communist hardliners saw organized crime as a result of Gorbachev's reforms, therefore vindicating socialist truths about the evils of capitalism; on the other hand, liberals saw the growth of organized crime as a function of the corruption inherent in socialism. Adherents of the latter view ignored the corrupting effects of capitalist enterprise, and instead regarded the failure of authorities to respond effectively to organized crime as a direct consequence of the criminogenic nature of the communist regime:

> Thus the sole explanation given for the proliferation of organized crime after the demise of communism is the inadequacy of law enforcement, again an implied criticism of the former regime within which these agencies were created. No reference is made to the vast array of opportunities made available to organized crime by capitalism.
>
> (Rawlinson 1998: 352)

Articulating a version of the symbiotic model, Rawlinson (1998: 357) shows how media coverage of Russian organized crime helped divert attention from some 'unpalatable home truths'. From the media's perspective, revealing the gray areas and overlaps that exist between licit and illicit behavior and activities – showing, for instance, how organized crime has penetrated legitimate structures, such as the world of finance and banking, politics and even the media itself – is undesirable not only because it is dangerous, but because there is a lack of graphic evidence, and the complexity of the issues do not make for dramatic and entertaining stories that audiences find attractive:

> It is more comfortable and profitable to concentrate on difference, on the easily definable, the distinguishable and the safe rather than face the revelations that might emerge from introspection and critical self-analysis. . . . And so the camera and tape-recorder are directed at the more orthodox areas of organized crime, the gang. Their activities and business are clearly illegal.
>
> (Rawlinson 1998: 351)

In conclusion, Rawlinson (1998: 357) says if we accept organized crime as 'an illegal entrepreneurial structure which responds to market dynamics of supply and demand', then the media's role in effectively denying the relationship between the extremely inequitable distribution of wealth that has proliferated in post-communist Russia and the rise of disaffection, unemployment, poverty, which intensifies demand for what organized crime can offer (e.g. drugs, arms, prostitution), is tantamount to playing a dangerous 'game of ostrich'. This act of 'willful blindness' bolsters the view presented at various points in the book apropos the criminogenic nature of the commercial mass media.

ORGANIZED CRIME-TERRORISM NEXUS

While old style 'modern' values, such as loyalty, honor and commitment have been seen as integral to the moral code of gangsters and, in particular, the Mafia, mobsters involved in organized crime have also been regarded folk devils and thereby connected to moral panics, the function of which has been, 'absolving mainstream society of responsibility for perceived decline in moral values and exaggerating the threat from an alien nebulous enemy' (Woodiwiss and Hobbs 2009: 106). In this way, political elites engineer moral panics by lumping a myriad of activities under the single category of 'organized crime' to create the impression the threat is far more forbidding and substantial than it really is (Woodiwiss and Hobbs 2009: 124).

Woodiwiss and Hobbs (2009: 121) observe that towards the end of the 1990s organized crime had become increasingly transnational in nature, and in the UK, for example, 'concerns about foreign gangsters, and, in the wake of the 2001 World Trade Center bombing, foreign terrorists, were being mixed up in a popular press-inspired panic involving those seeking asylum in Britain'. Certainly, the post-9/11 context provided fertile ground to conjure up such links. As we saw in Chapter 3, it gave politicians license to describe outlaw motorcycle gang members, or 'bikies', allegedly involved in organized crime as 'terrorists within our community' (Martin 2012: 210), and following the refugee crisis, it has facilitated a more or less persistent global moral panic 'where the figure of the Muslim-terrorist-refugee is constructed as a transnational folk devil' (Martin 2015b: 304). In this scenario, then, there has been a lumping together of refugees, organized criminals and terrorists, with 'people smugglers' embodying connections between transnational terrorism and organized crime.

Notwithstanding these examples, Levi (2007) has questioned the nexus between terrorism and organized crime. For a start, he argues, especially since the London bombings of 2005, it is now understood most of the terrorism affecting the UK, and indeed other countries, is 'home-grown', rather than emanating from a threat posed by foreign 'invaders'. Having said that, terrorism at home can be influenced by global events, such as attacks on Muslim countries, and external relationships, such as people spending time or training in countries where they 'convert' to terrorism (Levi 2007: 791; see also Kundnani 2014). Others have disputed the linkages between organized crime and terrorism on the basis of differing motives. Thus, whereas Mafia mobsters are likely to be motived by moneymaking, Islamic suicide bombers may be driven by revulsion at decadent Western values (Levi 2007: 792). Either way, and as already indicated by Woodiwiss and Hobbs (2009: 124), not only is there a tendency 'to impose a false (fantasy) grid of coherence on what is a very diverse set of people and activities' (Levi 2007: 794), but also an inclination to overgeneralize the relationship between terrorism and organized crime, 'to try to upgrade the harmfulness of undesired activities by stating that it (e.g. product counterfeiting, fraud, or Internet gambling) could finance terrorism (as indeed it sometimes does)' (Levi 2007: 792). For instance, the Provisional IRA traditionally obtained funds via illegitimate means (e.g. extortion), but also from legitimate sources, such as funding from the Irish diaspora via Noraid in the US (Levi 2007: 793).

Nuanced accounts like this do not always feature in media reports, which often rely on official interpretations that tend to conflate or ignore differences; for instance, applying the term 'Islamic terrorism' to 'a range of political affiliations, in addition to the conflicts between Sunni and Shi'a believers' (Levi 2007: 793). Hence, just as a multitude of activities may be lumped together under the category 'organized crime', so 'terrorism' can be used as a catch-all phrase masking a myriad of actors and activities. This goes to one of the problems Ross (2007) identifies with media coverage on terrorism: not only is it selective and often driven by sensationalism, but it can also be prone to disseminating misinformation, which is fed to reporters by national security agencies. Sometimes this can be done for selfish reasons by providing 'strategic leaks', as happened after 9/11, 'when federal agencies scrambled to do "damage control", hoping to prove to the American public that they were not sleeping on the job' (Ross 2007: 218). Indeed, as we will see shortly, this is precisely what happened when the Bush administration denied torture and abuse was taking place at Abu Ghraib prison following the invasion of Iraq in 2003, which, accordingly to Hamm (2007: 279), 'amounted to conscious disinformation intended to swindle the American public into thinking that the government's investigations should be taken at face value, in the hope that the media – and by implication, the nation – would move on'.

Similarly, David Altheide (2006: 417, 424–425) shows how news organizations' reliance on government officials as news sources directed the focus and language of news coverage after 9/11, and that a compliant news media (acting as a willing accomplice) played a key role in propagating fear of terrorism and 'the politics of fear'. Moreover, he says, the politics of fear did not begin with 9/11, but 'was extended from a long history associating fear with crime' (Altheide 2006: 426). And it was thus emotions rather than evidence that drove Bush supporters: 'emotions consonant with the mass-mediated politics of fear nurtured by decades of crime control efforts' (Altheide 2006: 416). Likewise, Mythen and Walklate (2006) argue the framing of the terrorist problem through media and political discourse about 'new terrorism' has built upon as well as escalated a cultural climate of fear and uncertainty since 9/11.

Another problem Ross (2007: 218) identifies with news media coverage of terrorism is that it can, from the perspective of those in power, obstruct counter-terrorist efforts, such as inadvertently hindering anti-terror initiatives like resolving hostage incidents. This type of criticism came to light in comments made by MI5 boss, Sir Andrew Parker, who implicated the *Guardian* newspaper in his first speech in the job. Referring to the material the newspaper published from former CIA contractor turned whistle-blower, Edward Snowden, which included revelations about the scale of the surveillance operations at the UK Government Communications Headquarters (GCHQ) and its US counterpart, the National Security Agency, he said: 'It causes enormous damage to make public the reach and limits of GCHQ techniques. Such information hands the advantage to the terrorists. It is the gift they need to evade us and strike at will' (Marshall 2013; see also Hopkins 2013). For this reason, the surveillance methods used by police and security-intelligence agencies are protected in law (Kumar et al. 2015: 1; Martin 2012: 194, 211). Similarly, information sharing between nation-states is safeguarded under what is known as the 'control principle', which provides, 'intelligence belonging to a foreign government may not be disclosed without its permission' (Scott Bray and Martin 2012: 126).

In light of the issues raised by Ross, two positions have emerged. First, it is suggested *government intervention* is required to control media coverage, although the obvious problem here is that this is seen as tantamount to censorship, representing curbs on free speech and democratic expression; an example being restrictions on press freedom recently introduced in Australia, where legislation prohibits media reporting of 'special intelligence operations', which may conceivably include the reporting of conditions in offshore refugee detention camps, to which new whistle-blowing offenses now attach. Further restrictions provide the executive branch of government with new powers to apply for 'journalist information warrants' that can compel telecommunications companies to surrender the metadata of journalists that may identify a source (Martin 2017c: 105). The second suggested response is for *self-regulation* by the media, although that will always be difficult, given what we know of the highly competitive media marketplace, which drives a race to the bottom to produce sensationalized or otherwise newsworthy stories.

BOX 9.2 ALLYING CRITICAL TERRORISM STUDIES AND CULTURAL CRIMINOLOGY

Given the complicity between state, organized crime and the mainstream media, as postulated by the symbiotic model, Keith Hayward proposes an alliance be forged between critical terrorism studies (CTS) and cultural criminology. It will be recalled from Chapter 2 that cultural criminology emerged partly out of a critique of so-called 'administrative criminology', which is the kind of criminological practice associated with official government bodies, such as the police and criminal justice agencies. Cultural criminology, by contrast, seeks to discover alternative perspectives, such as those of offenders, focusing on the emotions, experiences and situational aspects of transgression and rule-breaking. Accordingly, Hayward (2011: 60) says, as both challenge 'state-centric disciplinary norms', cultural criminology and CTS might prove allies:

> both sub-fields train their critical cross hairs firmly on the state. For CTS, the state itself is an agent of terror worthy of scholarly analysis, whereas cultural criminologists agitate for a 'cultural criminology of the state' capable of countering the discourse that surrounds the various 'wars' on drugs, gangs and crime, and the mass incarceration machinery that follows in their wake.
>
> (Hayward 2011: 59)

Hence, there needs to be some kind of re-orientation, with

> obvious examples being the heavy focus on al-Qaeda terrorist cells rather than rigorous analysis of Middle Eastern history politics in mainstream terrorism studies and the prioritization of street-level surveillance by government criminologists at the expense of any substantive concern with corporate or white-collar crime.
>
> (Hayward 2011: 60)

A good illustration of the CTS-cultural criminology nexus Hayward proposes is contained in Hamm's (2007) analysis of the atrocities committed at Abu Ghraib.

HIGH CRIMES, MISDEMEANORS AND CALAMITOUS FAILURES AT ABU GHRAIB

In this section, we take the symbiotic model of organized crime to its logical conclusion, proposing certain crimes of state, or high crimes, can be classified as *organized* crime by virtue of their programmed and systematic nature. Cases of ethnic cleansing and other forms of genocide, massacre and mass murder provide clear instances of state criminality or war crimes that contravene international law, and do so in a highly organized fashion. Such claims are by no means novel. In this ground-breaking study, Zygmunt Bauman (1989: 12, original emphasis) showed how rather than being seen as a failure of civilization, the Holocaust should be regarded a product of modernity: '*a rare, yet significant and reliable, test of the hidden possibility of modern society*'. Similarly, as we saw in Chapter 7, even though people suggest psychopaths could be involved in some of today's most serious crimes (Arrigo and Griffin 2004: 380; Gacono 2000: xix), Haggerty (2009) resists correlating psychopathy and serial killer, arguing instead that serial killing is a peculiarly modern phenomenon. Bauman (1989: 13, original emphasis) is likewise interested in developing a sociological explanation of the modern origins – though not *the* cause – of the Holocaust, saying, while 'modern civilization was not the *sufficient* condition; it was, however, most certainly its *necessary* condition'.

Without modern civilization and rational-bureaucratic organization the Holocaust would have been unthinkable: 'The Nazi mass murder of the European Jewry was not only the technological achievement of an industrial society, but also the organizational achievement of a bureaucratic society' (Browning 1983: 148, quoted in Bauman 1989: 13).

Hence, implementing the Final Solution was largely a matter of following routine bureaucratic procedures, 'of co-operation between various departments of state bureaucracy; of careful planning, designing proper technology and technical equipment, budgeting, calculating and mobilizing necessary resources: indeed, the matter of dull bureaucratic routine' (Bauman 1989: 16–17). Moreover, although Bauman (1989: 18, original emphasis) does not claim 'modern bureaucracy *must* result in Holocaust-style phenomena', he suggests 'that is was the spirit of instrumental rationality, and its modern, bureaucratic form of institutionalization, which had made the Holocaust-style solutions not only possible, but eminently "reasonable" – and increased the probability of their choice'. In this way, the Holocaust was unthinkable without bureaucracy: it 'was not an irrational outflow of the not-yet-fully-eradicated residues of pre-modern barbarity. It was a legitimate resident in the house of modernity; indeed, one who would not be at home in any other house' (Bauman 1989: 17).

Mark Hamm's analysis of the torture and abuse that occurred at Abu Ghraib following the US-led invasion of Iraq in 2003 chimes very much with these ideas, as well as Hayward's (2011) arguments about forming an allegiance between CTS and cultural criminology (Box 9.2), and, in particular, visual criminology, which, as we saw in Chapter 2, is a strand of cultural criminology. Hence, to Hamm (2007: 263), what makes Abu Ghraib exceptional is that the abuses were photographed. For him, the pictures of Abu Ghraib constitute the photographic record (and evidence) of a crime committed by the capitalist state: the 'high crime' of torture, or the 'deliberate, systematic, brutal torture carried out by American soldiers with appalling shamelessness' (Hamm 2007: 261). Importantly, however, Hamm argues the soldiers were not the ultimate culprits, since the command to 'take off the gloves' in prisoner interrogations, can be traced from George W. Bush and other top government officials through to the CIA, which was the lead agency, with army intelligence and military police units in supporting roles.

Senior military personnel at Abu Ghraib intended to 'Gitmo-ize' it (i.e. make it like the detention camp at Guantanamo Bay, Cuba) by attacking inmates' cultural sensitivity, and especially targeting sexual shame and humiliation, which were seen as the greatest weakness of Arab men. Techniques included: beatings, starving, asphyxiation, burning, stretching, sexual degradation, low-voltage electrocution, psychological manipulation and mutilation via dog bites. Prisoners were also raped, ridden, deprived of medical treatment and forced to eat pork and drink alcohol, which was against their religion. Victims included women and children.

The Red Cross reported the torture regime and interrogation methods were 'part of a process'; they were standard operating procedure, used by military personnel to extract confessions and intelligence. Hamm (2007: 273) argues the images of Abu Ghraib reveal 'a pattern of torture' that constituted a flagrant violation of international law. The 1985 UN Convention against Torture (ratified by the US) defines torture as: 'any act by which severe pain or suffering, whether physical or mental, is intentionally inflicted on a person for such purposes of obtaining from him or a third person information or a confession' (Hamm 2007: 265). The UN Convention also states: 'no exceptional circumstances . . . may be invoked as a justification of torture' (Hamm 2007: 266). Moreover, Article 3 of the Geneva Conventions prohibits 'violence to life and persons, in particular murder of all kinds, mutilation, cruel treatment and torture' (Hamm 2007: 266).

While grave breaches of these international standards amount to 'war crimes' (Hamm 2007: 266), the US narrowed the definition of torture 'almost to the vanishing point' (Hamm 2007: 268) to justify its action and accommodate its practices post-9/11 in places like Guantanamo Bay and Abu Ghraib. Based on a legal review, the White House Counsel and his associate built a 'theory of torture', stipulating

> that in order for an act to rise to the level of torture within the meaning of the UN and Geneva Conventions, 'it must inflict pain that is difficult to endure. Physical pain amounting to torture must be equivalent in intensity to the pain accompanying serious physical injury, such as organ failure, impairment of bodily function, or even death'.
>
> (Hamm 2007: 266)

Added to this, the interrogation policy was ambiguous about the rules of engagement, and there was uncertainty about who was and was not covered by the Geneva Conventions, which bred a climate whereby abuses could take place. Moreover, as mistreatment of detainees was deliberately kept from public view, it gave rise to a situation in which human rights abuses were probably inevitable (cp. Nethery and Holman 2016: 1019).

Most worryingly, the Red Cross found 70–90 percent of prisoners had been arrested by mistake, while the US Army estimated later that 85–90 percent offered no intelligence or were innocent of terrorism-related charges (Hamm 2007: 265), leading to the alarming conclusion that people had been 'tortured for nothing' (Hamm 2007: 273). And, although we will never comprehend the full effects of the US-led military action in the Middle East following 9/11, it has undoubtedly sparked the refugee crisis, and contributed to the rise of radicalization and home-grown terrorism in the West, and in the Middle East itself:

> We will never know how many Iraqi men were tortured by American forces at Abu Ghraib, though it was certainly hundreds, if not thousands: all for nothing. But of this we can be sure: once freed from prison, some of these men joined the insurgency, some joined death squads, and others became straight up al-Qaeda.
>
> (Hamm 2007: 282)

In order to make sense of what happened at Abu Ghraib, Hamm examines three theories, each of which were mobilized to explain the abuse. First, he disputes the theory promulgated by the US government the abuse at Abu Ghraib was perpetrated by a few 'bad apples' in the lower ranks of the military. Emphasizing individual acts rather than system failures the 'rotten apple theory' has been contrasted with the 'rotten barrel theory' in respect of corporate crime and police crime/corruption (Gottschalk 2012), and, in the Abu Ghraib case, was the view adopted by the Bush administration, which implicated a small group of morally corrupt 'rogue soldiers'. Hamm (2007: 269) also doubts the applicability of 'automatic brutality' theory, which, following Zimbardo's 1971 Stanford behavioral prison experiments (where students played roles of prisoners and guards in a simulated setting), attributed 'the abuse to a collapse of discipline in an over-strapped and unsupervised military unit'. According to this theory, soldiers became 'bad' because of chronic and dysfunctional conditions at Abu Ghraib – most of us would have behaved like this in similar circumstances; therefore, we are all 'latent torturers'.

In contrast, Hamm's assessment of the abuse supports McCoy's (2006) argument that the CIA was the lead agency in the abuse, and was supported by Army intelligence in its mission. McCoy shows how physical pain often produces heightened resistance in prisoners, and how the CIA understood this, having participated in such practices in South Vietnam in 1960s and Latin America in 1980s. Thus, 'the CIA designed a revolutionary two-phase form of torture that fused *sensory disorientation* and *self-inflicted pain*', and refined its 'tactics of sensory disorientation into a total assault on all senses and sensibilities – auditory, visual, thermal, sexual, and cultural' (Hamm 2007: 270, original emphasis).

To Hamm (2007: 270), the images of abuse at Abu Ghraib are best understood in the context of cultural criminology, since they depict 'both the thrills of sexual violence that were experienced by the immediate perpetrators of the torture, as well as the agony suffered by victims'. Indeed, the archive of the Army's Criminal Investigation Division 'reveals that the torture and the sexual humiliation of prisoners were often performed in conjunction with American soldiers having sex with prisoners, and with each other' (Hamm 2007: 270). This suggests there is 'a pornographic function of the torture scenarios' (Hamm 2007: 271).

The examples of two soldiers at the center of the Abu Ghraib scandal refute the bad apple theory and Zimbardo's theory, and support McCoy's theory. First, in the case of Sabrina Harman, Hamm (2007: 276) argues if the bad apple theory were to apply it would suggest she 'dreamed this treatment up herself' – that this 'untrained, lowly Army reservist, who had worked on the Hard Site for little more than two weeks, had the martial aptitude necessary to invent such cruelty'. Moreover, Zimbardo's theory offers no support as to how she learned such sophisticated torture techniques. McCoy's theory, on the other hand, suggests Harman's treatment of prisoners via the technique of 'Palestinian hanging' (i.e. prisoners suspended by the wrists, with arms hyper-extended behind their backs) was a CIA tactic in which sensory disorientation is fused with self-inflicted pain (i.e. the physical consequences of having to stand barefoot on a concrete floor for hours on end).

The example of Lynndie England also supports McCoy's theory. Prior to her deployment to Iraq, she had worked at a West Virginia chicken-processing plant, and, like Harman, 'did not possess the criminal tradecraft necessary to think up such things as the naked pyramid or Palestinian hanging' (Hamm 2007: 280). Thus, Hamm's conclusion is that these soldiers learned to torture; and, moreover, 'the most *refined* and *aggressive* interrogation methods used at Abu Ghraib were designed by the CIA' (Hamm 2007: 280, original emphasis). Crucially, Hamm argues that rather than the soldiers being responsible for what occurred at Abu Ghraib, ultimately the US president should have been held accountable:

> To the extent that this torture took place as a result of the President's policies or conduct, then George W. Bush may have violated both the War Crimes Act and the Geneva Conventions, and is therefore culpable of high crimes and misdemeanors.
>
> (Hamm 2007: 279)

Such culpability is easily proved, according to Hamm. The chain of command between the US President and the CIA is not complicated, and, at the time the abuses were taking place at Abu Ghraib, CIA Director George Tenet would have reported directly to the US President; indeed, the two 'spent hours together and developed a personal relationship' (Hamm 2007: 281). But anytime the CIA is involved in state criminality, says Hamm (2007: 281), 'it will use what the agency calls a "cut-out", a person or persons who will provide plausible deniability for the President's wrongdoing'. In this way, England and Harman were perfect foils for CIA operations at Abu Ghraib. While they had no intent to torture prisoners – intent is central to determining criminal responsibility in torture cases – 'they did have their sexuality. And this the CIA used to create a culture inside Abu Ghraib that exploited and debased women soldiers by having them behave like trollops' (Hamm 2007: 281). Ultimately, though, as they had never been given Geneva Conventions training, nor were there any camp rules or provisions of the Geneva Conventions posted in English or, for that matter, in the detainees' language, Hamm concludes, somewhat magnanimously, that the story of Abu Ghraib is one of:

> monumental administrative incompetence. Abu Ghraib was not an aberration. It was a symptom of a war in which the people in charge had no idea what they were doing. American efforts to rebuild looted schools and hospitals in Iraq, restore electricity and banking systems, train Iraqi police, and provide basic security have all been calamitous failures.
>
> (Hamm 2007: 281)

The example of Abu Ghraib confirms Cohen's (2001) thesis that nation-states are quite adept at employing strategies to deny and conceal their involvement in criminal activities. In the 'war on terror' that was demonstrated clearly in the practice of 'extraordinary rendition', whereby people designated 'enemy combatants' by the Bush administration were transported to countries with little or no human rights monitoring, so they could be secretly tortured. Outsourcing torture like this created a scenario analogous to the way corporations avoid liability, including criminal liability, by locating their operations in offshore tax havens and countries with few, if any, labor standards. Torture under a regime of extraordinary rendition, as well as other human rights abuses following 9/11 were justified by states on the basis that 'extreme times call for extreme measures'. Hence, what Agamben (2005) calls a 'state of exception' was created that gave rise to sites like the US detention facility at Guantanamo Bay, Cuba, which has been described as a 'legal black hole' (Steyn 2004) because it is a place wherein the rule of law is suspended.

From a visual criminology perspective (discussed in Chapter 2), Campbell (2010) has argued the legal excommunication of Muslims at Guantanamo has been made possible partly by the construction of a racist caricature in cultural imageries, such as film, which sets up an us/them binary, where the US is seen as essentially good and the Muslim-Other is regarded a dangerous enemy. Similarly, Carrabine (2011: 19) seeks to situate the images of Abu Ghraib within the 'history of violent representation that figures in the European classical art tradition, which all too frequently has justified imperial ambition, colonial conquest, and belief in racial superiority, while eroticizing bodies in pain'. Accordingly, his reading of the torture images of Abu Ghraib differs somewhat from Hamm's (2007), in that it explores the moral relations the images might cultivate in a much larger field of representation 'where the victorious pose with the vanquished to gratify the violence of the oppressor' (Carrabine 2011: 6). Hence, he suggests what happened at Abu Ghraib may be comparable to the popular practice among German soldiers during the Second World War of keeping photo albums containing atrocity images and 'trophy' photographs (Carrabine 2011: 9), including those taken by soldiers and policemen involved in the Holocaust (Morrison 2004a).

In other work, Morrison (2004b: 81) has shown how although the Holocaust involved killing on an industrial scale, it was nevertheless achieved by aggregates of individuals, some of whom 'clearly grew to enjoy the job', even taking photographs, 'which demonstrated the lack of distance between victim and killer as well as appearing to some critics to almost present a pornography of genocide'. Likewise, he shows how the fact the trophy images at Abu Ghraib were taken by reservists – taken from civilian life for a limited time – had the effect of creating 'little distance between these perpetrators and us', and thereby provided legitimation for 'the processes of authorization and routinization of the brutality done in the name of defending our civilized space' (Morrison 2010: 202). In a similar vein, Carrabine (2011: 14) draws parallels between the photographs of lynching at Abu Ghraib and public hangings of the nineteenth and twentieth century, which functioned as visual trophies or collective souvenirs justifying what was done.

CONCLUSION

The analogy that has been made in this chapter between state crime and corporate crime can be further extended in the context of the Abu Ghraib torture scandal for which individual state officials, according to Hamm, could be held accountable. Legal systems in capitalist societies have created a situation whereby corporations are treated as legal entities in their own right, meaning they might be held liable for wrongdoing, while CEOs and company directors can be absolved of any responsibility. Just as it is incredibly difficult to 'pierce the corporate veil' to prosecute CEOs and company directors for corporate wrongdoing, so it is with respect to world leaders like George W. Bush and Tony Blair, who, it is claimed by some, ought to be brought to trial for state crimes committed under their watch in the 'war on terror', including for the illegal invasion of Iraq. However, while nation-states attempt to deny and cover up human rights abuses and other crimes, it is increasingly less likely they will get away with so doing, given the intensified scrutiny of their activities by international non-governmental organizations comprising 'global civil society', such as Human Rights Watch, Amnesty International, Greenpeace and Médecins sans Frontières (Martin 2015a: 228–229).

Coupled with this are the activities of citizen journalists, who, as discussed in Chapter 8, can be highly influential in exposing state crimes and other abuses of power via various forms of counterveillance. In the case of leaks of government secrets post-9/11, though, the US state has behaved in a somewhat contradictory manner (Savage 2017). On the one hand, the Obama administration has prosecuted an unprecedented number of whistle-blowers for revealing state secrets, yet in his capacity to grant clemency as outgoing president, Barak Obama commuted all but four months of the remaining prison term of Chelsea Manning, who was the US army analyst convicted of disclosing sensitive information to Wikileaks.

The Manning case shows how, in the face of state crimes, some form of 'justice' might be achieved. Indeed, even if the prosecution of those in power is an unlikely prospect that is, after all, only one possible outcome among others. As we saw in Chapter 2, in their campaign to highlight the system of sex slavery they were subjected to as part of the Japanese army's war effort during the Second World War, surviving 'comfort women' sought to hold the Japanese government to account, even indicting Japan's late Emperor Hirohito. In the end, comfort women did receive recognition for their pain and suffering in a judgment made in The Hague in 2001, and, significantly for them, their stories are now told in Japanese school textbooks (Martin 2015a: 245–247).

Education and raising awareness, then, can be a desirable outcome, which in some cases of state crimes might manifest in the phenomenon of 'dark tourism'; that is, travel to sites associated with atrocities, death and suffering, or the macabre (Stone 2006: 146). So, in the paradigmatic example of the Holocaust, which was discussed earlier, places like the Auschwitz-Birkenau death-camp are symbols of evil. However, they are also sites of commemoration and remembrance, which, as discussed in Chapter 2, raises the importance of being mindful of the 'ethics of representation' when working with sensitive images and, in particular, when engaging social media at such sites, as we saw in the case of 'Yolocaust'. The mainstream media play a role here too: 'principally through increasing the geographic specificity of murder and violent death and, more recently, through global communication technology that televises events almost as they happen into people's "living rooms" around the world' (Stone 2006: 150; see also Miles 2011). Thus, while it is debatable whether we should preserve the homes of infamous serial killers – e.g. 25 Cromwell Street, Gloucester, UK, where Fred and Rose West committed sex crimes and serial murder – because that simply feeds people's morbid fascination and desire for entertainment, the case for preserving sites like Auschwitz-Birkenau is more compelling, since it clearly performs a positive societal function, acting as a means of trying to make sense and come to terms with death in extraordinarily tragic circumstances.

SUGGESTED FURTHER READING

While this chapter has adopted a broad and inclusive conception of organized crime, it is still useful to recall Edwin Sutherland's (1949: 9) original work on white-collar crime, which he defined as crime committed by 'a person of high status in the course of his occupation':

Sutherland, E. (1949) *White-Collar Crime*. New York, NY: Holt, Rinehart and Wilson.

The works by Chambliss and Tilly are useful places to start when thinking about state crime as organized crime:

Chambliss, W. J. (1989) 'State-organized crime – The American society of criminology, 1988 presidential address' *Criminology* 27(2): 183–208.

Tilly, C. (1985) 'War making and state making as organized crime' in P. B. Evans, D. Rueschemeyer and T. Skocpol (eds) *Bringing the State Back In*. Cambridge: Cambridge University Press, pp. 169–191.

In the following article, Keith Hayward addresses the claim that by concentrating on the transgressive acts of deviant edgeworkers cultural criminology fails to engage critically with state formations and harms caused by state agents:

Hayward, K. (2011) 'The critical terrorism studies-cultural criminology nexus: Some thoughts on how to "toughen up" the critical studies approach' *Critical Studies on Terrorism* 4(1): 57–73.

On the connections between organized crime and terrorism see:

Levi, M. (2007) 'Organized crime and terrorism' in M. Maguire, R. Morgan and R. Reiner (eds) *The Oxford Handbook of Criminology* (4th edition). Oxford: Oxford University Press, pp. 771–809.

CHAPTER 10

Conclusion

MULTIPLE MEDIA EFFECTS

The purpose of this final chapter is to consider some of the more prominent themes that have arisen in our explorations at the intersections of crime, media and culture. As discussed in Chapter 2, the framework of cultural criminology provides one of the key means of studying links between criminological and cultural inquiry, where the focus is on crime-media relations. Influenced by disciplines beyond criminology as well as critical approaches from within the criminological mainstream, cultural criminology rejects conventional approaches to studying 'crime and the media', including media effects models and quantitative research using content analysis. However, in striving to break free from the limitations and constraints of orthodox criminology and existing scholarship on the crime-media nexus, cultural criminologists have tended to oversimplify what they regard as 'this relatively formulaic [and] static received body of knowledge' (Hayward 2010: 5). While cultural criminology is indeed well placed to make sense of a contemporary world replete with mediated images of crime, and offer invaluable insights into the situated dynamics of crime and transgression using methods like 'criminological *verstehen*' (Ferrell 1997), it should not so readily dismiss the suggestion that analyzing media content, for instance, can illuminate relationships between crime and culture. David Green's (2008a) comparative study of responses to child-on-child killing in England and Norway, discussed in Chapter 6, provides one such case, which uses a text-based approach to highlight the contrasting press and political-economic cultures in the two countries.

Likewise, although the notion of a 'pure media effect' is somewhat implausible, as Allen et al. (1998: 55) suggest, we should not deny the existence of *any* media effects just because it is difficult to prove straightforward causal links between media and audiences. Media effects theories are quite rightly criticized for assuming audiences passively receive (and accept) any information or views the mass media broadcast or promulgate. Moreover, critics say, they take insufficient account of contextual factors, such as geographic locality, social class, gender, age and race, all of which impact upon people's mediated experiences of crime and justice. As we saw in Chapter 4, fear of crime research reveals the all-important role of context, with place of residence and community attachment among the most significant factors mitigating people's fear and beliefs regarding potential victimization.

Therefore, rather than discounting the notion of media effects, as cultural criminologists are prone to do, the concept of media effects ought instead to be interpreted and applied broadly, recognizing as we have throughout this book that media effects can be multifarious, complex and context-bound. That includes looking at the ways media can affect not only audiences but also legal processes and government agendas. In Chapter 3, for instance, we saw how David Garland (2008) has extended moral panic theory to examine what he terms the *productivity* of moral panics. It will be recalled that despite being sporadic and of short duration, Garland argues moral panics can have lasting effects, evident he says in the punitive turn and drift to a 'law and order' society. Although this is not a media effect in the narrow sense intended by the media effects model, it nevertheless constitutes a *real* effect, showing how media-induced moral panics can influence political and socio-legal structures.

Similarly, in Chapter 4 we saw how 'feedback loops' between media, fear of crime research and fearing subjects have real effects not only on people's behavior but also in shaping crime policy. Legislative measures designed to tackle anti-social behavior, for instance, are predicated on the *likelihood* certain behavior will cause harassment, alarm or distress. As such, they are based on people's often-mediated perceptions and fears, rather than on actual behavior or the commission of crimes. However, as with moral panics, although illusory and imagined, crime fear of this nature can still be productive and have real effects, such as contributing to the emergence of what Zedner (2007: 262) calls 'pre-crime society', wherein risk aversion measures are introduced to 'anticipate and forestall that which has not yet occurred and may never do so'. *Pre-empting* crime in this way, instead of *reacting* to it, reverses the way the criminal justice system has traditionally operated, meaning very real (criminal) consequences may accrue to people who are presumed guilty not innocent.

Even if we conceive of media effects in a more conventional sense, we see how media-audience relations are not simple and straightforward. Similar to Garland, Valverde (2006: 105) argues television shows such as *COPS* have a 'law and order effect', creating the impression crime and disorder is everywhere. Moreover, the broader 'political' effect of reality TV shows like *COPS* is to portray (mostly white) law enforcement officers in a positive light: as upholders of justice who restore law and order to the streets and suburbs overrun with uncivilized disorderly criminal hordes. Thus, by providing a restorative message and coherent narrative, these shows make the unintelligible world of crime intelligible to a middle class and respectable working-class audience, and thereby act to *reassure* viewers something is being done about the 'crime problem'. As we saw in Chapter 4, this suggests that, contrary to the media effects model, audiences are not passive cultural dopes, but might *actively select* crime shows precisely because they provide reassurance via a 'just' resolution (Sparks 1992a: 95, 148–150; Wakshlag et al. 1983; see also Allen et al. 1998: 55).

Variations in media effects are most clearly evident in research on the '*CSI* effect', which, it will be recalled, refers to the propensity of jurors who have watched forensic-themed television to accord greater leniency to defendants in criminal trials that do not yield the quantity and quality of scientific evidence as compared to shows like *CSI*. In Chapter 5, we saw how the existence of a simple *CSI* effect is contested on several grounds. For example, Cole and Dioso-Villa (2009: 1371) propose there is a '*CSI* effect effect', whereby jurors perceiving a media bias against prosecutors (the 'strong prosecutor's effect') sympathize with the prosecution case, which results in a tendency to convict rather than acquit defendants. Prosecutors themselves are also not immune from media influence, as we saw in relation to the concept of the 'weak prosecutor's effect', which points to the measures employed by prosecutors when faced with what they see as 'over-acquitting' juries. Techniques here include questioning jurors about *CSI* watching in voir dire or explaining the absence of forensic evidence in opening and closing addresses (Cole and Dioso-Villa 2007: 448).

Another effect, known as the 'defendant's effect', as it is proffered by defense attorneys, holds that the favorable portrayal of honest, skilled and heroic forensic scientists on shows like *CSI* increases their credibility as expert witnesses in real trial settings, and that this benefits the prosecution (Cole and Dioso-Villa 2009: 1344–1348). A further effect, known as the 'police chief's effect', suggests *CSI* educates criminals in ways to avoid detection, such as wearing gloves or cleaning crime scenes with bleach (Cole and Dioso-Villa 2009: 1344). A recent real-life example of the police chief's effect concerns the Dutch case of Michael P., who after raping and killing his victim, destroyed DNA trace evidence, including with chlorine because some think, he had seen this technique used on *CSI* (Pieters 2018).

Beyond this narrow educative effect, numerous studies reveal a wider function or effect of watching *CSI* and similar shows, which are believed to educate viewers generally about criminal investigations and police procedures. Although findings are mixed and studies have different emphases, all tend to suggest watching *CSI* and shows like it performs an *educative function*. For instance, in their study Schweitzer and Saks (2007) found *CSI* viewers are more skeptical of scientific evidence adduced at trial, as reflected in their being less likely to convict: 18 percent of *CSI* viewers likely to convict as compared to 29 percent of non-*CSI* viewers. Similarly, Maeder and Corbett (2015) found *CSI* viewers are more critical of forensic evidence than non-viewers. Shelton et al.'s (2006: 348) findings not only support the idea *CSI* educates audiences, but also that it is more likely to educate less educated viewers, as their '[r]espondents with less education tended to watch *CSI* more frequently than those who have more education'. Thus, as with content analysis studies, demographics and other contextual factors, including education, gender and political views, have some bearing on *CSI* research.

The idea that television shows might educate audiences is something we also considered in Chapter 5 when looking at reality TV shows like *Judge Judy*. Although reality TV is something of a misnomer in that case, as *Judy Judge* tends to conflate judging and entertainment, according to Marder (2012: 242) daytime television judges nevertheless perform a 'translator' function, enabling viewers to better understand specialized legal language, ideas and concepts, like 'hearsay' or 'credibility'. Furthermore, just as *COPS* provides an entertaining means of 'vicarious slum travel' (Valverde 2006: 107), so reality TV judge shows enable forms of voyeuristic gawping at participants who are presented in contradistinction to deserving neoliberal workers; that is, greedy, lazy, self-indulgent and ignorant, and thus victims worthy of scorn and punishment (Huws 2015).

Similar processes of media demonization occur in the creation of moral panics. Just as the participants in shows like *Judge Judy* present a discombobulating inversion of dominant societal norms and values (in that case, the virtue of work in the neoliberal economy), so the media can be instrumental in singling out certain groups as 'folk devils', which act as 'cultural scapegoats' for deep-seated societal fears and anxieties (Garland 2008: 15). However, while moral panics are defined according the *disproportionality* of the social reaction, towards the end of Chapter 3 we saw how 'good' moral panics might emerge around genuine social problems, and, in those cases, societal responses can be entirely *proportionate* to the deviance they condemn. We saw for instance how, following the bank-instigated GFC, bankers might be regarded as corporate criminals, who, along with expenses-fiddling politicians, should join the rogues' gallery of usual folk devil suspects. However, it has been argued bankers and other white-collar criminals are too powerful and will never be regarded enough of a threat to society's moral (neoliberal) order to be considered villainous folk devils. Indeed, it is doubtful whether corporate crime of this sort should be a legitimate source of moral panic research anyway, given the fallout from the banking crisis raised serious issues of global import.

As we saw in Chapter 3, Cohen himself recognized the expanding range of moral entrepreneurs and cultural workers that have succeeded in bringing new issues and concerns to media attention, including those relating to state crimes involving mass atrocities, corporate crime, environmental concerns and political suffering, such as that experienced by forced migrants and other refugees (Martin 2015b, 2018; Martin and Tazreiter 2017). Furthermore, the scope for positive and efficacious intervention is now far greater than ever, as citizen journalists, sometimes in conjunction with professional journalists working in established media organizations, harness social media and new digital technologies to effect change. We have seen several examples of this throughout the book, including in Chapter 6, when we discussed the way social media has been used to raise awareness of miscarriages of justice, such as in the campaign to overturn the convictions of Amanda Knox and Raffaele Sollecito. Another example considered in Chapter 8 concerned the death of Ian Tomlinson, in which citizen journalism and new media, allied to traditional newspaper reporting, acted as an extra-judicial means of transforming formal justice processes.

Another more recent case where online activism and social media campaigning has affected political change and law reform is #HomeToVote, which saw thousands of Irish woman living overseas fly back to Ireland in May 2018 to vote 'Yes' in a referendum to repeal the Eighth Amendment to the Irish constitution, thus paving the way to legalize abortion (McDonald et al. 2018). Many Irish women were inspired to return home to vote by an iconic photograph that was taken at a protest staged in 2016 by the London Irish Abortion Rights Campaign (https://londonirisharc.com/), depicting women marching to the Irish Embassy in London to demand a referendum to abolish the Eighth Amendment (Figure 10.1). As well as illustrating the growing significance of digital

© Alastair Moore/London Irish Abortion Rights Campaign

Figure 10.1 London Irish abortion rights campaigners march to the Irish Embassy, London, 2016

activism and the potential impact that might have on criminal justice issues, the #HomeToVote example highlights what cultural criminologists see as the power of the visual and of images in framing stories of crime and justice in contemporary society.

SYMBIOSIS, BLURRING AND CRIMINOGENIC MEDIA

Another theme we have encountered at various places in the book is the notion of symbiosis, and related ideas about the blurring of factual and fictional representations of crime and criminality. For example, in Chapter 5 we saw how a premise of Garland and Bilby's (2011) analysis of *Life on Mars* is that police dramas reflect dominant cultural conceptions of the criminal justice system, enabling audiences to reflect on real changes in police occupational culture that have occurred as a consequence, among other things, of equal opportunities discourse around race and gender. Resonance with a changing reality not only occurs in relation to police dramas but crime fiction generally. For instance, in addressing local anxieties arising from crimes of contemporary global significance, such as sex trafficking and cyberterrorism, Nordic noir dramas like *Wallander* address some of the challenges that are posed to the Scandinavian social democratic ideal. Nordic noir also registers social change in the way male and female police officers are represented: reversing traditional gender roles by depicting female detectives, such as *The Bridge*'s Saga Norén, as equivalent to their hard-boiled male counterparts in film noir. However, in other cases, like *The Fall*, 'progressive' depictions of the female detective have been critiqued on the basis they constitute a superficial nod to postfeminist 'gains' in the context of a show that fetishizes misogynistic violence and eroticizes dead women (Jermyn 2017; Penfold-Mounce 2016).

Similar to fictionalized accounts of police, gangster dramas can also serve 'as an index of much broader changes in social relations' (Hayward and Biro 2002: 209). As we saw in Chapter 9, for example, the depiction of a self-conflicted Tony Soprano in *The Sopranos* can be contrasted to earlier portrayals of gangsters in movies like *Goodfellas* and *The Godfather*. Here, *The Sopranos* acts as a means of signaling shifts from modernity to postmodernity; much in the way we saw in Chapter 7 the fictional serial killer in *American Psycho*, Patrick Bateman, represents a new kind of fractured and de-centered postmodern self railing against the routines and controls of modernity (King 2006). Like *The Sopranos*, *The Wire* has been credited with providing a realistic and authentic portrayal of crime and law enforcement in America, including depictions that invert stereotypical images of criminals and police: honorable gangsters and moral thieves versus corrupt and compromised cops. For that reason, *The Wire* has been described as an example of social science-fiction, because it blends journalism and social science in a fictional format (Penfold-Mounce et al. 2011).

The blurring of reality and fiction also has implications for media effects. In Chapter 5, we considered Maeder and Corbett's (2015) study of the relationship between people's *perceived realism* of television shows such as *CSI* and *frequency of watching*. They found continuous frequency of watching is directly related to guilt certainty in prosecution cases presenting DNA evidence, and that people who perceive crime television as more realistic tend to have positive attitudes to DNA evidence and are more influenced by it when it is presented at trial. As we have already seen, the idea that real effects or consequences might derive from people's perceptions resonates with crime fear and fear of crime research. Here too symbiotic relationships are constituted in a recursive looping process, or 'fear of crime feedback loop', with fear of crime, crime fear research, citizens' fears and government reactions operating in similar fashion to the loops (and spirals) cultural criminologists study, whereby images of crime created and consumed by criminals, media institutions and agencies of social control appear to bounce endlessly off one another, as if in 'an infinite hall of mirrors' (Ferrell 1999: 397).

In Chapter 7, we once again encountered the idea of symbiosis, this time exploring the slippage between fictional and non-fictional representations of serial killers and serial killing, as evident in the entwined relations between media, law enforcement agencies and serial killers themselves. Reveling in their own infamy and celebrity status, we saw how serial killers have been known to emulate their fictional counterparts. They have also courted media attention, which the media in turn uses to tap into people's fears and macabre fascination with crime of this kind. We also saw how the 'serial killer' category was essentially an invention of the FBI and criminal profilers influenced by popular culture and detective fiction. Indeed, as Jenkins (1994: 81, 223) has noted, while it is unclear whether changes in law enforcement preceded changes in popular culture or vice versa, what is certain is that the investigative priorities of law enforcement agencies have been shaped by public and legislative expectations, which have themselves been influenced by popular culture and news media. The symbiosis is further manifest in the converging interests of parties involved in the *business* of law enforcement including professional profilers, police, politicians, journalists and crime-fiction writers, all of whom have a stake in upholding the blurred boundaries between reality and fiction, joined as they are in a highly lucrative 'serial killer industry' (Soothill 1993: 341).

This leads to another instance of symbiosis, which we considered in Chapter 9 when looking at the blurring or gray zone between legitimate and illicit business activities. In that part of the book, we saw how orthodox ways of thinking about organized crime have been challenged from a symbiotic perspective, which posits relationships of mutual gain exist between organized crime, business, politicians and even media institutions. To interrogate that idea, however, we must move beyond limited definitions of crime as equivalent to acts violating criminal law, as well as debunk classic imagery of organized crime as synonymous with the shady dealings of underworld mobsters. In other words, we must adopt a more inclusive conception of what constitutes crime and who the criminals are. Indeed, just as shows like *The Wire* and *The Bridge* reverse stereotypical depictions of criminals and cops (including female detectives), so the symbiotic model suggests we ought to invert prevailing ideas about the actors and activities conventionally linked to organized crime.

By that logic, we should consider the possibility that states and state officials can be involved in crime (i.e. state crime), as took place at Abu Ghraib (Hamm 2007), and continues to occur at other sites, such as refugee detention centers (Martin 2018). In these cases, not only does the cruel and inhumane treatment of detainees breach international law but, as we saw in Chapter 9, it can also be conceived as 'state-organized crime', since it is part of a systematic and bureaucratically administered program of abuse. As mentioned in Chapter 9, this analysis goes some way to answering the criticism (flagged in Chapter 2) about the tendency of cultural criminologists to focus on the transgressive activities of deviant 'edgeworkers', while failing to develop critiques of state formations and harms perpetrated by states and state agents.

The symbiotic approach to organized crime does not limit the analysis to state agents, state officials and politicians, however, as business people and corporations can also be implicated. In this way, we can think of corporate crime as a species of organized crime. That, in turn, calls us to expand our view of what constitutes white-collar/corporate 'crime', given corporate activity may be legally compliant while simultaneously causing harm or injustice. A good example, here, would be the activities of bankers prior to the 2008 banking crisis. By promoting and selling 'subprime' mortgages, bankers engaged in an activity that was entirely legal. However, the conduct was immoral and unethical because bankers knew they were selling high-risk products to vulnerable clients. While not a crime in the technical sense, the activities of bankers nevertheless caused a great deal of harm to those who defaulted on mortgages and lost their homes. The harm was then multiplied when, following the GFC (which was precipitated by the banking crisis), governments implemented austerity measures, the adverse effects of which have been felt by ordinary people the most. In the example of the phone-hacking scandal, discussed in Chapter 9, we saw how senior executives at News International similarly turned a blind eye to the unethical conduct of journalists at one of its newspapers. Although 'willful blindness' does amount to a violation of law, that case provides a clear example of the symbiotic model in action; with the subsequent Leveson Inquiry revealing the depths of entanglement, collusion and corruption prevalent among senior politicians, police and journalists in Britain.

While the phone-hacking scandal is an extreme case of media involvement in organized crime (in the broad and inclusive sense of that term), it is also illustrative of a final key theme of this book, which pertains to the 'criminogenic' operation of the mass media as an institution in contemporary capitalist society. As with our treatment of media effects theories, the idea that the mass media is criminogenic ought to be read broadly on a number of levels and in multiple ways, though probably the most obvious and apparent way the mainstream media can be regarded criminogenic derives from its commercial drive to make profit by producing 'newsworthy' stories. This view chimes with various works cited throughout the book (Berrington and Honkatukia 2002; Critcher 2011; Green 2008a; Young 1971), which support a *political economy* reading of the mass media, recognizing its institutionalized need to produce provocative and shocking stories delivered to audiences as quickly and cheaply as possible in an highly competitive

24–7 global marketplace. In Chapter 1, we saw how in order to sell stories, and hence make profit, mass media institutions are animated by certain 'news values', which reflect particular interests and judgments made by journalists and editors about what they believe will appeal to the general public (Jewkes 2015: 46). As we have seen at various points in the book, that results in the media producing stories that are often sensationalized, and which provide a distorted picture of crime in society. In this sense, then, the media can be thought of as criminogenic for producing a false account of crime in society, which tends to exaggerate the incidence of certain crimes (e.g. sexual and violent crime) while ignoring those crimes deemed less appealing (e.g. corporate crime).

A broad reading of the mass media as criminogenic also connects to an expansive conception of media effects insofar as that involves some consideration of the criminogenic consequences of media representations. We have seen, for instance, how media-produced messages and imagery not only affect people's fear of crime and attendant behavior in daily life but how they have also been instrumental in generating a pervasive 'culture of fear' (Altheide 1997; Glassner 1999). As with moral panics, media-generated crime fear can produce a range of real effects. For instance, politicians can tap into widespread fear about crime to justify the introduction of punitive crime policy measures that might, in turn, fundamentally alter the way the criminal justice system operates. One outcome or effect of that process has been identified as 'overcriminalization' (Husak 2008), which, in Cohen's (1985) terminology, widens the net of deviancy control, leading as it does to 'an increased recourse to criminal law and penal sanctions to solve particular problems that may be better addressed through alternative means, such as increasing state resources or allocating them more efficiently' (Martin 2014: 537).

Thus, rather than engaging in serious debate about crime causation, crime policy and prevention, and issues that might point to systemic problems requiring long-term solutions, the mainstream mass media, and especially tabloid variants thereof, tend to be myopically focused on headline-grabbing stories. However, it is not all bad news, for, as was mentioned right at the beginning of the book, we must not treat 'the media' as a monolithic mass, but instead recognize media in the plural, as diverse and constituting a multifarious set of institutions, processes and practices, which are varied in composition, purpose and scope. Accordingly, the rise of digital technologies, newer media formats, such as social media, online activism and citizen journalism, now provide growing opportunities for democratic participation and openings for activism and other interventions around crime and justice issues, which, as we have seen, can be executed either in partnership with or without the help of older media.

REFERENCES

Abbott, A. (2007) 'Against narrative: A preface to lyrical sociology' *Sociological Theory* 25(1): 67–99.

Agamben, G. (2005) *State of Exception*. Chicago, IL: University of Chicago Press.

Agger, G. (2013) '*The Killing*: Urban topographies of a crime' *Journal of Popular Television* 1(2): 235–241.

Allen, J., Livingstone, S. and Reiner, R. (1998) 'True lies: Changing images of crime in British postwar cinema' *European Journal of Communication* 13(1): 53–75.

Altheide, D. L. (1997) 'The news media, the problem frame, and the production of fear' *The Sociological Quarterly* 38(4): 647–668.

Altheide, D. L. (2006) 'Terrorism and the politics of fear' *Cultural Studies ↔ Critical Methodologies* 6(4): 415–439.

Altheide, D. L. (2009) 'Moral panic: From sociological concept to public discourse' *Crime Media Culture* 5(1): 79–99.

Altheide, D. L. and Snow, R. (1991) *Media Worlds in the Post-Journalism Era*. New York, NY: Aldine de Gruyter.

Annesley, J. (1998) *Blank Fictions: Consumerism, Culture and the Contemporary American Novel*. London: Pluto.

Annunziato, S. (2011) 'The Amanda Knox case: The representation of Italy in American media coverage' *Historical Journal of Film, Radio and Television* 31(1): 61–78.

Anonymous. (1998) 'A serial killer's perspective' in R. M. Holmes and S. T. Holmes (eds) *Contemporary Perspectives on Serial Murder*. Thousand Oaks, CA: Sage, pp. 123–135.

Arlacchi, P. (1988) *Mafia Business: The Mafia Ethic and the Spirit of Capitalism*. Oxford: Oxford University Press.

Arrigo, B. A. and Griffin, A. (2004) 'Serial murder and the case of Aileen Wuornos: Attachment theory, psychopathy, and predatory aggression' *Behavioral Sciences and the Law* 22: 375–393.

Asimow, M. (ed.) (2009) *Lawyers in Your Living Room!: Law on Television*. Chicago, IL: ABA Publishing.

Baker, J. (2008) 'Crime Inc's riders' *The Sydney Morning Herald*, 12 January, available at: <www.smh.com.au/news/national/crime-incs-riders/2008/01/11/1199988590155.html>

Baker, R. and Bachelard, M. (2018) 'Phoebe's death could prompt big changes in the Coroner's court' *The Age*, 15 February, available at: <www.theage.com.au/national/victoria/phoebe-s-death-could-prompt-big-changes-in-the-coroner-s-court-20180215-p4z0eo.html>

Baker, S. A. (2012) 'Policing the riots: New social media as recruitment, resistance, and surveillance' in D. Briggs (ed.) *The English Riots of 2011: A Summer of Discontent.* Sherfield: Waterside Press, pp. 169–190.

Banks, C. (2000) *Developing Cultural Criminology: Theory and Practice in Papua New Guinea.* Sydney: Sydney Institute of Criminology.

Banks, M. (2005) 'Spaces of (in)security: Media and fear of crime in a local context' *Crime Media Culture* 1(2): 169–187.

Barretta, A. G. (2000) 'Tony Soprano as postmodern gangster: Controlling identities and managing self-disclosure' *The New Jersey Journal of Communication* 8(2): 211–220.

Bauman, Z. (1989) *Modernity and the Holocaust.* Ithaca, NY: Cornell University Press.

Baumer, T. L. (1978) 'Research on fear of crime in the United States' *Victimology* 3(3–4): 254–264.

Beck, B. (2000) 'The myth that would not die: *The Sopranos*, mafia movies, and Italians in America' *Multicultural Perspectives* 2(2): 24–27.

Becker, H. S. (1963) *Outsiders: Studies in the Sociology of Deviance.* New York, NY: Free Press.

Becker, H. S. (1974) 'Photography and sociology' *Studies in the Anthropology of Visual Communication* 1(1): 3–26.

Becker, H. S. (1995) 'Visual sociology, documentary photography and photojournalism: It's (almost) all a matter of context' *Visual Sociology* 10(1–2): 5–14.

Bergmann, K. (2014) *Swedish Crime Fiction: The Making of Nordic Noir.* London: Mimesis International.

Berrington, E. and Honkatukia, P. (2002) 'An evil monster and a poor thing: Female violence in the media' *Journal of Scandinavian Studies in Criminology and Crime Prevention* 3(1): 50–72.

Bhatia, M., Poynting, S. and Tufail, W. (eds) (2018) *Media, Crime and Racism.* Cham, Switzerland: Palgrave Macmillan.

Biber, K. (2013) 'In crime's archive: The cultural afterlife of criminal evidence' *British Journal of Criminology* 53(6): 1033–1049.

Biressi, A. (2001) *Crime, Fear and the Law in True Crime Stories.* Houndmills: Palgrave Macmillan.

Bourgois, P. (2003) *In Search of Respect: Selling Crack in El Barrio* (2nd edition). Cambridge: Cambridge University Press.

Boyd, M. S. (2013) 'Representation of foreign justice in the media: The Amanda Knox case' *Critical Approaches to Discourse Analysis across Disciplines* 7(1): 33–50.

Boyle, P. and Haggerty, K. D. (2009) 'Spectacular security: Mega-events and the security complex' *International Political Sociology* 3(3): 257–274.

Bradshaw, E. A. (2013) 'This is what a police state looks like: Sousveillance, direct action and the anti-corporate globalization movement' *Critical Criminology* 21(4): 447–461.

Branson, A. L. (2013) 'African American serial killers: Over-represented yet underacknowledged' *The Howard Journal* 52(1): 1–18.

Braudy, L. (1986) *The Frenzy of Renown: Dame and Its History.* New York, NY: Oxford University Press.

Brewer, D. D., Dudek, J., Potterat, S. M., Roberts, J. M. and Woodhouse, D. (2006) 'Extent trends and perpetrators of prostitution-related homicide in the United States' *Journal of Forensic Sciences* 15(5): 1101–1108.

Brophy, P. (1986) 'Horrality – the textuality of contemporary horror films' *Screen* 27(1): 2–13.

Brown, A. P. (2004) 'Anti-social behaviour, crime control and social control' *The Howard Journal* 43(2): 203–211.

Brown, D. (2016) 'The sentencing of Harriet Wran: Tabloid press induced extra curial punishment as mitigation' *Alternative Law Journal* 41(4): 275–278.

Brown, M. (2014) 'Visual criminology and carceral studies: Counter-images in the carceral age' *Theoretical Criminology* 18(2): 176–197.

Brown, M. and Carrabine, E. (2017a) 'Introducing visual criminology' in M. Brown and E. Carrabine (eds) *Routledge International Handbook of Visual Criminology*. Abingdon: Routledge, pp. 1–9.

Brown, M. and Carrabine, E. (eds). (2017b) *Routledge International Handbook of Visual Criminology*. Abingdon: Routledge.

Brown, S. (2003) *Crime and Law in Media Culture*. Buckingham: Open University Press.

Brown, S. (2006a) 'Virtual criminology' in E. McLaughlin and J. Muncie (eds) *The Sage Dictionary of Criminology*. London: Sage, pp. 224–258.

Brown, S. (2006b) 'The criminology of hybrids: Rethinking crime and law in technosocial networks' *Theoretical Criminology* 10(2): 223–244.

Browne, S. (2015) *Dark Matters: On the Surveillance of Blackness*. Durham, NC: Duke University Press.

Browning, C. R. (1983) 'The German bureaucracy and the Holocaust' in A. Grobman and D. Landes (eds) *Genocide: Critical Issues of the Holocaust*. Los Angeles, CA: The Simon Wiesenthal Center, pp. 145–149.

Brunsdon, C. (1998) 'Structure of anxiety: Recent British television crime fiction' *Screen* 39(3): 223–243.

Brunton-Smith, I. (2011) 'Untangling the relationship between fear of crime and perceptions of disorder: Evidence from a longitudinal study of young people in England and Wales' *British Journal of Criminology* 51(6): 885–899.

Burnham, D. (1997) *Above the Law: Secret Deals, Political Fixes, and Other Misadventures of the US Department of Justice*. New York, NY: Scribner.

Cameron, D. (1994) 'Sti-i-i-i-ll going . . . The quest for Jack the Ripper' *Social Text* 40: 147–154.

Campbell, A. (2010) 'Imagining the "war on terror": Fiction, film, and framing' in K. Hayward and M. Presdee (eds) *Framing Crime: Cultural Criminology and the Image*. Abingdon: Routledge, pp. 98–114.

Campbell, D. (2013) 'Fun-loving criminals' *New Statesman*, 29 March–11 April, pp. 34–37.

Carlen, P. (1976) 'The staging of magistrates' justice' *British Journal of Criminology* 16(1): 48–55.

Carney, N. (2016) 'All lives matter, but so does race: Black Lives Matter and the evolving role of social media' *Humanity & Society* 40(2): 180–199.

Carrabine, E. (2008) *Crime, Culture and the Media*. Cambridge: Polity Press.

Carrabine, E. (2011) 'Images of torture: Culture, politics and power' *Crime Media Culture* 7(1): 5–30.

Carrabine, E. (2012) 'Just images: Aesthetics, ethics and visual criminology' *British Journal of Criminology* 52(3): 463–489.

Carrabine, E. (2014) 'Seeing things: Violence, voyeurism and the camera' *Theoretical Criminology* 18(2): 134–158.

Carrabine, E. (2016a) 'Changing fortunes: Criminology and the sociological condition' *Sociology* 50(5): 847–862.

Carrabine, E. (2016b) 'Picture this: Criminology, image and narrative' *Crime Media Culture* 12(2): 253–270.

Carrabine, E. (2017) 'Social science and visual culture' in M. Brown and E. Carrabine (eds) *Routledge International Handbook of Visual Criminology*. Abingdon: Routledge, pp. 23–39.

Carter, C. and Weaver, C. K. (2003) *Violence and the Media*. Buckingham: Open University Press.

Cavender, G. (1999) 'Detecting masculinity' in J. Ferrell and N. Websdale (eds) *Making Trouble: Cultural Constructions of Crime, Deviance and Control*. Hawthorne, NY: Aldine de Guyter, pp. 157–175.

Cavender, G. and Deutsch, S. K. (2007) '*CSI* and moral authority: The police and science' *Crime Media Culture* 3(1): 67–81.

Chadee, D. and Ditton, J. (2005) 'Fear of crime and the media: Assessing the lack of relationship' *Crime Media Culture* 1(3): 322–332.

Chambliss, W. J. (1989) 'State-organized crime – The American Society of Criminology, 1988 Presidential Address' *Criminology* 27(2): 183–208.

Chan, K-W. (2013) 'An investigation into the CSI effect on the Malaysian population' *Australian Journal of Forensic Sciences* 45(4): 417–430.

Chesney-Lind, M. (1999) 'Media misogyny: Demonizing "violent" girls and women' in J. Ferrell and N. Websdale (eds) *Making Trouble: Cultural Constructions of Crime, Deviance and Control*. Hawthorne, NY: Aldine de Guyter, pp. 115–141.

Chesney-Lind, M. (2007) 'Beyond bad girls: Feminist perspectives on female offending' in C. Sumner (ed.) *The Blackwell Companion to Criminology*. Malden, MA: Blackwell Publishing, pp. 255–267.

Chesney-Lind, M. and Eliason, M. (2006) 'From invisible to incorrigible: The demonization of marginalized women and girls' *Crime Media Culture* 2(1): 29–47.

Chibnall, S. (1977) *Law and Order News: Crime Reporting in the British Press*. London: Tavistock.

Chiricos, T., Padgett, K. and Gertz, M. (2000) 'Fear, TV news, and the reality of crime' *Criminology* 38(3): 755–785.

Christie, N. (1986) 'The ideal victim' in E. A. Fattah (ed.) *From Crime Policy to Victim Policy: Reorienting the Justice System*. Houndmills: Palgrave Macmillan, pp. 17–30.

Clarke Dillman, J. (2014) *Women and Death in Film, Television and News: Dead but Not Gone*. Basingstoke: Palgrave Macmillan.

Clemente, F. and Kleinman, M. B. (1976) 'Fear of crime amongst the aged' *The Gerontologist* 16(3): 207–210.

Clifford, K. (2014) 'Amanda Knox: A picture of innocence' *Celebrity Studies* 5(4): 504–507.

Cohen, A. K. (1955) *Delinquent Boys: The Subculture of the Gang*. Chicago, IL: Free Press.

Cohen, A. K. (1965) 'The sociology of the deviant act: Anomie theory and beyond' *American Sociological Review* 30(1): 5–15.

Cohen, S. (1972/2002) *Folk Devils and Moral Panics* (3rd edition). London: Routledge.

Cohen, S. (1985) *Visions of Social Control: Crime, Punishment and Classification*. Cambridge: Polity Press.

Cohen, S. (2001) *States of Denial: Knowing About Atrocities and Suffering*. Cambridge: Polity Press.

Cohen, S. (2011) 'Whose side are we on? The undeclared politics of moral panic theory' *Crime Media Culture* 7(3): 237–243.

Cole, S. A. and Dioso-Villa, R. (2007) '*CSI* and its effects: Media, juries, and the burden of proof' *New England Law Review* 41: 435–469.

Cole, S. A. and Dioso-Villa, R. (2009) 'Investigating the "*CSI* effect" effect: Media and litigation crisis in criminal law' *Stanford Law Review* 61: 1335–1374.

Conlon, G. (1990) *Proved Innocent: The Story of Gerry Conlon and the Guildford Four*. New York, NY: Plume.

Cook, T. D., Fremming, J. and Tyler, T. (1981) 'Criminal victimization of the elderly: Validating the policy assumptions' in G. M. Stephenson and J. M. Davis (eds) *Progress in Applied Social Psychology*. New York, NY: John Wiley, pp. 223–251.

Copes, H. and Ragland, J. (2016) 'Considering the implicit meanings in photographs in narrative criminology' *Crime Media Culture* 12(2): 271.

Creeber, G. (2015) 'Killing us softly: Investigating the aesthetics, philosophy and influence of *Nordic Noir* television' *Journal of Popular Television* 3(1): 21–35.

Critcher, C. (2011) 'For a political economy of moral panics' *Crime Media Culture* 7(3): 259–275.

Crone, T. (2002) *Law and the Media: An Everyday Guide for Professionals* (4th edition). Oxford: Focal Press.

David, M., Rohloff, A., Petley, J. and Hughes, J. (2011) 'The idea of moral panic – Ten dimensions of dispute' *Crime Media Culture* 7(3): 215–228.

Davis, J. E. (ed.) (2002) *Stories of Change: Narrative and Social Movements*. Albany, NY: State University of New York Press.

Davis, K. and Morrissey, B. (2003) 'Utilities and utilitarianism' *Continuum* 17(4): 387–395.

Davis, M. (1998) *The Ecology of Fear: Los Angeles and the Imagination of Disaster*. London: Verso.

de Lint, W. and Hall, A. (2009) *Intelligent Control: Developments in Public Order Policing in Canada*. Toronto: University of Toronto Press.

della Porta, D., Andretta, M., Mosca, L. and Reiter, H. (eds) (2006) *Globalization from Below: Transnational Activism and Protest Networks*. Minneapolis, MN: University of Minnesota Press.

Denham, J. (2016) 'The commodification of the criminal corpse: "Selective memory" in posthumous representations of criminal' *Morality* 21(3): 229–245.

Dennis, K. (2008) '*Keeping a close watch* – The rise of self-surveillance and the threat of digital exposure' *The Sociological Review* 56(3): 347–357.

de Zwart, M. (2013) 'Whistle-blowers and the media: Friends or "frenemies"?' *Alternative Law Journal* 38(4): 250–254.

Dietz, M. L. (1996) 'Killing sequentially: Expanding the parameters of the conceptualization of serial and mass murder' in T. O'Reilly-Fleming (ed.) *Serial and Mass Murder*. Toronto: Canadian Scholar's Press, pp. 109–122.

Ditton, J., Chadee, D., Farrall, S., Gilchrist, E. and Bannister, J. (2004) 'From imitation to intimidation: A note on the curious and changing relationship between the media, crime and fear of crime' *British Journal of Criminology* 44(4): 595–610.

Ditton, J. and Duffy, J. (1983) 'Bias in the newspaper reporting of crime news' *British Journal of Criminology* 23(2): 159–165.

Ditton, J., Farrall, S., Bannister, J. and Gilchrist, E. (1998) 'Measuring fear of crime' *Criminal Justice Matters* 31: 10–12.

Dominick, J. (1978) 'Crime and law enforcement in the mass media' in C. Winick (ed.) *Deviance and Mass Media*. London: Sage, pp. 105–128.

Doob, A. and MacDonald, G. (1979) 'Television viewing and the fear of victimization: Is the relationship causal?' *Journal of Personality and Social Psychology* 37(1): 170–179.

Downes, D. and Rock, P. (2007) *Understanding Deviance: A Guide to the Sociology of Crime and Rule-Breaking* (5th edition). Oxford: Oxford University Press.

Doyle, A. (2011) 'Revisiting the synopticon: Reconsidering Mathiesen's "The Viewer Society" in the age of Web 2.0' *Theoretical Criminology* 15(3): 283–299.

Durkheim, E. (1897/1970) *Suicide: A Study in Sociology*. London: Routledge & Kegan Paul.

Egger, S. A. (2002) *The Killers Among Us: Examination of Serial Murder and its Investigations*. Upper Saddle River, NJ: Prentice Hall.

Elias, N. (1982) *The Civilizing Process*, Vol. 2, *State Formation and Civilization*. Oxford: Blackwell Publishing.

Elias, N. (1987) *The Civilizing Process*, Vol. 1, *The History of Manners*. Oxford: Blackwell Publishing.

Ellis, B. E. (1991) *American Psycho*. London: Picador.

Elmer, G. (2003) 'A diagram of panoptic surveillance' *New Media and Society* 5(2): 231–247.

Eschholz, S., Chiricos, T. and Gertz, M. (2003) 'Television and fear of crime: Programme types, audience traits and the mediating effect of perceived neighbourhood racial composition' *Social Problems* 50(3): 395–415.

Faludi, S. (1991) *Backlash: The Undeclared War Against American Women*. New York, NY: Anchor Doubleday.

Farrall, S. (2004a) 'Revisiting crime surveys: Emotional responses without emotions? Or look back at anger' *International Journal of Social Research Methodology* 7(2): 157–171.

Farrall, S. (2004b) '*Can* we believe our eyes? A response to Mike Hough' *International Journal of Social Research Methodology* 7(2): 177–179.

Farrall, S., Bannister, J., Ditton, J. and Gilchrist, E. (1997) 'Questioning the measurement of the "fear of crime": Findings from a major methodological study' *British Journal of Criminology* 37(4): 658–679.

Fernandez, L. A. (2008) *Policing Dissent: Social Control and the Anti-Globalization Movement*. New Brunswick, NJ: Rutgers University Press.

Fernandez, L. A. and Huey, L. (2009) 'Is resistance futile? Thoughts on resisting surveillance' *Surveillance & Society* 6(3): 198–202.

Ferrell, J. (1996) *Crimes of Style*. Boston, MA: Northeastern University Press.

Ferrell, J. (1997) 'Criminological *verstehen*: Inside the immediacy of crime' *Justice Quarterly* 14(1): 3–23.

Ferrell, J. (1999) 'Cultural criminology' *Annual Review of Sociology* 25: 395–418.

Ferrell, J. (2004) 'Boredom, crime and criminology' *Theoretical Criminology* 8(3): 287–302.

Ferrell, J. (2010) 'Cultural criminology: The loose canon' in E. McLaughlin and T. Newburn (eds) *The Sage Handbook of Criminological Theory*. London: Sage, pp. 303–318.

Ferrell, J. (2013) 'Cultural criminology and the politics of meaning' *Critical Criminology* 21(3): 257–271.

Ferrell, J. (2015) 'Cultural criminology as method and theory' in J. Miller and W. R. Palacios (eds) *Advances in Criminological Theory: The Value of Qualitative Research for Advancing Criminological Theory*. Abingdon: Routledge, pp. 293–310.

Ferrell, J. and Hamm. M. (eds) (1998) *Ethnography at the Edge: Crime, Deviance and Field Research*. Boston, MA: Northeastern University Press.

Ferrell, J., Hayward, K., Morrison, W. and Presdee, M. (eds) (2004) *Cultural Criminology Unleashed*. London: Glasshouse Press.

Ferrell, J., Hayward, K. and Young, J. (2008) *Cultural Criminology: An Invitation*. Los Angeles, CA: Sage.

Ferrell, J., Hayward, K. and Young, J. (2015) *Cultural Criminology: An Invitation* (2nd edition). Los Angeles, CA: Sage.

Ferrell, J. and Sanders, C. R. (eds) (1995) *Cultural Criminology*. Boston, MA: Northeastern University Press.

Ferrell, J. and Van de Voorde, C. (2010) 'The decisive moment: Documentary photography and cultural criminology' in K. Hayward and M. Presdee (eds) *Framing Crime: Cultural Criminology and the Image*. New York, NY: Glasshouse Press, pp. 36–52.

Ferrell, J. and Websdale, N. (eds) (1999) *Making Trouble: Cultural Constructions of Crime, Deviance, and Control*. Hawthorne, NY: Allen de Gruyter.

Field, F. (2003) *Neighbours from Hell: The Politics of Behaviour*. London: Politico's Publishing.

Force, W. R. (2010) 'The code of Harry: Performing normativity in *Dexter*' *Crime Media Culture* 6(3): 329–345.

Forshaw, B. (2012) *Death in a Cold Climate: A Guide to Scandinavian Crime Fiction*. London: Palgrave Macmillan.

Fortin, V., Lemonde, L., Poisson, J. and Poisson, M. (2013) *Repression, Discrimination and the Student Strike: Testimonies and Analysis*, available at: <http://liguedesdroits.ca/wp-content/fichiers/repression-report-2012-final-web.pdf>

Foucault, M. (1976/1990) *The History of Sexuality*, Vol. 1. London: Penguin.

Foucault, M. (1977/1991) *Discipline and Punish: The Birth of the Modern Prison*. London: Penguin.

Freiberg, A. (2001) 'Affective versus effective justice: Instrumentalism and emotionalism in criminal justice' *Punishment & Society* 3(2): 265–278.

Freiberg, A. and Carson, W. G. (2010) 'The limits of evidence-based policy: Evidence, emotion and criminal justice' *The Australian Journal of Public Administration* 69(2): 152–164.

Freud, S. (1949) *The Ego and the Id*. London: Hogarth.

Freud, S. (1961) *Civilization and Its Discontents*. New York, NY: Norton.

Freud, S. (2001) *Totem and Taboo*. London: Routledge.

Gacono, D. B. (2000) *The Clinical and Forensic Assessment of Psychopathy: A Practitioner's Guide*. Mahwah, NJ: Lawrence Erlbaum.

Galloway K. and Ardill, A. (2014) 'Queensland: A return to the moonlight state?' *Alternative Law Journal* 39(1): 3–8.

Galtung, J. and Ruge, M. H. (1965) 'The structure of foreign news: The presentation of the Congo, Cuba and Cyprus crises in four Norwegian newspapers' *Journal of Peace Research* 2(1): 64–91.

Garfinkel, H. (1967) *Studies in Ethnomethodology*. Englewood Cliffs, NJ: Prentice Hall.

Garland, D. (2008) 'On the concept of moral panic' *Crime Media Culture* 4(1): 9–30.

Garland, J. and Bilby, C. (2011) ' "What next, dwarves?": Images of police culture in *Life on Mars*' *Crime Media Culture* 7(2): 115–132.

Gekoski, A. (1998) *Murder by Numbers: British Serial Killers Since 1950*. London: Andre Deutsch.

Gerbner, G. and Gross, L. (1976) 'Living with television: The violence profile' *Journal of Communication* 26(1): 173–199.

Gerbner, G., Gross, L., Eleey, M. F., Jackson-Beeck, M., Jeffries-Fox, S. and Signorielli, N. (1977) 'TV violence profile no. 8: The highlights' *Journal of Communication* 27(2): 171–180.

Gerbner, G., Gross, L., Morgan, M. and Signorielli, N. (1980) 'The mainstreaming of America: Violence profile no. 11' *Journal of Communication* 30(3): 10–29.

Gerbner, G., Gross, L., Morgan, M. and Signorielli, N. (1994) 'Growing up with television: The cultivation perspective' in J. Bryant and D. Zillman (eds) *Media Effects: Advances in Theory and Research*. Hillsdale, NJ: Lawrence Erlbaum, pp. 17–41.

Gies, L. (2017) 'Miscarriages of justice in the age of social media: The Amanda Knox and Raffaele Sollecito innocence campaign' *British Journal of Criminology* 57(3): 723–740.

Gilboa, E. (2005a) 'The CNN effect: The search for a communication theory of international relations' *Political Communication* 22(1): 27–44.

Gilboa, E. (2005b) 'Global television news and foreign policy: Debating the CNN effect' *International Studies Perspectives* 6(3): 325–341.

Gilchrist, E., Bannister, J., Ditton, J. and Farrall, S. (1998) 'Women and the "fear of crime": Challenging the accepted stereotype' *British Journal of Criminology* 38(2): 283–299.

Gilman Srebnick, A. (2005) 'Does the representation fit the crime? Some thoughts on writing crime history as cultural text' in A. Gilman Srebnick and R. Lévy (eds) *Crime and Culture: An Historical Perspective*. Aldershot: Ashgate, pp. 3–19.

Girling, E., Loader, I. and Sparks, R. (2000) *Crime and Social Change in Middle England: Questions of Order in an English Town*. London: Routledge.

Giroux, H. A. (2000) 'Brutalised bodies and emasculated politics: *Fight Club*, consumerism, and masculine violence' *Third Text* 14(53): 31–41.

Glassner, B. (1999) *The Culture of Fear: Why Americans are Afraid of the Wrong Things*. New York, NY: Basic Books.

Goffman, E. (1959) *The Presentation of Self in Everyday Life*. Garden City, NY: Anchor Doubleday.

Goffman, E. (1963) *Stigma: Notes on the Management of Spoiled Identity*. New York, NY: Touchstone.

Goffman, E. (1979) *Gender Advertisements*. New York, NY: Harper & Row.

Goldsmith, A. (2010) 'Policing's new visibility' *British Journal of Criminology* 50(5): 914–934.

Goode, E. and Ben-Yehuda, N. (1994) *Moral Panics: The Social Construction of Deviance*. Oxford: Blackwell Publishing.

Goodey, J. (1997) 'Boys don't cry: Masculinities, fear of crime and fearlessness' *British Journal of Criminology* 37(3): 401–418.

Gordon, D. (1990) *The Justice Juggernaut: Fighting Street Crime, Controlling Citizens*. New Brunswick, NJ: Rutgers University Press.

Gorringe, H. and Rosie, M. (2008) 'It's a long way to Auchterarder! "Negotiated management" and mismanagement in the policing of G8 protests' *British Journal of Sociology* 59(2): 187–205.

Gotsis, T. (2015) *Protests and the Law in NSW: Briefing Paper No 7/2015*, available at: <www.parliament.nsw.gov.au/researchpapers/Documents/protests-and-the-law-in-nsw/Protests%20and%20the%20law%20in%20NSW.pdf>

Gottschalk, P. (2012) 'White-collar crime and police crime: Rotten apples or rotten barrels?' *Critical Criminology* 20(2): 169–182.

Grabe, M. E. and Drew, D. (2007) 'Crime cultivation: Comparisons across media genres and channels' *Journal of Broadcasting and Electronic Media* 51(1): 147–171.

Grabe, M. E., Trager, K. D., Lear, M. and Rauch, J. (2006) 'Gender in crime news: A case study test of the chivalry hypothesis' *Mass Communication and Society* 9(2): 137–163.

Graber, D. (1980) *Crime News and the Public.* New York, NY: Praeger.

Gray, E. (2014) 'In/between place: Connection and isolation in *The Bridge*' *Aeternum: The Journal of Contemporary Gothic Studies* 1(1): 73–85.

Green, D. A. (2008a) 'Suitable vehicles: Framing blame and justice when children kill a child' *Crime Media Culture* 4(2): 197–220.

Green, D. A. (2008b) *When Children Kill Children: Penal Populism and Political Culture.* Oxford: Oxford University Press.

Greenfield, S., Osborn, G. and Robson, P. (2009) '*Judge John Deed*: British TV lawyers in the 21st century' in M. Asimow (ed.) *Lawyers in Your Living Room!: Law on Television.* Chicago, IL: ABA Publishing, pp. 205–215.

Greer, C. (2003) *Sex Crime and the Media: Sex Offending and the Press in a Divided Society.* Cullompton: Willan Publishing.

Greer, C. (2005) 'Crime and media: Understanding the connections' in C. Hale, K. Hayward, A. Wahadin and E. Wincup (eds) *Criminology.* Oxford: Oxford University Press, pp. 157–182.

Greer, C. (2010) 'News media criminology' in E. McLaughlin and T. Newburn (eds) *The Sage Handbook of Criminological Theory.* London: Sage, pp. 490–513.

Greer, C. and McLaughlin, E. (2011) ' "Trial by media": Policing, the 24–7 news mediasphere and the "politics of outrage" ' *Theoretical Criminology* 15(1): 23–46.

Greer, C. and McLaughlin, E. (2012a) 'Media justice: Madeleine McCann, intermediatization and "trial by media" in the British press' *Theoretical Criminology* 16(4): 395–416.

Greer, C. and McLaughlin, E. (2012b) 'Trial by media: Phone-hacking, riots, looting, gangs and police chiefs' in J. Peay and T. Newburn (eds) *Policing, Politics, Culture and Control: Essays in Honour of Robert Reiner.* Oxford: Hart Publishing, pp. 135–154.

Grice, A. (2017) 'Fake news handed Brexiteers the referendum – and now they have no idea what they're doing' *The Independent*, 18 January, available at: <www.independent.co.uk/voices/michael-gove-boris-johnson-brexit-eurosceptic-press-theresa-may-a7533806.html>

Guild, E. (2009) *Security and Migration in the 21st Century.* Cambridge: Polity Press.

Gumpert, R. and Goodman, A. (2012) 'Robert Gumpert: Take a picture, tell a story' *Crime Media Culture* 8(1): 95–106.

Gunter, B. (1987) *Television and the Fear of Crime.* London: John Libbey.

Gunter, J. (2017) ' "Yolocaust": How should you behave at a Holocaust memorial' *BBC News*, 20 January, available at: <www.bbc.com/news/world-europe-38675835>

Haggerty, K. D. (2009) 'Modern serial killers' *Crime Media Culture* 5(2): 168–187.

Haggerty, K. D. and Ericson, R. V. (2000) 'The surveillant assemblage' *British Journal of Sociology* 51(4): 605–622.

Haines, F. (2017) 'White-collar and corporate crime' in D. Palmer, W. de Lint and D. Dalton (eds) *Crime and Justice: A Guide to Criminology* (5th edition). Pyrmont: Thomson Reuters, pp. 173–192.

Hale, C. (1996) 'Fear of crime: A review of the literature' *International Review of Victimology* 4(2): 79–150.

Hale, R. and Bolin, A. (1998) 'The female serial killer' in R. M. Holmes and S. T. Holmes (eds) *Contemporary Perspectives on Serial Murder*. Thousand Oaks, CA: Sage, pp. 33–58.

Hall, S., Critcher, C., Jefferson, T., Clarke, J. and Robert, B. (1978) *Policing the Crisis: Mugging, the State and Law and Order*. London: Palgrave Macmillan.

Hall, S. and Winlow, S. (2015) *Revitalizing Criminological Theory: Towards a New Ultra-realism*. London: Routledge.

Halsey, M. (2008) 'Narrating the chase: Edgework and young peoples' experiences of crime' in T. Anthony and C. Cunneen (eds) *The Critical Criminology Companion*. Sydney: Hawkins Press, pp. 105–117.

Hamm, M. (1995) *The Abandoned Ones: The Imprisonment and Uprising of the Mariel Boat People*. Boston, MA: Northeastern University Press.

Hamm, M. (2007) '"High crimes and misdemeanors": George W. Bush and the sins of Abu Ghraib' *Crime Media Culture* 3(3): 259–284.

Harcup, T. and O'Neill, D. (2001) 'What is news? Galtung and Ruge revisited' *Journalism Studies* 2(2): 261–280.

Harding, T. (2001) *The Video Activist Handbook* (2nd edition). London: Pluto Press.

Harris, T. (1997) *The Silence of the Lambs*. London: Mandarin.

Hasan, M. (2011) 'Sadiq Kahn: Champion of the underdog' *New Statesman*, 14 February, available at: <www.newstatesman.com/uk-politics/2011/02/shadow-cabinet-khan-labour>

Hawkins, R. and Pingree, S. (1980) 'Some processes in the cultivation effect' *Communication Research* 7(2): 193–226.

Hayward, K. (2002) 'The vilification and pleasures of youthful transgression' in J. Muncie, G. Hughes and E. McLaughlin (eds) *Youth Justice: Critical Readings*. London: Sage, pp. 80–94.

Hayward, K. (2004) *City Limits: Crime, Consumer Culture and the Urban Experience*. London: Glasshouse Press.

Hayward, K. (2010) 'Opening the lens: Cultural criminology and the image' in K. Hayward and M. Presdee (eds) *Framing Crime: Cultural Criminology and the Image*. New York, NY: Glasshouse Press, pp. 1–16.

Hayward, K. (2011) 'The critical terrorism studies-cultural criminology nexus: Some thoughts on how to "toughen up" the critical studies approach' *Critical Studies on Terrorism* 4(1): 57–73.

Hayward, K. (2016) 'Cultural criminology: Script rewrites' *Theoretical Criminology* 20(3): 297–321.

Hayward, K. (2017) 'Documentary criminology: A cultural criminological introduction' in M. Brown and E. Carrabine (eds) *Routledge International Handbook of Visual Criminology*. Abingdon: Routledge, pp. 135–150.

Hayward, K. and Presdee, M. (eds) (2010) *Framing Crime: Cultural Criminology and the Image.* New York, NY: Glasshouse Press.

Hayward, K. and Yar, M. (2006) 'The "chav" phenomenon: Consumption, media and the construction of a new underclass' *Crime Media Culture* 2(1): 9–28.

Hayward, K. and Young, J. (2004) 'Cultural criminology: Some notes on the script' *Theoretical Criminology* 8(3): 259–273.

Hayward, K. and Young, J. (2007) 'Cultural criminology' in M. Maguire, R. Morgan and R. Reiner (eds) *The Oxford Handbook of Criminology* (4th edition). Oxford: Oxford University Press, pp. 102–121.

Hayward, S. and Biro, A. (2002) 'The eighteenth Brumaire of Tony Soprano' in D. Laverty (ed.) *This Thing of Ours: Investigating the Sopranos.* New York, NY: Columbia University Press, pp. 203–214.

Heath, L. (1984) 'Impact of newspaper crime reports on fear of crime: Multi-methodological investigation' *Journal of Personality and Social Psychology* 47(2): 263–276.

Heath, L. and Petraitis, J. (1987) 'Television viewing and fear of crime: Where is the mean world?' *Basic and Applied Social Psychology* 8(1–2): 97–123.

Heffernan, M. (2011) 'Wilful blindness – why we ignore the obvious at our peril' *New Statesman,* 8 August, available at: <www.newstatesman.com/ideas/2011/08/wilful-blindness-essay-news>

Holmes, R. M. and DeBurger, J. E. (1998) 'Profiles in terror: The serial murderer' in R. M. Holmes and S. T. Holmes (eds) *Contemporary Perspectives on Serial Murder.* Thousand Oaks, CA: Sage, pp. 5–16.

Holmes, R. M., DeBurger, J. E. and Holmes, S. T. (1998a) 'Inside the mind of the serial murderer' in R. M. Holmes and S. T. Holmes (eds) *Contemporary Perspectives on Serial Murder.* Thousand Oaks, CA: Sage, pp. 113–122.

Holmes, S. T., Hickey, E. and Holmes, R. M. (1998b) 'Female serial murderesses' in R. M. Holmes and S. T. Holmes (eds) *Contemporary Perspectives on Serial Murder.* Thousand Oaks, CA: Sage, pp. 59–70.

Holmes, R. M. and Holmes, S. T. (1998a) 'Preface' in R. M. Holmes and S. T. Holmes (eds) *Contemporary Perspectives on Serial Murder.* Thousand Oaks, CA: Sage, pp. vii–ix.

Holmes, R. M. and Holmes, S. T. (eds) (1998b) *Contemporary Perspectives on Serial Murder.* Thousand Oaks, CA: Sage.

Holmes, R. M. and Holmes, S. T. (2010) *Serial Murder* (3rd edition). Los Angeles, CA: Sage.

Hoogenboom, B. (2010) *The Governance of Policing and Security: Ironies, Myths and Paradoxes.* Basingstoke: Palgrave Macmillan.

Hopkins, N. (2013) 'MI5 chief: GCHQ surveillance plays vital role in fight against terrorism' *The Guardian,* 9 October, available at: <www.theguardian.com/uk-news/2013/oct/08/gchq-surveillance-new-mi5-chief>

Hough, M. (2004) 'Worry about crime: Mental events and mental states' *International Journal of Social Research Methodology* 7(2): 173–176.

Houlihan, A. (2012) 'Stranger danger? Sadistic serial killers on the small screen' in P. Robson and J. Silbey (eds) *Law and Justice on the Small Screen.* Oxford: Hart Publishing, pp. 441–453.

Howe, A. (1995) 'Chamberlain revisited: The case against the media' in N. Naffine (ed.) *Gender, Crime and Feminism*. Aldershot: Dartmouth, pp. 175–181.

Howe, A. (1999) '"The war against women": Media representations of men's violence against women in Australia' in J. Ferrell and N. Websdale (eds) *Making Trouble: Cultural Constructions of Crime, Deviance and Control*. Hawthorne, NY: Aldine de Guyter, pp. 142–156.

Huey, L. (2010) '"I've seen it on *CSI*": Criminal Investigators' perceptions about the management of public expectations in the field' *Crime Media Culture* 6(1): 49–68.

Hughes, G. (2006) 'Foreword' in R. Birch (ed.) *Todmorden Album 4: People Places and Events*. Todmorden: Woodlands Press.

Hughes, M. (1980) 'The fruits of cultivation analysis: A re-examination of some effects of television watching' *Public Opinion Quarterly* 44(3): 287–302.

Hunter, R. and Tyson, D. (2017) 'Justice Betty King: A study of feminist judging in action' *UNSW Law Journal* 40(2): 778–805.

Husak, D. (2008) *Overcriminalization: The Limits of Criminal Law*. Oxford: Oxford University Press.

Huws, U. (2015) 'Saints and sinners: Lessons about work from daytime TV' *International Journal of Media & Cultural Studies* 11(2): 143–163.

Jacobs, J. (2005) 'Violence and therapy in *The Sopranos*' in M. Hammond and L. Mazdon (eds) *The Contemporary Television Series*. Edinburgh: Edinburgh University Press, pp. 139–158.

Jameson, F. (1979) 'Reification and utopia in mass culture' *Social Text* 1(Winter): 130–148.

Jameson, F. (1991) *Postmodernism or the Cultural Logic of Late Capitalism*. London: Verso.

Jarvis, B. (2007) 'Monsters Inc.: Serial killers and consumer culture' *Crime Media Culture* 3(3): 326–344.

Jasper, J. M. (1997) *The Art of Moral Protest: Culture, Biography and Creativity in Social Movements*. Chicago, IL: University of Chicago Press.

Jaycox, V. (1978) 'The elderly's fear of crime: Rational or irrational' *Victimology* 3(3–4): 329–334.

Jefferson, T. (1993) 'Pondering paramilitarism: A question of standpoints?' *British Journal of Criminology* 33(3): 374–381.

Jenkins, H. (2006) *Convergence Culture: Where Old and New Media Collide*. New York, NY: New York University Press.

Jenkins, P. (1994) *Using Murder: The Social Construction of Serial Homicide*. New York, NY: Aldine de Gruyter.

Jenkins, P. (2002) 'Catch me before I kill more: Seriality as modern monstrosity' *Cultural Analysis* 3: 1–17.

Jenks, C. (2003) *Transgression*. London: Routledge.

Jenks, C. (2011) 'The context of an emergent and enduring concept' *Crime Media Culture* 7(3): 229–236.

Jermyn, D. (2017) 'Silk blouses and fedoras: The female detective, contemporary TV crime drama and the predicaments of postfeminism' *Crime Media Culture* 13(3): 259–276.

Jewkes, Y. (2015) *Crime and Media* (3rd edition). Los Angeles, CA: Sage.

Johnson, D. (2009) 'Anger about crime and support for punitive criminal justice policies' *Punishment & Society* 11(1): 51–66.

Jones, P. J. and Wardle, C. (2008) '"No emotion, no sympathy": The visual construction of Maxine Carr' *Crime Media Culture* 4(1): 53–71.

Jones, P. J. and Wardle, C. (2010) 'Hindley's ghost: The visual representation of Maxine Carr' in K. Hayward and M. Presdee (eds) *Framing Crime: Cultural Criminology and the Image*. New York, NY: Glasshouse Press, pp. 53–67.

Kane, S. C. (1998) 'Reversing the ethnographic gaze: Experiments in cultural criminology' in J. Ferrell and N. Websdale (eds) *Making Trouble: Cultural Constructions of Crime, Deviance and Control*. Hawthorne, NY: Aldine de Guyter, pp. 132–145.

Kane, S. C. (2004) 'The unconventional methods of cultural criminology' *Theoretical Criminology* 8(3): 303–321.

Karstedt, S. (2002) 'Emotions and criminal justice' *Theoretical Criminology* 6(3): 299–317.

Karstedt, S. and Farrall, S. (2006) 'The moral economy of everyday crime: Markets, consumers, citizens' *British Journal of Criminology* 46(6): 1011–1036.

Karstedt, S., Loader, I. and Strang, H. (eds) (2014) *Emotions, Crime and Justice*. Oxford: Hart Publishing.

Katz, J. (1987) 'What makes crime news?' *Media, Culture and Society* 9(1): 47–75.

Katz, J. (1988) *Seductions of Crime: Moral and Sensual Attractions in Doing Evil*. New York, NY: Basic Books.

Katz, J. (2016) 'Culture within and culture about crime: The case of the "Rodney King Riots"' *Crime Media Culture* 12(2): 233–251.

Keene, C. (1992) 'Fear of crime in Canada – An examination of concrete and formless victimization' *Canadian Journal of Criminology* 34(2): 215–224.

Kelling, G. L. and Wilson, J. Q. (1982) 'Broken windows: The police and neighborhood safety' *The Atlantic Monthly*, March, 249(3): 29–38, available at: <www.theatlantic.com/magazine/archive/1982/03/broken-windows/304465/>

Kidd, J. (2015) 'NSW police issued body cameras to record interactions, gather video evidence' *ABC News*, 17 September, available at: <www.abc.net.au/news/2015-09-17/nsw-police-to-wear-body-cameras/6783862>

Kim, Y. S., Barak, G. and Shelton, D. E. (2009) 'Examining the "CSI-effect" in the cases of circumstantial evidence and eyewitness testimony: Multivariate and path analyses' *Journal of Criminal Justice* 37(5): 452–460.

King, A. (2006) 'Serial killing and the postmodern self' *History of the Human Sciences* 19(3): 109–125.

King, B. (2009) 'Underbelly – A true crime story or just sex, drugs and rock and roll?' *Medico-Legal Society of Victoria, The Melbourne Club, Victoria*, 13 November, available at: <http://mlsv.org.au/meetings/justice-betty-king/>

Kinney, E. (2015) 'Victims, villains, and valiant rescuers: Unpacking sociolegal constructions of human trafficking and crimmigration in popular culture' in M. João Guia (ed.) *The Illegal Business of Human Trafficking*. Cham, Switzerland: Springer, pp. 87–108.

Kooistra, P. (1989) *Criminals as Heroes: Structure, Power and Identity*. Bowling Green, OH: Bowling Green State University Popular Press.

Koskela, H. (1999) '"Gendered exclusions": Women's fear of violence and changing relations to space' *Geografiska Annaler: Series B, Human Geography* 81(2): 111–124.

Kubrin, C. (2008) 'Making order of disorder' *Criminology and Public Policy* 7(2): 203–214.
Kumar, M., Martin, G. and Scott Bray, R. (2015) 'Secrecy, law and society' in G. Martin, R. Scott Bray and M. Kumar (eds) *Secrecy, Law and Society*. Abingdon: Routledge, pp. 1–19.
Kundnani, A. (2014) *The Muslims are Coming! Islamophobia, Extremism and the Domestic War on Terror*. London: Verso.
Lartey, J. (2016) 'Film-makers demand inquiry into "targeting" of people who record police' *The Guardian*, 12 August, available at: <www.theguardian.com/film/2016/aug/10/film-makers-citizen-journalists-justice-department-investigation>
Lawler, S. (2005) 'Introduction: Class, culture and identity' *Sociology* 39(5): 797–806.
Lemert, E. (1951) *Social Pathology: A Systematic Approach to the Theory of Sociopathic Behavior*. New York, NY: McGraw-Hill.
Lemert, E. (1964) 'Social structure, social control and deviation' in M. B. Clinard (ed.) *Anomie and Deviant Behaviour: A Discussion and a Critique*. New York, NY: Free Press, pp. 57–97.
Lebowitz, B. (1975) 'Age and fearlessness: Personal and situational factors' *Journal of Gerontology* 30(6): 696–700.
Lee, H. (1960) *To Kill a Mocking Bird*. Philadelphia, PA: J. B. Lippincott & Co.
Lee, M. (2001) 'The genesis of "fear of crime"' *Theoretical Criminology* 5(4): 467–485.
Lee, M. (2007) *Inventing Fear of Crime: Criminology and the Politics of Anxiety*. Cullompton: Willan Publishing.
Levi, M. (2007) 'Organized crime and terrorism' in M. Maguire, R. Morgan and R. Reiner (eds) *The Oxford Handbook of Criminology* (4th edition). Oxford: Oxford University Press pp. 771–809.
Levi, M. (2009) Suite revenge? The shaping of folk devils and moral panics about white-collar crimes' *British Journal of Criminology* 49(1): 48–67.
Librett, M. (2008) 'Wild pigs and outlaws: The kindred worlds of policing and outlaw bikers *Crime Media Culture* 4(2): 257–269.
Lichter, S. R., Lichter, L. S. and Rothman, S. (1994) *Prime Time: How TV Portrays American Culture*. Washington, DC: Regnery.
Lijphart, A. (1998) 'Consensus and consensus democracy: Cultural, structural, functional, and rational-choice explanations' *Scandinavian Political Studies* 21(2): 99–108.
Lijphart, A. (1999) *Patterns of Democracy: Government Forms and Performance in Thirty-Six Countries*. London: Yale University Press.
Linnemann, T. (2017) 'Bad cops and true detectives: The horror of police and the unthinkable world' *Theoretical Criminology*, available at: <https://doi.org/10.1177/1362480617737761>
Liska, A. E. and Baccaglini, W. (1990) 'Feeling safe by comparison: Crime in the newspapers *Social Problems* 37(3): 360–374.
Liska, A. E., Sanchirico, A. and Reed, M. D. (1988) 'Fear of crime and constrained behaviour Specifying and estimating a reciprocal effects model' *Social Forces* 66(3): 827–837.
Livingston, S. (1997) 'Beyond the "CNN effect": The media-foreign policy dynamic' in P. Norris (ed.) *Politics and the Press: The News Media and Their Influences*. Boulder, CO Lynne Rienner, pp. 291–318.
Lloyd, A. (1995) *Doubly Deviant, Doubly Damned: Society's Treatment of Deviant Women*. London: Penguin.

Loughnan, A. (2010) 'Drink spiking and rock throwing: The creation and construction of criminal offences in the current era' *Alternative Law Journal* 35(1): 18–21.

Lyng, S. (1990) 'Edgework: A social psychological analysis of voluntary risk taking' *American Journal of Sociology* 95(4): 851–886.

Lyon, D. (1994) *The Electronic Eye: The Rise of Surveillance Society*. Minneapolis, MN: University of Minnesota Press.

Lyon, D. (2001) *Surveillance Society: Monitoring Everyday Life*. Buckingham: Open University Press.

Lyon, D. (ed.) (2006) *Theorizing Surveillance: The Panopticon and Beyond*. Cullompton: Willan Publishing.

Lyon, D. (2007) *Surveillance Studies: An Overview*. Malden, MA: Polity Press.

Machado, H. and Santos, F. (2009) 'The disappearance of Madeleine McCann: Public drama and trial by media in the Portuguese press' *Crime Media Culture* 5(2): 146–167.

Mader, S. (2009) 'Law & Order' in M. Asimow (ed.) *Lawyers in Your Living Room!: Law on Television*. Chicago, IL: ABA Publishing, pp. 117–128.

Maeder, E. M. and Corbett, R. (2015) 'Beyond frequency: Perceived realism and the *CSI* effect' *Canadian Journal of Criminology and Criminal Justice* 57(1): 83–114.

Manheim, J. B. (1998) 'The news shapers: Strategic communication as a third force in news making' in D. Gruber, D. McQuail and P. Norris (eds) *The Politics of News, the News of Politics*. Washington, DC: Congressional Quarterly Press, pp. 94–109.

Mann, S. (1998) '"Reflectionism" and "diffusionism": New tactics for deconstructing the video surveillance superhighway' *Leonardo* 31(2): 93–102.

Marder, N. S. (2012) 'Judging reality television judges' in P. Robson and J. Silbey (eds) *Law and Justice on the Small Screen*. Oxford: Hart Publishing, pp. 229–249.

Marsh, H. L. (1991) 'A comparative analysis of crime coverage in newspapers in the United States and other countries from 1960–1989: A review of the literature' *Journal of Criminal Justice* 19(1): 67–79.

Marshall, C. W. and Potter, T. (2009) '"I am the American dream": Modern urban tragedy and the borders of fiction' in T. Potter and C. W. Marshall (eds) *The Wire: Urban Decay and American Television*. New York, NY: Continuum, pp. 1–14.

Marshall, T. (2013) 'MI5 boss warns of growing UK terror threat' *Sky News*, 8 October, available at: <https://news.sky.com/story/mi5-boss-warns-of-growing-uk-terror-threat-10432073>

Martin, G. (2002) 'Conceptualising cultural politics in subcultural and social movements studies' *Social Movement Studies* 1(1): 73–88.

Martin, G. (2009) 'Subculture, style, chavs and consumer capitalism: Towards a critical cultural criminology of youth' *Crime Media Culture* 5(2): 123–145.

Martin, G. (2010) 'No worries? Yes worries! How New South Wales is creeping towards a police state' *Alternative Law Journal* 35(3): 163–167.

Martin, G. (2011a) 'Tackling "anti-social behaviour" in Britain and New South Wales – A preliminary comparative account' *Current Issues in Criminal Justice* 22(3): 379–397.

Martin, G. (2011b) 'Why the UK riots have more to do with austerity than criminality' *On Line Opinion*, 15 August, available at: <www.onlineopinion.com.au/view.asp?article=12470>

Martin, G. (2011c) 'Showcasing security: The politics of policing space at the 2007 Sydney APEC meeting' *Policing & Society* 21(1): 27–48.

Martin, G. (2012) 'Jurisprudence of secrecy: *Wainohu* and beyond' *Flinders Law Journal* 14(2): 189–230.

Martin, G. (2014) 'Outlaw motorcycle gangs and secret evidence: Reflections on the use of criminal intelligence in the control of serious organized crime in Australia' *Sydney Law Review* 36(3): 501–539.

Martin, G. (2015a) *Understanding Social Movements*. London: Routledge.

Martin, G. (2015b) 'Stop the boats! Moral panic in Australia over asylum seekers' *Continuum* 29(3): 304–322.

Martin, G. (2017a) 'Youth and crime' in D. Palmer, W. de Lint and D. Dalton (eds) *Crime and Justice: A Guide to Criminology* (5th edition). Pyrmont: Thomson Reuters, pp. 103–128.

Martin, G. (2017b) 'Digital democracy' in B. S. Turner, C. Kyung-Sup, C. Epstein, P. Kivisto, W. Outhwaite and J. M. Ryan (eds) *The Wiley-Blackwell Encyclopedia of Social Theory*. Oxford: Wiley-Blackwell.

Martin, G. (2017c) 'Secrecy's corrupting influence on democratic principles and the rule of law' *International Journal for Crime, Justice and Social Democracy* 6(4): 100–115.

Martin, G. (2017d) 'Criminalizing dissent: Social movements, public order policing and the erosion of protest rights' in L. Weber, E. Fishwick and M. Marmo (eds) *The Routledge International Handbook of Criminology and Human Rights*. Abingdon: Routledge, pp. 280–290.

Martin, G. (2018) 'Turning the detention centre inside out: Counterveillance of state-organized crimmigration in Australia', paper presented at Center for Global Constitutionalism, WZB Berlin Social Science Center, 8 January; and TC Beirne School of Law, University of Queensland, 19 July.

Martin, G. and Scott Bray, R. (2015) 'Secret isle? Making sense of the Jersey child abuse scandal' in G. Martin, R. Scott Bray and M. Kumar (eds) *Secrecy, Law and Society*. London: Routledge, pp. 251–272.

Martin, G. and Tazreiter, C. (2017) 'Seeking asylum in Australia: The role of emotion and narrative in state and civil society responses' in D. C. Brotherton and P. Kretsedemas (eds) *Immigration Policy in the Age of Punishment: Detention, Deportation and Border Control*. New York, NY: Columbia University Press, pp. 97–115.

Martin, P. (2004) 'Culture, subculture and social organization' in A. Bennett and K. Kahn-Harris (eds) *After Subculture: Critical Studies in Contemporary Youth Culture*. Houndmills: Palgrave Macmillan, pp. 21–35.

Marx, G. T. (2009) 'A tack in the shoe and taking off the shoe: Neutralization and counter-neutralization dynamics' *Surveillance & Society* 6(3): 294–306.

Marx, G. T. (2013) 'The public as partner? Technology can make us auxiliaries as well as vigilantes' *IEEE Security & Privacy*, September/October: 56–61, available at: <http://web.mit.edu/gtmarx/www/marx-publicas.html>

Mathiesen, T. (1997) 'The viewer society: Michel Foucault's "panopticon" revisited' *Theoretical Criminology* 1(2): 215–234.

Mattley, C. (1998) '(Dis)courtesy stigma: Fieldwork among phone fantasy workers' in J. Ferrell and N. Websdale (eds) *Making Trouble: Cultural Constructions of Crime, Deviance and Control* Hawthorne, NY: Aldine de Guyter, pp. 146–158.

Matza, D. (1964) *Delinquency and Drift*. New York, NY: John Wiley.

Matza, D. and Sykes, G. M. (1961) 'Juvenile delinquency and subterranean values' *American Sociological Review* 26(5): 712–719.

McBarnet, D. (2006) 'After Enron will "whiter than white-collar crime" still wash?' *British Journal of Criminology* 46(6): 1091–1109.

McCabe, J. (2017) 'Locating justice in *Wallander*: Trading TV stories, local jurisdictions and global injustice in the Swedish and UK *Wallanders*' in M. Aristodemou, F. Macmillan and P. Tuitt (eds) *Crime Fiction and the Law*. Abingdon: Birkbeck Law Press, pp. 55–70.

McCahill, M. (2002) *The Surveillance Web: The Rise of Visual Surveillance in an English City*. Cullompton: Willan Publishing.

McCoy, A. W. (2006) *A Question of Torture: CIA Interrogation, from the Cold War to the War on Terror*. New York, NY: Metropolitan Books.

McDonald, H., Graham-Harrison, E. and O'Carroll, L. (2018) 'Ireland votes by landslide to legalise abortion' *The Guardian*, 27 May, available at: <www.theguardian.com/world/2018/may/26/ireland-votes-by-landslide-to-legalise-abortion>

McRobbie, A. and Thornton, S. L. (1995) 'Rethinking moral panic for multi-mediated social worlds' *British Journal of Sociology* 46(4): 559–574.

Meloy, J. R. (1992) *The Psychopathic Mind: Origins, Dynamics, Treatment* (2nd edition). Northvale, NJ: Aronson.

Merton, R. K. (1938) 'Social structure and anomie' *American Sociological Review* 3(5): 672–682.

Middleweek, B. (2017) 'Deviant divas: Lindy Chamberlain and Schapelle Corby and the case for a new category of celebrity for criminally implicated women' *Crime Media Culture* 13(1): 85–105.

Miethe, T. D. and Lee, G. R. (1984) 'Fear of crime among older people: A reassessment of the predictive power of crime-related factors' *The Sociological Quarterly* 25(3): 397–415.

Miles, A. (2011) 'When disaster strikes, remember – this is not your drama' *New Statesman*, 28 March, available at: <www.newstatesman.com/international-politics/2011/03/tourism-japan-tsunami-million>

Miller, E. M. (1991) 'Assessing the risk of inattention to class, race/ethnicity, and gender: Comment on lyng' *American Journal of Sociology* 96(6): 1530–1534.

Miller, W. B. (1958) 'Lower class culture as a generating milieu of gang delinquency' *Journal of Social Issues* 14: 5–19.

Mills, C. W. (1959) *The Sociological Imagination*. Oxford: Oxford University Press.

Mirabella, J. G. (2012) 'Scales of justice: Assessing Italian criminal procedure through the Amanda Knox trial' *Boston University International Law Journal* 30(1): 229–260.

Mock, B. (2016) 'The right to film cops comes into question' *CITYLAB*, 24 February, available at: <www.citylab.com/equity/2016/02/there-is-no-first-amendment-right-to-film-cops/470670/>

Monahan, T. (2006) 'Counter-surveillance as political intervention' *Social Semiotics* 16(4): 515–534.

Morgan, G., Dagistanli, S. and Martin, G. (2010) 'Global fears, local anxiety: Policing, counterterrorism and moral panic over "bikie gang wars" in New South Wales' *Australian and New Zealand Journal of Criminology* 43(3): 580–599.

Morgan, M. and Shanahan, J. (2010) 'The state of cultivation' *Journal of Broadcasting and Electronic Media* 54(2): 337–355.

Morrison, W. (2004a) '"Reflections with memories": Everyday photography capturing genocide' *Theoretical Criminology* 8(3): 341–358.

Morrison, W. (2004b) 'Criminology, genocide, and modernity: Remarks on the companion that criminology ignored' in C. Sumner (ed.) *The Blackwell Companion to Criminology*. Oxford: Blackwell Publishing, pp. 68–88.

Morrison, W. (2010) 'A reflected gaze of humanity: Cultural criminology and images of genocide' in K. Hayward and M. Presdee (eds) *Framing Crime: Cultural Criminology and the Image*. Abingdon: Routledge, pp. 189–207.

Mythen, G. and Walklate, S. (2006) 'Communicating the terrorist risk: Harnessing a culture of fear?' *Crime Media Culture* 2(2): 123–142.

Nethery, A. and Holman, R. (2016) 'Secrecy and human rights abuse in Australia's offshore immigration detention centres' *The International Journal of Human Rights* 20(7): 1018–1038.

Neuweiler, S. (2017) 'Ms Dhu's family to sue state over death in custody' *ABC News*, 20 July, available at: <www.abc.net.au/news/2017-07-20/ms-dhu-family-to-sue-wa-over-death-in-custody/8728620>

Newburn, T., Deacon, R., Diski, B., Cooper, K., Grant, M. and Burch, A. (2018) '"The best three days of my life": Pleasure, power and alienation in the 2011 riots' *Crime Media Culture* 14(1): 41–59.

Norris, C. and Armstrong, G. (1999) *The Maximum Surveillance Society: The Rise of CCTV*. New York, NY: Berg.

Norris, C. and Armstrong, G. (2009) 'Working rules and the social construction of suspicion' in C. Greer (ed.) *Crime and Media: A Reader*. London: Routledge, pp. 522–538.

Northrop, A., Kramer, K. and King, J. L. (1995) 'Police use of computers' *Journal of Criminal Justice* 23(3): 259–275.

Nurse, A. (2012) 'Decoding the dark passenger: The serial killer as a force for justice. Adapting Jeff Lindsay's *Dexter* for the small screen' in P. Robson and J. Silbey (eds) *Law and Justice on the Small Screen*. Oxford: Hart Publishing, pp. 403–423.

Obasogie, O. K. and Newman, Z. (2016) 'Black lives matter and the respectability politics in local news accounts of officer-involved civilian deaths: An early empirical assessment' *Wisconsin Law Review* 3: 541–574.

O'Brien, M. (2005) 'What is *cultural* about cultural criminology?' *British Journal of Criminology* 45(5): 599–612.

O'Carroll, L. (2014) 'Andy Coulson jailed for 18 months for conspiracy to hack phones' *The Guardian*, 4 July, available at: <www.theguardian.com/uk-news/2014/jul/04/andy-coulson-jailed-phone-hacking>

O'Keefe, G. J. and Reid-Nash, K. (1987) 'Crime news and real-world blues: The effects of the media on social reality' *Communication Research* 14(2): 147–163.

Oltermann, P. (2017) '"Yolocaust" artist provokes debate over commemorating Germany's past' *The Guardian*, 20 January, available at: <www.theguardian.com/world/2017/jan/19/yolocaust-artist-shahak-shapira-provokes-debate-over-commemorating-germanys-past>

Pain, R. (1997) 'Social geographies of women's fear of crime' *Transactions of the Institute of British Geographers* 22(2): 231–244.

Pain, R. (2000) 'Place, social relations and the fear of crime: A review' *Progress in Human Geography* 24(3): 365–387.

Parker, M. (2012) *Alternative Business: Outlaws, Crime and Culture.* London: Routledge.

Patterson, J. (2016) 'From serial to making a murderer: Documentaries renew hope for justice' *The Guardian*, 14 August, available at: <www.theguardian.com/culture/2016/aug/13/making-murderer-serial-jinx-crime-documentaries-brendan-dassey>

Pauwels, L. (2017) 'Key methods of visual criminology: An overview of different approaches and their affordances' in M. Brown and E. Carrabine (eds) *Routledge International Handbook of Visual Criminology.* Abingdon: Routledge, pp. 62–73.

Peelo, M. (2006) 'Framing homicide narratives in newspapers: Mediated witness and the construction of virtual victimhood' *Crime Media Culture* 2(2): 159–175.

Penfold-Mounce, R. (2009) *Celebrity Culture and Crime: The Joy of Transgression.* Houndmills: Palgrave Macmillan.

Penfold-Mounce, R. (2016) 'How the rise in TV "crime porn" normalizes violence against women' *The Conversation*, 24 October, available at: <https://theconversation.com/how-the-rise-in-tv-crime-porn-normalises-violence-against-women-66877>

Penfold-Mounce, R., Beer, D. and Burrows, R. (2011) '*The Wire* as social science-fiction?' *Sociology* 45(1): 152–167.

Perry, B. and Alvi, S. (2011) ' "We are all vulnerable": The *in terrorem* effects of hate crimes' *International Review of Victimology* 18(1): 57–71.

Perry, B. and Dyck, D. R. (2014) ' "I don't know where it is safe": Trans women's experiences of violence' *Critical Criminology* 22(1): 49–63.

Peters, C. (2005) *Harold Shipman: Mind Set on Murder.* London: Carlton Books.

Pieters, J. (2018) 'Suspect could face 28 years for killing Anne Faber' *NL Times*, 13 June, available at: <https://nltimes.nl/2018/06/13/suspect-face-28-years-killing-anne-faber>

Podlas, K. (2006) ' "The CSI effect": Exposing the media myth' *Fordham Intellectual Property, Media & Entertainment Law Journal* 16: 429–466.

Podlas, K. (2007) 'The "*CSI* effect" and other forensic fictions' *Loyola of Los Angeles Entertainment Law Review* 27: 87–126.

Pogue, A. (1999) '1984 photograph of the "gay wing" of a Texas state prison' *International Journal of Qualitative Studies in Education* 12(5): 563.

Polletta, F. and Amenta, E. (2001) 'Conclusion: Second that emotion? Lessons from once-novel concepts on social movement research' in J. Goodwin, J. M. Jasper and F. Polletta (eds) *Passionate Politics: Emotions and Social Movements.* Chicago, IL: University of Chicago Press, pp. 303–316.

Poster, M. (1990) *The Mode of Information.* Chicago, IL: University of Chicago Press.

Potter, W. J. (1988) 'Three strategies for elaborating the cultivation hypothesis' *Journalism Quarterly* 65(4): 930–939.

Potter, W. J. (2014) 'A critical analysis of cultivation theory' *Journal of Communication* 64(6): 1015–1036.

Potter, W. J., Vaughan, M. W., Warren, R., Howley, K., Land, A. and Hagemeyer, J. C. (1995) 'How real is the portrayal of television aggression in television programming?' *Journal Broadcasting and Electronic Media* 39(4): 496–516.

Potter, W. J., Vaughan, M. W., Warren, R., Howley, K., Land, A. and Hagemeyer, J. C. (1997) 'Aggression in television entertainment: Profiles and trends' *Communication Research Reports* 14(1): 116–124.

Powell, A., Henry, N. and Flynn, A. (2018) 'Image-based sexual abuse' in W. S. DeKeseredy and M. Dragiewicz (eds) *Routledge Handbook of Critical Criminology* (2nd edition). Abingdon: Routledge, pp. 305–315.

Powell, A., Stratton, G. and Cameron, R. (2018) *Digital Criminology: Crime and Justice in Digital Society*. London: Routledge.

Pratt, J. (2006) 'The dark side of paradise: Explaining New Zealand's history of high imprisonment' *British Journal of Criminology* 46(4): 541–560.

Pratt, J. (2007) *Penal Populism*. London: Routledge.

Presdee, M. (2004a) 'Cultural criminology: The long and winding road' *Theoretical Criminology* 8(3): 275–285.

Presdee, M. (2004b) 'The story of crime: Biography and the excavation of transgression' in J. Ferrell, K. Hayward, W. Morrison and M. Presdee (eds) *Cultural Criminology Unleashed*. London: Glasshouse Press.

Presser, L. (2009) 'The narratives of offenders' *Theoretical Criminology* 13(2): 177–200.

Presser, L. (2010) 'Collecting and analyzing the stories of offenders' *Journal of Criminal Justice Education* 21(4): 431–446.

Presser, L. (2016) 'Criminology and the narrative turn' *Crime Media Culture* 12(2): 137–151.

Presser, L. and Sandberg, S. (eds) (2015a) *Narrative Criminology: Understanding Stories of Crime*. New York, NY: New York University Press.

Presser, L. and Sandberg, S. (2015b) 'Conclusion: Where to now?' in L. Presser and S. Sandberg (eds) *Narrative Criminology: Understanding Stories of Crime*. New York, NY: New York University Press, pp. 287–299.

Presser, L. and Sandberg, S. (2015c) 'Research strategies for narrative criminology' in J. Miller and W. R. Palacios (eds) *Advances in Criminological Theory: The Value of Qualitative Research for Advancing Criminological Theory*. Abingdon: Routledge, pp. 85–99.

Rafter, N. (2007) 'Crime, film and criminology: Recent sex-crime movies' *Theoretical Criminology* 11(3): 403–420.

Rafter, N. (2014) 'Introduction to special issue on visual culture and the iconography of crime and punishment' *Theoretical Criminology* 18(2): 127–133.

Ramshaw, S. (2012) '"McNutty" on the small screen: Improvised legality and the Irish-American cop in HBO's *The Wire*' in P. Robson and J. Silbey (eds) *Law and Justice on the Small Screen*. Oxford: Hart Publishing, pp. 361–379.

Rawlinson, P. (1998) 'Mafia, media and myth: Representations of Russian organized crime' *The Howard Journal* 37(4): 346–358.

Reid-Henry, S. (2011) 'Norway: The mourning after' *New Statesman*, 1 August, <www.newstatesman.com/europe/2011/08/wing-extremism-norway-breivik>

Reiner, R. (2007) 'Media-made criminality: The representation of crime in the mass media' in M. Maguire, R. Morgan and R. Reiner (eds) *The Oxford Handbook of Criminology* (4th edition). Oxford: Oxford University Press, pp. 302–337.

Rickford, R. (2016) 'Black lives matter: Towards a modern practice of mass struggle' *New Labor Forum* 25(1): 34–42.

Ritzer, G. and Jurgenson, N. (2010) 'Production, consumption, prosumption: The nature of capitalism in the age of the digital "prosumer"' *Journal of Consumer Culture* 10(1): 13–36.

Roberts, M. (2001) 'Just noise? Newspaper crime reporting and the fear of crime' *Criminal Justice Matters* 43: 12–13.

Robertson, J. (2016) 'Mining protestors could face seven years' jail under Baird government CSG plans' *The Sydney Morning Herald*, 11 March, available at: <www.smh.com.au/nsw/mining-protesters-face-seven-years-jail-under-baird-government-csg-plans-20160310-gnfdi8.html>

Robinson, P. (1999) 'The CNN effect: Can news media drive foreign policy?' *Review of International Studies* 25(2): 301–309.

Robinson, P. (2005) 'The CNN effect revisited' *Critical Studies in Media Communication* 22(4): 344–349.

Robson, P. and Silbey, J. (eds) (2012) *Law and Justice on the Small Screen*. Oxford: Hart Publishing.

Romer, D., Hall Jamieson, K. and Aday, S. (2003) 'Television news and the cultivation of fear of crime' *Journal of Communication* 53(1): 88–104.

Rose, N. (1999) *The Powers of Freedom*. Cambridge: Cambridge University Press.

Roshier, B. (1973) 'The selection of crime news by the press' in S. Cohen and J. Young (eds) *The Manufacture of News*. London: Constable, pp. 40–51.

Ross, J. I. (2007) 'Deconstructing the terrorism-media relationship' *Crime Media Culture* 3(2): 215–225.

Rothe, D. L. and Steinmetz, K. F. (2013) 'The case of Bradley Manning: State victimization, realpolitik and Wikileaks' *Contemporary Justice Review* 16(2): 280–292.

Rourke, A. (2012) 'Australian coroner finds dingo took baby Azaria in 1980' *The Guardian*, 12 June, available at <www.theguardian.com/world/2012/jun/12/dingo-took-baby-azaria-chamberlain>

Rushe, D. (2013) 'Former Goldman Sachs trader "Fabulous Fab" goes on trial' *The Guardian*, 15 July, available at: <www.theguardian.com/business/2013/jul/14/goldman-sachs-fabulous-fab-trial>

Sacco, V. F. (1990) 'Gender, fear and victimization: A preliminary application of power-control theory' *Sociological Spectrum* 1(4): 485–506.

Salter, M. (2017) *Crime, Justice and Social Media*. London: Routledge.

Salter, M., Crofts, T. and Lee, M. (2013) 'Beyond criminalization and responsibilization: Sexting, gender and young people' *Current Issues in Criminal Justice* 24(3): 301–316.

Sandberg, S. (2016) 'The importance of stories untold: Life-story, event-story and trope' *Crime Media Culture* 12(2): 153–171.

Sandberg, S. and Ugelvik, T. (2016) 'The past, present, and future of narrative criminology: A review and an invitation' *Crime Media Culture* 12(2): 129–136.

Savage, C. (2017) 'Chelsea Manning to be released early as Obama commutes sentence' *The New York Times*, 17 January, available at: <www.nytimes.com/2017/01/17/us/politics/obama-commutes-bulk-of-chelsea-mannings-sentence.html?mcubz=0>

Schanz, K. and Salfati, C. G. (2016) 'The CSI effect and its controversial existence and impact: A mixed methods review' *Crime Psychology Review* 2(1): 60–79.

Schclarek Mulinari, L. (2017) 'Contesting Sweden's Chicago: Why journalists dispute the crime image of Malmö' *Critical Studies in Media Communication* 34(3): 206–219.

Schechter, H. (2003) *The Serial Killer Files*. New York, NY: Ballantine Books.

Schmid, D. (2005) *Natural Born Celebrities: Serial Killers in American Culture*. Chicago, IL: University of Chicago Press.

Schulz, K. (2016) 'Dead certainty: How "Making a Murderer" goes wrong' *The New Yorker*, 25 January, available at: <www.newyorker.com/magazine/2016/01/25/dead-certainty>

Schweitzer, N. J. and Saks, M. J. (2007) 'The *CSI* effect: Popular fiction about forensic science affects the public's expectations about real forensic science' *Jurimetrics* 47: 357–364.

Scott Bray, R. (2013) 'Paradoxical justice: The case of Ian Tomlinson' *Journal of Law and Medicine* 21(2): 447–472.

Scott Bray, R. (2014) 'Rotten prettiness? The forensic aesthetic and crime as art' *Australian Feminist Law Journal* 40(1): 69–95.

Scott Bray, R. (2017) 'Images of fatal violence: Negotiating the dark heart of death research' *Mortality* 22(2): 136–154.

Scott Bray, R. (2018) 'Visual criminology and the southern crime scene' in K. Carrington, R. Hogg, J. Scott and M. Sozzo (eds) *The Palgrave Handbook of Criminology and the Global South*. Cham, Switzerland: Palgrave Macmillan, pp. 415–432.

Scott Bray, R. and Martin, G. (2012) 'Closing down open justice in the United Kingdom?' *Alternative Law Journal* 37(2): 126–127.

Scraton, P. (2003) 'The demonization, exclusion and regulation of children: From moral panic to moral renewal' in A. Boran (ed.) *Crime: Fear or Fascination?* Chester: Chester Academic Press, pp. 9–39.

Seltzer, M. (1998) *Serial Killers: Death and Life in America's Wound Culture*. New York, NY: Routledge.

Shaw, C. R. (1930/1966) *The Jack-Roller: A Delinquent Boy's Own Story*. Chicago, IL: Chicago University Press.

Shelton, D. E., Kim, Y. S. and Barak, G. (2006) 'A study of jurors expectations and demands concerning scientific evidence: Does the "*CSI* effect" exist?' *Vanderbilt Journal of Entertainment and Technology Law* 9(2): 331–268.

Sherwin, R. K. (2004) 'Law and popular culture' in A. Sarat (ed.) *The Blackwell Companion to Law and Society*. Oxford: Blackwell Publishing, pp. 95–112.

Signorielli, N. (1990) 'Television's mean and dangerous world: A continuum of the cultural indicators perspective' in M. Morgan and N. Signorielli (eds) *Cultivation Analysis: New Directions in Media Effects Research*. Newbury Park, CA: Sage.

Simkin, S. (2013) '"Actually evil. Not high school evil": Amanda Knox, sex and celebrity crime' *Celebrity Studies* 4(1): 33–45.

Simmel, G. (1903/1950) 'The metropolis and mental life' in K. H. Wolff (ed.) *The Sociology of Georg Simmel*. New York, NY: Free Press, pp. 409–424.

Simpson, P. L. (2000) *Psycho Paths: Tracking the Serial Killer Through Contemporary American Film and Fiction*. Edwardsville, IL: Southern Illinois University Press.

Skeggs, B. (2005) 'The making of class and gender through visualizing moral subject formation' *Sociology* 39(5): 965–982.

Smith, G. J. D. (2007) 'Exploring relations between watchers and watched in control(led) systems: Strategies and tactics' *Surveillance & Society* 4(4): 280–313.

Smith, G. J. D. (2015) *Opening the Black Box: The Work of Watching*. London: Routledge.

Smith, S. M., Stinson, V. and Patry, M. W. (2011) 'Fact or fiction? The myth and reality of the CSI effect' *Court Review: The Journal of the American Judges Association*, Paper 355: 4–7, available at: <http://digitalcommons.unl.edu/ajacourtreview/355>

Snell, L. (2008) *Protest, Policing, Protection: The Expansion of Police Powers and the Impact on Human Rights in NSW – The Policing of APEC as a Case Study*. Sydney: Combined Community Legal Centres Group (NSW) and Kingsford Legal Centre.

Soothill, K. (1993) 'The serial killer industry' *The Journal of Forensic Psychiatry* 4(2): 341–354.

Soothill, K. (2001) 'The Harold Shipman case: A sociological perspective' *Journal of Forensic Psychiatry* 12(2): 260–262.

Soothill, K. and Wilson, D. (2005) 'Theorising the puzzle that is Harold Shipman' *Journal of Forensic Psychiatry & Psychology* 16(4): 685–698.

Sparks, R. (1992a) *Television and the Drama of Crime: Moral Tales and the Place of Crime in Public Life*. Buckingham: Open University Press.

Sparks, R. (1992b) 'Reason and unreason in "left realism": Some problems in the constitution of the fear of crime' in R. Matthews and J. Young (eds) *Issues in Realist Criminology*. London: Sage, pp. 119–135.

Squires, P. (2006) 'New Labour and the politics of anti-social behaviour' *Critical Social Policy* 26(1): 144–168.

Stanko, E. A. and Hobdell, K. (1993) 'Assault on women's safety in Britain' *British Journal of Criminology* 33(3): 400–415.

Stach, R. (2014) 'Death by data: How Kafka's The Trial prefigured the nightmare of the modern surveillance state' *New Statesman*, 16 January, available at: <www.newstatesman.com/2014/01/death-data-how-kafkas-trial-prefigured-nightmare-modern-surveillance-state?page=518&title=&text=>

Stasio, M. (2009) 'A Swedish cop, not a Danish prince, but still melancholy' *The New York Times*, 10 May, available at: <www.nytimes.com/2009/05/10/arts/television/10stas.html>

Sterling, C. (1991) *The Mafia*. London: Grafton.

Steyn, J. (2004) 'Guantanamo Bay: The legal black hole' *The International and Comparative Law Quarterly* 53(1): 1–15.

Stinson, V., Patry, M. W. and Smith, S. M. (2007) 'The *CSI* effect: Reflections from police and forensic investigators' *The Canadian Journal of Police & Security Services* 5(3–4): 125–133.

Stone, P. R. (2006) 'A dark tourism spectrum: Towards a typology of death and macabre related tourist sites, attractions and exhibitions' *Tourism* 54(2): 145–160.

Stratton, G., Powell, A. and Cameron, R. (2017) 'Crime and justice in digital society: Towards a "digital criminology"?' *International Journal for Crime, Justice and Social Democracy* 6(2): 17–33.

Streib, V. (1994) 'Death penalty for lesbians' *National Journal of Sexual Orientation Law* 1(1): 40–52.

Sullivan, A. (2015) '*The Fall*: The most feminist show on television' *The Atlantic Monthly*, 23 January, available at: <www.theatlantic.com/entertainment/archive/2015/01/the-fall-the-most-feminist-show-on-television/384751/>

Surette, R. (2015) *Media, Crime and Criminal Justice: Images, Realities and Policies* (5th edition). Stamford, CT: Cengage Learning.

Surette, R. and Gardiner-Bess, R. (2014) 'Media, entertainment, and crime' in B. A. Arrigo and H. Y. Bersot (eds) *The Routledge Handbook of International Crime and Justice Studies*. London: Routledge, pp. 373–396.

Sutherland, E. (1949) *White-Collar Crime*. New York, NY: Holt, Rinehart and Wilson.

Sykes, G. M. and Matza, D. (1957) 'Theories of neutralization: A theory of delinquency' *American Sociological Review* 22(6): 664–670.

Tallerico, B. (2017) 'The real FBI agents and serial killers who inspired Netflix's *Mindhunter*' *Vulture*, 19 October, available at: <www.vulture.com/2017/10/mindhunter-netflix-real-serial-killers.html>

Tilly, C. (1985) 'War making and state making as organized crime' in P. B. Evans, D. Rueschemeyer and T. Skocpol (eds) *Bringing the State Back In*. Cambridge: Cambridge University Press, pp. 169–191.

Timberg, S. (2016) 'The trial-by-Netflix age: "Making a Murderer", "Serial" and the mixed blessings of media justice' *Salon*, 20 August, available at: <www.salon.com/2016/08/20/the-trial-by-netflix-age-making-a-murderer-serial-and-the-mixed-blessings-of-media-justice/>

Treanor, J. (2010) 'Goldman Sachs investigation could put Wall Street under microscope' *The Guardian*, 20 April, available at: <www.theguardian.com/business/2010/apr/19/sec-questions-paulson-deal-unique>

Trottier, D. (2015) 'Vigilantism and power users: Police and user-led investigations on social media' in C. Fuchs and D. Trottier (eds) *Social Media, Politics and the State: Protest, Revolutions, Riots, Crime and Policing in the Age of Facebook, Twitter and YouTube*. London: Routledge, pp. 209–226.

Tyler, I. (2008) '"Chav mum, chav scum": Class disgust in contemporary Britain' *Feminist Media Studies* 8(1): 17–34.

Tyler, T. R. (2006) 'Viewing *CSI* and the threshold of guilt: Managing the truth and justice in reality and fiction' *Yale Law Journal* 115(5): 1050–1085.

Ugelvik, T. (2016) 'Techniques of legitimation: The narrative construction of legitimacy among immigration detention officers' *Crime Media Culture* 12(2): 215–232.

Umphrey, M. M. and Shuker-Haines, T. (1991) 'The mystery of gender: The female hard-boiled detective' *Michigan Feminist Studies* 6: 3–16.

Valentine, G. (1989) 'The geography of women's fear' *Area* 21(4): 385–390.

Valverde, M. (2006) *Law and Order: Images, Meanings, Myths*. New Brunswick, NJ: Rutgers University Press.

Vitale, A. S. (2005) 'From negotiated management to command and control: How the New York police department polices protest' *Policing & Society* 15(3): 283–304.

Waade, A. M. and Jensen, P. M. (2013) 'Nordic noir production values: *The Killing* and *The Bridge*' *akademisk kvarter* 7: 189–201.

Wainwright, S. (2017) 'Copwatch program empowers aboriginal communities to film interactions with police' *ABC News*, 22 August, available at: <www.abc.net.au/news/2017-08-22/watching-the-watchers-copwatch-program-launches-in-broken-hill/8828570>

Waiton, S. (2008) *The Politics of Antisocial Behaviour: Amoral Panics*. New York, NY: Routledge

Wakeman, S. (2014) '"No one wins. One side just loses more slowly": *The Wire* and drug policy' *Theoretical Criminology* 18(2): 224–240.

Wakshlag, J., Vial, V. and Tamborini, R. (1983) 'Selecting crime drama and apprehension about crime' *Human Communication Research* 10(2): 227–242.

Walker, J. (2004) 'David Simon says' *Reason Online*, October, available at: <www.reason.com/news/show/29273.html>

Walklate, S. (1997) 'Risk and criminal victimization: A modernist dilemma?' *British Journal of Criminology* 37(1): 35–45.

Walton, P. L. and Jones, M. (1999) *Detective Agency: Women Rewriting the Hard-boiled Tradition.* Berkeley, CA: University of California Press.

Warr, M. (1984) 'Fear of victimization: Why are women and the elderly more afraid?' *Social Science Quarterly* 65(3): 681–702.

Warwick, A. (2006) 'The scene of the crime: Inventing the serial killer' *Social & Legal Studies* 15(4): 552–569.

Weaver, J. and Wakshlag, J. (1986) 'Perceived vulnerability to crime, criminal victimization experience, and television viewing' *Journal of Broadcasting and Electronic Media* 30(2): 141–158.

Weber, M. (1949) *The Methodology of the Social Sciences.* New York, NY: Free Press.

Webber, C. (2007) 'Background, foreground, foresight: The third dimension of cultural Criminology?' *Crime Media Culture* 3(2): 139–157.

Websdale, N. (1999) 'Predators: The social construction of "stranger-danger" in Washington State as a form of patriarchal ideology' in J. Ferrell and N. Websdale (eds) *Making Trouble: Cultural Constructions of Crime, Deviance and Control.* Hawthorne, NY: Aldine de Guyter, pp. 91–114.

Welch, M. (2011) 'Counterveillance: How Foucault and the Groupe d'Information sur les Prisons reversed the optics' *Theoretical Criminology* 15(3): 301–313.

Wells, H. and Wills, D. (2009) 'Individualism and identity: Resistance to speed cameras in the UK' *Surveillance & Society* 6(3): 259–274.

Whyte, D. (ed.) (2015) *How Corrupt Is Britain?* London: Pluto Press.

Wiest, J. B. (2016) 'Casting cultural monsters: Representations of serial killers in the US and UK news media' *Howard Journal of Communications* 27(4): 327–346.

Wilby, P. (2012) 'Alan Rusbridger: The quiet evangelist' *New Statesman*, 4 June, available at: <www.newstatesman.com/media/media/2012/05/guardian-editor-alan-rusbridger-peter-wilby>

Wilde, J. (2009) 'Why *The Wire* is the greatest TV show ever made' in S. Busfield and P. Owens (eds) *The Wire Re-Up.* London: Guardian Books.

Wilkins, L. T. (1964) *Social Deviance.* London: Tavistock.

Williams, G. (2015) 'The legal assault on Australian democracy' *Sir Richard Blackburn Lecture, ACT Law Society*, 12 May, available at: <www.actlawsociety.asn.au/documents/item/1304>

Williams, P. and Dickinson, J. (1993) 'Fear of crime: Read all about it? The relationship between newspaper crime reporting and fear of crime' *British Journal of Criminology* 33(1): 33–56.

Willing, R. (2004) '"*CSI* effect" has juries wanting more evidence' *USA Today*, 5 August, available at: <http://usatoday30.usatoday.com/news/nation/2004-08-05-csi-effect_x.htm>

Wilson, D. (2009) *A History of British Serial Killing.* London: Sphere.

Wilson, D. and Serisier, T. (2010) 'Video activism and the ambiguities of counter-surveillance' *Surveillance & Society* 8(2): 166–180.

Wilson, D., Tolputt, H., Howe, N. and Kemp, D. (2010) 'When serial killers go unseen: The case of Trevor Joseph Hardy' *Crime Media Culture* 6(2): 153–167.

Wilson, J. R. (2014) 'Shakespeare and criminology' *Crime Media Culture* 10(2): 97–114.

Winlow, S., Hall, S., Treadwell, J. and Briggs, D. (2015) *Riots and Political Protest: Notes from the Post-Political Present*. London: Routledge.

Wise, J. (2010) 'Providing the *CSI* treatment: Criminal justice practitioners and the *CSI* effect' *Current Issues in Criminal Justice* 21(3): 383–399.

Wood, L. J. (2014) *Crisis and Control: The Militarization of Protest Policing*. London: Pluto Press.

Wood, M. (2014) 'Lessons from *The Wire*: Epistemological reflections on the practice of sociological research' *The Sociological Review* 62(4): 742–759.

Woodcock, J. and Johnson, M. R. (2018) 'Gamification: What it is, and how to fight it' *The Sociological Review* 66(3): 542–558.

Woodiwiss, M. (2005) *Gangster Capitalism: The United States and the Global Rise of Organized Crime*. London: Constable and Robinson.

Woodiwiss, M. and Hobbs, D. (2009) 'Organized evil and the Atlantic alliance: Moral panics and the rhetoric of organized crime policing in America and Britain' *British Journal of Criminology* 49(1): 106–128.

Wright, S. (2015) 'Moral panics as enacted melodramas' *British Journal of Criminology* 55(6): 1245–1262.

Wright, A. and Myers, S. (1996) 'Introduction' in A. Myers and S. Wright (eds) *No Angels. Woman Who Commit Violence*. London: Pandora, pp. xi–xvi.

Wright Monod, S. (2017) 'Portraying those we condemn with care: Extending the ethics of representation' *Critical Criminology* 25(3): 343–356.

Yardley, E., Wilson, D. and Kennedy, M. (2017) '"TO ME ITS [SIC] REAL LIFE": Secondary victims of homicide in newer media' *Victim & Offenders* 12(3): 467–496.

Young, A. (1996) *Imagining Crime: Textual Outlaws and Criminal Conversations*. London: Sage.

Young, A. (2014) 'From object to encounter: Aesthetic politics and visual criminology' *Theoretical Criminology* 18(2): 159–175.

Young, J. (1971) 'The role of the police as amplifiers of deviancy, negotiators of reality and translators of fantasy: Some consequences of our present system of drug control as seen in Notting Hill' in S. Cohen (ed.) *Images of Deviance*. Harmondsworth: Penguin, pp. 27–61.

Zajko, M. and Béland, D. (2008) 'Space and protest policing at international summits' *Environment and Planning D: Society and Space* 26(4): 719–735.

Zedner, L. (2007) 'Pre-crime and post-criminology?' *Theoretical Criminology* 11(2): 261–281.

Zillman, D. and Wakshlag, J. (1987) 'Fear of victimization and the appeal of crime drama' in D. Zillman and J. Bryant (eds) *Selective Exposure to Communication*. Hillsdale, NJ: Lawrence Erlbaum, pp. 141–156.

Ziv, S. (2017) 'The story of Yolocaust, the Holocaust memorial selfie that shocked and vanished' *Newsweek*, 3 February, available at: <www.newsweek.com/story-yolocaust-holocaust-memorial-selfie-project-shocked-and-vanished-552247>

INDEX

Page numbers in *italics* indicate figures on the corresponding pages.